ENVIRONMENTAL ECONOMICS AND POLICY

ENVIRONMENTAL ECONOMICS AND POLICY

Paul B. Downing
Florida State University

LITTLE, BROWN AND COMPANY
Boston   Toronto

Library of Congress Cataloging in Publication Data

Downing, Paul B.
  Environmental economics and policy.

  Bibliography: p.
  1. Environmental policy. 2. Pollution—Economic aspects. I. Title.
HC79.E5D69   1984   338.4'33637   83-19554
ISBN 0-316-19180-9

Copyright © 1984 by Paul B. Downing

All rights reserved. No part of this book may be reproduced in any form or by any electronic or mechanical means including information storage and retrieval systems without permission in writing from the publisher, except by a reviewer who may quote brief passages in a review.

Library of Congress Catalog Card No. 83-19554

ISBN 0-316-19180-9

9 8 7 6 5 4 3 2 1

MV

Published simultaneously in Canada by Little, Brown & Company (Canada) Limited

Printed in the United States of America

The author gratefully acknowledges permission to use the following material:
  Table 2.1. From Henry M. Peskin, Environmental Policy and the Distribution of Benefits and Costs," in P. Portnoy, ed., *Current Issues in U.S. Environmental Policy,* Table 5-6. Published for Resources for the Future, Inc. by The John Hopkins University Press. By permission.
  Figure 5.1. From Paul B. Downing, *The Economics of Urban Sewage Disposal* (N.Y.: Praeger, 1969). Reprinted by permission.
  Figure 5.2. From Paul B. Downing, "The Cost and Effectiveness of Retrofit Programs for Used Cars," *Water, Air, and Soil Pollution,* 3:95 (1974). Reprinted by permission.
  Table 2.1. From Paul B. Downing, "Controlling Oxidents in Los Angeles," *Environmental Affairs,* 4: 733–734 (fall 1975). Reprinted by permission of Boston College Environmental Affairs Law Review.
  Figure 6.1. From Thomas R. Dye, *Understanding Public Policy,* 4th ed., © 1981, p. 27. Adapted by permission of Prentice-Hall, Inc., Englewood Cliffs, N.J.

To Bobbi

Preface

This is a text intended for undergraduate students interested in the economic aspects of pollution control. It assumes that the student has some background in microeconomics (a principles course), but students without such a background should be able to comprehend most of this text with occasional remedial reading. While this book is intended to present the central economic issues in environmental policy, it explicitly acknowledges that economics is closely interlinked with politics in policy formulation. Any understanding of current environmental issues requires that the student be knowledgeable about how economics and politics interact. Thus, this book does not present economic theory in a vacuum. Rather, it uses simple theory to explain why various individuals behave as they do. This political economy perspective is drawn from the literature in public choice and bureaucracy theory.

The book also explicitly acknowledges that economic theory is useful only if it can be brought to bear on practical issues. I discuss practical issues at length and demonstrate how simple economic theory can be employed to understand these practical issues as well as to offer practical solutions. To ensure that the discussions are related to real situations, I establish the connection between emissions and environmental quality. This helps to keep clear the distinction between environmental policy and emission control policy.

While the book employs simple theory, it does deal with complex issues. These issues are presented simply at the beginning of the text and with increasing complexity as new concepts are introduced. In some cases this methodology has called for repeated explanations — a simple explanation of a phenomenon first, and a more complex one later on. Even though the level of economic tools employed is relatively simple, the subjects discussed involve subtle interrelationships. Thus, the book should be useful to more advanced students as well as to those just beginning the study of environmental economics. In addition, I have included an extensive bibliography to provide students with a start on further investigation in this field.

Acknowledgments

No book comes into being without the influence and help of many individuals. I was first introduced to this subject while an undergraduate student, when Mason Gaffney gave me a prepublication draft of Allen Kneese's 1964 book, *The Economics of Regional Water Quality Management*. I have learned a great deal in personal discussions with these gentlemen as well as from their writings. In the early 1970s Tom Crocker had the office next to mine at the University of California — Riverside. My initial investigations of enforcement and the political aspects of pollution control started after conversations with Tom. While at EPA I learned a great deal about the economics, politics, and bureaucracy of pollution control from Larry Ruff, William Watson, and Allen Carlin. At Virginia Polytechnic Institute and State University Charles Goetz, T. Nicolaus Tideman, Arthur Denzau, and Gordon Tullock provided support and education. While at VPI, I was blessed with a number of very capable students who worked with me on several issues discussed in this book. They include David Barnes, Michael Marlow, and James O'Toole who wrote dissertations under me, and James Kimball and Gordon Brady with whom I co-authored several studies that served as a basis for parts of this book. I wish to thank the Ford Foundation for support during this period. A special note must be added about Gordon Brady. My association with him has continued over the years and includes several studies done since we left VPI. While Gordon did not help me write this book, he influenced every word. In 1979 and again in 1982 I worked with Ken Hanf, Frank Mueller, Peter Knoepfel, Arieh Ullmann, Helmut Weidner, Gabriele Knodgen, and others at the International Institute for Environment and Society in Berlin. It was there that I started to develop the political economy of implementation model. At Florida State I have renewed my discussions with Richard Wagner. As with any listing of this sort the above is obviously incomplete, and to those whom I have omitted, I apologize.

During the writing of this book I have had the benefit of careful and helpful reviews by Richard Caves, Thomas Crocker, David Fractor, John Miranowski, and Richard Porter. The book is better for the advice they offered.

I owe a great debt to Mary Schneider who translated my poor writing into readable prose and who kept asking questions until my explanations made sense.

Finally I wish to thank my wife Bobbi, who remained cheerful and supportive throughout the whole process.

Contents

Chapter 1 The Context of the Environmental
          Problem   1

The Clean Air Act   2
The Federal Water Pollution Control Act   5
The 1977 Amendments   7
The Proposed Amendments   7
Hazardous Wastes   8
Ten Years of "Progress" in Environmental Quality
    Improvement   9
Some Institutional Questions   16
Statement of the Issues   18
Study Questions   19
Suggested Readings   20

Chapter 2 Basic Concepts in Economics and Pollution
          Control   21

Scarcity and Opportunity Cost   21
Behavioral Assumptions   22
Efficiency in Individual Consumption Decisions   23
Economic Efficiency in the Economy   24
Economic Efficiency and Distributional Equity   26
Benefit/Cost Analysis in Pollution Control   26
    The Costs of Preventing Pollution   27
    Benefits from Controlling Pollution   29
    Efficiency in Pollution Control   30
    An Example of Benefit/Cost Analysis   33
The Environmental Problem as One Economist Sees It   35
Study Questions   36
Suggested Readings   37

ix

x   Contents

Chapter 3 Pollution and the Private Market   38

The Basics of a Market Economy   38
  Consumption Choices   39
  Production Choices   42
  Profit Maximization   44
  Firm and Market Equilibrium   45
  Market Adjustments   45
Pollution Externalities   48
  Externalities   48
  Externalities and the Misallocation of Resources   49
  Implications of Pollution Externalities for the Allocation of
    Resources in the Private Market   52
Environmental Quality as a Public Good   52
  Private Goods   52
  Public Goods   52
  Exclusion   56
  Free Riders   56
  Efficiency and Lindahl Taxes   57
  The Environment as a Public Good   58
Summary   59
Study Questions   60
Suggested Readings   60

Chapter 4 Control of Pollution   62

Controlling Emissions in a Plant   62
Emissions and Environmental Quality   67
Benefits of Controlling Emissions   70
Simple Benefit/Cost Analysis   72
More than One Source of Emissions   76
More than One Benefiting Group   79
Changing Location   82
Summary   83
Study Questions   85
Suggested Reading   85

Chapter 5 Measuring the Benefits and Costs of
             Environmental Improvements   86

Discounting   86
Estimating Costs   88

Regression and Economies of Scale   89
Linear Programming, Pollutant Mix, and Technical Feasibility   91
Simulation and Degradation over Time   94
Neglected Alternatives and Bias   95
Estimating Benefits   96
   Technical Coefficients and the Value of Human Life   96
   Epidemiological Studies   99
   Property Value and Air Pollution   99
   Survey Techniques: Incentives to Tell the Truth   102
   Selecting Techniques   103
Uncertainty and the Range of Outcomes   104
   Uncertainty   104
A National Estimate of Water Pollution Control Benefits   106
Alternatives to Benefit/Cost Analysis   109
   Arbitrary Standards   109
   Cost Effectiveness   109
   Policy Trade-off Analysis   110
Summary   114
Study Questions   115
Suggested Readings   115

Chapter 6   Government Action to Control Pollution   117

Government Action   117
   The Balancing of Interests and Power   118
   Utility Maximization in Government   119
Political Pressures in Pollution Control   121
   The Emitters' Lobby   121
   The Recipients' Lobby   124
   Political Pressures and Pollution Policy   126
   Ways to Change Control Efforts After Passage of a Law   129
Does the System Oversupply or Undersupply Pollution Control?   133
Study Questions   136
Suggested Readings   136

Chapter 7   Some Recent Policy Issues   138

Hazardous Wastes   138
The Appropriateness of Benefit/Cost Analysis   139

Damages Are Not Infinite (Usually)   139
Costs of Controlling Toxic Waste Release   142
Prohibition May Be Efficient   142
Policy Applications   143
The Control of New Releases   143
Current Policy   145
Executive Order 12291   148
Acid Rain   151
Summary   153
Study Questions   154
Suggested Readings   154

Chapter 8   The Regulatory Approach to Controlling Pollution   155

The Regulatory Approach   155
Environmental Quality Standards   155
Effluent Standards   158
Efficient Regulation/Inefficient Practice   160
Efficient Environmental Quality Standards   160
Efficient Emission Standards   162
Enforcing Emission Standards   164
Interrelationships Among Standards   165
Inefficient Practice   165
Implementation Structure   166
Who Sets Standards?   166
National versus Regional Standards   168
Agency Responsibility   169
Summary   171
Study Questions   171
Suggested Readings   172

Chapter 9   An Economic Incentive System for Pollution Control   173

Effluent Fees   173
Effect of Effluent Fees on Control Efforts   174
Effect on Firm Output   175
Efficient Effluent Fees   177
The Simple Case   177
Many Sources, Many Emissions   178
Choice of an Efficient Location   178

Efficient Timing 178
Dynamic Efficiency 179
Revenue Implications 179
Subsidies 181
Effluent Fees, Subsidies, and Regulation Compared 181
  Emission Level 182
  Costs of Control and Residual Payments 182
  Output of Final Goods and Profit 182
  The Market for Final Goods 184
  Shifting of Effluent Fees 185
  Environmental Quality 187
  Effects on Innovation 189
Property Rights Implications 193
Summary 194
Study Questions 195
Suggested Readings 196

Chapter 10 Practical Problems in Pollution Control 197

Imperfect Information 197
  Uncertainty in Information 197
  Errors and Adjustments 200
  Flexibility to Change 202
Some Practical Alternatives 204
  Transferable Permits 205
  Practical Effluent Fees 210
  The Sulfur Tax 211
  Economic Incentives in the Clean Air Act of 1977 212
Political Implications of Economic Incentive Systems 213
  Who Pays? 213
  Who Receives the Revenue? 216
Practical Solutions with Practical Problems 218
Uncertainty and Information Under Policy Alternatives 219
Summary: There Is No Perfect System 223
Study Questions 224
Suggested Readings 224

Chapter 11 Pollution Control Policy in Practice 226

Passage of a Pollution Control Law 227
  Perceived Benefits and Shifting Costs 227

Distribution of Costs and Benefits in the Passage of the Clean Air Act of 1970   228
Regional Development and Passage of the 1970 Act   233
Implementing the Clean Air Act   235
Complex Bargaining   240
Summary   241
Study Questions   242
Suggested Readings   242

Chapter 12   The Political Economy of Implementation   244

The Behavior of Policy-Makers   244
   Agency Behavior   244
   Source Behavior   253
   CIG Formation and Behavior   254
Interaction and Bargaining   258
   Toward Equilibrium   258
   Political Benefit/Cost Analysis   259
The Origin and Funding of CIGs   263
Summary   268
Study Questions   268
Suggested Readings   268

Chapter 13   Enforcing Pollution Control Laws   270

The Economics of Enforcement   270
   Incentives to Comply   270
   Effective Penalty   273
   Agency Response   275
Current Practice in Enforcement   275
   Setting a Standard   276
   Detecting Violations   278
   Court Referral and Conviction   281
   Fines   283
   The Control Agency's Prosecution Effort   284
   A Source's Decision to Control   285
Summary: Lessons Learned   289
Study Questions   290
Suggested Readings   290

Chapter 14 Where Do We Go from Here?   292

Considering Basic Issues   292
   The Role of Government   292
   Who Owns the Environment?   293
   Efficiency and Equity in Pollution Control   294
   Acting in the Social Interest   294
   Cost of Errors   295
   Growth and Change   295
A Comparison of Options   296
Summary   300
Study Questions   302

Appendix to Chapter 14 A Proposal for a Practical Alternative   303

The Basic System   303
   Determining an Environmental Quality Goal   303
   Transferable Permits   304
   Enforcement   308
   Agency Structure and Financing   308
   Interregional Control   312
An Example of the Proposal   313
Conclusion   317

Basic Terms   318

Bibliography   322

Index   329

1
The Context of the Environmental Problem

Pollution has been with us since human beings built the first fire. Smoke rising from the fire and ashes left on the ground changed the natural environment, reducing the site's desirability to those early inhabitants. When air and water pollution became a problem in one location, people moved to a new, unpolluted area. After a time, the polluted site returned to its natural state. As long as people could move to newer, cleaner sites easily, pollution was not considered a problem. When population increased, when it became more concentrated in cities, and when technology began to require more stationary production sites, pollution began to build. It then became a matter of concern to society.

Concern for environmental quality has led to major efforts to control the undesirable effects of pollution. In the middle of the nineteenth century, cities began to install sewer systems to dispose of unwanted human and industrial wastes. The Rivers and Harbors Act of 1899 was designed to control water quality throughout the nation. In the twentieth century, states and localities have adopted many laws designed to control damage from pollution. Since the 1950s, major efforts have been underway to solve the air pollution problems of Pittsburgh, New York, Los Angeles, and most other large cities. At the same time, Wisconsin and other states have adopted comprehensive water pollution control laws.

The federal government had enacted a number of air, water, land, and hazardous waste pollution control laws earlier, but not until 1970 was a specific agency formed to organize and coordinate federal efforts in pollution control. The formation of the U.S. Environmental Protection Agency (EPA) was followed closely by the passage of the Clean Air Act of 1970. This Act provided for a major federal role in determining how clean the air should be, who should control emissions to make it clean, and when the task should be completed. In 1972 a companion law, the Federal Water Pollution Control Act, was passed. This law gave the major responsibility for water pollution control to EPA. Major efforts to control the release of toxic substances and to control waste disposal on land were initiated in 1976 with the Resource Conservation and Recovery Act. These efforts were expanded in the Comprehensive Environmental Response, Compensation, and Liability Act of 1980.

THE CLEAN AIR ACT

The Clean Air Act of 1970, passed at the height of the environmental movement with virtually no dissent, substantially federalized air pollution control and promised clean air by 1977. It contained two institutional innovations that were designed to force states and automobile manufacturers to move swiftly to control pollution.

The "date certain" provision placed pressure on each state and on EPA to adopt plans to meet the goal of clean air by 1977. Such a plan would specify a sequence of steps toward control and a date by which each step was to be completed. Section 107 of the Act required EPA to designate air quality control regions within ninety days of passage. Section 108 required EPA to publish Criteria Documents and Control Techniques within twelve months of passage. Criteria Documents discuss relevant technical studies of the effects of air pollutants on public health and welfare. Control Techniques present the technologies currently available to control the various pollutants produced by coal-fired power plants, steel mills, and other such industrial centers. Section 109 required EPA to propose national primary air quality standards within thirty days of passage and to promulgate them ninety days later. National air quality standards were to be based on the Criteria Documents and were to protect human health from any adverse effects from air pollution, with an adequate margin of safety. (The current standards are listed in Table 1.1.) Section 110 required that each state produce and submit a State Implementation Plan (SIP) to EPA for approval not more than nine months after the national air quality standards were promulgated. This SIP would have to show how the state was going to meet these standards by 1975. If, however, a state could show that the

TABLE 1.1 National Ambient Air Quality Standards

Pollutant	Averaging Time	Primary Standard Levels	Secondary Standard Levels[a]
Particulate matter	Annual (geometric mean)	75 μg/m^3	60 μg/m^3
	24 hours[b]	260 μg/m^3	150 μg/m^3
Sulfur oxides	Annual (arithmetic mean)	80 μg/m^3 (0.03 ppm)	—
	24 hours[b]	365 μg/m^3 (0.14 ppm)	—
	3 hours[b]	—	1300 μg/m^3
Carbon monoxides	8 hours[b]	10 mg/m^3 (9 ppm)	10 mg/m^3 (9 ppm)
	1 hour[b]	40 mg/m^3 (35 ppm)[c]	40 mg/m^3 (35 ppm)[c]
Nitrogen dioxide	Annual (arithmetic mean)	100 μg/m^3 (0.05 ppm)	100 μg/m^3 (0.05 ppm)
Ozone	1 hour[b]	240 μg/m^3 (0.12 ppm)	240 μg/m^3 (0.12 ppm)
Hydrocarbons (nonmethane)[a]	3 hours (6:00 to 9:00 A.M.)	160 μg/m^3 (0.24 ppm)	160 μg/m^3 (0.24 ppm)
Lead	3 months	1.5 μg/m^3	1.5 μg/m^3

Source: Council on Environmental Quality, *Environmental Quality*, Eleventh Annual Report (Washington, D.C.: U.S. Government Printing Office, 1980), p. 172. μg/m^3 = micrograms per cubic meter; ppm = parts per million; and mg/m^3 = milligrams per cubic meter.
[a] Not a health-related standard; used as a guide for ozone control.
[b] Not to be exceeded more than once a year.
[c] EPA has proposed a reduction of this standard to 29 mg/m^3 (25 ppm).

application of "reasonably available alternative" control techniques would not meet the air quality standards within three years, the administrator of EPA could grant a delay to 1977.

In the event that a state did not comply with these requirements, EPA was mandated to produce the required SIP. If a state did not promulgate, implement, and enforce the SIP, EPA was required to complete the task. Section 113 allowed EPA to assume the enforcement of SIP provisions against any or all sources if the administrator determined that a state had failed to enforce the SIP effectively. Section 116 allowed states to adopt and enforce more stringent emission standards than those required by the EPA, but prohibited them from adopting or enforcing less stringent standards.

The effect of these requirements is clear: Each state had to adopt control plans that satisfied EPA, or EPA would take over. The power behind the SIP plan was the threat of federal preemption and the refusal to allow extensions beyond 1977, regardless of the cost, technical feasibility, or social impact of cleaning up the air. This "date certain" system would, it was thought, guarantee that EPA's definition of clean air would be achieved by 1977 at the latest.

The "technology forcing" provisions of the 1970 Act applied to many pollution sources, but can be illustrated best by the new automobile emission standards. Section 202 set a series of emission standards for new automobiles, which became progressively more stringent until 1976. By that year, new cars were to emit no more than 10 percent of the amount of certain pollutants they emitted in 1970. Since cars for the 1970 model year already controlled emissions somewhat, this amounted to a reduction of 98 percent of the uncontrolled level of emissions. This reduction required a degree of control that many specialists thought would not be technologically feasible within the time allotted, if ever. Congress argued that automobile manufacturers in the United States had been deliberately slow in developing emission control technology. By passing a law that required such controls and by imposing the loss of the right to sell cars in the United States as a penalty for failure, Congress believed it could force the automobile manufacturers to develop the required technology. It did not happen. Neither the date certain provision nor technology forcing worked as Congress had planned.

There are many reasons why the Clean Air Act of 1970 did not meet its 1977 goal. These will be discussed later in this book, after we examine the circumstances of pollution and pollution control at the time, and the effects of competing incentives to pollute and not to pollute. At this time I wish to stress one point: Congress was fully aware of the fact that it was passing a law that would not succeed. The Senate committee report on the Act specifically rejected concerns about technological feasibility and cost. In fact, it recognized that meeting the ambient air quality standards suggested by federal administrators in 1970 would require a reduction in automobile traffic of as much as 75 percent in some metropolitan areas.[1] The committee also argued that existing emitters should clean up, regardless of the cost, or be closed down. Reducing traffic by 75 percent and controlling emissions without regard to costs were not likely to

---

[1] S. Rep. No. 91-1196, 91st Cong., 2nd Sess. 2 (1970).

be socially desirable or politically viable solutions. I leave as a question for the future why Congress would pass such an impractical law.

By 1976 it became obvious that the Clean Air Act of 1970 was going to fail. Congress, at EPA's urging, initiated efforts to amend the law. A filibuster killed the 1976 amendments, but in 1977 Congress did pass a set of Amendments to the Clean Air Act. It would seem reasonable that Congress and the EPA would have been aware of the shortcomings of the 1970 Act and would have adopted an approach that worked better. Instead, the 1977 Amendments adopted the same "date certain" approach that had failed previously. The 1977 Amendments required states to produce SIPs that would demonstrate compliance with the original 1970 national air quality standards by December 31, 1982. Most areas of the country missed this deadline and are now in violation of the 1977 version of the Act. In areas with severe carbon monoxide or ozone (smog) problems, EPA can approve a state request to delay the deadline until 1987, with the proviso that the state will implement significant controls in the intervening years. These controls must be "reasonably available" (not excessively costly), and not have "serious adverse social and economic impacts." It was left up to EPA and the courts to interpret the meaning of these ambiguous terms.

The 1977 Act does nothing to change the basic enforcement tool — federal preemption. Like its predecessor, the 1977 Act provides for federal action whenever a state fails, even though the threat of federal intervention, and its actual occurrence in many cases, did not yield the desired result in the 1970 Act. Under these circumstances one can reasonably predict continued delays in institution of control.

THE FEDERAL WATER POLLUTION CONTROL ACT

In 1972 Congress passed extensive amendments to the Federal Water Pollution Control Act (FWPCA). The 1972 Amendments called for a significant federalization of water pollution control efforts, as the Clean Air Act of 1970 had for air pollution control. The approach to controlling emissions from individual sources was somewhat different, but the intent was to place significant time constraints on the process. The FWPCA required that all sources install the "best practicable technology" (BPT) by 1977 and the "best available technology" (BAT) by 1983. Where this level of control was insufficient to render receiving waters swimmable and fishable, even more extensive controls would be required. The 1972 Amendments set a goal of zero discharge of any pollutant into the country's waters by 1985. The enforcement mechanism was again federal preemption. But in this case EPA was to define BPT and BAT, and each state was assigned the task of enforcing the EPA regulations.

The process of defining BPT became complex very quickly. Technology is "practicable" only under specific circumstances. This led EPA to define BPT according to the type and size of industry. Thus there are separate BPT standards for "poultry packing — chicken" and "poultry packing — turkey"; for "raw sugar processing — Louisiana," "raw sugar processing — Hilo-Hamakua," and "raw sugar processing — Puerto Rico"; and many others.[2] Divisions like these were made for each of the twenty-eight major industry groups. Many of the proposed BPT regulations were opposed by industry. EPA's response was to add or drop subcategories and generally weaken the BPT standards. The more effective an industry's political pressure on EPA, the more specialized subcategories that industry would receive and the less stringent their BPT schedules. Even so, after final promulgation of the BPT regulations EPA was sued by several industry groups. Many of the standards were still in court in 1977, when the BPT standards were to have been implemented. The result of these cases was an even further weakening of the standards. The BPT standards have no relationship to cost of control. Some industry groups would be controlling at very high marginal costs while others would be controlling at very low marginal costs. This leads to a waste in the country's resources.

The BAT standards suffered a different fate. In 1977 several powerful industries campaigned in Congress to delay or eliminate the BAT standards. Their argument was that industry had met BPT requirements but that municipalities had not. It was unfair and inefficient, they argued, for industry to control while municipalities lagged behind in their efforts. Enforcement studies indicate that in fact industry was often not in compliance with the BPT standards at the time. Nevertheless, Congress granted a delay in implementing BAT until 1984 with further delays at EPA's discretion.

---

[2] A. J. Krupnick and W. Harrington, "Decision Rules Used in the Promulgation of Federal Regulations: The Case of EPA Effluent Discharge Standards," in P. B. Downing and K. I. Hanf, eds., *Implementing Pollution Laws: International Comparisons*, Vol. I (Tallahassee, Fla.: Florida State University, 1981).

THE 1977 AMENDMENTS

The 1977 Amendments to the Clean Air Act and the Federal Water Pollution Control Act retained the same basic philosophy as the earlier legislation but weakened and delayed its impact. Economists have argued for an alternative to the regulatory approach now employed. They contend that an economic incentive approach is much preferred to the regulatory approach. This book will deal with these approaches in detail, so I will not discuss them here. It is interesting to note, however, that some elements of the incentive approach were included in the 1977 Amendments to the Clean Air Act. These provisions include (1) a delayed compliance penalty designed to make it more expensive for a source to delay installation of control equipment; (2) emission offsets, which require a new source entering an area to negotiate with existing sources in the area for a corresponding reduction in their emissions; and (3) the bubble concept, which allows all the processes in a factory to be treated as a group rather than process by process, thus allowing less expensive control. Studies on the actual effectiveness of these changes have not been completed, so it is too early to tell if they have worked better than the regulatory approach.

THE PROPOSED AMENDMENTS

Congress was expected to amend both the Clean Air Act and the FWPCA in 1981 and again in 1982, but it did not act. Congress had still failed to act as 1983 drew to a close. If and when it does, recent shifts in political strength and philosophy probably mean that both Acts will be further weakened. At the same time, economic incentives may replace more of the regulatory aspects of these laws.

The Reagan administration has sought to weaken these pollution control laws, and has justified this effort on two grounds. First, they claim that the existing regulatory system is inefficient in its methods of controlling emissions, and that greater control can be achieved — and pollution control costs reduced — by adjusting control requirements to make them more flexible.[3] Second, they argue that the level of control required by the Acts has a severe impact on

---

[3] "Behind the Push to Ease Pollution Laws: An Interview with Anne M. Gorsuch, Administrator, EPA," *U.S. News and World Report,* October 19, 1981, p. 48.

the economy, making the production of goods and services more costly and slowing economic growth.

Economists would generally agree with the first point. They find the current regulatory approach wasteful and inefficient. Their solution, however, would differ from that of the Reagan administration. Instead of deregulation, most economists would favor a switch in the form of regulation. On the second point economists are split. Some agree that environmental regulations, with their excessive costs and regulatory delays, reduce economic growth. Others claim that control improves growth because it increases the health and productivity of the population and provides jobs in the pollution control industry that partially or fully offset losses in production.[4]

HAZARDOUS WASTES

The environmental problem with the greatest potential for long-term detrimental effects may well be the production and release of hazardous and toxic wastes. Released into the air, such wastes fall to the ground to be ingested directly by plants and animals or find their way into surface waters, where they affect the entire food chain and contaminate drinking water. Direct water disposal has the same effects. Land disposal has been considered the safest alternative because it isolates these materials from the air and the water. Yet poorly designed land disposal sites have allowed toxic chemicals to seep into the ground and find their way into surface or underground water supplies. This has been happening with some regularity in old, poorly designed, often abandoned disposal sites.

In order to solve this problem, Congress has enacted two laws: the Resource Conservation and Recovery Act of 1976, which regulates the design and operation of land disposal sites, and the Comprehensive Environmental Response, Compensation, and Liability Act of 1980, which provides means for cleaning up accidental spills of toxic materials and past unregulated disposal sites that are causing environmental dangers. The cleanup is financed by a $1.6 billion Superfund. This law was passed in part as a response to the Love Canal problem in Niagara City, New York; but EPA has since found more than twenty sites worse than Love Canal.[5] To date EPA has

[4] See H. Peskin, P. Portney, and A. Kneese, eds., *Environmental Regulation and the U.S. Economy* (Baltimore: Johns Hopkins University Press, 1981).
[5] L. Brown and C. Pope, *Hazardous Waste in America* (San Francisco: Sierra Club Books, 1982).

designated 435 Superfund sites. It has also found it necessary to close down an entire town — Times Beach, Missouri — because of dioxin contamination from waste oil spread in 1973.

The potential dangers of toxic wastes are very serious. Past disposal of hazardous wastes has created a large number of sites throughout the country that could cause water contamination, many of which have not yet been identified. This is a fast-changing and important area of pollution control.

TEN YEARS OF "PROGRESS" IN ENVIRONMENTAL QUALITY IMPROVEMENT

Since the passage of the Clean Air Act of 1970, the federal government has had the major responsibility for the control of pollution. One might well ask what progress has been made during that period. Because this federalization represented a significant departure from the state-originated programs of the past, and because the Reagan administration appears to want to return primacy to the state programs, one might also like to know the effects of these different emphases on progress over the past twenty years. If federalization has led to a more proenvironmental administration of pollution control laws, as its proponents claim, then one would expect to find that environmental quality has improved faster in the 1970s than it did in the 1960s. A survey of available data indicates that these questions are very difficult, if not impossible, to answer.

Let us look first at expenditures for pollution control. Systematic data on expenditures were not compiled before 1972. Figure 1.1 presents estimates, produced by the Bureau of Economic Analysis (BEA) of the U.S. Department of Commerce, of pollution control expenditures since 1972. In current (inflated) dollars, expenditures on pollution control increased rapidly in the 1970s (an increase of 166 percent). In constant (noninflated) dollars, however, the growth in expenditures has been a more modest 43 percent. The growth in expenditures in constant dollars for air pollution control (56 percent) has been greater than the growth in expenditures for water pollution control (35 percent).

These BEA figures represent expenditures on pollution control required by federal, state, and local environmental regulations. The Council on Environmental Quality (CEQ) generates cost estimates somewhat differently. Their estimates represent the annual costs of operating pollution control equipment and of the capital invested in

FIGURE 1.1 Pollution Control Expenditures in the United States

Since the passage of major federal pollution control legislation, the expenditure of goods and services in our economy has increased rapidly, both in current dollars and in constant dollars (controlling for inflation). In 1981 the growth trend was reversed, primarily because of a reduction in water pollution control expenditures.

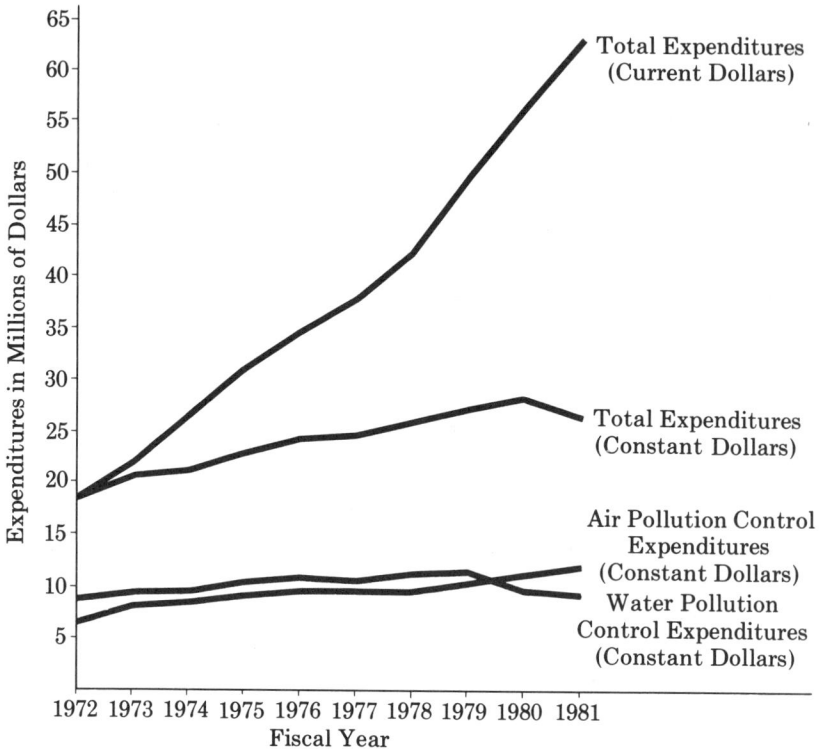

Source: G. Rutledge and S. Lease-Trevathan, "Pollution Abatement and Control Expenditures, 1972-1981," *Survey of Current Business* 63 (February 1983) 15-23.

pollution control. This figure reflects the economic costs of pollution control more accurately. CEQ estimates that the total annual cost of pollution abatement in 1979 was $55.9 billion,[6] or 3.4 percent of the GNP; the BEA estimate is $48.5 billion. In looking ahead, CEQ estimates that we will spend $92.9 billion in 1988 and $755 billion over the ten years from 1979 to 1988.

The next question one might ask is what effect these expenditures have had on environmental quality. There are two steps to improving environmental quality. The first step is to reduce emissions of pollutants. The second and most important step is to determine what effects the reduced emissions have had on improving environmental quality. After all, improved environmental quality is the goal of our pollution control efforts. As was the case with data for expenditures, there is little information on environmental quality available for the years before 1970.

Estimates of air pollutant emissions from 1940 to 1976 are presented in Figure 1.2. Emissions generally increased from 1940 to 1970, with the lone exception being total suspended particulates (TSP), which have been declining since 1950. TSPs are commonly produced by smokestacks, especially the ones that carry off the smoke of burning coal, and in the 1950s and 1960s many state and local governments had initiated smoke control programs. Since 1970 the trend in emissions of air pollutants is generally downward. The exception is emissions of nitrogen oxides (NO_X), which have increased. Since 1960 the ratio of NO_X emissions from mobile sources (automobiles, trucks, and airplanes) to emissions from stationary sources (fuel combustion and industrial processes) has remained relatively constant. Growth in both mobile and stationary sources has more than offset attempts to control NO_X.

The reduction in emissions since 1970 has not been sufficient to return total emissions to the 1950 levels. Recent controls appear to have overcome recent growth, but they have not been able to overcome pollution resulting from past growth in the economy.

Reductions in emissions do not necessarily indicate improvements in environmental quality. The relationship between emissions and environmental quality is a complex one; chemical reactions depend on so many natural factors and emissions from so many other sources. Reducing emissions that do not affect people

---

[6] Council on Environmental Quality, *Environmental Quality*, Eleventh Annual Report (Washington, D.C.: U.S. Government Printing Office, 1980), Table 10-2.

FIGURE 1.2 Nationwide Total Air Pollution Emission Estimates

As a result of government efforts to control air pollution, total emissions of most air pollutants have declined since 1970. Nitrogen oxide (NO_x) emissions, however, continued to rise through the 1970s, and hydrocarbon (HC) and sulfur oxide (SO_x) emissions have increased after an initial decline.

Source: EPA, *National Air Pollutant Emission Estimates, 1940–1976* (U.S. Environmental Protection Agency, July 1978), Table 1; EPA, *National Air Pollutant Emission Estimates, 1970–1978* (U.S. Environmental Protection Agency, 1980), Table 1.

[a] CO data is in terms of 10^7 metric tons per year.

adversely does not reduce pollution. EPA has developed an index of air quality, the pollutants standard index (PSI). It defines "unhealthful air" as air that exceeds national ambient air quality standards in one or more of five pollutants: sulfur dioxide (SO_2), nitrogen dioxide (NO_2), carbon monoxide (CO), ozone (O_3), and TSP. "Very unhealthful air" is defined as air that has significant adverse health effects, especially to such susceptible segments of the population as the elderly and people with existing heart or lung diseases. CEQ has compiled air quality statistics according to this index for twenty-three standard metropolitan statistical areas (SMSAs) from 1974 to 1978. Figure 1.3 indicates the average number of days these cities were found to have unhealthful air between 1974 and 1978.

Between 1974 and 1978 the average number of days of "unhealthful air" in the twenty-three cities declined from 86.3 days to 71.2 days, a 17 percent improvement. Very unhealthful days declined from 23.8 to 15.6 days, a 34 percent improvement. Hazardous days have declined by well over 50 percent. This indicates that the federal and state control efforts have reduced the severity of air pollution episodes more than the total number. Since more damage is done by the severe episodes, we can conclude that for these twenty-three cities at least, and perhaps for the rest of the country as well, damages from air pollution have been reduced by as much as 50 percent.

These data demonstrate an improvement between 1974 and 1978, but they also make clear that the goal of the Clean Air Act of 1970 — zero health effects, which translates into a PSI of less than 100 — has not been met. In fact, all twenty-three cities in the CEQ reports were in violation of the air quality standards for at least some time every year. Los Angeles, Riverside-San Bernardino, Ontario (California), and New York were in violation more than half the days of the year. Even the trend differs from city to city. Seven cities have clearly identifiable improvements in air quality, while four cities have become more polluted. The remaining twelve cities have mixed results, improving in some years and worsening in others. In comparing the 1980 CEQ report to its predecessors, one finds that many of the same cities are covered but that the data are inconsistent. In the 1978 CEQ report, for example, Los Angeles was reported to have had approximately 170 days with a PSI above 100 in 1976. In the 1980 report, the corresponding figure for 1976 was 260 days. Similar discrepancies can be found for all the cities that are covered in both reports. This demonstrates the difficulties a student of environmental policy has in determining air quality

FIGURE 1.3 Average Number of Days of Polluted Air in Twenty-three SMSAs

The expenditure of resources to control air pollution has resulted in a decline in the number of days per year that the populations of major cities have been exposed to seriously polluted air.

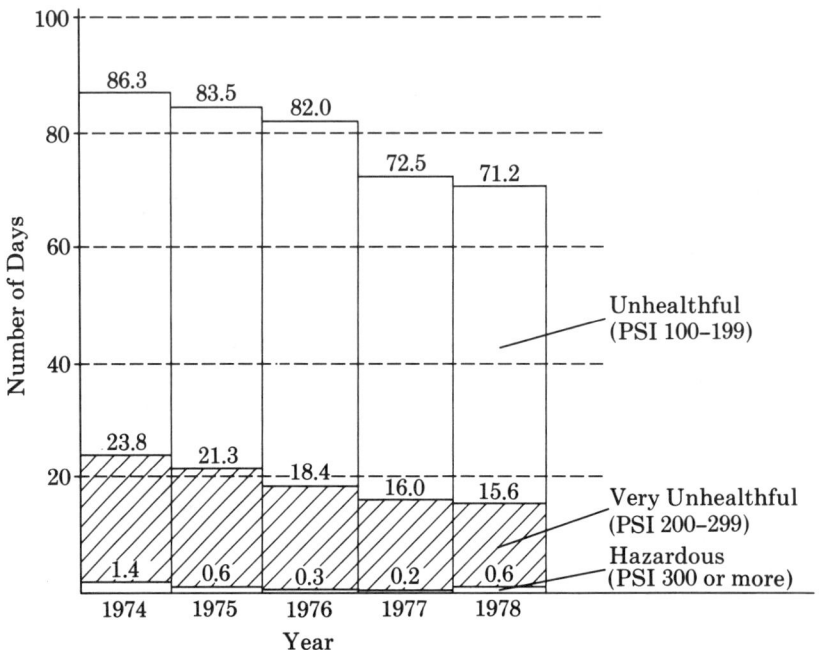

Source: Council Environmental Quality, *Environmental Quality,* Eleventh Annual Report (Washington, D.C.: U.S. Government Printing Office, 1980), Figure 4-2.

trends. Data are scarce, often unreliable, and generally not comparable across years.

Past data are even more difficult to obtain. The 1976 CEQ report presents data on photochemical oxidant (O_3) levels at three stations in Los Angeles from 1963 to 1974.[7] These data show that the aver-

[7] Council on Environmental Quality, *Environmental Quality*, Seventh Annual Report (Washington, D.C.: U.S. Government Printing Office, 1976), p. 234.

age of the worst five days has declined somewhat at each station, although yearly variations make the trend uncertain. The average daily one-hour maximums have generally declined over the period. The data do not show a significant improvement in the trend since the passage of the 1970 Act — but they extend only to 1974. It could be argued that the data contained in the 1980 CEQ report support the contention that the 1970 Act has significantly accelerated the rate of improvement, but the data from the two reports are not comparable.

The 1976 CEQ report presents data on TSP and SO_2 for the years 1960 to 1972. For ninety-five urban stations there has been a consistent decline in TSP over the period, with no sign of acceleration after 1970. The trend for SO_2 is similar.

Our survey of available air quality data shows that the trend is unclear. There appear to have been some improvements over the past twenty years, yet many areas of the country are in worse shape now. Clearly, the goals of the 1970 Act have not been met. In fact, the available data do not suggest that the rate of improvement in air quality has been affected in any way by the federalization of emission controls.

The data on water quality present the same sort of picture. The 1980 CEQ report summarizes the situation as follows: "In some localities there has been substantial improvement in water quality, but the quality of surface waters nationally has not changed much in the last five years."[8] This conclusion covered most of the years the FWPCA of 1972 had been in effect.

The data on water quality improvement before 1972 indicate that there was continual improvement after 1963. The 1974 CEQ report summarized data on twenty-two major waterways. Some of the findings are presented in Table 1.2. While the data indicate improvement, the report notes that violations of reference level water quality values, an indication of water quality in these major rivers, were observed in 14 percent of the reaches of these major waterways between 1968 and 1972. The 1976 CEQ report updates this information. In a study covering only twelve of the major waterways, it found that some showed continued improvement from 1968 to 1975. Others showed no discernible trend or even some decline in quality.

Again, as with the air quality data, a consistent set of data from

---

[8] Council on Environmental Quality, *Environmental Quality*, Eleventh Annual Report (Washington, D.C.: U.S. Government Printing Office, 1980), p. 100.

TABLE 1.2 Water Quality Trends in Twenty-two Major Waterways, 1963–1972

Water Quality Parameter	Percentage of Reaches Showing Improvement
Suspended Solids	82
BOD_5	74
Fecal Coliforms	70
Temperature	67
Dissolved Oxygen	61
Odor	60
Color	33

Source: Council on Environmental Quality, *Environmental Quality*, Fifth Annual Report (Washington, D.C.: U.S. Government Printing Office, 1974), p. 285.

which to judge trends is not readily available. There appears to have been improvement before the major federalization in 1972, but recent data indicate no new progress.

At this point it is useful to note that improvements in environmental quality need not always be good. Suppose the value to society of an improvement in environmental quality is $100, but the cost of obtaining that improvement is $200. Then it would not pay society to make the improvement. This being the case, it is not possible to determine whether the lack of improvement in environmental quality at any given location means that the political and administrative system has not functioned well or that it was not economical to seek additional control. Most economists would argue that the existing system for controlling pollution ignores the necessity of balancing costs and benefits. This being the case, current controls, whether they meet legal requirements or not, are likely to waste money; that is, be inefficient.

SOME INSTITUTIONAL QUESTIONS

We have undergone a major philosophical change on pollution control since 1970. Major responsibility for controlling both air and water pollution, and for controlling noise pollution, toxic wastes, solid wastes, and pesticides, has been given to one federal agency,

EPA. We have spent a substantial portion of the nation's resources on controlling emissions. Yet the data we have reviewed show that it is difficult to document significant progress. Furthermore, the rate of progress in air pollution control has not increased and in water pollution control it may, in fact, have been brought to zero. The country does not seem to have benefited greatly from this massive federal effort. One might reasonably ask why not.

There are a number of possible answers to this question. I address this basic issue repeatedly throughout this book, so I will only suggest a few answers at this time.

1. *Growth.* In spite of EPA's best efforts, the growth of the economy and thus the increase in potential emissions has taken place faster than EPA has been able to reduce existing emissions.
2. *Inadequate staffing and funding.* Congress and the executive have not given EPA the resources necessary to implement existing pollution control laws fully. Even though pollution laws are inefficient, greater funding could have generated more control.
3. *Recalcitrant state agencies.* It is true that EPA has major responsibility for administering pollution control laws, but EPA must depend on state environmental agencies to do the bulk of the enforcement of these laws. States have been reluctant to enforce these stringent laws because they fear the loss of businesses.
4. *Political pressure.* EPA has faced substantial political pressure to go slow in implementing these laws. It is worth it for firms to become more active in resisting control during the implementation of these laws because it saves them money.
5. *Bureaucracy.* Either through bureaucratic incompetence or through conflicting bureaucratic incentives, EPA has wasted resources and pursued other goals instead of implementing and enforcing these pollution laws effectively.
6. *Technological infeasibility.* EPA realizes that the requirements of these pollution control laws are not technologically feasible, and that as a result the country cannot reach the goals of these laws.
7. *Economic irrationality.* These laws were passed with explicit and purposeful disregard for the economic realities of pollution control, its costs and its benefits. EPA realized that these laws went too far, requiring controls that have costs far in excess of benefits produced, and it reduced its efforts in order to bring about the proper economic balance.

The answers presented here are not mutually exclusive. The full answer to the question why pollution control laws have not met their goals includes elements of all seven.

STATEMENT OF THE ISSUES

We are now faced with an interesting set of observations. Society perceives environmental problems to be of such concern that Congress has passed major federal legislation to control pollution in all media. It has created a separate agency to oversee the implementation of those laws and provided that agency with substantial funding. Yet the results of this major effort over the last ten years are disappointing. We have not had the major increases in environmental quality we had hoped for. At the same time, new problems with hazardous wastes and acid rain suggest that there is much more to be accomplished.

Superimposed on this history is the growing realization that economics and politics play a significant role in the formation of environmental policy. The goal of cleaning up the environment to the point where there are virtually no adverse effects is unrealistic and technically impossible. Furthermore, the cost of such a massive effort would far exceed the benefit society would obtain from this high a level of environmental quality. While economics places one constraint on the quality of our environment, politics places another. Policy is not made by an unbiased analyst. It is made in a political process, where individuals are influential and compromise among competing interests is the way to reach agreement. It is impossible to separate the economics of environmental issues fully from the politics. Polluting firms act politically to influence control policy because such policy is costly to them. Environmentalists act politically because politicians control the means through which they can improve the environment. Special interests abound on both sides, and these are influenced by the economic implications of policy choices.

The issue of why government action has not achieved society's goals is a most interesting one. Without going into the detail we will go into later, it is sufficient to emphasize two related points. Each individual acts in his or her own self-interest. This leads individuals to seek government actions that will make them better off. Firms and other polluters (whom we will call emitters) may find it in their self-interest to seek reductions in the effectiveness of pollution control laws. Alternatively, they may seek subsidies for the costs they incur in controlling emissions. Recipients — those who consume environmental quality — may find it in their self-interest to seek more control over environmental quality and to require someone else, such as emitters, to pay for the necessary actions.

Self-interest is closely associated with the question of who pays. I might very well prefer high environmental quality. But the greater the share of the costs I must pay, the less I will actually demand. In other words, environmental quality has individual and market demands just like other goods. The amount of environmental quality an individual demands declines as the price he or she pays increases. If I can act politically to require another to pay for improvements in environmental quality, the price is lower to me and I will demand more than if I had to pay for improvements myself. If I could get you to pay for my car, I would be driving the Ferrari rather than a Mazda RX-7. Self-interest and the related issue of who pays are at the heart of all political decisions on the environment. Each side would be delighted to have a cleaner environment, provided the other side pays.

Indeed, the message of this book is that pollution policy is the result of interaction between the economics and the politics of environmental quality. Hence the title, *Environmental Economics and Policy*. In the chapters that follow I will explore these issues and their interaction.

STUDY QUESTIONS

1. If Congress knew that various provisions of the Clean Air Act of 1970 were not technically feasible and that the Act would fail to meet its 1977 objective, why did it pass an obviously defective law? Facing the same problems in 1977, did Congress correct these problems? It is reasonable to predict that Congress will remain reluctant to act effectively. How might this problem be solved?
2. Progress in improving environmental quality has not been as great as one might desire. What are some economic, technical, and political reasons why progress is slow? How might progress be speeded up? Is it desirable to increase our control effort?

3. "Self-interest and the related issue of who pays for pollution control are at the heart of all political decisions on the environment." Do you agree with this statement? How might self-interest be used to help solve the pollution problem?

SUGGESTED READINGS

1. The most recent issue of *Environmental Quality*, the annual report of the Council on Environmental Quality.
2. John Quarles, *Cleaning Up America* (Boston: Houghton Mifflin, 1976) presents an insider's view of EPA during the first Ruckelshaus administration.
3. Bruce Ackerman, Susan Rose-Ackerman, James Sawyer, Jr., and Dale Henderson, *The Uncertain Search for Environmental Quality* (New York: The Free Press, 1974) presents a case study of water pollution policy in the Delaware estuary.
4. J. Krier and E. Ursin, *Pollution and Policy* (Berkeley: University of California Press, 1977) presents a detailed discussion of automotive emission control policy in California.

2

Basic Concepts in Economics and Pollution Control

We have seen that current efforts to control pollution are not making great progress. We have also noted that existing laws tend to ignore economic principles. This may be a source of the problem. Before we explore what economics can tell us about how much control society should seek, I will develop the basic principles upon which the economic understanding of pollution control rests. Several basic concepts of economics are central to a discussion of the economics of pollution control. In this section I will briefly review these concepts and apply them to pollution control.

SCARCITY AND OPPORTUNITY COST

In our everyday lives we observe one of the basic concepts of economics: *scarcity*. Goods are scarce when there are not enough of them to go around at a price of zero. The productive capacity of our economy is limited and cannot fill the virtually unlimited wants of people. With limited resources, we must choose which goods to produce. A decision to produce more of one good necessarily requires a reduction in the output of some other good.

One corollary of scarcity is the notion of opportunity cost. Limited resources require us to give up one good in order to produce another. The cost to society of producing one good is the loss of the other good. This lost opportunity to produce the other good is called the *opportunity cost* of producing the first good. In a market economy where many goods are produced, it is convenient to measure opportunity cost in some common unit. We could use shoes or some other goods as the common measure, but it is easier to use the symbolic measure called money. If a good costs one dollar to produce, the opportunity cost of producing this good is one dollar's worth of some other good that could have been produced instead.

As an example, suppose an automobile manufacturer employs 100 hours of labor and $1,000 of capital equipment and materials to build a small car. These same productive resources could be used to produce bicycles instead. Suppose fifty bicycles could be produced with these resources. Then the opportunity cost of one automobile could be seen as the fifty bicycles that might have been produced. Of course, we do not measure opportunity cost in bicycles. Instead, the market places a value on them through the mechanism of prices. If the market price of a bicycle is $125.00, then the opportunity cost of one automobile is fifty times that, or $6,250.00. The opportunity cost is the dollar value of the alternative goods that could have been produced. Scarcity implies that those 100 hours of labor and that $1000 of capital can produce one automobile *or* fifty bicycles, but not both.

Scarcity and opportunity cost are important concepts in environmental economics. Because resources are scarce, using more of them in an effort to improve the environmental quality means that fewer will be available to produce other goods. The opportunity cost of an improved environment is a loss of output of other goods. This opportunity cost can be measured in money.

BEHAVIORAL ASSUMPTIONS

Economics starts from the basic behavioral assumption that *individuals act so as to maximize their own self-interest.* Individuals as consumers allocate their scarce income among consumption opportunities so as to obtain the greatest possible satisfaction. Individuals as producers of goods and services organize production so as to maximize profit. Profit is then returned to the owner, who can use it for consumption and thus achieve greater satisfaction.

It is useful to apply this assumption of maximization to environmental quality issues. When dealing with pollution, each individual will operate so as to maximize his or her self-interest. The definition of what is in an individual's self-interest will depend on that individual's circumstances. An individual who owns a plant may find it in his or her self-interest to release pollutants into the environment, because release is less expensive than control and would serve to increase the plant's profits. If that same individual were working as a control agency bureaucrat, he or she might find it in his or her self-interest to attempt to reduce the plant's emissions. For a politician the rewards are different — publicity, campaign contributions, votes, re-election. Individual politicians must choose which course of action is in their best interests. Even environmental activists who seek greater control of emissions can be seen to act according to their own self-interest.

The process of maximizing one's self-interest has two sides. Individuals must be able to define the set of circumstances that will make them happier. This is known as the individual's *utility* or goal function, and it is what the individual seeks to maximize. In maximizing utility, the individual operates under *constraints* that originate from various sources. Income constraints might prevent the individual from purchasing a desired good. Institutional constraints might prohibit an action that is seen as highly desirable. The introduction of nonsmoking sections in restaurants and on airplanes is an example of an institutional constraint; while it improves the environment it prevents the individual smoker from maximizing his or her self-interest.

Constraints need not be absolute; some are best understood as a kind of cost. In essence, most laws are of this sort. Robbery may be in an individual's self-interest, but society (through its government) has ruled such behavior illegal. The constraint a potential robber faces is the expected cost of being caught and sent to jail. The individual will weigh the benefits of robbery (the *utility* of all that money) against the costs (the potential *constraint* of going to jail). The penalty constrains behavior and reduces the number of robberies.

The basic behavioral assumption we apply to individual behavior in this book is that the individual seeks to maximize his or her self-interest, subject to constraints. One implication of this is that a change in constraints will generate a change in the behavior of the individual.

EFFICIENCY IN INDIVIDUAL CONSUMPTION DECISIONS

Maximization of personal utility requires that the individual compare the marginal utility per dollar of an additional unit of one good with the marginal utility per dollar of all others. When all marginal utilities per dollar are equal and the consumer has expended all of her budget, she has obtained the maximum level of satisfaction possible. An increase in the price of one good will usually cause the consumer to reduce the consumption of that good and increase the consumption of other goods. An increase in the consumer's budget will usually cause an increase in the consumption of all goods. The increase in consumption of some goods, however, will be more than proportional to the consumer's increase in income.

Goods whose consumption increases more than the proportional increase in relation to income are said to have *income-elastic demand functions*. This is an important concept in environmental economics, because it is generally argued that the demand for environmental quality is income-elastic. This observation suggests an interesting phenomenon. As the income of a population increases, the demand for environmental quality improvements is likely to increase more rapidly. This argument has been used to suggest why there has been a substantial growth in environmental concerns in the United States since the 1950s. If environmental demand curves are indeed income-elastic throughout the world, we can expect growing global concern for environmental quality, because world income is growing. We are beginning to see the signs of this growing awareness in the international concern for acid rain and the depletion of the ozone layer. We can expect an acceleration of this trend as world income grows in real terms.

To summarize, consumers want to maximize their own satisfaction from consumption. Each consumer is subject to a limited budget (also called a budget constraint), and has preferences for (that is, derives utility from) various consumption goods. Maximization requires that the consumer choose combinations of goods to the point where marginal utility per dollar is equal and the full budget is spent. Any increase in budget (that is, in the consumer's income) will increase consumption. Any increase in the price of one product will cause the consumer to consume less of that good and, if possible, more of other goods.

ECONOMIC EFFICIENCY IN THE ECONOMY

Because individuals have utility functions and budget constraints, the combination of actions that maximizes their self-interest can be said to be efficient. Efficiency implies that maximization is taking place. No other option could do better at meeting the stated goals, given the costs of the alternatives.

In the purely competitive market that economists call perfect competition, the self-interests of all the actors in the economy lead to an efficient outcome for the whole economy. This maximization is achieved by what Adam Smith called the "invisible hand" of the marketplace. Individual consumers maximize their utility given their income and the prices of goods and services. Owners of plants organize output so as to maximize their profit, since profit is returned to them and increases their income and the total utility available to them. In order to maximize profits, each plant will produce products at the lowest possible cost. That is, it will combine inputs of land, labor, and capital (machinery) to get the largest possible output for a given cost. The plant owner's incentives ensure that the consumer purchases goods produced at the lowest possible cost. The consumers' incentives ensure that plant owners produce the goods the society wants. Efficiency is automatically generated.

This perfectly competitive model is not fully applicable, however, in the case of pollution. This is because in generating pollution a plant imposes costs on others — costs the plant owner does not have to pay. The result is that the plant does not reflect these pollution costs in the prices of the goods it produces. Consumers are misled by the low prices and consume more of these polluting goods than they would if the prices reflected the costs of pollution. In other words, a private market with pollution will produce an inefficient combination of goods. The invisible hand does not work.

This inefficiency in the market can be corrected in several ways. The regulatory approach taken in existing federal pollution laws is one way to move the private market toward an efficient allocation of resources. It does this by regulating the quantity of emissions a source may release. If the appropriate quantity is dictated, the result will be efficient. Economists have suggested a somewhat different approach, which would employ some elements of the market system: They suggest that pollution be priced. Emissions would be controlled indirectly because the price makes it more expensive to pollute than not to pollute. Because individuals respond to differences in the costs of alternatives, it follows that self-interested plant owners would reduce emissions as the cost of polluting rose. The result would be an efficient economy. There is considerable difference of opinion among students of environmental policy, however, over whether the regulatory or the economic approach would work best in solving the inefficiency of distributing the costs of pollution that exists in the private market. This issue will be explored in depth in this book.

ECONOMIC EFFICIENCY AND DISTRIBUTIONAL EQUITY

In theory, the private market leads to an efficient allocation of resources in the absence of pollution. It also leads to a particular distribution of income within the society. People are paid according to the value society, through the market, places on the output of their work. If a particular worker is good at producing shoes, his or her income will be higher than other, less productive workers. Those with little or no ability to produce goods and services that are valued by society will receive little or no income. If their lack of productivity is not their fault, our society typically makes the judgment that the market distribution of income is unfair. Under these circumstances society may choose to interfere with the market distribution of income. This change in distribution is usually accomplished through government action. The goal of such redistribution is to increase the income of people with lower incomes transferring to them some of the income of people with higher incomes. The progressive income tax is one example of an effort to redistribute income in this way.

The purpose of government action to control pollution is not a redistribution of income, but such government actions do in fact affect the distribution of income. A regulation that requires owners of all automobiles to install pollution control devices, for example, is more likely to affect the income of the poor adversely than is a policy of controlling emissions from new cars, because poor people are more likely to own old cars. Society might decide to modify its pollution control policies if they affect the distribution of income adversely. Even if a society does not seek to modify government actions, it might want to determine the effects of pollution control laws on income distribution. This information could be useful in determining whether other remedial policies are required.

BENEFIT/COST ANALYSIS IN POLLUTION CONTROL

Benefit/cost analysis applies the same logic to public decisions as is applied by the market to private decisions. Benefits, which represent demand, are compared with cost, which represents supply. In this section is discussed the use of benefit/cost analysis to determine the efficient level of environmental quality.

The Costs of Preventing Pollution

In producing, transporting, and consuming goods and services, society generates unwanted by-products. When these unwanted by-products are released into the environment, they can cause damage. To prevent such damage, it is necessary to do one of three things. First, the source could refrain from releasing the waste. The simplest — but not necessarily the best — way to accomplish this would be to refrain from producing. Other possibilities for reducing the amount of waste released include changing production techniques and installing control devices. Second, the source could modify the form of the waste, the time of its release, or the location of its release to reduce the damage it does to the environment. Third, the ability of the environment to absorb waste without adverse effects could be improved.

The prevention of environmental damage is costly. Workers must be employed to operate pollution control equipment. Capital must be invested in the equipment. Land must be used to locate the equipment or to hold wastes for future release. All of these factors of production could be used to produce other goods and services instead. The cost of pollution control is the opportunity cost of the resources (land, labor, and capital) used; that is, the amount of shoes, bicycles, or other goods that could be produced with those resources.

The total cost of pollution control depends on how effective the control process is at removing damaging wastes. Figure 2.1 shows a typical pollution control cost curve. This curve relates the *total costs of controlling emissions (TTC)* to the quality of the environment. *TCC* increases at an increasing rate because higher levels of emission control are more expensive to obtain than lower levels. Essentially, a source of emissions will select easy, and therefore less expensive, controls to achieve small reductions. For bigger reductions, more sophisticated equipment is required. Automobile exhaust emissions can be reduced somewhat, for example, by simple changes in carburetion. To achieve higher levels of control it is necessary to install more complex equipment, such as air pumps and catalytic converters. This means that costs increase at an increasing rate.

FIGURE 2.1 Total and Marginal Costs of Pollution Control

Controlling pollution requires the use of resources. The total cost of control (*TCC*) increases after some improvements occur in environmental quality because more sophisticated and complex technologies must be used to achieve later improvements. The marginal cost of control (*MCC*) is the change in total cost of control (*TCC*) for each incremental improvement in environmental quality. When *TCC* is increasing rapidly, *MCC* is also increasing, which is usually the case at very comprehensive levels of pollution control.

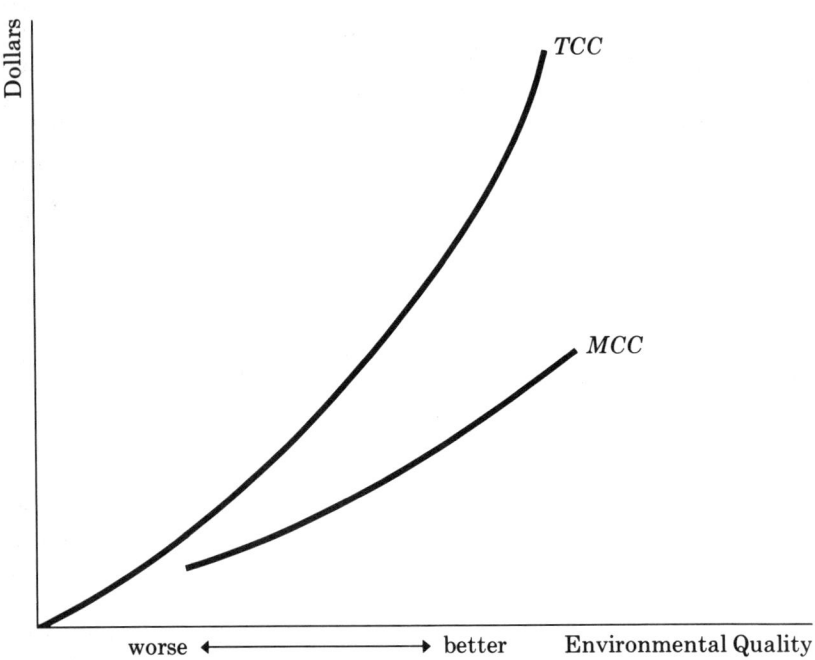

Marginal cost is the change in total cost for each small increase in environmental quality. It can be expressed as the slope of the *TCC* curve at any given level of environmental quality, or the change in *TCC* as environmental quality is increased by a certain small amount. The fact that *TCC* increases at an increasing rate implies that the *marginal cost of control (MCC)* increases as environmental quality improves.

Benefits from Controlling Pollution

The worsening of environmental quality as a result of emissions causes damage to people, plants, animals, and physical assets. People may suffer from the effects of pollution on health; poor air quality, for example, can trigger asthma attacks. People may also suffer reductions in the satisfaction they get from consuming the environment; they might, for example, lose a view of some distant mountains. People also suffer damages if plants or animals are adversely affected. Pollution can cause disease and lack of growth in plants and animals. It can also reduce the aesthetic value of plants by causing them to lose leaves, spot, or lose their flowers prematurely. Plants and animals are of value to people, so people suffer damages from these adverse environmental effects.

The benefit of pollution control is a reduction in these losses when the environment is improved. Benefit is another term for the satisfaction or utility gained from consuming the environment; it is another way of labeling *demand* for environmental quality. Suppose an orange tree produces five hundred oranges in a poor environment. As the environment is improved, production will increase. Small improvements generate substantial increases in the output of oranges if the original environmental quality is poor. Once environmental quality has been improved, additional small improvements will increase production, but by a lesser amount. Thus total production of oranges increases, but at a decreasing rate. We can measure the benefits of pollution control by the increased output of oranges. This output can be translated into dollars by multiplying the increase in output by the price of oranges. In this way we can express the benefits of pollution control in the same unit we express costs in: money.

Pollution control reduces other damages as well. Every damage that is avoided can be quantified in dollars, at least conceptually. The result is a *total benefits of control* function, which often looks like the curve labeled *TBC* in Figure 2.2. After the first improvements, *TBC* increases at a decreasing rate. At some point, further improvements in environmental quality will have no further effect on benefits and the *TBC* curve will become flat. The *marginal benefit of control (MBC)* is the slope of the *TBC* curve.

FIGURE 2.2 Total Benefit and Margin of Pollution Control

The total benefit from controlling pollution (*TBC*) represents improvements in human health, plant and animal health and productivity, and natural beauty. These benefits increase rapidly when control efforts begin. At later stages of control, however, *TBC* increases less rapidly. The marginal benefit of control (*MBC*) declines as the rate of growth in *TBC* lessens.

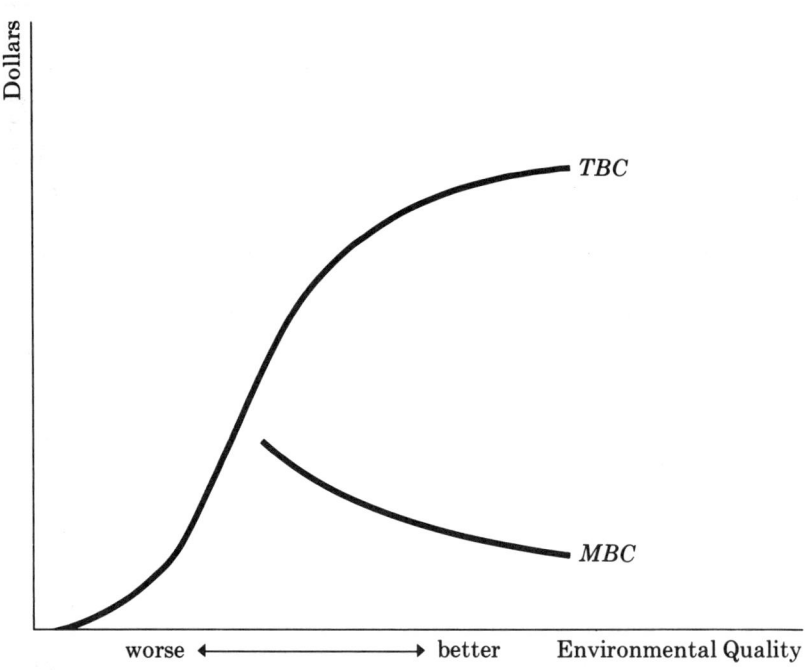

Where *TBC* increases at a decreasing rate, the *MBC* curve has a negative slope, because the marginal benefit is decreasing.

Efficiency in Pollution Control

To justify the expenditure of scarce resources on improvements in environmental quality, it is necessary to show that the resultant improvements are more valuable than the forgone goods and services. This is accomplished through *benefit/cost analysis*. With the help of Figure 2.3, we can discover the most efficient way to use

FIGURE 2.3 The Efficient Level of Environmental Quality

The efficient level of control of pollution is the point where the difference between TBC and TCC, called total net benefit (TNB), is greatest. This is at environmental quality EQ* where MBC equals MCC. Requiring a positive net benefit or — what amounts to the same thing — a positive benefit-to-cost ratio might seem to be a good rule for social decisions, but it allows any environmental quality between EQ_0 and EQ_1. Only one point in this range — EQ^* — is truly efficient.

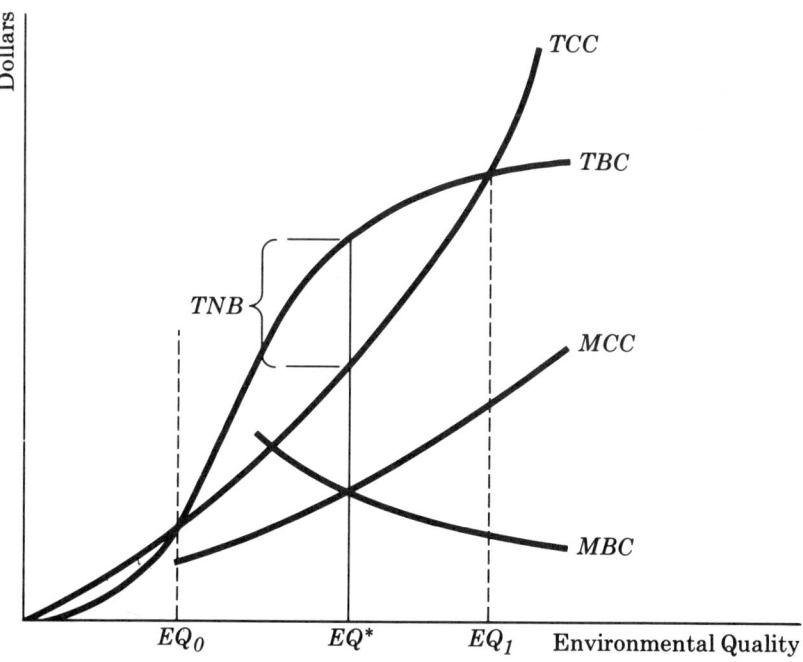

society's resources to control pollution. The total cost of control (*TCC*) curve and the marginal cost of control (*MCC*) curve indicate the opportunity costs of controlling emissions and improving environmental quality. This is because the cost of the land, labor, and capital employed in controlling emissions reflects the value these productive resources would have if they were used to produce some other good or service valued by society. The total benefit of control (*TBC*) curve and the marginal benefit of control (*MBC*) curve indicate the value to society of improvements in environmental quality.

How clean should the environment be? Two criteria should be used together to answer this question. First, *TBC* must be greater than *TCC*. The logic of this criterion is straightforward. *TBC* represents the value of all the resources used to generate the improvement in the environment, and *TCC* represents the value all these resources would have if they were used to produce other goods and services. Clearly, society would be worse off if we were to undertake a pollution control project whose *TCC* was greater than its *TBC*. Society would be giving up other goods that it valued more highly than the improved environmental quality. While this simple logic is helpful in determining the most desirable level of environmental quality, it does not go far enough. In Figure 2.3, any environmental quality between EQ_0 and EQ_1 would meet this criterion.

A second criterion is that *MBC* should equal *MCC*. In other words, the *efficient level of environmental quality* (represented by EQ^*) occurs at the point where *MBC* and *MCC* intersect. Again the logic of this criterion is rather simple. To the left of EQ^* the benefits of a small increase in *EQ* are greater than the costs. Society gets some additional net benefit (excess of benefits over costs) if pollution control is increased. Society will clearly be better off if the environment is improved somewhat, because the gain in the value of the environment is greater than the loss in the value of the other goods and services that could be produced with the same resources. At any point to the right of EQ^*, however, a small decrease in environmental quality will save more in costs than it will sacrifice in benefits. Net benefits will increase as environmental quality is reduced toward EQ^*. In fact, the *total net benefit* (*TNB*, obtained by subtracting *TCC* from *TBC*) is maximized where *MBC* equals *MCC*, which is at EQ^*. *TNB* represents the net gain society receives from using resources on environmental quality. At any point other than EQ^* this gain would be lower, and the society would be less well off. EQ^* represents the best society can do. Any other allocation is inefficient because the society is giving up some net benefit.

Both of the criteria stated above are necessary for the efficient achievement of environmental quality. Suppose instead that we decided to equate *TBC* and *TCC*. This is equivalent to having a benefit-to-cost ratio of one to one. In many public debates, people assume that a B/C (benefit/cost) ratio of one is the correct criterion. In fact, it is inefficient. *TBC* and *TCC* are equal at EQ_0 and at EQ_1. At EQ_1, *MCC* is greater than *MBC*. Society would be better off giving up some environmental quality. At EQ_0 the opposite is true.

Requiring a benefit/cost ratio of more than one is equivalent to requiring TBC to be greater than TCC. We have already seen that this criterion is insufficient because it allows acceptance of any value between EQ_0 and EQ_1. Likewise, it is possible for MBC to equal MCC while TBC is smaller than TCC. An environmental quality project with these characteristics should not be undertaken.

Another criterion suggested in public debate is cost effectiveness. This requires that one seek the least costly method of attaining a particular environmental quality. Any number of different methods of control could be used to produce a particular level of environmental quality. Adding the cost of each factor of production yields the total cost of employing that method. One method of control will prove less costly than the others for obtaining that particular level of environmental quality. Doing this sort of analysis for all levels of environmental quality produces the TCC curve in Figure 2.1. Thus all an analysis of cost effectiveness tells us is whether we are at or above TCC. This is useful information, because any cost in excess of the lowest possible cost is a waste of resources and therefore inefficient. It does not, however, tell us what level of effectiveness we should choose. In other words, ensuring that society is reaching any particular level of environmental quality in a cost-effective manner does not settle the question of what is the efficient level of environmental quality.

An Example of Benefit/Cost Analysis

The logic of benefit/cost analysis is simple, clear, and unavoidable. In practice, however, it is difficult and expensive to develop the full cost and benefit functions depicted in Figure 2.3. Instead, only a partial estimate or a point estimate is made. An example of a benefit/cost analysis that produced a point estimate is a study conducted by H. M. Peskin on the benefits and costs of meeting federal air quality standards.[1]

In Table 2.1 we present Peskin's estimates of the total benefit, total cost, and total net benefit of meeting the air quality requirements of the Clean Air Act of 1970. The figures are presented as percentages of income for various income groups. Several interesting conclusions can be drawn from these data. First, total net benefit

---

[1] H. M. Peskin, "Environmental Policy and the Distribution of Benefits and Costs," in P. R. Portney, ed., *Current Issues in U.S. Environmental Policy* (Baltimore: Johns Hopkins University Press, 1978).

TABLE 2.1 Distribution of Benefits and Costs of Federal Air Pollution Control Requirements among Income Groups (Percentage of Income)

					Income Group					
	Less than $3,000	$3,000 to $3,999	$4,000 to $4,999	$5,000 to $7,999	$8,000 to $9,999	$10,000 to $11,999	$12,000 to $14,999	$15,000 to $19,999	$20,000 to $24,999	$25,000 and over
Total Benefits	8.0	5.1	4.1	3.5	3.4	3.0	2.9	2.5	2.2	1.3
Total Costs	8.2	6.0	5.1	4.4	3.9	3.6	3.4	3.0	2.7	1.8
Total Net Benefits	−0.2	−0.9	−1.0	−0.9	−0.5	−0.6	−0.5	−0.5	−0.5	−0.5

Source: Henry M. Peskin, "Environmental Policy and the Distribution of Benefits and Costs," in P. R. Portney, ed., *Current Issues in U.S. Environmental Policy* (Baltimore: Johns Hopkins University Press, 1978), Table 5-6.

is negative for all income classes. This must mean that for society as a whole the total net benefit of meeting federal air quality standards is negative. Recall that this violates one of the conditions of efficient allocation of resources in benefit/cost analysis. In other words, Peskin's estimates indicate that federal air quality standards are to the right of EQ_1 in Figure 2.3.

Second, note that the distribution of benefits is not equal among income groups. Lower-income groups receive more benefits as a percentage of income than do higher-income groups. One possible reason for this is that people with lower incomes currently live in more polluted areas. Controlling air pollution will have a greater effect on these areas than on the relatively clean areas where people with higher incomes live. The fact that people with lower incomes live in dirtier areas is not surprising. The reduced environmental quality makes these places less desirable. People who can afford cleaner options move elsewhere. The price of property in the dirty areas is reduced, making it more accessible to lower-income groups. Note also that cleaning up the low-income areas can have the effect of causing prices to rise. Lower-income groups may move out of these areas when higher-income groups move in.

Third, the costs of pollution control are also distributed so that lower-income groups pay a greater percentage of their income for air pollution control. The cost of pollution control to people with low incomes is greater than its benefits, so its net benefit is negative. Net benefit is less (or loss is greater) for lower-income groups than for higher-income groups. If this pattern were to hold for an efficient level of control, air pollution control as currently approached in the Clean Air Act would tend to redistribute wealth from lower-income groups to higher-income groups. Such a redistribution is termed *regressive*. Such regressivity is commonly found in studies that analyze both the costs and benefits of government programs, but it is contrary to the professed ideals of the society. One might reasonably ask why this is true. We will explore this issue later in this book.

THE ENVIRONMENTAL PROBLEM AS ONE ECONOMIST SEES IT

Our society is faced with scarce resources, which must be used to fill virtually unlimited wants. Not everything desired by society can be accomplished. To improve environmental quality, society must forgo other goods and services. This simple idea of opportunity cost is central to the environmental problem and its solution. Attempts by government to solve the environmental problem without reference to opportunity costs cannot succeed.

In deciding how much it is willing to give up to obtain improvements in environmental quality, a society should seek efficient solutions. Efficiency requires that any chosen level of environmental quality be achieved at the lowest possible cost. Efficiency also requires that the level of environmental quality sought should be the quantity at which total net benefits are maximized. Meeting federal air quality standards that call for "zero health effects" will be inefficient and therefore undesirable if Peskin's study is correct.

The environmental problem thus appears to be that people are willing to give up some other goods and services to get improved environmental quality, but the private market does not provide them with a mechanism for doing so. The public market, or government, makes the choice between environmental quality and other goods possible. Existing laws, however, do not appear to be operating efficiently.

Finally, it is worthwhile to note that the pollution problem is general, but its solution in any particular area will be unique. EQ^* will be different in Los Angeles from what it is in Albuquerque. The relationship between emissions and environmental quality might also be different, so that it will take more pounds of emissions in Albuquerque to have the same effect on such air quality indicators as visibility. This suggests that MCC will be lower in Albuquerque than in Los Angeles. At the same time, people in Albuquerque might be more willing to pay for improvements in quality. This will increase MBC. If both of these assumptions were true, the efficient level of environmental quality would be higher in Albuquerque than in Los Angeles.

STUDY QUESTIONS

1. Instead of releasing wastes into the environment, a firm can recycle those wastes. Suppose that it costs $5.00 per pound to recycle wastes and the firm can sell the recycled wastes for $2.00. Is it economical for the firm to recycle? Suppose that environmental damage from the release of wastes is $6.00. Is it efficient for the society to recycle the waste?

2. Los Angeles is known for its smog and massive freeway system, while Albuquerque is known for its clean air and view of the mountains. Some economists argue that the efficient air quality in Albuquerque is much cleaner than the efficient air quality in Los Angeles. What factors could cause this to be the case?
3. In Table 2.1 it is shown that total net benefit of meeting the federal air quality control requirements in all areas of the country is negative for all income groups. What does this imply about the efficiency of the federal requirements as applied to any single area?

SUGGESTED READINGS

1. H. M. Peskin, "Environmental Policy and the Distribution of Benefits and Costs," in P. R. Portney (ed.), *Current Issues in U.S. Environmental Policy* (Baltimore: Johns Hopkins University Press, 1978) is instructive on how benefit/cost analysis is done.
2. E. Mishan, *Cost-Benefit Analysis* (New York: Praeger): Various editions present in detail the logic and pitfalls of benefit/cost analysis.

3

Pollution and the Private Market

Economic analysis reveals that private decision-makers will not choose to control pollution at the efficient level without government interference. This inefficiency has two closely related causes: externalities and public goods. But before we begin to look at the details of this economic analysis, it may be helpful to present a simple explanation of the private market economy. This explanation can then be used in analyzing the effect of externalities and public goods on the allocation of resources.

THE BASICS OF A MARKET ECONOMY

The following explanation of the workings of a market economy is presented to review how a simple private market would allocate resources efficiently.[1] I would not argue that markets work exactly as this idealized system suggests; in fact, I know that they do not. This simplified view is helpful, however, because it allows us to concentrate on a few essential elements in our analysis of pollution policy.

In this section I will present a graphic model of the private market for one good; let's say cola. In this simplified market all colas are identical, no matter who produces them. There are no labels or brand names. Every cola is indistinguishable from every other cola.

---

[1] If this material is new to you, you might want to review a good principles book. R. Dorfman, *Prices and Markets* (Englewood Cliffs, N.J.: Prentice-Hall, 1978), provides an excellent treatment in a short book.

This assumption is not essential, but it does make the analysis much easier. The principles derived for this simple model would also apply if colas were distinguishable. We assume that there are so many consumers of cola that individuals believe they have no effect on the price of cola, no matter how much or how little they consume. Similarly, we assume that there are so many producers of cola that each producer believes it has no effect on the price at which cola is sold, no matter how much or how little it produces. All consumers and producers do, however, attempt to maximize their own utility, and these individual actions to maximize self-interest cause the market economy to produce exactly what society wants.

Consumption Choices

Individuals seek to allocate their consumption between cola and other goods so as to obtain the maximum satisfaction from their available resources. This is accomplished when the consumer equates the marginal utility (MU) per dollar for each of the goods and spends his or her full income for the period. Generally, marginal utility declines as more units of a good are consumed. Picture yourself on a hot summer day. You have been playing tennis and you are very thirsty. The amount of utility (or benefit) you receive from the first glass of cola is very high. The utility you receive from the second glass is not so great. After perhaps three glasses you don't want any more. At this point the marginal utility of consuming an additional glass of cola is zero.

With declining marginal utility, it is possible to maximize your utility while spending all your income on the two goods X and Y, by employing Equation 3.1.

$$\frac{MU_X}{P_X} = \frac{MU_Y}{P_Y} \qquad 3.1$$

where:

MU_X = the marginal utility of the last unit of good X consumed.
P_X = the price of good X.
MU_Y = the marginal utility of the last unit of good Y consumed.
P_Y = the price of good Y.

Suppose that good X is cola and suppose that P_X is one dollar. After tennis you would prefer to have two glasses of cola, but you choose to consume only one because the price is so high. If the price were only fifty cents you would probably decide to have a second glass of cola. This illustrates the law of demand.

The *law of demand* states that the number of units of a good consumed by an individual during a specified period of time is inversely related to the price of the good. As the price declines, consumption increases. This behavior is consistent with Equation 3.1. Suppose that MU_X for one cola equals ten and P_X equals one dollar. Suppose also that the MU_Y (assume that good Y is popcorn) equals five and its price (P_Y) is fifty cents. These numbers satisfy Equation 3.1. If the price of a cola goes down to fifty cents, the MU per dollar's worth of cola (twenty) is higher than that of popcorn (ten). Your satisfaction (utility) would be increased by consuming more cola and less popcorn, given your budget.

Figure 3.1 presents the demand curve for a typical consumer of cola. This curve is designated by d (short for demand). Note that this individual demands less cola as its price increases.

The position of the demand curve d depends on three things:

1. The utility the individual derives from cola.
2. The individual's income.
3. The price of other goods.

The tennis game increased the utility derived from the cola. This increase in utility shows up as a shift of d to the right (to d', for example). This means that you will want to consume more cola at each possible price after the tennis game than you would normally. An increase in your income will also shift your demand curve to the right. Recall that we assumed that Equation 3.1 was satisfied *and* that all your income was spent. With more income, you will purchase more cola and more popcorn at the existing prices. Finally, an increase in the price of popcorn (P_Y) will lead to the consumption of more cola. This again shifts d for cola to the right.

Remember that consumers relate the satisfaction received from one good to the opportunity forgone by the reduction in their consumption of other goods. Thus the demand curve represents the marginal utility (or benefit) the consumer receives, and the price paid represents the opportunity cost of units of popcorn forgone to consume the last unit of cola.

An individual demand curve is logically equivalent to the marginal benefit of control (MBC) function developed in Chapter 2. We saw that improved environmental quality generated a lower MBC for additional control. The MBC function can be thought of as the demand for environmental quality. It shares all the characteristics

FIGURE 3.1 Typical Demand Curves

The law of demand states that the number of units of a good consumed by an individual during a specified period is inversely related to the price of the good. Thus, the demand curve d_x for the product X slopes downward to the right. This is comparable to the MBC curve discussed in Chapter 2. When such underlying factors as income and the price of other goods change, the whole demand curve shifts. A shift in demand to d' could be caused by an increase in the consumer's income, or by an increase in the prices of other goods.

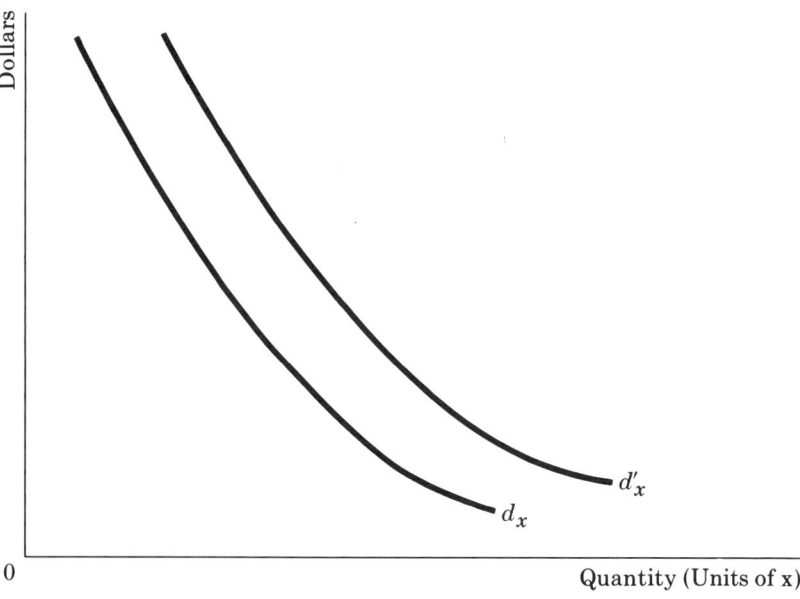

of the demand for cola: It depends on the utility the individual gains from improved environmental quality; as income increases, *MBC* shifts to the right just as d' does in Figure 3.1; and as the price of environmental quality increases, demand goes down. If the price of other goods were to rise, demand for environmental quality would increase because people would prefer the lower-priced activities and goods that are dependent on environmental quality to the other, now more expensive activities and goods.

Production Choices

Production of goods is organized by economic units called firms. A firm is owned by one or more individuals who produce and sell a good, pay the costs of production, and keep any residual. The residual is called *profit*. The organizers of a firm will seek to maximize their profit because this increases their income and, if more is better than less, increases in income are desired.

In order to maximize profit, a firm must do two things: Choose the correct number of units to produce and sell, and produce those units at the lowest possible cost. Let us first examine the costs of production.

A firm employs people, machinery, and land to produce its final product. These inputs are called *factors of production*. The factor of production that represents the employment of workers is labor (L). Let us assume that all labor is identical. Machinery, plants, materials, and equipment are called capital (K). Again for simplicity, assume that all capital is identical. The space on which production takes place is called land (A).

The marginal physical product (*MPP*) generated by a factor declines as more of it is used in conjunction with fixed amounts of the other factors. This phenomenon is true in all forms of production, including production of environmental quality. This phenomenon is called the *law of diminishing marginal productivity*. The task of the firm manager is to employ the combination of land, labor, and capital that will produce the desired output at the lowest possible cost. This will be accomplished when *MPP* per dollar is equal for all three factors of production. Equation 3.2 shows this condition.

$$\frac{MPP_L}{P_L} = \frac{MPP_K}{P_K} = \frac{MPP_A}{P_A} \qquad 3.2$$

where:

MPP_L = the marginal physical product of labor (and MPP_K of capital, and MPP_A of land).
P_L = the price of labor, or *wage* (and P_K of capital, and P_A of land — the *interest* and *rent*, respectively).

A firm can determine the total cost (*TC*) of production by employing the formula in Equation 3.3.

$$TC = Q_L P_L + Q_K P_K + Q_A P_A \qquad 3.3$$

where:

TC = total costs.
Q_L = the quantity of labor (or Q_K of capital, or Q_A of land) employed.
P_L = the price of labor (or P_K of capital, or P_A of land).

A typical TC function is presented in Figure 3.2.

Total cost is of interest, but two alternative cost concepts will also be useful in further discussion. Average cost (AC) is the total cost divided by the quantity produced. Geometrically, it is the slope of a line from the origin (0) to the TC function at the output quantity. In Figure 3.3 we see that the slope of such a line decreases at low quantities of output and increases at higher outputs. It is lowest

FIGURE 3.2 Total Cost Curve

The total cost of producing a good in the private economy (TC) increases as more is produced by a plant.

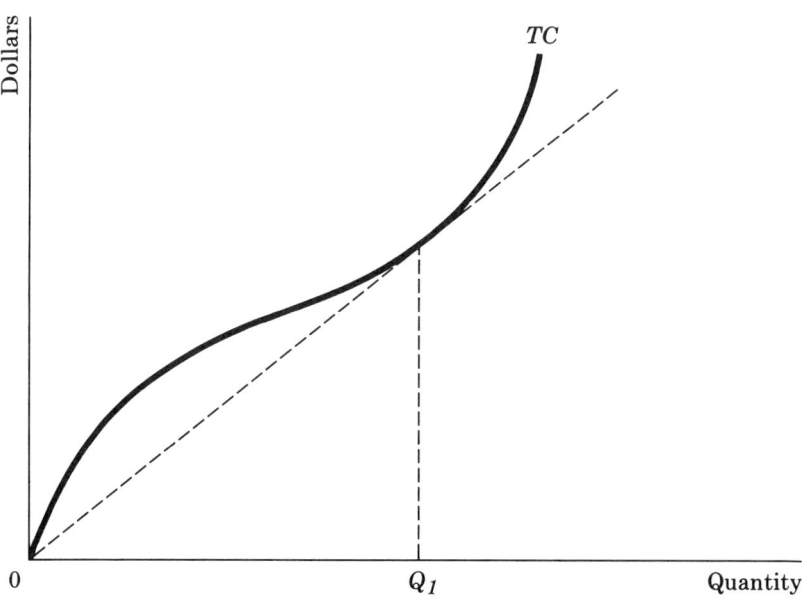

at output Q_1. The AC curve in Figure 3.3 is derived from the TC curve in Figure 3.2. Marginal cost is the change in cost as output is increased by the same small amount. Geometrically, it is the slope of the tangent to TC at each output. Initially, TC increases at a decreasing rate, so MC declines. At greater output, MC increases because TC increases at an increasing rate. MC equals AC at Q_1 because the line from the origin is tangent to TC at this point.

Profit Maximization

We can now analyze the profit-maximizing decision of the firm. The firm faces a market price for its product. This price is not affected by the firm's actions, because each firm's output is only a portion of the

FIGURE 3.3 Average and Marginal Cost Curves

The average cost of producing a good ($AC = TC/Q$) declines initially, reaches a minimum, and begins to increase as plant output increases. The marginal cost of production (MC) increases but remains below AC as AC declines, is equal to AC when AC is at its minimum, and is higher than AC when AC is increasing.

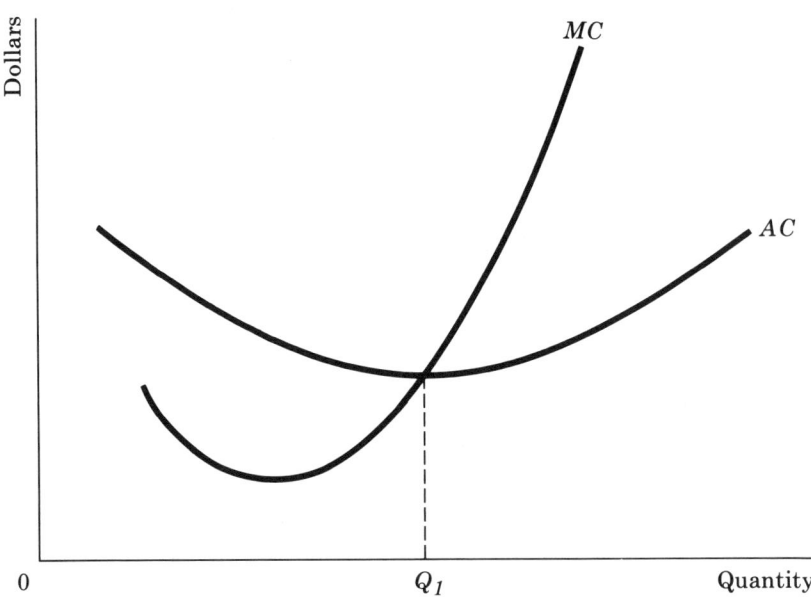

total output of this product. Thus the firm can sell any amount it chooses at the market price. In effect, the firm faces a horizontal demand curve for its product. The total revenue (TR) the firm receives is equal to the price received (P) times the quantity sold (Q_1). Profit (π) equals $TR - TC$.

Firm and Market Equilibrium

In a perfectly competitive market like the one we have been discussing, market price and quantity are determined by the interaction of demand and supply. The individual demand curve is derived from the utility or benefit an individual receives from the product as compared to the benefit he or she receives from other goods. Thus individual demand reflects the marginal benefit (MB) of consuming additional units of the good. Market demand is the horizontal sum of individual demand curves. Thus it reflects the marginal benefit received by all people in the market. Each firm supplies the good according to its marginal cost (MC). The market supply is the horizontal sum of these firms' MC functions, so it also reflects the marginal cost of producing this good. Market equilibrium results when the quantity demanded equals the quantity supplied. This equilibrium is a long-run equilibrium when the market price allows firms to cover all costs but have profits of zero. Such an equilibrium is depicted in Figure 3.4.

This market equilibrium automatically equates the benefits to society of producing a good with the opportunity costs of doing so. Recall that the factors of production are paid according to their value in producing other goods valued by society. The value of those other goods and the price they sell for is determined by their demand or marginal benefit. Thus the return that factors would earn if they produced a second good reflects the value society places on that good. That is, it measures the opportunity cost of producing the first good, which is the value to society of the amount of the second good not produced. At market equilibrium the price of any good equals the marginal benefit of producing it and the marginal cost of producing it — that is, the opportunity cost of forgoing another good valued by society.

Market Adjustments

The remarkable thing about the market we have just described is the way it responds to the desires of society without the necessity of

FIGURE 3.4 Firm and Market Equilibrium

A firm is producing at maximum profit when it equates the market price it sells its product at (P) with its MC. The market is in long-run equilibrium when the market price, determined by the intersection of demand (D) and supply (S), produces zero profit for all firms. At this point, no additional firms have an incentive to enter this market.

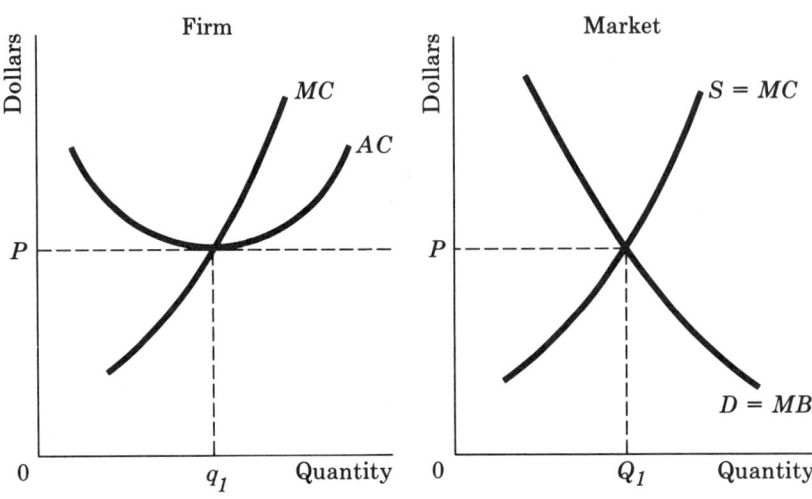

government intervention. To see how the market does this, we will examine the process of adjustment.

In Figure 3.5 we see the market for cola in equilibrium at a price of P_C and a quantity of Q_C. An individual firm produces q_1 units of cola and makes zero profits, just covering all costs. Now suppose society decides, for some external reason like an increase in GNP, that it wants more cola. The market demand curve will shift to D'. At the existing price, the quantity of cola demanded will be greater than the quantity supplied. Price will increase toward P'_C. As this happens, each of the firms currently producing cola will respond to the new demand, increase its output toward q_2, and earn a profit. This profit will induce other firms not already in the business to produce cola because of the return to be earned. The addition of more firms will shift the supply curve to the right. Eventually, it will shift sufficiently (to S') to make the price of cola return to its original

FIGURE 3.5 Market Adjustment

Suppose a market is initially in equilibrium at price (P_C). Now suppose that for some reason market demand increases to D'. This will cause an initial increase in the market price to P'_C. Existing firms will respond to the higher price by producing more and will earn a profit. This profit will attract new firms into the industry, increasing supply and lowering market price, until there is no longer a profit to be made. This equilibrating process causes the market to produce those products most desired by consumers.

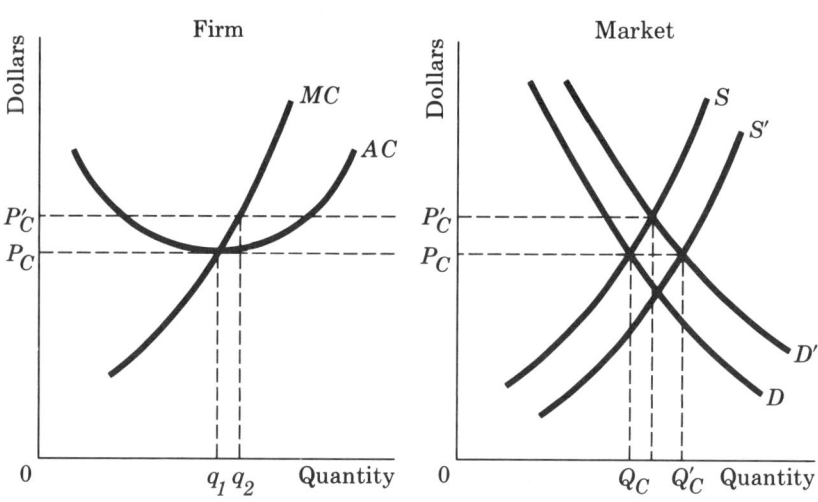

level.[2] At this point all the old firms and all the firms that have just entered the market are again making zero profits while total output has increased to Q'_C. There is no further incentive for new firms to become cola manufacturers.

Society's increased demand adjusted prices and generated profits. Profits generated increased supplies to satisfy the increase in demand. This is the automatic adjustment mechanism of a private market. No government action is necessary. The individuals acting through the market are guided by what Adam Smith called the invisible hand of self-interest to produce what society desires.

---

[2] This assumes that there are no unique inputs in the production of cola, so firm cost curves do not shift up or down as market output increases.

48 Pollution and the Private Market

The relationship between this market mechanism and the rules of benefit/cost analysis should now be evident. Market demand reflects the marginal benefit (MB) of consuming additional units of a good. Market supply reflects the marginal costs (MC) of producing those additional units of goods. Those marginal costs reflect the forgone opportunities to produce other goods valued by society. The private market automatically equates MB and MC through price competition. For two reasons, however, the private market does not work for environmental quality the way it works for cola. These reasons are *externalities* and *public goods*. We will turn to externalities first.

POLLUTION EXTERNALITIES

The private market allocates resources efficiently only when all individuals affected by the market decision are involved in making those decisions. This section explores the fact that the private market will not allocate resources efficiently because individuals who are affected by pollution do not participate in the market decision-making process.

Externalities

In the production of any good, unwanted by-products are generated. Suppose the production of cola creates wastes, which are released into a river. The adverse effect of these wastes reduces the number of fish living in the river and therefore the number that can be caught by the commercial fishing industry. If the firm decides to produce more cola, it will release more wastes into the river. Its decision to increase production does not take into account the costs to society of the release of wastes into the river. In an unregulated private market, such environmental costs are not reflected in the firm's marginal cost.

The production and sale of cola involves market agreements between the producing firm and the owners of the factors of production, and between the producing firm and the purchasers of cola. At no time does it include agreements with the fishing industry. Fishing is external to all agreements the firm enters when producing cola, yet the fishers are directly affected by the firm's decisions. This effect on parties not directly involved in market agreements is called an *externality*.[3]

Externalities can be either positive or negative. The previous example is of a negative externality. Most pollution cases involve negative externalities, representing changes in physical conditions that reduce the value of the environment for third parties. There are, however, positively valued effects on the environment as well. The San Onofre nuclear power plant on the California coast near San Clemente, for example, releases thermal waste into the Pacific Ocean. The higher temperature increases the production of microorganisms, small fish, and consequently, game fish. This increase in sport fish is a benefit from the production and release of unwanted waste. In this book we will generally be dealing with the negative effects of pollution, but the reader should not forget that positive effects sometimes occur as well.

Externalities and the Misallocation of Resources

The problem with externalities is that they cause the private market to misallocate resources. In our cola example, the manufacturer produces an excessive amount of cola and pollution. The full cost of producing cola includes the damages to the fish, but the firm does not consider these external costs and thus believes costs to be lower than they actually are. Responding to these lower private costs, the firm will produce a larger output of cola than it would if it had to pay for the damage to the fishing industry. This increased output increases the amount of pollution, which increases the damage to the fish, which increases costs, and so on.

A further example of an externality may be helpful. Suppose a firm built Lake View Apartments on the flat land along a lake. The view of the lake increases the benefit renters derive from the apartments. Consequently, rents are higher than for an equivalent apartment without a lake view. Now suppose that a second builder constructed Lake Shore Condominiums on the shore of the lake and that the new building interfered with the view from the previously built Lake View Apartments. The value of Lake View Apartments

---

[3] An excellent discussion of externalities can be found in A. V. Kneese and B. T. Bower, *Managing Water Quality: Economics, Technology, Institutions* (Baltimore: Johns Hopkins University Press, 1968), pp. 77–94.

has declined because the loss of view has caused renters to reduce the amount they are willing to pay. This loss in value was not considered by the builder of Lake Shore Condominiums, because the unregulated private market does not require it. Suppose the cost of building the Lake Shore Condominiums was $10 million and that they were sold for $10 million. (Remember that costs include the necessary return to the builder.) In a private market without regulation, the builder would proceed with the project. The $10 million cost, however — which we shall call the private cost of the building — does not include all the costs. The loss in the value of Lake View Apartments is also a cost, but it is external to the builder of Lake Shore Condominiums. If this external cost were included in the builder's decision, the condominiums would not be built. Thus an unregulated private market with externalities will produce an excessive amount of the externality-producing good, and resources will be allocated inefficiently.

In Figure 3.6 we see the situation faced by the cola manufacturer. The costs incurred directly by the firm, which we previously called marginal costs, we will now call the *marginal private costs* (*MPC*), to reflect the fact that they do not include the externalities. These private costs include the payments made by the firm for land, labor, and capital. These payments stem from the agreements between the manufacturer and the factors of production. But remember that these costs do not include the cost of the use of the environment. In a private market without government intervention there is no clear ownership of the environment, and therefore no market for it. The damage done by the release of wastes causes a reduction in environmental quality and an accompanying decrease in benefits. Such damages are called the *marginal externality costs* (*MEC*) of waste release. These marginal external costs are equal to the marginal benefits forgone as environmental quality deteriorates.

The full cost of production to society is the vertical sum of *MPC* plus *MEC*. This full cost, which is called the *marginal social cost* (*MSC*), is shown in Figure 3.6. These curves show that *MEC* increases with the output of cola. The firm would produce Q_C cola in the unregulated private market at the point where the market price for cola (P_C) equals *MPC*. The full cost to society of an additional cola, however, is E. Since P_C represents the benefits to society of one more cola, it is obvious that the firm has produced too much cola, because $P_C = MB = MPC < MSC$. The efficient level of cola production is at Q^*_C where $MSC = MB = P^*_C$. In the unregulated private

FIGURE 3.6 Externalities and the Efficient Output of Cola

The marginal private costs (MPC) reflect all the costs of producing cola except those external to the decision-maker. The marginal externality costs (*MEC*) represent the damages done by waste released in the process of producing cola. When the private market ignores these externalities, output is at Q_C and market price is at P_C. At this output, marginal social costs ($MSC = MPC + MEC$) are greater than marginal benefits (*MB*). The market is producing an inefficiently large output. The efficient output is at Q^*_C, where $MB = MSC$.

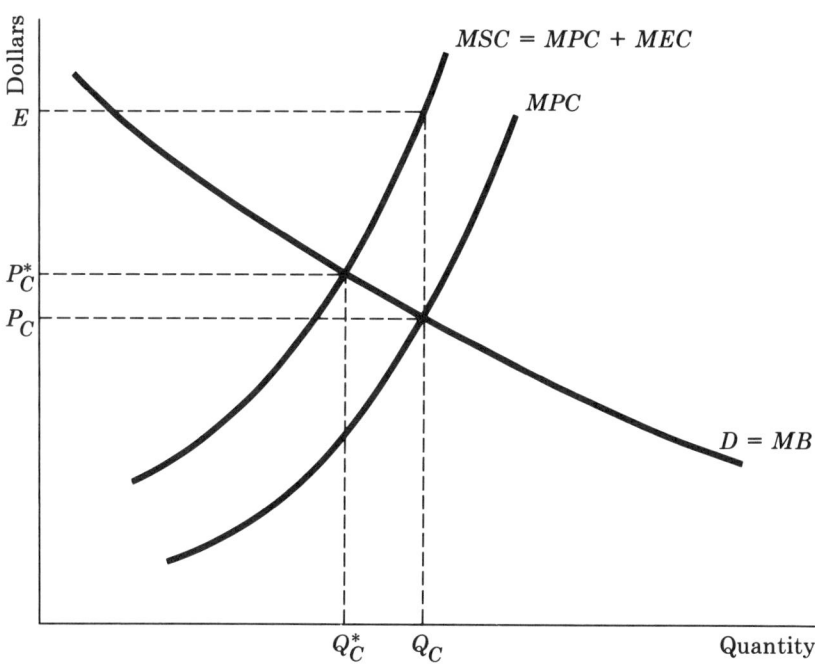

market there is no incentive for the firm to reduce its output because it does not directly pay *MEC*. Resources are misallocated. This misallocation is one reason given for government intervention in the private market to reduce pollution. In a private market without pollution *MEC* would be zero, so $MPC = MSC = MC$ and there would be no misallocation.

Implications of Pollution Externalities for the Allocation of Resources in the Private Market

We have shown that with no government intervention an individual firm that generates negative externalities in a private market will overproduce. Because all firms in an industry are likely to generate such externalities, the industry will produce an excessive amount of the good (Q_C) at too low a price (P_C). This leads consumers to overconsume the good and underconsume environmental quality and other goods. The extra environmental damage causes a reduction in the supply of fish and of other goods and services affected by wastes. This reduced supply, which can be represented as a shift to the left in the market supply function for fish, increases the price of fish (and other affected goods). Too few fish are produced and consumed at too high a price.

ENVIRONMENTAL QUALITY AS A PUBLIC GOOD

The second reason why the private economy does not allocate goods efficiently is that pollution and pollution control have the characteristics of a public good. In this section I explain what a public good is, show why pollution control is a public good, and discuss what effect this has on efficient supply of pollution control.

Private Goods

Goods commonly produced in the private market are called *private goods*. They are rival in consumption. That is, the consumption of one unit of the good by a particular individual precludes the consumption of that same unit of the good by another individual at the same time. Colas are a private good.

Public Goods

Goods that are not rival in consumption are called *public goods*. If one individual consumes one unit of the good, another individual can consume that same unit at the same time. A streetlight is an example of a public good. Walking down a street at night, I consume the services of a streetlight to avoid falling into a hole in the sidewalk. My companion also avoids the hole because she has the services of the same streetlight available to her at the same time. My consumption does not preclude her consumption. Whether or not I am there consuming the services of the streetlight, it is available to her. When the consumption of a good by one individual does not reduce the availability of that same unit of the good to others, the good is called nonrival in consumption. There is no rivalry over who gets the good because both can have it simultaneously.

Because of the nonrival nature of the consumption of public goods, the market demand for a public good is derived by adding individual demands vertically. In contrast, demands for private goods are added horizontally. The reason for horizontal addition of demands for private goods can be stated thus: If two separate individuals are to be provided with one unit of the good each, a total of two units is required. Each consumer must pay the same price for the unit he or she consumes, and the value each receives is equal to that price. The situation is different in the case of public goods. If I consume a unit of streetlight, it is still available for my companion to consume. It is not necessary to supply a second unit. Thus my willingness to pay for the public good can be added to hers. We both share the good, and total willingness to pay is the sum of our individual willingnesses.

When I want to consume a cola produced by the private market, I acquire access to it by paying the market price P_C. For my companion to consume a cola she must pay P_C for it as well. Total consumption is two units and total payment is $2P_C$. Neither of us gains access to a cola unless we pay the opportunity cost of providing it. The situation for the streetlight is different. Suppose I am willing to pay ten dollars for the availability of a streetlight because the marginal benefit to me of avoiding the hole in the sidewalk is equal to ten dollars. Further, suppose the cost of providing the streetlight is fifteen dollars. If I were the only person to benefit from the streetlight, it would be inefficient to supply it, because the value to society (ten dollars) is less than the opportunity cost (fifteen dollars). But I am not the only person to benefit from that particular streetlight; my companion benefits as well. Suppose her benefit is five dollars. Since she and I both benefit from the same streetlight, the total social benefit equals the sum of our individual benefits ($10 + $5 = $15), which just equals the opportunity cost of producing it. It is efficient to produce the streetlight.

A problem in the market provision of public goods now becomes clear. If I want to consume a private good like cola, I have to pay the opportunity cost of producing it. When I pay an amount equal to my benefit, I receive the cola and cover the opportunity cost of producing it. It is an efficient decision that involves only the producer and me. In order to consume the streetlight, I would have to pay the opportunity cost of producing it — fifteen dollars. I benefit only ten dollars' worth, however, so it does not increase my utility to supply the streetlight. A private decision between the producer and me would result in the streetlight not being produced. My companion, however, benefits by five dollars. If I could somehow get her to share in the cost of provision, the light would be produced and efficiency would result. But this requires the cooperation of three people: The producer, my companion, and I must agree that the streetlight will be purchased, and we must share the costs. The market for cola does not require such agreement to be efficient. This fundamental difference results in the private market failing to produce the efficient output of such public goods as streetlights. This failure of the private market creates problems for the environment, as we shall see.

Figure 3.7 presents the demands of three individuals (d_1, d_2, and d_3) for a public good. The curve labeled D is the vertical sum of the individual demands. The efficient level of supply of a public good is found at the intersection of the total demand and supply functions. These functions are the equivalent of market functions, but as we shall see, there is no market for a public good. This intersection requires an output of ten units at a cost of twenty-five dollars per unit. For individual 1, the marginal benefit of the tenth unit, and therefore his or her willingness to pay, is equal to eight dollars. For individuals 2 and 3, the willingnesses to pay are seven dollars and ten dollars, respectively. These marginal willingnesses to pay add up to twenty-five dollars. Thus they equal the costs of production. Since the individuals' demand curves equal their marginal benefits, the sum of those curves equals the marginal benefit for society. At an output of ten units, $MB = MC$.

The marginal values for the individuals in our example are not equal at the equilibrium level of output, or indeed at any other level. It is possible that MB for some individuals will be zero or negative. Note that in our example, MB_3 is zero beyond fifteen units. It is also possible that the willingness of an individual to pay will be relatively high at low outputs and low at high outputs, as d_3 demonstrates. Nor does the fact that a good is a public good necessarily imply that none of it will be produced in a private market. In Figure 3.7, demand d_3 is sufficient to induce a private market to supply two units of the public good, because at that level a purely private deci-

FIGURE 3.7 Demand and Supply of a Public Good

The aggregate demand for a public good (D) is the vertical sum of the demands of each individual. The efficient output, where $D = S = MC$, is ten units. At this output the marginal willingness to pay for output of the public good is \$8 per unit for individual 1, \$7 for individual 2, and \$10 for individual 3.

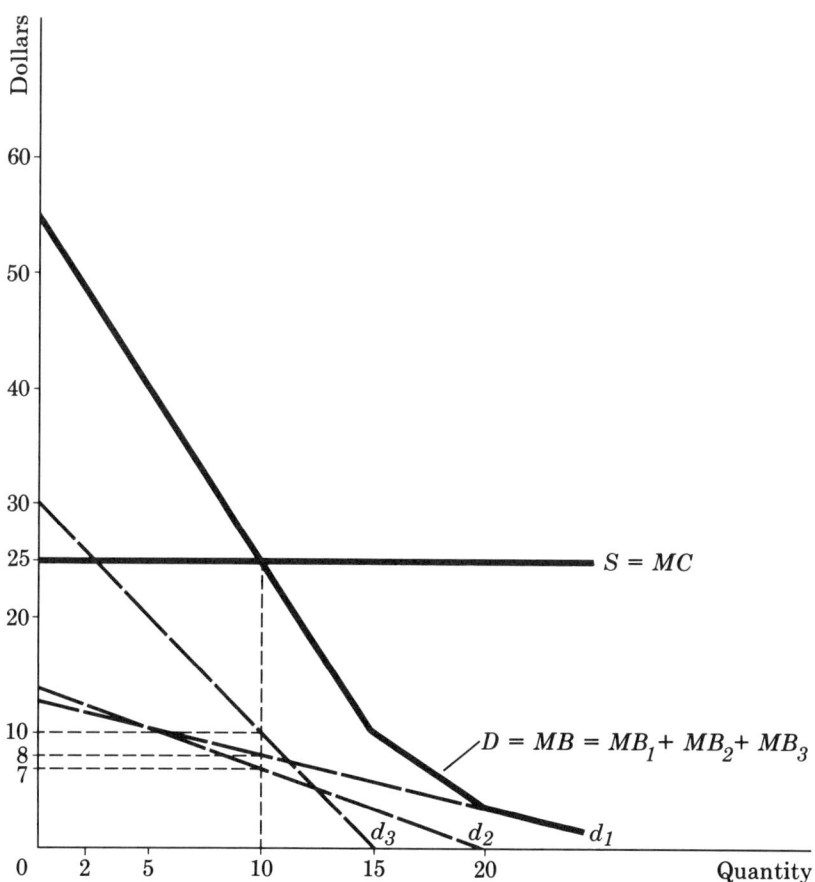

sion between individual 3 and the producer would create a marginal benefit to individual 3 equal to the opportunity cost of producing an additional unit of the good. Total benefit, however, is greater than the opportunity cost, so the private solution still undersupplies the public good.

Exclusion

A number of goods have the characteristics of being nonrival in consumption but are produced efficiently in the private market. A rock concert is a good example. Suppose your favorite group was performing outdoors in an area with no fences, so anyone could come to hear them. Then the rock concert would have the characteristics of a public good. You could enjoy the concert regardless of whether I was there listening or not. My consumption does not reduce the availability of the concert to you. Produced in this way, the rock concert is a public good.[4]

Now suppose that the rock concert was presented in a local auditorium with a limited number of seats. By holding the concert in an auditorium, the promoter can charge admission. Those with *MB* equal to or greater than the admission price will pay and attend. Others will be excluded. This exclusion can be used to make the rock concert a profitable operation. Those who attend pay for the costs of providing the rock concert. It is supplied in the same way cola is supplied, through a market. Those who attend are those who value the rock concert most highly, as measured by their willingness to pay to attend. The payment in this case could also include the personal costs of camping out all night in front of the ticket window. The fan who does that must value the concert more than the one who is willing to risk not getting a ticket and arrives at the ticket window after sunup.

Free Riders

Without exclusion, the concert would not be produced. Assume again that the rock concert is being held outdoors and that you and I are attending along with 998 others. The cost of producing the concert is $5,000, which implies a cost of five dollars per person attend-

---

[4] We are ignoring the possible crowding effects of an open-access concert, which might reduce, or might even increase, the benefits to an attendee. Crowding makes the open rock concert a less than perfect public good.

ing. There was no exclusion, because we did not have to pay before attending. But during the rock concert the promoter comes around asking for donations to cover costs. What will be my response?

The following logic might run through my mind: The rock concert is already supplied. It will not be stopped if I do not pay. Furthermore, others will pay for it. Therefore, even though I benefit by more than five dollars, I will assert that my benefit is low and refuse to make a donation. (After all, I am a professor, and everyone knows that professors don't like rock concerts.) In this way, I act as a free rider; that is, I enjoy the benefit free, assuming others will pay. Everyone else will have a similar incentive to act as a free rider. The result will be that the promoter will collect less than the expenses of putting on the concert and less than the concert is worth to society. Having learned from this experience, the promoter will not organize an open-access rock concert again. (The Woodstock rock festival in 1969, to cite a famous example, was intended to be a closed-access event until thousands of people broke down the fences.)

The fact that people tend to act as free riders when exclusion is not exercised explains why public goods are not provided in the private market. Society turns to government to solve this problem of inefficient output in cases where exclusion is prohibitively expensive or is deemed not socially desirable.

Efficiency and Lindahl Taxes

If the government is to supply public goods, it should do so at the efficient level. In the example in Figure 3.7, the efficient output is ten units. These ten units can be financed in various ways, but the most efficient way is to charge each individual an amount equal to his or her marginal benefit. In our example, the charges would be eight dollars, seven dollars, and ten dollars, respectively. This set of charges, equal to each individual's marginal benefit, is called a Lindahl tax, after the originator of the concept, E. Lindahl, a nineteenth century Swedish economist.[5] At this charge, each individual is in equilibrium; that is, each prefers the chosen output to any alternative. The marginal benefit of the public good equals the payment each individual makes. Thus everyone is happy with this output.

Other methods of financing do not share this characteristic. Charging each individual a third of the total cost, or $8.33, will

[5] D. C. Mueller, *Public Choice* (New York: Cambridge University Press, 1979), p. 24

cause all three to be out of equilibrium. At this cost, individuals 1 and 2 would want less than ten units because their *MB* would be less than their payment at ten units. Individual 3 would prefer more at this price because his *MB* would be greater than his payment. Any other tax scheme will have a similar disequilibrium characteristic. The issues of exclusion and efficient pricing of government-provided goods and services are very important in pollution control.

The Environment as a Public Good

The environment is a public good, nonrival in consumption. If I am enjoying a particularly nice environmental setting, such as a view of snowcapped mountains or a clear trout stream, you can enjoy the same view at the same time. My consumption does not preclude yours.

It is important to maintain a clear distinction between emissions and environmental quality. At a given level of environmental quality, my consumption of the environment does not preclude your consumption of the environment. We both see the same view. Emissions from a plant may reduce the environmental quality available to us both. The use of the environment as a waste disposal site precludes, or at least reduces in value, the use of the environment for other purposes.

Let's see how all this pertains to our friend the fish. Suppose 1,000 pounds of fish are available at a particular level of water quality. If I fish and take 500 pounds of them, only 500 pounds are available to you. It would seem that fishing is not a public good, since my consumption reduces the amount available to you. This is true, but it misses the point. Without exclusion, 1,000 pounds of fish are available at this level of environmental quality. Whether I intend to fish or not does not alter the fact that a certain number of fish are available to us collectively. My decision to fish only reallocates the available fish among people who benefit from pollution control. My benefit is still added to yours vertically to get the total benefit (1,000 fish) at this level of environmental quality. It is the environmental quality, not the fishing, that is nonrival.

Likewise, improvements in environmental quality are nonrival. If I take political action to reduce air pollution and consequently improve my view of the mountains, I receive benefits. At the same time, you receive benefits from my actions because your view of the mountains is also improved. It follows that in the absence of exclusion I will undersupply political action favoring pollution control, just as promoters would undersupply rock concerts. I will promote control to the point where my private *MB* equals my private *MC*. At that point, however, society's *MB* is greater than its *MC*. In Figure 3.7, if individual 3 took independent action to produce the public good, he would produce approximately two units at a marginal cost of approximately twenty-five dollars each because this is the point where his private marginal benefit (reflected in d_3) equals his private marginal cost. At this output, individuals 1 and 2 have positive *MB*. Thus the public *MB* (the vertical sum of d_1, d_2, and d_3) is greater than the *MC*, and the public good is undersupplied.

In some cases, it is possible to apply exclusion to environmental quality. One person, for example, might own a small lake. He can control access to the lake by fencing it and allowing only those who pay to use it. With exclusion, the owner will equate the *MC* of controlling emissions to the *MB* of the improved quality to the lake users, because he can collect that *MB* in the form of entry fees. The lake will have an efficient environmental quality.

Exclusion, however, is expensive for an owner to accomplish. A fence must be built and maintained; an attendant must be hired. As exclusion becomes more expensive, its cost might outweigh the benefits of the improved environmental quality. Large regions would require prohibitively expensive exclusion. Furthermore, they would require one owner. Imagine one individual owning all of the Los Angeles air basin or the Mississippi River water basin, and not allowing anyone into it who did not pay a fee. Exclusion may be conceptually possible, but it is not practical except in a few cases.

SUMMARY

In a private market without pollution, the self-interest of each individual leads the economy to produce the efficient output for the society. This output is determined by the intersection of the demand function and the supply function. The benefit/cost criteria we have suggested for pollution control decisions employs the logic of the market in that it equates the demand for environmental quality (the marginal benefit of control) to the supply of environmental quality (the marginal cost of control).

If pollution were just like cola, a market would exist for environmental quality. Externalities would not exist and the efficient outcome would be generated by the private market. But this is not the case. Because of the practical difficulties of providing exclusion in most cases of environmental damage, a market usually does not exist. The result is externalities and an inefficiently high output of goods that use and alter the environment. The environment is not like cola because the consumption of a given level of environmental quality by one individual does not preclude the consumption of that same level of environmental quality by others. The environment has the characteristics of a public good. Political action to induce government to control pollution is also a public good. This creates problems in finding a political solution, as we shall see later in this book.

STUDY QUESTIONS

1. The release of unwanted wastes can have both positive and negative effects on the environment. For example, the thermal waste at San Onofre increases sport fish species in the immediate area but may reduce other species and cause other damage. How would you determine the efficient level of environmental quality with both positive and negative externalities?
2. Suppose that a single firm owns a lake and all the surrounding land and there is no flow of water from the lake so that others are not affected by pollution in the lake. The lake can be used to dispose of wastes from the firm's plant and for recreational swimming. Will the firm use the lake in a socially efficient way? Hint: Don't forget about the cost of exclusion.
3. A public good can be transformed into a private good by the device of excluding those who do not pay from the benefits of the provision of the good. Political action which has the effect of improving environmental quality has the characteristics of a public good. Can political action be transformed into a private good through exclusion?

SUGGESTED READINGS

1. A. V. Kneese and B. T. Bower, *Managing Water Quality: Economics, Technology, Institutions* (Baltimore: Johns Hopkins University Press, 1968), pp. 77–94 provides an excellent discussion of externalities.

2. T. Crocker and A. Rogers, *Environmental Economics* (Chicago: Dryden, 1971) provides a very readable and brief discussion of externalities and the efficient level of control of pollution.
3. R. Dorfman and N. Dorfman (ed.), *Economics of the Environment: Selected Readings* (New York: Norton, 1977) contains several of the classic articles on this subject including papers by L. Ruff, O. Davis and M. Kamien, and R. Turvey.
4. J. Buchanan and C. Stubblebine, "Externality," *Economica* 29 (1962): 371–384 provides the classic discussion of when it is economic to adjust to externalities.
5. G. Hardin, "The Tragedy of the Commons," *Science* 162 (1968): 1243–1248 presents a simple explanation of the public goods nature of environmental issues in a classic article.

4

Control of Pollution

In the previous chapters you learned the essence of the economic problem of pollution control. Individuals have preferences for environmental quality and for other goods, and they are willing to pay for the goods they prefer. The private market does not generate the efficient level of environmental quality. The problem is to determine what level is efficient. How much environmental quality will society forgo in order to have certain goods, and what goods will society forgo in order to achieve a certain level of environmental quality? A natural state with no emissions is not likely to be the most preferred policy because pollution control carries with it opportunity costs, and at a high level of control the goods and services forgone are sure to be more valued by society than the additions to environmental quality. I have suggested that benefit/cost analysis be used to address the question of how clean to make the environment. In this chapter we will see the benefit/cost model substantially expanded. We will examine the control of emissions in a plant, the relationship between emissions and environmental quality, and the determination of an efficient level of environmental quality in a simple case involving one emitting plant and one person suffering damage. I will then expand the example to show how the same model can be used to deal with cases involving many plants and many people.

CONTROLLING EMISSIONS IN A PLANT

The owner of a plant retains as profit any difference between the cost of producing a good and the price at which it sells. The price of a good is determined in a market over which the producer generally has no control. The goal of the plant owner is to produce any particular level of output at the lowest possible cost, because decreases in the cost of production mean increases in profits. Thus the plant owner has an incentive to minimize costs.

Most production processes generate unwanted by-products. The burning of fuel produces needed heat, but it also produces waste gases. Painting a car leaves residual paint and solvents. The printing of this book generated waste paper in the folding and trimming processes. The list could go on, but the point is clear: Unwanted by-products are unavoidable, and they must be disposed of in some way. Matter cannot be created or destroyed. This fact has spawned a whole approach to the pollution problem, called the *materials balance approach*, which explicitly recognizes that these wastes must go somewhere. Where they go and in what form dictates the damage they do — that is, the pollution they create.[1]

The owner of the plant, wanting to maximize profit, will seek to dispose of these wastes in the least expensive manner possible. The least expensive method of disposing of wastes in an unregulated private economy is to dump them into the environment. Airborne wastes can be blown out of the plant and allowed to disperse in the atmosphere. Waterborne wastes can be released into a nearby river, lake, or ocean. Solid wastes can be dumped on the land. All of these methods carry with them, however, the potential for polluting the environment. This is where the considerations of profit maximization and benefits versus costs come into play. A plant owner who is not allowed to release these wastes directly into the environment will seek the least costly combination of land, labor, and capital necessary to stop the release.

The rule for determining the least costly technique is remarkably similar to the rule for maximizing a consumer's utility. Suppose that dust emissions (formally called particulates) can be controlled by the use of a filter system on the smokestack of a plant. The device can be made to remove dust more effectively in two ways. The size of the filter can be increased (which requires capital), or the frequency and quality of maintenance can be increased (which requires labor). If the size of the filter is increased but a fixed amount of maintenance labor is maintained, the number of pounds of dust removed

---

[1] An excellent book on this subject is A. Kneese, R. Ayres, and R. d'Arge, *Economics and the Environment: A Materials Balance Approach* (Baltimore: Johns Hopkins University Press, 1970).

increases, but it increases at a decreasing rate. In other words, the additional amount of dust collected per dollar of capital spent declines as more capital is invested. The dust collected is called the physical product of capital, and the change in physical product as more capital is invested is called the *marginal physical product of capital* (MPP_K). The same declining rate of increase holds true for labor. With a fixed capital investment (filter size), more hours of labor will increase the amount of dust collected, but the amount will increase at a decreasing rate. The *marginal physical product of labor* (MPP_L) will decline.

We can now address the question of how best to control the dust from the smokestack. Suppose that the plant owner wants to remove fifty pounds of dust per day. This can be done by using a number of different combinations of filter size and hours of maintenance labor. The least costly combination will be that quantity of capital and labor for which the $MPP_K/P_K = MPP_L/P_L$, where P_K is the price of capital and P_L is the price of labor. Having determined the least costly combination of capital and labor for one level of control, we can expand the inquiry to ask how much it would cost to control at different levels by applying the same rule. An example of the results of such an analysis is presented in Figure 4.1. Differing amounts of labor and capital will be found to be the least expensive solution at different levels of emissions. As with other cost functions, the *marginal emission reduction cost* (*MERC*) increases at an increasing rate as higher levels of control are reached.

The origin of the *MERC* curve — that is, the level of waste that would be produced if there were no control of emissions, is depicted as 300 tons per day in Figure 4.1. The firm would dispose of wastes to the point where the *MPP* of waste disposal equals zero, because the unregulated price of emissions is zero. This is the extensive margin of the production function. Note that this origin depends on the final production level of the plant. An increase in final production will increase the amount of waste generated and shift the *MERC* curve to the right. This function has all the characteristics common to all cost functions. It is drawn, however, so that the origin is at the right of the diagram and emission reductions are movements to the left. Thus, as with other cost functions, *MERC* increases at an increasing rate as emissions are reduced. This reversal from the usual form may be somewhat confusing, but it will serve a purpose later in the chapter when we examine the relationship between emission reductions and environmental quality. In Figure 2.1 (page 28) we depicted a cost function called the marginal costs of

FIGURE 4.1 Hypothetical Marginal Emission Reduction Cost Function

The marginal emission reduction cost (*MERC*) function represents the cost of reducing the release of pollutants into the environment. Control is achieved by the least expensive combination of substitution of inputs, changes in production processes, treatment at the end of the production process, and adjustments in output. The *MERC* function begins at the level of emissions that would exist if there were no control (300 tons per day in this case). As control increases and emissions are reduced, the *MERC* increases.

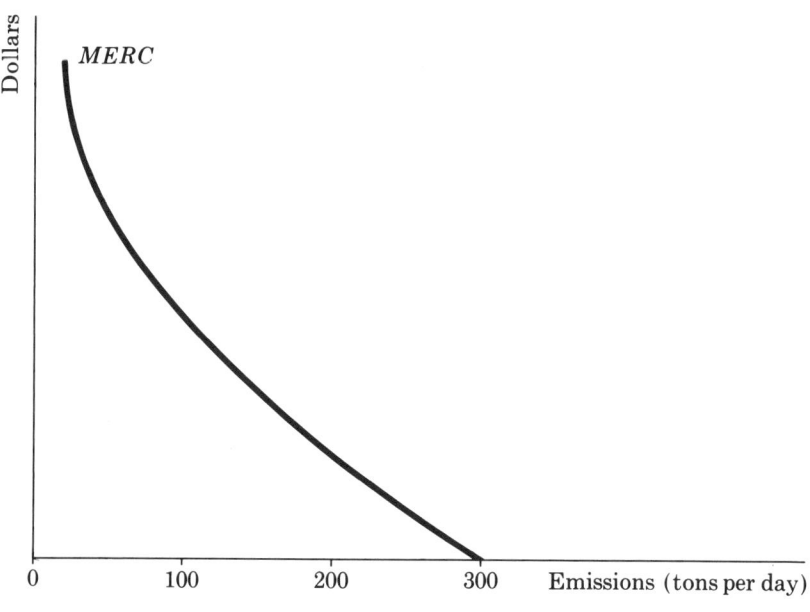

control (*MCC*) as sloping upward to the right, just the opposite of the *MERC* function depicted in Figure 4.1; but note that the horizontal axis represents environmental quality in the first figure and emissions in the second. We will need to translate the level of emissions into a level of environmental quality, which we will do after some additional discussion of the *MERC* function.

The presentation so far has been limited to a simple case with only maintenance labor and, as capital equipment, an end-of-process filtering device being used to control emissions. It will be useful to raise several issues at this point.

First, other factors of production are involved in operating a filter. In the real world, a dust filter must use space that could be used for other purposes, so land should be included in our calculations. A filter spread over more space may be less expensive to build (and thus save capital) or easier to maintain (and thus save labor). The effectiveness of the filter could be increased by using different types of materials or by using a forced air system. Such changes in the character of the filter could require different kinds of labor for its operation. A more sophisticated system might require a trained operator, who would earn more money per hour because of the higher opportunity cost of her time. The plant management might have to spend time overseeing the operation of the filter. In the case of the forced air system, a different type of capital (a fan and electricity) would be required. The plant owner must take all of these trade-offs into consideration in finding the least costly method of filtering dust, but our simple rule still applies: When the marginal physical product for each input is divided by the price of that input ($MPP/_P$), and the quotient is the same for all inputs, the efficient level has been reached.

Filtering is not the only way to reduce emissions. Fuel that produces less dust can be used, the shape of the combustion chamber can be changed, or the fuel can be washed or oiled. If any of these alternatives is less expensive than the marginal cost (MC) of increasing filter capacity, it would pay to undertake them to the point where their MC per unit of emissions reduced equals that of the filter system. The ability to use these fuel and combustion changes allows the plant owner to save on filter costs by installing a smaller, less expensive filter.

Likewise, it may be possible to change the production process of the plant to one that requires the burning of less fuel. Suppose some of the heat is used to dry paint. Using less heat and allowing the paint to dry more slowly would reduce potential emissions. The savings in fuel costs and emission reduction costs would be offset, however, by an increase in production time. Suppose automobile bodies placed in a drying oven dry in eight hours, but if they are allowed to dry naturally it takes three days. The cost to the plant is the value of the inventory that is delayed by the slower drying process and the value of the space required for the bodies to sit. If the plant used heat in the absence of emission control requirements, it must have been the least expensive option. Efforts to control emissions from fuel combustion may, however, make natural drying — or at least a slower drying process that requires less heat — the least expensive option.

Another option should be considered. The total amount of emissions depends on the total output of the plant. If more automobiles are produced, more fuel is burned and more dust is emitted. Dust emissions can be controlled by reducing output. The cost of reducing output is the profit lost by not producing and selling the additional units. If this proves to be the least expensive option, output will be reduced to the point where the loss in profit just equals the savings from reduced pollution control costs.

The true *MERC* curve a plant faces when considering emission reduction options will be the least costly combination of changes in process, changes in output, and controls added at the end of the process. From now on, when I talk about a plant's *MERC* curve I will be referring to this more complex curve.

EMISSIONS AND ENVIRONMENTAL QUALITY

Now that we have developed estimates of the cost of controlling emissions, we must relate emission reductions to changes in environmental quality. This relationship can be rather simple, but more often it is quite complex.

One of the simplest relationships between emissions and environmental quality is the effect of water pollutants on the level of oxygen in a river. Organic wastes, including domestic sewage and chemical wastes, are oxidized by the oxygen that is dissolved in the water. A standard test called the biochemical oxygen demand (BOD) test measures the amount of oxygen used up by wastes. BOD, stated in pounds, is one simple measure of the waste load released by a plant, and could be used as a measure of emissions in Figure 4.1.

When wastes are released into a river, oxidation takes place over time, depleting the oxygen in the river water. Because river water moves, the effects are felt downstream from the point of release. Figure 4.2 presents a typical relationship between emissions of BOD and water quality downstream, with the point of release at *A*. Suppose there were a constant release of twenty pounds of BOD per day, and suppose the dissolved oxygen would have remained at twelve parts per million (ppm) if there had been no release of wastes. Water quality declines initially as the wastes are oxidized and the water flows downstream. But the stream has a natural ability to

FIGURE 4.2 Hypothetical Oxygen Sag Curves

The oxygen sag curves presented here are an illustration of the effects of emissions on the environment. Here the effects of emissions into a river are felt at various locations along the river. The extent of the effects depends on the amount of pollution released, higher emissions having a greater adverse effect on environmental quality (represented here by the amount of dissolved oxygen in the river) than do lower emissions.

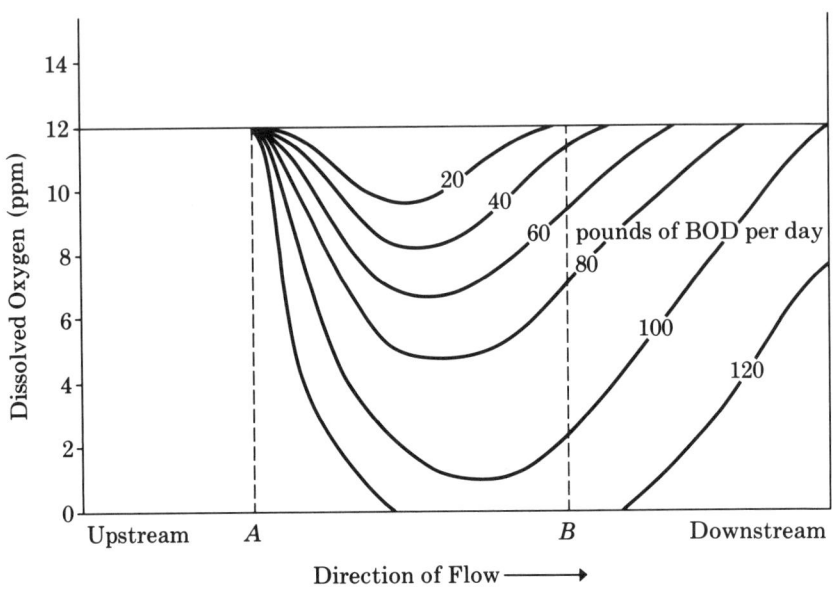

recharge its oxygen content through contact with the air and through the release of oxygen by photosynthesizing plants. When a substantial portion of the waste has been oxidized, the use of oxygen slows down. As the wastes are further degraded (oxidized) the water absorbs more oxygen than is being used up, and water quality improves, finally returning to its original level. Higher levels of emissions of BOD will lead to a greater depletion of oxygen and a longer recovery period. Dissolved oxygen will consequently be lower at each downstream location as emissions at A are increased.[2]

[2] For more discussion of the relationship between discharge and water quality, see A. Kneese and B. Bower, *Managing Water Quality: Economics, Technology, Institutions* (Baltimore: Johns Hopkins University Press, 1968), Chapter 2.

We can now determine the relationship between emissions of BOD and environmental quality at some downstream location. Let us focus on water quality at location B. At low levels of BOD emissions, the water quality returns to 12 ppm before it reaches location B. At somewhat higher levels of emissions, water quality at B is affected. When forty pounds of BOD are emitted at A, dissolved oxygen at B is reduced to 11.2 ppm. The effects on water quality are greater as emissions increase until waste releases surpass 110 pounds of BOD. At this point dissolved oxygen is completely depleted, and further emissions of BOD will have no further effect on

FIGURE 4.3 Emission Transformation Function

The oxygen sag curves are an example of an emission transformation function (*ETF*). The *ETF* relates emissions of a pollutant at one location to environmental quality at another location.

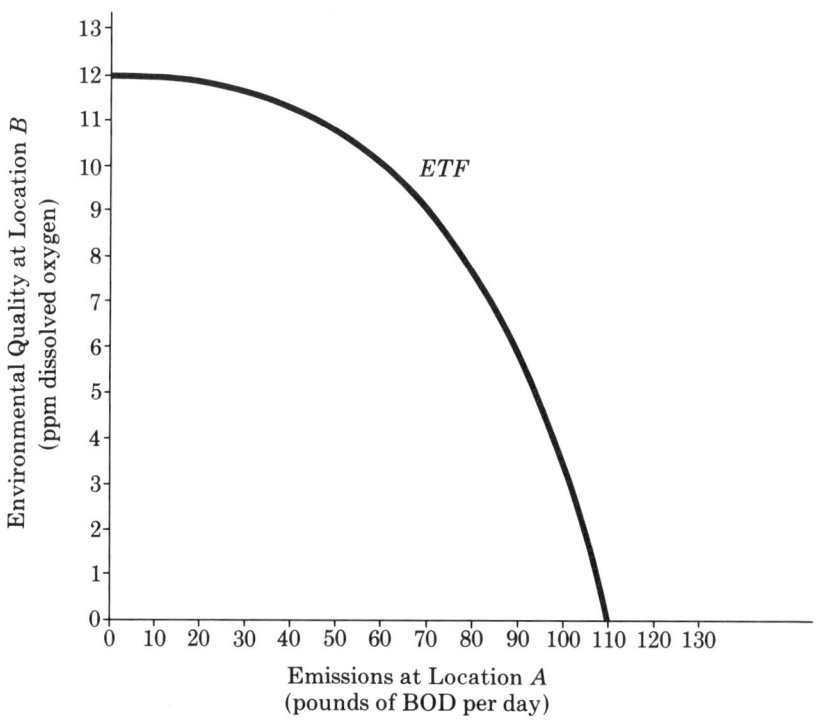

this measure of water quality at B. The relationship between emissions at A and water quality at B can be summarized in the curve presented in Figure 4.3, which is derived from the information in Figure 4.2. We will call this curve the *emission transformation function (ETF)* because it will be used throughout this book to transform emissions data into effects on environmental quality.

The relationship presented by the *ETF* is a simplification of the real situation. Let us look at some of its characteristics as they might affect emission control policy. In addition to reducing emissions at A, another way to improve environmental quality at B would be to move the site of emissions release. If the emission site is moved upstream from A, any particular level of emissions will have less effect on environmental quality at B. If the emission site is moved downstream from A, the effect on B will be larger for a small move but will decline as the emission site approaches B. Of course, if the emission site were below B, there would be no relationship between emissions and environmental quality at B. This seems like a good arrangement for people at B, but it must be remembered that there may be reasons for society to be concerned with water quality downstream from B.

We have assumed only one source of emissions and only one location where environmental damages are of concern, but in the real world this is not the case. There are many sources of emissions, and there are also many points where people use the river and so are concerned with water quality. Doing a complete analysis of all sources and all locations becomes complex — needlessly so for our present purposes. Some discussion of the issues raised in generalizing from a simple benefit/cost analysis to cover a situation with many sources and many people will be presented after we complete the discussion of this simple case.

BENEFITS OF CONTROLLING EMISSIONS

In Chapter 2 we saw that the benefit society receives from controlling emissions represents the gain in utility generated by an improved environment. Now we will explore this concept more fully.

Let us assume that the only use society has for the river at location B is commercial fishing. There is a direct relationship between the level of dissolved oxygen in the river and the river's ability to support fish. At low levels of oxygen, only a few kinds of fish with little commercial value will survive; at still lower levels even these fish will die. The number of fish a commercial fishing boat can catch during a year will increase as water quality at B increases. Table 4.1 presents hypothetical data on the amount of fish caught by one fishing boat at location B at various levels of water quality.

Once we determine the quantity of fish that will be caught at each level, our problem is to determine the benefits society derives from these fish. Consumers consume goods up to the point where their marginal utility divided by the price (MU/P) of a unit of one good is equal to MU/P for the other goods available. As the price of a product increases, MU/P declines and fewer units of the good are purchased. Thus the price an individual is willing to pay for a good reflects the MU derived from that good.

To see this, examine Equation 4.1, which is a solution to the general rule discussed in Chapter 3.

$$P_X = \frac{MU_X}{MU_Y}(P_Y) \qquad 4.1$$

In this form, the equation allows us to determine the price an individual is willing to pay for X given P_Y, MU_Y, and MU_X. If MU_Y and P_Y are held constant, the price P_X is determined by MU_X. In a market economy the price of any commodity is determined by the value to each consumer of consuming one more unit of that good. Thus the price of fish reflects the MU each consumer of fish derives from consuming the last unit of it.

Because price reflects MU to each consumer, it can be used to measure the benefits society gains from having more of a good available. We have been calling this gain in utility the *benefit*. Multiplying the total catch at each level of water quality by the price of fish gives us the total benefit to be realized from each level of dissolved oxygen. The third column of Table 4.1 presents this total benefit when the price of fish is seventy-five cents per pound. The marginal benefit can be derived from this information by subtracting from the total for a given level of water quality the total for the next lower level of water quality. The result of this operation is presented in the fourth column of Table 4.1. Note that MB declines as environmental quality improves.

In this example and in Table 4.1, I have assumed two things that should be stated clearly. First, I have assumed that the price of fish does not change as more fish are caught. This would be true if fish supplied from this river were so small a part of the total market for

TABLE 4.1 Hypothetical Benefit Function for Commercial Fishing at Location B

Quality (ppm dissolved oxygen)	Pounds of Fish Caught (1,000 lbs/yr)	Total Value of Fish Caught, at 75¢ per Pound ($1,000/yr)	Marginal Benefit of Control ($1,000/yr)
1	16.0	12.0	
2	29.3	22.0	12.0
3	40.9	30.7	10.0
4	52.5	39.4	8.7
5	61.2	45.9	7.5
6	68.8	51.6	6.5
7	75.2	56.4	5.7
8	80.5	60.4	4.8
9	85.2	63.9	4.0
10	89.1	66.8	3.5
11	91.9	68.9	2.9
12	94.1	70.6	2.1
			1.7

fish that they do not affect the price. If this were not the case, control of emissions would shift the supply curve for fish to the right. This would result in a downward movement in the price of fish. A complete benefit estimate would have to take this reduction in price into account. If it did not, the estimate of benefits would be too high. Second, I have assumed that the fish are caught without any additional effort by the fisherman. The availability of more fish, however, means that the marginal payoff (profit) for each additional unit of fishing effort has increased. The fishers will increase their fishing effort until the value of an additional unit of effort just equals the price received for the fish. The benefit of the emission reductions will then be an increase in the number of fish caught times the new lower price of fish, less the increase in fishing costs caused by the increase in fishing effort. From now on, when we discuss an *MBC* function we will mean this more completely specified benefit function.

SIMPLE BENEFIT/COST ANALYSIS

We have developed a cost function relating costs to emission reductions, an emission transformation function relating emissions to environmental quality, and a benefit function relating benefits to environmental quality. Now we will see how this information can be combined to produce a benefit/cost analysis.[3]

A typical *MERC* curve is presented in panel A of Figure 4.4. In order to compare these costs with the benefits of control (*MBC* in panel D) it is necessary to employ the *ETF* (emission transfer function), shown in panel B. A point on the curve in panel D relating the marginal costs of control (*MCC*) to environmental quality at location *B* is derived by dropping a vertical line from *MERC* in panel A to *ETF* in panel B (point *W* to point *X*), drawing a horizontal line from that intersection to point *Y* on the 45° line in panel C, and then drawing a vertical line to point *Z* in panel D. The intersection of that vertical line with a horizontal line from point *W* on the *MERC* curve in panel A determines a point on the *MCC* curve. Using this procedure for a number of emission levels allows us to develop an *MCC* function.[4]

The *MBC* function can be drawn in panel D using the data presented in Table 4.1. No environmental transformation function is required because the data were developed to reflect environmental quality at location *B*. The intersection of the *MBC* function and the *MCC* function determines the efficient level of environmental quality given the circumstances of this particular case. The efficient environmental quality is at 9.6 ppm dissolved oxygen. The marginal cost of control is $3,000 per year and the efficient level of emissions at location *A* is sixty pounds of BOD per day.

The marginal cost of control (*MCC*) is uniquely determined by the shape and location of the *MERC* and *ETF* functions. An increase in the output of the plant shifts the *MERC* function to the right. This translates through the *ETF* to a shift of *MCC* to the right. Likewise, a change in the shape or location of *ETF* would affect the shape and location of the *MCC* function. Often reductions in emissions have very little effect on environmental quality at the initial levels of control but have a much bigger effect after substantial control has been achieved. In such a case the *ETF* would bow inward (it would be convex) rather than outward (concave). If this convexity

---

[3] This technique for showing the relationship between MERC and MCC is adapted from a similar method presented in A. M. Freeman, *The Economics of Pollution Control and Environmental Quality* (General Learning Press, 1971), p. 13.

[4] Throughout this book I am assuming that MCC functions are strictly separable. However, in the real world they are not. The effect of the emissions of one plant on the environment depends upon the level of emissions of other plants. This creates a complexity which cannot be easily solved. For the classic writing on this problem, see H. Green, *Aggregation in Economic Analysis: An Introductory Survey* (Princeton: Princeton University Press, 1963).

FIGURE 4.4 Basic Benefit/Cost Analysis

This rather complex diagram shows how to derive a marginal cost of control (*MCC*) function, which relates cost to improvements in environmental quality, from a *MERC* function which relates costs to emissions. To derive the *MCC* you must use the *ETF*. The procedure for establishing a point on MCC is to draw a horizontal line from a point *W* on MERC (panel A) and draw a vertical line from *W* to the intersection with the *ETF* in panel B (point *X*). Next draw a horizontal line to the 45° line in panel C. Then draw a vertical line from that intersection to panel D. The intersection of the vertical and horizontal lines in panel D establishes one point on the *MCC* function. By selecting other points on the *MERC* function and repeating this procedure, you can derive a complete MCC function.

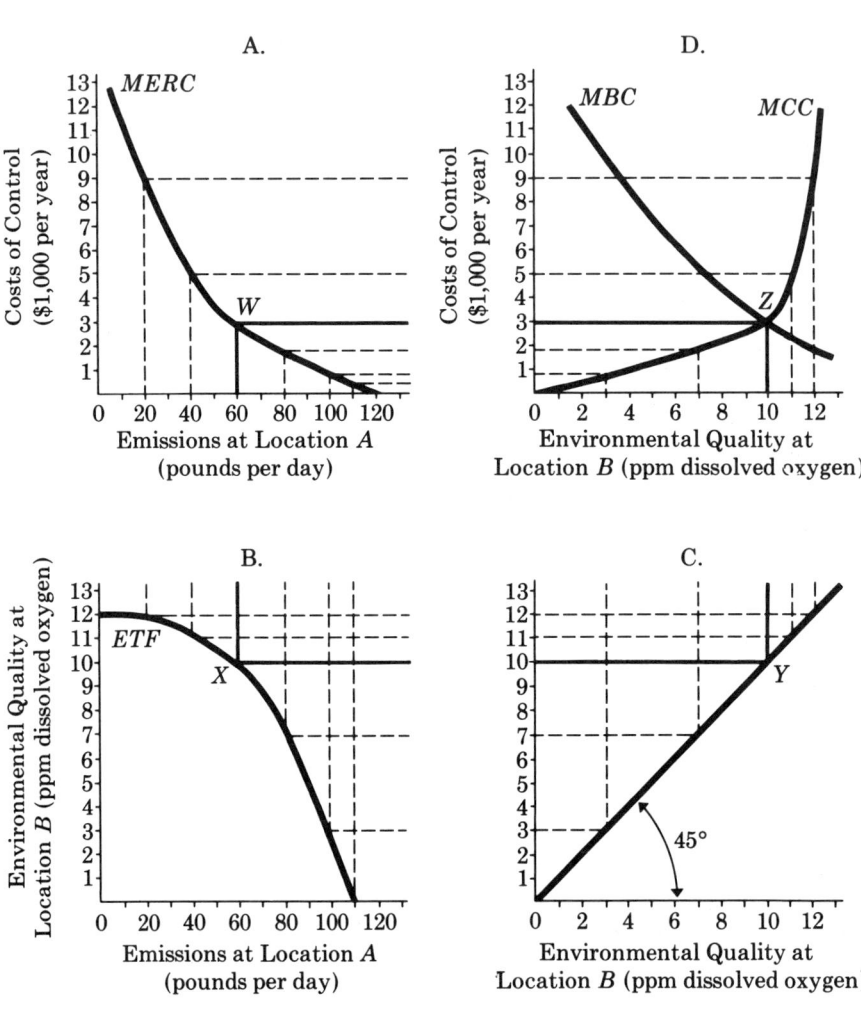

were not too great, the *MCC* function would still slope upward to the right. As the convexity of the *ETF* increased, however, the *MCC* would slope downward to the right. This would create the possibility that there would be two intersections of *MBC* and *MCC*. Which intersection would be the efficient one? The rule is that the intersection where the *MBC* function crosses the *MCC* function from above is the efficient output.

Such a set of functions is depicted in Figure 4.5. Intersection *A* represents an inefficient level of environmental quality, while intersection *B* represents the efficient level. This issue is important because there are many real-world examples where *ETF* is convex. An

FIGURE 4.5 Efficiency and Convexity

Under certain circumstances it is possible that the *MCC* function and the *MBC* function will intersect at two different levels of environmental qualities. One intersection, *B*, produces the efficient level of control.

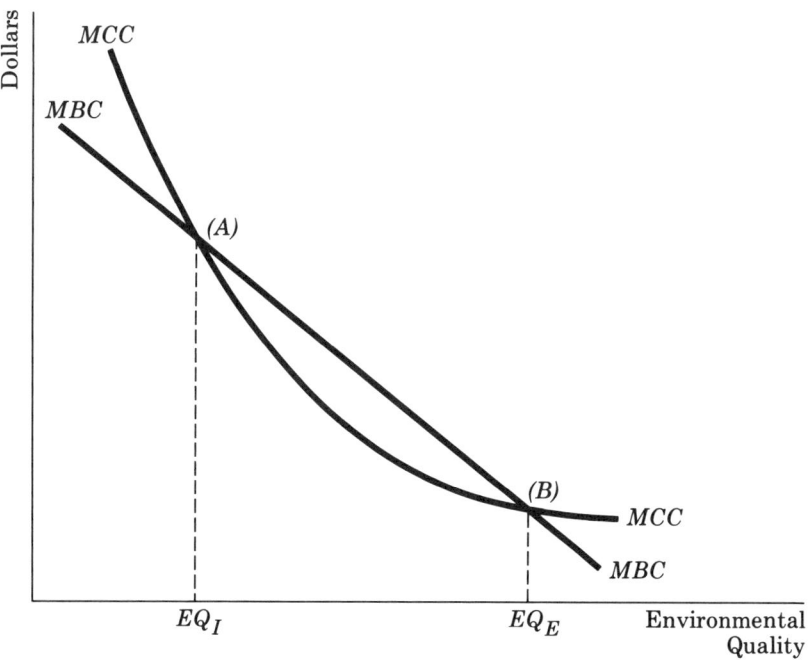

MORE THAN ONE SOURCE OF EMISSIONS

In the simple analysis discussed thus far in this chapter, we have assumed only one plant at one location that emits pollutants and one industry at one location that benefits specifically from pollution control. Now we will expand this analysis to show how to deal with more than one emitter at location A.

When there is more than one source of emissions, it is necessary to determine both the efficient amount of total emissions and the efficient mix of emissions among sources. The efficient mix is the combination of controls that generates the efficient total of emissions at the lowest total cost. A simple rule allows us to determine this least costly mix of controls. All sources should control to the level at which their MERC equals that of all other sources. This rule is stated in Equation 4.2.

$$MERC_1 = MERC_2 = \ldots = MERC_{n-1} = MERC_n \qquad 4.2$$

The subscripts refer to individual sources, and n is the total number of sources.

The logic of this rule can be explained in a simple numerical example. Figure 4.6 presents the MERC curves for two sources, both located at A. The marginal emission reduction cost curve for both sources ($MERC_{1\,\&\,2}$) is derived as follows. If neither source controlled emissions, the total emissions would be $120 + 100 = 220$ pounds per day. This defines the starting point for $MERC_{1\,\&\,2}$, with no control costs. Now suppose that both sources controlled to the level where their MERC equaled \$2,000 per year. Source 1 would emit seventy-six pounds and source 2 would emit seventy pounds of BOD per day. Total emissions would be 146 pounds per day at a $MERC_{1\,\&\,2}$ of \$2,000 per year. The reason $MERC_1$ and $MERC_2$ are not added is that *each* represents the marginal cost of reducing emissions by one pound per day. If they were added, they would represent the marginal cost of reducing emissions by *two* pounds per day. To generate the rest of the $MERC_{1\,\&\,2}$ curve, follow the same procedure. Table 4.2 presents in numerical terms the figures that $MERC_{1\,\&\,2}$ in Figure 4.6 present graphically.

Using these data, we can demonstrate why the equal marginal cost rule works. If we want to reduce emissions to sixty-two pounds

FIGURE 4.6 Efficient Emission Control Mix

To determine the least expensive combination of controls for two sources at one location, it is necessary to ensure that they control at an equal *MERC*. The aggregate *MERC* function ($MERC_{1\ \&\ 2}$) is derived by horizontal addition of individual emission quantities. For example, using control methods that cost $6,000 per year, source 1 would produce emissions of thirty-five pounds per day and source 2 would produce twenty-seven pounds per day. Thus the aggregate emissions at this cost are sixty-two pounds per day.

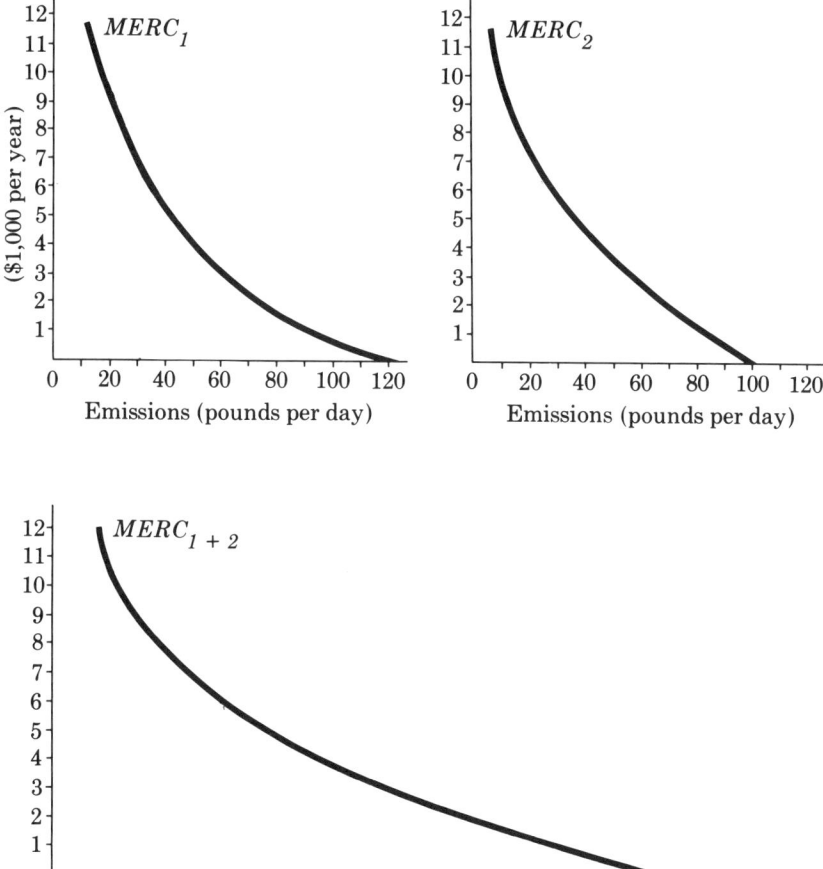

TABLE 4.2 Total Cost of Control from Two Sources

MERC ($1,000/pounds/yr)	Source 1		Source 2		Total Sources	
	Emissions (pound/day)	$TERC_1$ ($1,000/yr)	Emissions (pound/day)	$TERC_2$ ($1,000/yr)	Emissions (pound/day)	$TERC_{1\&2}$ ($1,000/yr)
0	120	0	100	0	220	0
2	76	51	70	40	146	91
4	50	135	45	123	95	258
6	35	224	27	228	62	452
8	25	304	14	331	39	635
10	16	393	8	441	24	834

per day, Table 4.2 tells us that source 1 should emit thirty-five pounds per day and source 2 should emit twenty-seven pounds per day. Many other combinations would meet the sixty-two-pound-per-day requirement, but they would not equate the two *MERC*s. Suppose we adopted the rule that both sources should emit the same amount. Source 1 would control at a marginal cost of $6,800 per pound per year and a total cost of $252,000 per year, while source 2 would control at a marginal cost of $5,600 per pound per year and a total cost of $202,000 per year. The combined total cost for both sources is $454,000 per year — $2,000 per year more than the result for controlling at equal marginal costs, as shown in Table 4.2. The reason for the difference in total costs can be seen from the differences in marginal costs. A reduction of one pound in emissions from source 2 would cost $5,600 a year, but if total emissions are kept constant would allow source 2 to increase its emissions by one pound and save $6,800 a year — a net saving of $1,200 a year. Clearly the equal emissions rule is undesirable because it wastes resources that can be better used elsewhere. The equal marginal cost rule will save those resources.

To determine the efficient level of environmental quality with two sources at location A, all you need to do is insert $MERC_{1\ \&\ 2}$ from Figure 4.6 into panel A of Figure 4.4. Total emissions for any marginal cost will be higher than they were when only one source was at location A. The *ETF* has not changed because it expresses a physical relationship dependent only on the total number of pounds emitted. Translating $MERC_{1\ \&\ 2}$ into panel D would generate a new *MCC* curve, which would then imply that a poorer environmental quality is efficient when a second source of emissions is located at A. Figure 4.7 presents this result. The efficient level of environmental quality is reduced to 6.8 ppm and the *MERC* is increased to $4,800 per year. The efficient emission level for source 1, the original source, has been reduced and its total costs increased by the addition of a second source. This result has important implications, which will be explored in subsequent chapters. Note that this result depends on the second plant being located at A. That may not be the efficient location for it. We will explore that possibility shortly.

MORE THAN ONE BENEFITING GROUP

Thus far we have been assuming that the fishing industry is the only recipient to benefit from improved environmental quality at

FIGURE 4.7 Efficient Environmental Quality with Two Sources at Location A

When a second emitting source is added at location A, the $MERC$ function is shifted up and to the right (to $MERC_{1 \& 2}$ in panel A). This in turn shifts the MCC curve up and to the left ($MCC_{1 \& 2}$ in panel D), which suggests that a lower level of environmental quality is now efficient.

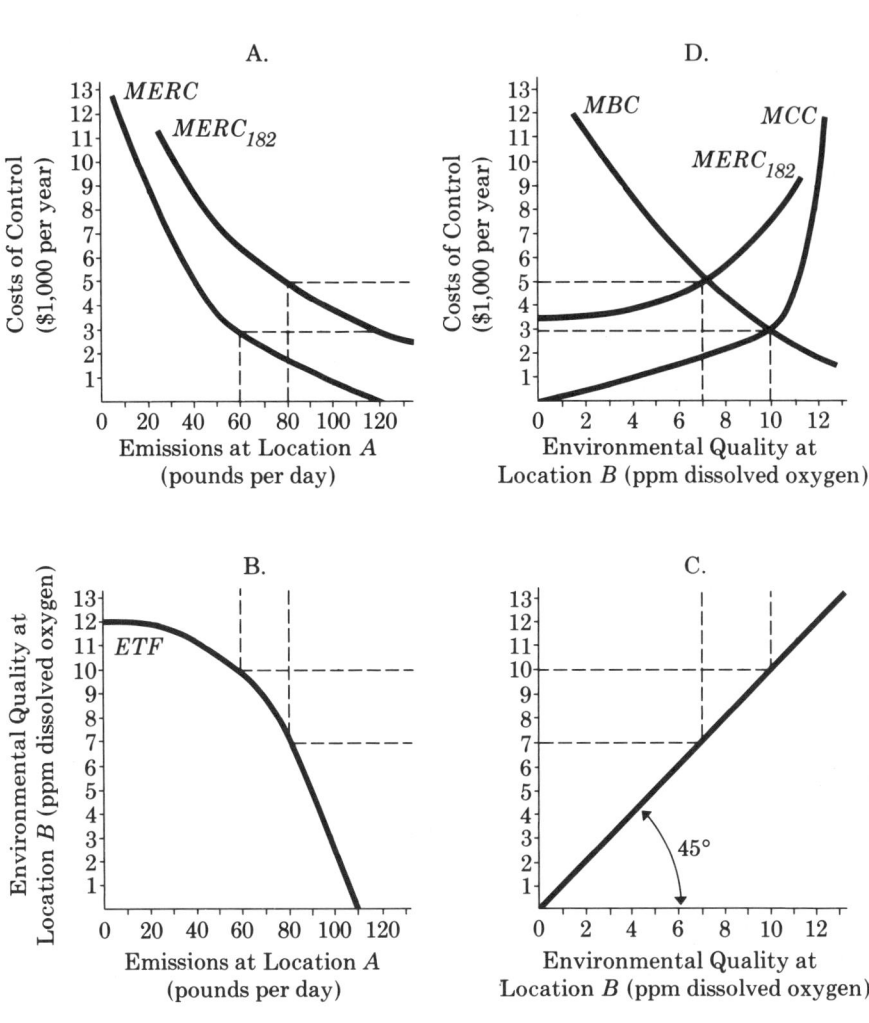

location B. Now we will turn our attention to the case where many different entities benefit from pollution control.

The rule for the addition of benefits is different from the one we employed for the addition costs. When a certain level of environmental quality is reached, the number of pounds of fish that can be caught is determined. We can estimate the benefits to society of this level of environmental quality. Now suppose that a plant located at B uses the river water for cooling. The level of dissolved oxygen in the water determines the speed of the corrosion of the plant's water pipes — the less oxygen in the water, the more corrosive it is. The benefits of reducing corrosion can be estimated by first determining the reduced frequency of maintenance and replacement, and then placing a dollar value on this saving. A particular increase in the level of dissolved oxygen generates both increased fish and reduced corrosion. Thus the benefits to both groups should be added together to determine the total benefit and the marginal benefit of that environmental quality. The sum of marginal benefit of control can be derived by using Equation 4.3.

$$MBC_T = MBC_1 + MBC_2 + \ldots + MBC_{n-1} + MBC_n \qquad 4.3$$

The subscript T represents the total, and n represents the number of individuals benefiting.

An example of this is presented in Figure 4.8. MBC_1 is the benefit function generated by the data in Table 4.1, and MBC_2 is the benefit function for the reduction in corrosion at the plant located at B. At a level of 1 ppm dissolved oxygen, the marginal benefit of an improvement is $12,000 a year for the fisherman and $8,000 a year for the plant, making the total marginal benefit of control (MBC_{1+2}) $20,000 a year. The MBC_{1+2} function is the vertical sum of MBC_1 and MBC_2. This is because the benefit functions are for a public good so that quality provided to 1 is also provided to 2.

This new MBC_{1+2} function could be superimposed on Figure 4.4. The additional benefit would cause MBC_{1+2} to be above MBC (which is the same as MBC_1 in Figure 4.8). Consequently, MBC_{1+2} would intersect MCC to the right of the previous intersection and the efficient level of environmental quality would be increased. The efficient $MERC$ would also increase, and emissions from the source at location A would have to be reduced. The source would have to pay additional costs because of the additional benefiter. This is an important finding, and one we will return to throughout this book.

FIGURE 4.8 Benefits with Two Benefits at Location B
Environmental quality has the characteristics of a public good: The presence of more than one individual who benefits from improved environmental quality requires that an aggregate benefit function (MBC_{1+2}) be derived. This is done by the vertical addition of the benefits of all individuals, because all consume the same environmental quality.

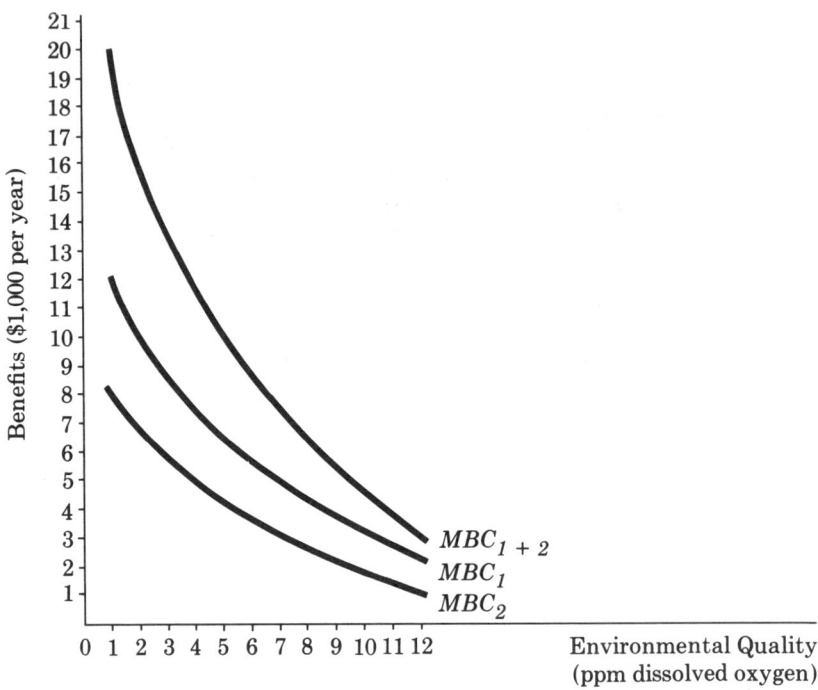

CHANGING LOCATION

We have discussed the efficient levels of environmental control and emissions given that the source of emissions is at A. There is, however, another way of solving the problem of environmental damages at B. The emitting source could move. If the emitter were below B, the level of dissolved oxygen at B would clearly be 12 ppm and damages would be zero. Moving the emission source might be the most efficient solution. Let's take a look at this possibility.

If the emitter were to relocate below B, its emissions would have an effect further downstream. Assume for the moment that society does not care about this effect. Does it pay (is it efficient for society) to move the source? The answer depends on the costs and the benefits. If the emitter were to move from A to the new location C, it would save $TERC_A$, but it would incur relocation costs TRC_{AC}. Society would gain the benefit of the increased catch of fish. This gain in benefits would be the difference between the total benefit of control to 12 ppm and the total benefit of control to the efficient level when the emitter is located at A. Let us call this difference the gain in benefits from relocation (TGB_B). Using Equation 4.4, we can determine if society has a net gain from the move (NGM).

$$NGM = TERC_A + TGB_B - TRC_{AC} \qquad 4.4$$

Remember that $TERC_A$ represents the control costs the firm saves by moving — a benefit in this circumstance. Society will be better off and the move will be efficient if NGM is positive. If NGM is negative, the source should not move.

If society does want to avoid adverse consequences downstream, we must extend the analysis somewhat. We must do a benefit/cost analysis for the new location to determine the efficient level of environmental quality at the adversely affected location D. Location D would lose benefits (TLB_D) because of the reduction in dissolved oxygen from 12 ppm to the efficient level. The emitter would also incur some costs in achieving the efficient level of control at C ($TERC_C$). The NGM equation now looks like Equation 4.5.

$$NGM = TERC_A + TGB_B - TRC_{AC} - TERC_C - TLB_D \qquad 4.5$$

The rule remains the same: If NGM is positive, the source should move from A to C; if not, it should remain at A.

SUMMARY

In this chapter we have explored in substantial detail the use of benefit/cost analysis to determine the efficient level of environmental quality. First we analyzed the cost of controlling emissions at a plant. We saw that the least costly method of controlling would be found where the marginal physical product of each factor input divided by the price of that input was equal for all inputs. Each point on the marginal emission reduction cost (*MERC*) function represents one of these least-cost combinations. The marginal emission reduction cost function increases as the source emits less pollution.

Next we examined the relationship between emissions and environmental quality. We found that the emission transformation function (*ETF*) expresses this relationship. With this function we could relate the source's control costs to environmental quality.

Next we developed the rationale for a benefit function. Benefits can be measured by the prices people are willing to pay for goods and services. Using these prices we were able to create a relationship between money benefits and environmental quality. Armed with benefit and cost relationships we were able to determine the efficient level of environmental quality and the efficient level of emissions from the source.

Extending the analysis to more than one emitter is relatively simple. The efficient mix of emissions from each source is the point at which the marginal emission reduction costs are equal for all sources. This rule means that any given total emission is generated at the lowest cost to the society. In analyzing this issue, we noted that the location of a new emitting source in an area caused the efficient level of environmental quality to decline while the efficient level of control of emissions, and consequently the costs incurred, increased for the source already located in the area. This outcome is important in the politics and economics of pollution control.

Extending the analysis to more than one benefiting entity required a different rule. The benefit of control to society is the sum of the benefits to each individual, because each individual consumes the same environmental quality. (We will have more to say about this notion in Chapter 5.) When an individual or business sensitive to environmental changes moves into an area, it adds to the benefits of control. This increases the efficient level of environmental quality and the efficient level of control of emissions.[5] We will use this important result later in the book.

In analyzing the possibility of solving an environmental problem by moving the source of emissions, we developed a new rule: The source should move if the net gain from moving is positive. This is

---

[5] Several more complex models of the economics of control take multiple emitters, multiple receptors, and location differentials into account. See, for example, T. H. Tietenberg, "Derived Decision Rules for Pollution Control in a General Equilibrium Space Economy," *Journal of Environmental Economics and Management* 1 (June 1974): 3–16, and W. Baumol and W. Oates, *The Theory of Environmental Policy* (Englewood Cliffs, N.J.: Prentice-Hall, 1975).

similar to the rule that total net benefits at any given location should be maximized, but is extended to take into consideration gains at one location and losses at another. When one area gains from a move and another loses, the move has important implications in the politics of pollution control.

The logic of economic efficiency is quite simple. The results that society prefers should be generated. Benefits measure the value society places on the improved environmental quality it gets. Costs represent the value to society of the other goods forgone for the sake of the improvement in environmental quality. Requiring a positive net gain is simply requiring that what society gets is worth at least as much as what it loses.

STUDY QUESTIONS

1. A certain level of control of emissions results in such high costs to a firm that it is no longer economical to operate the plant at its given location. Under what circumstances is it efficient to control emissions to such a level that one or more plants in an area close?
2. It is possible to improve the waste assimilating capacity of a stream by the process of low flow augmentation where heavy spring runoff water is retained in reservoirs and released during the late summer months. This reduces the oxygen sag (Figure 4.2) during the summer. Low flow augmentation is costly. Develop a rule for how much low flow augmentation is efficient in terms of the benefits and costs to be obtained with improved environmental quality.
3. There are positive and negative externalities resulting from the plant location choice made by a firm. In the absence of government influence (control), will the firm make the socially efficient choice? What are all the effects which should be included in this choice of plant location?

SUGGESTED READING

1. E. Stokey and R. Zeckhauser, *A Primer for Policy Analysis* (New York: W. W. Norton, 1978) provides discussion of numerous issues in the technique of policy analysis.

5

Measuring the Benefits and Costs of Environmental Improvements

We have developed a detailed methodology for generating a benefit/cost analysis of environmental quality improvements. In this chapter we turn our attention to the practical problems of quantifying such a system.[1] Because pollution control projects generate costs and benefits over time, it is necessary to discuss how to make these costs and benefits comparable. This process is called discounting. We will examine various methods of estimating the costs and benefits of pollution control. These methods do not generate ideal information, so it will be necessary to explore some practical variants of full benefit/cost analysis: cost-effectiveness analysis and policy trade-off analysis.

DISCOUNTING

Suppose I offered to give you a dollar exactly one year from today or seventy-five cents today. Which would you take? The dollar will buy more, but you won't get to use it until next year. Are two drinks of cola next year worth more than one today? The answer depends on your time preference — and your patience.

The calculation that generalizes this question is presented in Equation 5.1. It presents the simple discounting formula used to

---

[1] For a further discussion of the practical problems of benefit/cost analysis, see E. M. Gramlich, *Benefit/Cost Analysis of Government Programs* (Englewood Cliffs, N.J.: Prentice-Hall, 1981).

determine the *present value* (*PV*) of a gain (*g*) or loss received some time in the future, when *i* represents your time preference.

$$PV = \frac{g}{1 + i}. \qquad 5.1$$

Present value is defined as the amount of money in the present that would provide the same utility to you as would some money received at some future date.

We generally prefer the present to the future. You would prefer having a dollar now to having it some time in the future. This dollar could be used now or it could be saved for future consumption. To be compensated for the loss of benefit from current consumption, you try to receive a larger benefit at the time of future consumption. The degree to which you insist on receiving a higher benefit in the future is your time preference. If you must receive a dollar and a quarter in benefits next year to be as well off — that is, to have as high a present utility from the consumption — as for a dollar now, your time preference is 25 percent. Thus the ratio of current value to value one year in the future is 1/1.25. Stated alternatively: To be equally well off in future consumption, you must get what you would consume now plus your time preference (1 + .25), or 1.25 times as much. With a 25 percent time preference, will you take my offer of one dollar next year? Using the discounting formula, you calculate that the *PV* of my offer of a dollar next year is eighty cents (1/1.25 × $1.00). This is greater than the alternative of seventy-five cents now, so you accept the offer of a dollar next year. In fact, your time preference would have to be above 42 percent for you to accept the offer of seventy-five cents now (unless, of course, you had good reason to doubt I would come through next year).

Society as a whole has a rate of time preference as well. In theory, this time preference is reflected in the market interest rate — that is, the rate of return to capital. Capital is supplied by individuals who voluntarily give up current consumption for future gain. The higher the gain in the future, the more capital people are willing to supply. The market interest rate determines the amount of capital supplied by society, so the market interest rate represents the social rate of time preference. This interest rate should in theory be used in *PV* calculations for environmental projects. In fact, however, there are many reasons to believe that the market interest rate does not reflect the true time preference of society. Government interventions in the capital market through the actions of the Federal Reserve and the sale of government debt clearly alter the market interest rate. The rate must be adjusted for inflation, and there are other problems as well. These problems lead to uncertainty about the true social rate of time preference, but it is clear that some rate above zero is appropriate.

The benefit/cost formula can be changed to reflect the fact that benefits and costs are generated at different times. Equation 5.2 presents this reformulation.

$$PVTNB = \sum_{t=0}^{t=T} \left[\frac{TB_t}{(1+i)^t} - \frac{TC_t}{(1+i)^t} \right] \qquad 5.2$$

The *present value of total net benefit* (*PVTNB*) is the sum of the discounted total benefit of (*TB*) in each year (*t* being used to indicate time in years) and the discounted total cost (*TC*) in each year over the life of the pollution control project. *T* is the life of the project. The rules of benefit/cost analysis are unchanged by this formulation, but they are now stated according to present value; equate *PVMC* with *PVMB* and adopt any pollution control project with a positive *PVTNB*. We can now return to the notation employed in Chapter 4 with the understanding that we mean this present value formulation.

Before we leave the subject of discounting future costs and benefits, though, two points should be raised. Projects for controlling emissions typically have a disproportionate share of their costs in the early years of the project's life and a disproportionate share of their benefits in the later years. This means that *PVTNB* will be affected by the interest rate. A high interest rate reduces the importance of future benefits and costs relative to the earlier benefits and costs, so it tends to reduce the *PVTNB* of projects with long lives more than that of projects of short duration. Pollution control projects vary in their distributions of costs and benefits over time. Suppose two projects had the same *PVTNB* at a 10 percent interest rate. Because of their differences in time distribution of benefits and costs, at lower interest rates one of the projects may have a higher *PVTNB* (the one with greater future benefits or lower present costs), while at higher interest rates the other will have the higher *PVTNB*. Finally, higher interest rates will tend to reduce the total number of projects with positive *PVTNB*.

ESTIMATING COSTS

A number of techniques can be used in estimating the costs of pollution control. The choice of a method depends on the problem encountered and the data available for analysis. In this section we will discuss several of the commonly used techniques. Our goal is merely to become familiar with these alternatives, not to become experts on how to use them.

Regression and Economies of Scale

In some cases, many sources have installed and operated similar pollution control equipment. Data can be collected from each source detailing costs, removal or emission rates, and other important technical details that affect costs. These data can then be analyzed statistically, using regression techniques, to determine the relationships between these technical details and costs.

Domestic sewage treatment plants are a good example to use in applying regression analysis to costs. Thousands of these plants have been built in this country over the last fifty or so years. Collecting their data and analyzing them through regression yields cost functions like those in Figure 5.1.

The analysis in Figure 5.1 reveals several interesting points. It shows that the total cost of control (TCC) increases as the degree of removal of BOD in municipal sewage treatment plants increases. It also shows that larger plants are more efficient than smaller plants in treating sewage. That is, it is less costly (per unit of sewage of equal incoming strength) to remove a given percentage in a large plant than in a smaller one. This phenomenon, called economies of scale, is quite common in the analysis of pollution control.

If it is less expensive to treat sewage in larger facilities, it would appear desirable to accomplish municipal and industrial treatment at central regional facilities. There are pros and cons to regional treatment, however, and these must be weighed. Suppose there are three emitting sources on a river. Each could treat its own wastes at the efficient level, depending on the location of the release of these wastes. Connecting these sources and treating the wastes at the location furthest downstream could save treatment costs, but it would generate costs for the sewer pipe necessary to connect the sources. This additional cost would offset the savings in treatment cost either partially or fully. But offsetting costs are not the only consideration. The efficient level of treatment at the regional plant might be less desirable because of the larger volume of wastes being released there. With a constant percentage of removal, more BOD would be released at the regional site than at any individual site; we can assume that the BOD level would be three times greater. Environmental quality would be improved at some locations, but it

FIGURE 5.1 Regression Analysis for Domestic Sewage Plants: Cost of Biochemical Oxygen Demand (BOD) Removal

The cost of controlling emissions of biochemical oxygen demand (BOD) from sewage depends on the extent of removal (high control being more expensive) and the size of the treatment plant (larger plants costing less per unit). At high levels of control, costs increase quite rapidly.

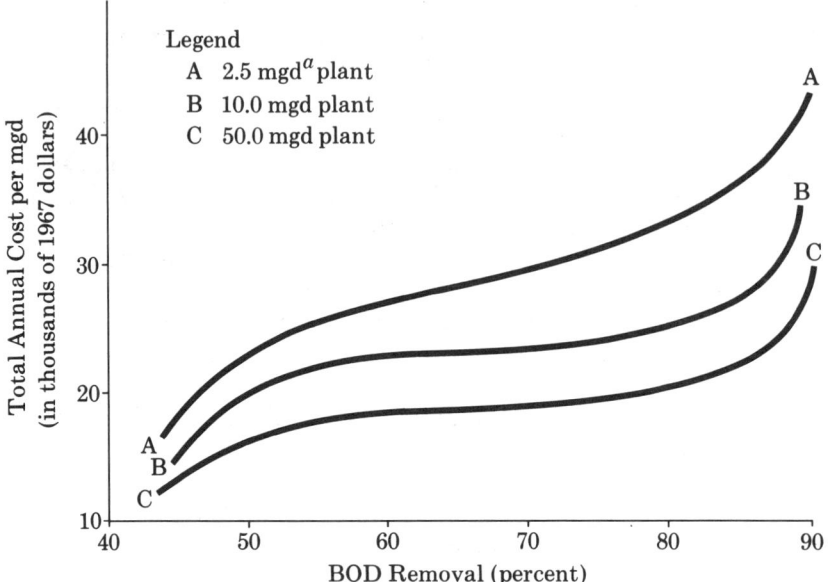

Source: Paul B. Downing, *The Economics of Urban Sewage Disposal* (New York: Praeger, 1969), Figure 2.

a mgd = millions of gallons per day of sewer water treated.

would be decreased at others. Thus there are simultaneous gains and losses in the regional treatment system. In choosing between a central treatment plan and an individual plan, remember that the most desirable alternative is the one with the greatest net benefit.[2]

[2] For further discussion of water treatment alternatives and their costs, see A. Kneese and B. Bower, *Managing Water Quality: Economics, Technology, Institutions* (Baltimore: Johns Hopkins University Press, 1968), Chapter 4.

Linear Programming, Pollutant Mix, and Technical Feasibility

Linear programming is another method of estimating the costs of control. The basic sources of input data are the estimates of the cost of controlling individual sources or processes at various levels. The object of linear programming is to determine which sources should be controlled at which levels in order to generate each total emission level at the lowest cost.

Figure 5.2 presents estimates of total cost functions for the con-

FIGURE 5.2 Automotive Control Cost Estimates Using Linear Programming

Control of automotive emissions also exhibits the characteristic of rapidly increasing costs at high levels of control. In addition, costs depend on the mix of pollutants being controlled.

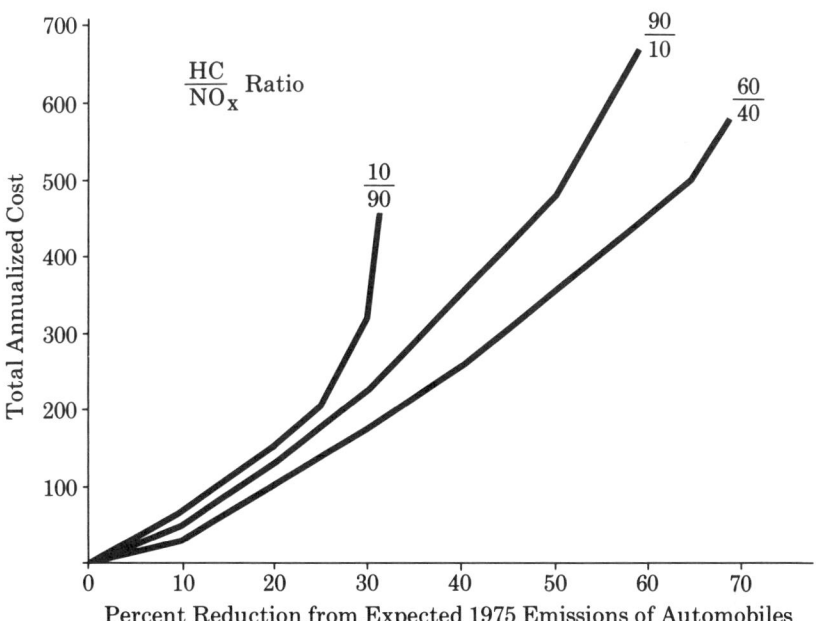

Source: Paul B. Downing, "The Cost and Effectiveness of Retrofit Programs for Used Cars," *Water, Air, and Soil Pollution* 3 (1974): 95.

trol of emissions from used cars. This study was intended to solve a particular problem. The Clean Air Act of 1970 required that the Los Angeles area clean up its air pollution as much as possible by 1975. Various devices were then available, or could have been made available, to reduce emissions from used cars substantially. The task of this analysis, conducted in 1972, was to determine which combination of these devices would produce a given level of control of emissions from used cars at the lowest cost. The annual cost of a device depended on various characteristics of the car on which it would be installed. A device that cost $100 would have had a higher annual cost if it was installed on an older car headed for the junk yard than if it was installed on a newer used car that could be expected to last eight more years or so. More effective devices were also more expensive, and some devices could not be used on certain types of cars or in combination with other devices. To complicate the problem even further, some devices controlled hydrocarbon emissions (HC) and others controlled nitrogen oxides (NO_x), two components of the Los Angeles smog problem.

The linear programming technique determined the least costly combination of devices and automobile models needed to meet a particular level of control and mix of HC and NO_x, using a solution technique that incorporated the "equal marginal cost" principle discussed in Chapter 4. The repeated application of this type of analysis with different emission control goals generated the cost estimates presented in Figure 5.2.

Two interesting results are evident in Figure 5.2. First of all, a 60/40 mix of control of HC and NO_x is obviously less expensive than either a concentration on HC (90/10) or a concentration on NO_x (10/90), for any rate of reduction. In addition, the 60/40 mix generates the highest percentage of removal at its technological maximum level of control. The endpoint of each cost line is the point beyond which further control is technologically impossible with available devices. Concentration on NO_x has the highest cost and the lowest technological maximum. One reason automobile manufacturers are currently seeking relaxation of NO_x standards is the high cost of compliance.

Given that the 60/40 mix is less expensive and can control more, it would seem to be the preferred mix. This is not necessarily the case, however, for these cost curves deal only with levels of emissions, not with environmental quality. There is a great deal of controversy over the form of the emission transformation function in this case. Some scientists say that HC is the crucial element in the formation of photochemical oxidants, which are primarily ozone and are commonly called smog. If this is the case, the 90/10 cost curve might be the appropriate one. Other scientists of equal repute say that NO_x is the key element in smog formation, thus making the 10/90 cost function more appropriate. In the absence of new knowledge, it is impossible to determine which group is correct. If neither group is correct and the truth is somewhere in the middle, the 60/40 curve or something like it may be the best choice. The point is that the least costly mix of controls for emissions is not necessarily the least costly combination for improving environmental quality. That determination depends on both *MERC* and *ETF*.

The mix of controls and the expense to individual car owners differed substantially depending on the level of control and the mix of pollutants. Let us assume a goal of 30 percent overall removal and a 60/40 mix. While the average additional reduction in emissions would have been 30 percent, the economical distribution of burdens among car age groups would have required reductions of more than 30 percent from newer and older cars, with lower reductions from the intermediate age group. Previously uncontrolled cars built between 1960 and 1965 would have required relatively inexpensive devices. Newer cars (1971 to 1974) with moderately effective assembly-line controls would have required very expensive catalytic converter systems. The intermediate age group of cars (1966 to 1970) would have required virtually nothing, because they had the inexpensive controls and would not last long enough to make the expensive retrofits economical. While this solution might have been effective, it would have been difficult to implement because of the political reaction it would have generated. It would seem inequitable that owners of newer cars would have to pay more for controls than would owners of older cars. After all, the higher prices of those newer cars had included the cost of required emission controls. By the same token, the financial burden of achieving compliance would probably be most difficult for the owners of older cars, mainly people with lower incomes. These political considerations became apparent when the state of California attempted to require the installation of pollution control devices on some model years. The plan proceeded as far as approving devices and installing them on a few cars. Then it was on-again off-again until the affected model became virtually extinct and the feasibility of the plan became a moot question.

Simulation and Degradation over Time

Pollution control costs often depend on the functioning of the actual equipment and the activities of the emission source. Mathematical models of the control process can be designed. The values of variables which determine levels of performance in such models can be estimated and the model can be solved to determine costs and outputs. The model is designed to simulate the actual functioning of the process mathematically, so this procedure is called simulation.

When values for variables in the model are uncertain, a range of likely alternative values can be chosen and the model solved for each set. The results of these successive simulations can then be summarized by statistical regression techniques. The difference between this method of cost estimation and the regression analysis discussed earlier is that the base data in this case come from a model rather than from actual experience.

The results of a simulation of particulate control in coal-fired electric power plants using electrostatic precipitators indicate that control of these emissions has certain cost characteristics common also to sewage treatment and automotive emission control.[3] The study demonstrates that costs increase at an increasing rate, and it displays the existence of economies of scale. Another interesting characteristic of the use of electrostatic precipitators is that their ability to collect particulate matter declines with usage. This degradation of effectiveness can be reversed by replacing broken electrodes, but this requires that the power plant be shut down. Standard operating procedure is to accomplish this maintenance at the time the plant is shut down for annual maintenance. Emissions from the plant are lower after annual maintenance and higher as time goes on. There are several ways to increase the effectiveness of an electrostatic precipitator. It can be increased in size, thus reducing emissions at all times during the cycle. It can be repaired more frequently, thus limiting the period of lower performance. It can be modified to shift electricity from broken electrodes to neighboring ones, thus slowing down the rate of degradation. To determine the least costly option, an investigator must make estimates of the cost of all these alternatives. The correct solution will depend on the size of the plant and the effects on the environment — the benefits — of

---

[3] See P. B. Downing and W. D. Watson, Jr., "The Economics of Enforcing Air Pollution Controls," *Journal of Environmental Economics and Management* 1 (November 1974): 219–236.

the variations in emissions. All of these options can be considered in a simulation method.

Neglected Alternatives and Bias

The estimating techniques we have discussed thus far are fairly typical and have been used effectively by many researchers. One drawback is that each analyzes only one part of the control problem and neglects certain other possibilities. Process changes have been neglected: It is possible to change the way cola is made so as to reduce the amount of BOD released to the sewage treatment plant. Input changes can be made: The use of coal with a low ash content could effectively reduce particulate emissions. Outputs could be reduced: Automobiles could be driven less. Ignoring the possibility of such changes in process may result in control costs being overstated. In fact, some sources faced with pollution control requirements have learned that they can control at virtually no cost by recovering valuable resources previously released into the environment.[4] This tendency to overstate costs when doing benefit/cost analyses could bias environmental decisions toward a lower level of environmental quality than is desirable.

There is another perplexing problem with estimating costs. Suppose a plant changes its production process, as a consequence increasing the quality of its product *and* reducing the quantity of pollution produced. How much of the cost of designing and implementing this new process is attributable to pollution control? If the increase in the quality of the good results in an increase in the price received or the volume sold (or both), at least some of the change in process is attributable to the change in product. Yet existing economic models do not allow us to separate the joint production of improvements in the quality of final goods and of pollution control. It is not possible to say how much of the increase in costs can be attributed to either output of the change in process.[5] This is a general problem in estimating pollution control costs, and it leads to a great deal of uncertainty in cost estimation.

---

[4] "Dow Cleans Up Pollution at No Net Cost," *Business Week,* January 1, 1972, pp. 32–34.

[5] For a discussion of these problems, see R. Kopp and V. K. Smith, "The Perceived Role of Materials in Neoclassical Models of Production Technology," in V. K. Smith and J. Krutilla, eds., *Explorations in Natural Resources Economics* (Baltimore: Johns Hopkins University Press, 1982).

ESTIMATING BENEFITS

Estimating the costs of pollution control is technically complex and time-consuming, but it is easier than estimating benefits. A pollutant like asbestos can cause cancer many years after exposure. People may not recognize that the wilting and brown spots on their roses are attributable to air pollutants. Thus the reduction of these adverse effects (the benefits of control) may not be directly felt or quickly or accurately perceived by those affected. It is not easy to assign economic values to such things as a beautiful garden. Nonetheless, economists have developed various techniques to attempt to measure benefits.

Technical Coefficients and the Value of Human Life

One method of estimating benefits uses technical relationships between environmental quality and effects on people, plants, animals, or physical objects. These relationships are derived experimentally by exposing study objects to pollutants in a laboratory. The result is a physical or biological function, called a *dose-response function*, which relates damages to pollution levels. The physical or biological damages are then converted into economic costs by multiplying by prices. Suppose, for example, that a particular level of smog is found to reduce the orange yield of a tree by twenty pounds. If oranges would sell for fifty cents per pound if there had been no pollution, the damage from that level of smog is ten dollars per tree. Finally, the individual dollar damages for all physical and biological effects are added together to obtain a total damage estimate. Such damage estimates can be made for various levels of environmental quality. The benefit function is the reduction in estimated damages as environmental quality improves.

The generation of dose-response functions is particularly difficult to estimate in cases of human health. It is simply not morally possible to expose human beings to pollutants in a laboratory to see what levels cause illness or death. One alternative, which we will deal with later, is to study the responses of people exposed in the natural environment. A second method of generating dose-response functions is to use laboratory animals, usually rats.

Using rats in experimentation has some substantial advantages. Rats are easy and inexpensive to raise, so large numbers can be used. They are small enough that equipment for studying them is easy to design and construct. And rats can be interbred to reduce genetic variability. But such experiments also have a disadvantage: The physiology of a rat is much different from that of a human. Consequently, the results of rat experiments cannot be directly related to the dose-response reactions of humans. In particular, since rats' lungs do not work the way ours do, the relationship between rat experiments and human reality is suspect in studies of the effects of air pollution. In addition, the experiments usually employ high dosages and short response times. The levels of pollution experienced in the real world are typically low dosages over long durations. A relationship between experimental dosages and actual exposure must be assumed. This leads to an additional potential error in dose-response functions.

Even when dose-response functions can be established, there are other problems when human lives and human well-being are at stake. The analyst must somehow put a dollar value on illness and death caused by exposure to pollutants. Suppose we estimate that at a specific level of air pollution one person more in a million will die than would die normally over a designated period. How much is it worth to society to save this one individual? If the person involved is you or one of your loved ones, your response would be that society should pay whatever is necessary to prevent the death. This is a reasonable emotional response, but society's behavior is not consistent with that reaction.

One example of the value placed on human life can be found in laws pertaining to highway safety. Many steps that are not presently required could reduce traffic injuries and deaths. Cushioning could be placed around bridge abutments, and the abutments themselves could be moved farther away from the road. Passive restraints could be required in new automobiles. Speed limits could be reduced and enforced. (Just think how few people would be killed if the speed limit were zero!) Society does not do everything in its power to reduce traffic deaths, and from that we can assume that society does not put an infinite value on human life.

If human life is not of infinite value, how might we value it? One way is to estimate the discounted present value of the earning power of each individual. These earnings are a measure of the value to society of the goods and services the individual produces. In other words, it measures opportunity costs of the individual's premature death. There are other problems. For the single individual, the evaluation might be rejected easily; a retired person would have no value; a baby would be valued less than a young adult.[6] But as a way of arriving at an average for society, this method can be defended. Assigning the value of the average loss of earnings to any loss of life reflects the opportunity cost of the premature death of the average individual. In the case of illness, we must add the cost of care to the loss of earnings.

There is a further problem with this form of evaluation. Premature loss of life creates pain and suffering to the individual, and also to relatives, friends, and indeed all of society. Evaluating this pain and suffering in dollar terms is difficult. But attempts have recently been made to do so. Generally, relatives are more damaged the closer they are to the individual with the health problem. Also, younger individuals are valued more highly by relatives than are older people. A man of seventy years is valued 80 percent less than a newborn baby boy. Women are valued more by relatives than are men, even though men have a higher embodied capital value.[7]

Determining opportunity costs is but one method of valuing human life as it relates to the costs and benefits of pollution control. An alternative to this method is to ask how much society is willing to spend to save lives in other areas. Traffic safety programs, health services, and other such activities have the goal of saving lives. We could assume that the dollar expenditure per life saved in each such program is the implicit value society places on human life. This sort of analysis has been done, but unfortunately the results have not been consistent or satisfactory. The values derived in this way range from a few hundred dollars to millions of dollars. While there is no truly satisfactory calculation of the value of a human life, some value must be adopted if we are to estimate benefits in dollars.

Estimating benefits by using technical coefficients reflects the opportunity costs of losses in human health, and of physical damage to plants, animals, and objects. But it cannot measure such aesthetic losses as a view of some mountains. This and other limitations have led researchers to search for other alternatives.

---

[6] One study of the present value of premature death estimated that the present value of earnings was largest for the 25–29 age group, at $171,000 (1972 dollars) each. The present value of earnings for someone in the 65–69 age group was $18,000. The present value for the average person who died in 1972 was $29,000. See B. S. Cooper and D. P. Rice, "The Economic Cost of Illness Revisited," *Social Security Bulletin* 39 (1976): 28.

[7] L. Needelman, "Valuing Other People's Lives," *The Manchester School of Economics and Social Studies* 44 (December 1976): 330.

Epidemiological Studies

An alternative method of determining the relationship between pollutant exposures and human health effects is to study the incidence of diseases in the population. A statistical method of doing this has been developed by L. B. Lave and E. P. Seskin.[8] They have collected extensive data on the incidence of various diseases in various cities and related them to air pollution and such additional explanatory variables as climate and age, sex, income, and other socioeconomic indicators. Statistically significant relationships between mortality and certain air pollutants were revealed. These regressions indicate that "if the [regression] relationship were causal, a 50 percent abatement of suspended particulates and sulfates would be estimated to increase life expectancy by slightly less than one year."[9] Nitrates, nitrogen dioxide, and sulfur dioxide were found to be much less closely related to mortality than were sulfates and suspended particulates. Photochemical oxidants, which are potentially important air pollutants, were not included in this study.

Once morbidity and mortality relationships have been determined by using this methodology, it is still necessary to develop estimates of the dollar value of the human health effects of air pollution. Lave and Seskin did this using the economic loss estimates generated by B. S. Cooper and D. P. Rice. They conclude that "our 'best' estimate of the benefits of a 58 percent abatement of particulates and an 88 percent abatement of sulfur oxides, in terms of improvements in health, is $1.61 billion (1973 dollars) for 1979."[10]

Property Value and Air Pollution

Real estate values depend on various factors, including aesthetics and the level of pollution experienced at the site. Suppose you are considering buying a lot in a recreational development. You would be willing to pay more for a lot on the lake than for an interior lot of equal size. A view of the mountains would also command a premium. A lot on a clean lake with plenty of trout would be worth more to you than a lot on a polluted lake with plenty of green algae.

---

[8] L. B. Lave and E. P. Seskin, *Air Pollution and Human Health* (Baltimore: Johns Hopkins University Press, 1977).

[9] Lave and Seskin, p. 157.

[10] Lave and Seskin, p. 225. These percentages represent the control necessary to meet the requirements of the Clean Air Act of 1970.

Your reaction, combined with that of other lot purchasers, would cause the price of the preferred lots to be higher than the price of the less preferred lots. This market reaction provides us with some measure of the value people place on a less polluted environment.

Suppose two sites were otherwise identical in important characteristics, but one site had an air quality twice as good as the other. In deciding how much you would be willing to pay for the dirty site, you would consider the damages done by the air pollution. If the sites were to be used for orange production, the difference in land value would reflect the difference in orange production resulting from the pollution. (This example is obviously for California; Florida's orange-growing areas are never polluted.) The difference in the market price can be used as a measure of the present value of future production losses attributable to the air pollution. By systematically comparing the prices of land in areas with different levels of air pollution, we could obtain a measure of the productivity gains from cleaner sites. This market price difference is a measure of the value to society of the cleaner site.

This simple market response principle has been used by economists to estimate the benefits of air pollution control. Air pollution reduces visibility, increases the aging of materials, adversely affects plants, and increases human morbidity and mortality. In theory at least, differences in land values reflect the values people place on all these adverse affects. To measure these values in a particular city, researchers must gather data on the value of various sites throughout the city. They must also adjust this value for all factors other than air pollution that affect a site's value. These factors include locational desirability, quality of improvements, quality of neighborhood, and numerous others. A statistical method of controlling for all these other factors is regression. Regressions can explain the value of property as it is affected by air pollution and all these other variables.

Actually, the problem of conducting such a study is complex. It is necessary to be able to distinguish the demand for property from its supply. The data used consist of property characteristics as they now exist and the prices of property. These do not tell us how the property would be used if the pollution were reduced. Suppose, for example, that the property on a polluted river bank is now devoted to low-income housing. Another area is relatively free from pollution, and is developed into expensive resort condominiums. The additional investment in buildings affects the value of the property, as does the reduced pollution. It is impossible to sort out exactly how much each factor contributes to value. Furthermore, reducing pollution at the first site might cause it to be converted to resort condominiums. This increase in the supply of resort property can be expected to reduce the price at which it sells at the newly developed site and at the older site. This price adjustment, similar to the one we discussed in Chapter 3, must be included if a correct estimate is to be derived. So must the social cost of the eviction of low-income tenants, especially if low-priced housing is in short supply.

There is a related problem with these studies. In reacting to the existing situation, an individual will adjust investments so as to minimize the effect of the pollution at a site. Such adjustments could include installing fewer windows overlooking the river, locating the building farther from the bank, or including air conditioning instead of windows that open to avoid odor problems. When pollution is reduced, these investments may become inefficient. This loss in value reduces the benefits of pollution control. Furthermore, the relatively long-lived nature of these adjustments makes it difficult to adjust after pollution has been reduced. At the same time, some benefits of the environmental quality improvements are not captured in a current development. Consequently, they cannot be reflected in property value studies. Suppose the improvement in water quality spawned a new theme park. Existing property value differences would provide no estimate of this benefit.

In a review of the findings of these air pollution–property value studies, A. M. Freeman III, shows that most studies have found a significant negative relationship between property value and air pollution.[11] These results show that people do consider environmental quality when settling on the price of real property. Most of these studies are of sulfate and particulate pollution, and they cover St. Louis, Pittsburgh, Philadelphia, Boston, Kansas City (Missouri), Toronto, Chicago, and Washington, D.C. All show that these pollutants have a significant depressing effect on property values. Four studies of photochemical oxidants (in Washington, D.C., Boston, Los Angeles, and San Mateo County, California) also show that oxidants contribute significantly to reductions in property values.

These studies have been criticized for underestimating the benefits of pollution control. For an individual to decide that a polluted site is less valuable than a clean site, he or she must know that one

---

[11] A. M. Freeman III, *The Benefits of Environmental Improvement* (Baltimore: Johns Hopkins University Press, 1979), pp. 156–160.

site is more polluted than another *and* that the pollution is causing damages. Individual perceptions of the relative pollution loads of different sites are not always accurate. A study conducted in Los Angeles illustrates this fact. Residents were asked whether the area they lived in was more or less polluted than another area. In paired comparisons of responses to this question, respondents in area *A* thought area *B* was more polluted, while respondents in area *B* thought area *A* was more polluted. In fact, both areas were about equally polluted.[12] Individual perceptions of pollution levels clearly are not very accurate.

Individuals' knowledge of the effects of pollutants is also typically incomplete, especially in the case of human health effects. You might live in an area where you are exposed to a variety of pollutants, but it is unlikely that you would be aware of the possible adverse effects unless they became obvious. While such eye-opening effects do occur, subtle health hazards are more common.

The lack of knowledge about exposures to pollutants and their effects leads us to conclude that property value studies provide a minimum estimate of benefits. They do, however, reflect the aesthetic effects of pollution — something technical coefficient and epidemiological studies do not do.

Survey Techniques: Incentives to Tell the Truth

If our goal is to know how much people value improvements in environmental quality, why not simply ask them? After all, public opinion polls have been used for virtually every other purpose. There are problems, however, with this approach. For one thing, people are not used to thinking about environmental quality and may not know how to respond, especially on the spur of the moment. The lack of knowledge discussed above would also cast doubt on the accuracy of the responses. But even more important than these considerations, respondents might think it advantageous to misrepresent their true feelings purposely.

A good pollster knows that the way a question is asked will affect the response. If you ask an individual how much he or she would be willing to pay to clean up the environment, they may expect to have to pay. This could lead to a systematic underestimat-

---

[12] H. Molotch and R. C. Follett, "Air Pollution as a Problem for Sociological Research," in Paul B. Downing, ed., *Air Pollution and the Social Sciences* (New York: Praeger, 1971).

ing of benefits as respondents attempt to avoid the payment. Alternatively, if you were to ask individuals how much emitting firms should pay to clean up the environment, they might perceive that they would get environmental improvements without paying. This could lead to a systematic overestimation of benefits.

An alternative, less questionable survey method would be to ask how individuals have altered their consumption behavior because of pollution. Questionnaires might seek to determine, for example, whether people in polluted areas paint their houses more frequently than do people in relatively clean areas. With this type of information and estimates of the cost of painting, an analyst could generate a benefit estimate. In other words, through questionnaire techniques an equivalent to technical coefficients can be estimated, and benefit estimates can be generated employing the same dollar values.

Selecting Techniques

We have suggested four techniques for estimating the benefits of pollution control. Each technique has its advantages and disadvantages. Technical coefficient studies provide definite results, but they may not reflect reactions outside the laboratory. Epidemiological studies have the advantage of relating health effects to pollution in the real world, but reactions to pollution are often so subtle that standard statistical techniques cannot isolate them from other factors. Technical coefficient and epidemiological studies share the problem of placing a dollar value on human life. Property value studies are the only source of information about true willingness to pay for improved environmental quality, but they depend on the level of public knowledge of the effects of pollution. Public opinion polls get directly at the people affected, but may themselves be prejudicial toward one response or another.

There is yet another alternative, suggested by T. E. Waddel, which I feel is most valid for air pollution.[13] He suggests that studies of health effects that use epidemiological data primarily be combined with data on property value differences. The reasoning behind this alternative is that property owners are probably good at assessing physical and aesthetic damages, but they are generally unaware of health effects and so underestimate them. Adding health

---

[13] T. E. Waddell, *The Economic Damages of Air Pollution*, EPA Socioeconomic Environmental Studies (Washington, D.C.: U.S. Government Printing Office, 1979).

effects to property value differences could double-count benefits, but it is equally probable that property value studies undercount nonhealth benefits. These offsetting errors should make such estimates just about right.

UNCERTAINTY AND THE RANGE OF OUTCOMES

It is not possible to estimate benefits and costs perfectly in pollution control. Uncertainty in these estimates generates a range of potentially efficient outcomes. In the following section I show how this uncertainty can affect pollution control policies.

Uncertainty

The techniques available for estimating the costs and benefits of pollution control generate substantial uncertainty. Changes in process might make control costs lower than estimates of the cost of end-of-process controls suggest, and unanticipated technical difficulties might cause real costs to be greater than estimated. But in all of this, one cost category is not usually included in estimates: the cost to the emitting firm and the government of administering the control program. All of this leads to the uncertainty associated with estimates of the marginal cost of control (MCC). On the benefit side there is even greater uncertainty. The effects of pollutants on plants, animals, and humans is still not well understood. Placing a dollar value on such items — and thus on the marginal benefit of control (MBC) — is difficult, to say the least.

All this uncertainty makes it impossible to specify precise MCC and MBC functions, so we must settle for a range of estimates. The extent of the range reflects the degree of uncertainty in quantifying the relationship: The greater the uncertainty, the greater the range in estimates. Generating a range of estimates for both MCC and MBC will generate a range of desired environmental qualities and associated costs. In Figure 5.3, hypothetical ranges are presented with the analyst's best estimates of these functions designated by a subscript ($_B$), and the range of uncertainty is represented by high ($_H$) and low ($_L$) estimates of both functions.

The range of outcomes is determined by the intersections of these functions. The analyst's best estimate of the desired environmental quality for the area would be determined by the intersection

FIGURE 5.3 Uncertainty and the Range of Outcomes in Environmental Quality

There is substantial uncertainty in estimating both *MCC* and *MBC*. This figure presents hypothetical ranges of estimates (H = high, B = best, L = low) and a possible range of estimated environmental qualities and prices. The intersection of MBC_B and MCC_B produces the best estimate, or the one most likely to be the efficient outcome (EQ_B at price P_B). The low range of *EQ* is determined by the intersection of MBC_L and MCC_H. It represents the low end of the range of expected efficient levels of environmental quality. The high range is determined by the intersection of MBC_H and MCC_L (at EQ_H). Given this uncertainty in benefits and costs, we expect that EQ_B is the efficient level of quality, but that efficient level of quality could be anywhere between EQ_L and EQ_H.

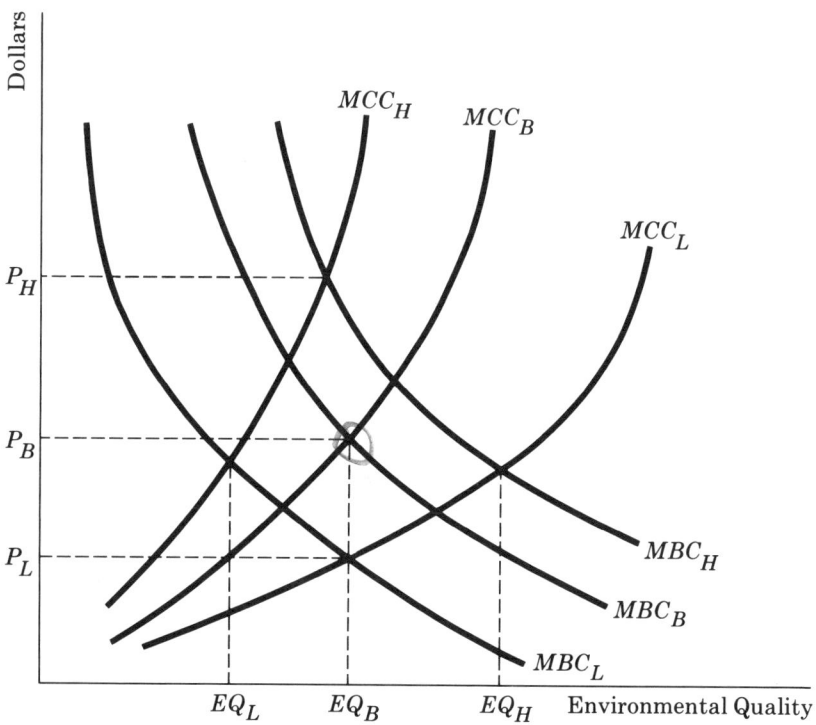

of the MCC_B and MBC_B functions (EQ_B at a price of P_B). Combining the low benefit estimate (MBC_L) with the high cost estimate (MCC_H) generates a minimum estimate of the desired environmental quality. This is designated as EQ_L. The maximum estimate (EQ_H) is generated by the intersection of MCC_L and MBC_H. Uncertainty is created in the price paid for pollution control. Combining MCC_H and MBC_H generates a maximum estimate of the cost of control (P_H), while using the lower estimates for both generates P_L, the minimum cost estimate.

There are some ways uncertainty can be reduced: More information on health effects could be gathered, or more extensive studies of costs could be completed. The problem is that all these efforts require time and resources (read *money*) that could be used for other things, including controlling emissions. Society may be willing to accept greater uncertainty in order to save resources for other uses. The level of expenditure on studies is itself an economic decision.

A NATIONAL ESTIMATE OF WATER POLLUTION CONTROL BENEFITS

The benefits of a national program to control water pollution come in several ways. First, emission control generates an improvement in water quality, which increases the mass of fish available. This relationship is captured in the oxygen sag curve presented in Figure 4.2 (page 68), and summarized in the range of benefits listed in Table 4.1 (page 72). Second, the quality of the fish available will be increased. Bass, trout, and other game fish are much more valued for recreational purposes than are carp, which are more likely to survive in polluted waters. Third, the improved aesthetics of the body of water increase the value of the recreational fishing experience. All these factors provide a difficult estimating task, but they are not the whole story. A national control program will increase the number of sites for fishing, with some of the improved sites closer to major populations. The improved availability of fishing experiences can be expected to increase participation. And a substitution among sites, from more distant, high-quality game fishing sites to closer sites, can be expected as well.

A recent effort to consider all these factors has produced estimates of the total benefit of water pollution control efforts to recreational fishing in the United States.[14] Employing data from a survey of active fishermen, Clifford Russell and William Vaughan estimate a range of annual benefits from improved recreational fishing to be from $307 million to $966 million. The level of estimated benefits depends on the degree of control achieved. If the nation were to meet the best practicable technology (BPT) standard required in the Federal Water Pollution Control Act (FWPCA), which has not yet been fully implemented, the total annual benefits to recreational fishing would fall in a range estimated between $307 million and $683 million. With the addition of sediment control for cropland to reduce the washing of suspended solids into surface water, and pH control to reduce the toxicity of that water, the range of benefits would increase from $363 million to $810 million. Further control to the best available technology (BAT) standard required by the FWPCA would increase the range of total annual benefits from $433 million to $966 million.

This study demonstrates the range of uncertainty involved in estimating benefits, even using the latest and most sophisticated techniques. For the BAT alternative, the high estimate is 123 percent higher than the low estimate.[15] The marginal benefit estimates show this same range. As we saw in Figure 5.3, this range can create substantial uncertainty about the desired level of environmental quality. Because of the slope of the MC function, the range of uncertainty for any estimate of MCC would be less than 123 percent. (See Figure 5.4.) The curves MBC_L and MBC_H represent the range of estimates found in the Russell and Vaughan study. The MCC_E function represents an easily expanded pollution control effort. Economists call such a cost function-elastic — in fact, it is perfectly elastic in this case. The range of desired environmental quality runs from EQ_L to EQ_{HE}, and would be the full 123 percent if MCC_E were perfectly elastic. In a more realistic case there would be additional control efforts increasing the marginal costs of control. Such a curve is

---

[14] Clifford Russell and William Vaughan, "The National Recreational Fishing Benefits of Water Pollution Control," *Journal of Environmental Economics and Management* 9 (December 1982): 328–354.

[15] In a recent study of recreation benefits for specific sites, the range of uncertainty was only 40 percent. This lower range suggests that the uncertainty of benefit/cost analysis at the local level would be lower than for benefit/cost analysis used in setting national policy. See Ann Fisher and Robert Raucher, "Estimating the Benefits of Improving Environmental Quality: Evidence from the Application of Alternative Models to Specific Waterbodies," paper presented at the Southern Economics Association Meetings, Atlanta, November 11, 1982.

FIGURE 5.4 Elasticity and the Range of Uncertainty in Desired Environmental Quality

A more elastic *MCC* function, such as MCC_E, leads to a broader range of possible efficient levels of environmental quality (EQ_L to EQ_{HE}) than does the more inelastic MCC_I, whose range runs from EQ_L to EQ_{HI}.

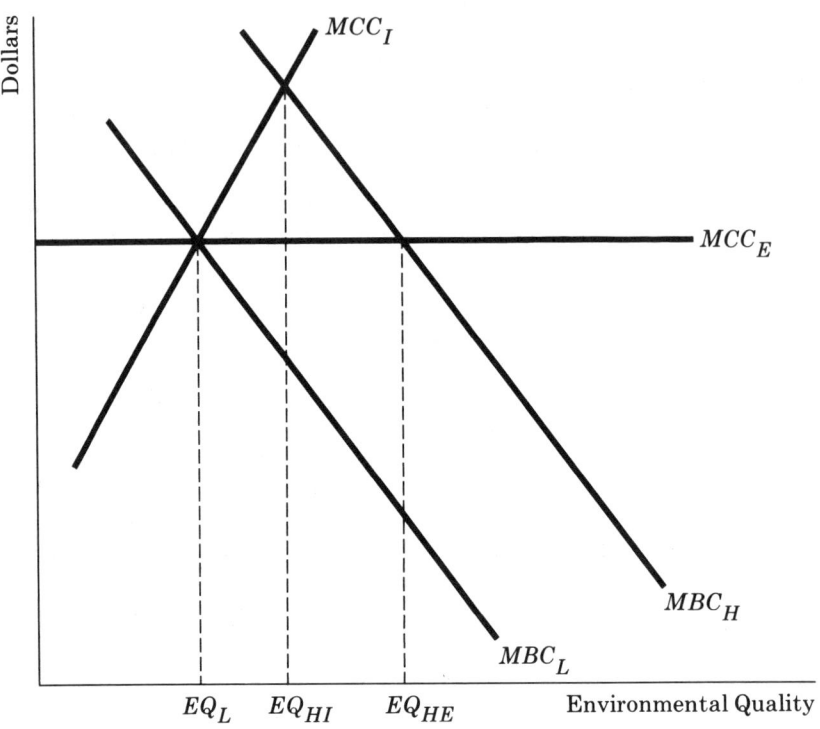

presented as MCC_I. This curve is less elastic than MCC_E, and may be inelastic (as the $_I$ indicates). Clearly a less elastic (more inelastic) *MCC* function will lower the range of uncertainty in any range of benefit estimates. In our example, EQ_{HI} is to the left of EQ_{HE}, thus lowering the range of uncertainty. The more inelastic *MCC* is, the steeper it will be, and the smaller the difference between EQ_L and EQ_H.

ALTERNATIVES TO BENEFIT/COST ANALYSIS

Costs and benefits are so uncertain that you might ask why we even bother with benefit/cost analysis. Why don't we substitute something more reliable? The answer is that we can and do use alternative techniques for determining desired levels of environmental quality and controls of individual sources. These alternatives do not, however, solve the problems we have been discussing. Instead, most hide them.

Arbitrary Standards

In Chapter 1 we discussed the system of determining environmental quality goals adopted by Congress in the Clean Air Act of 1970. Congress determined that air quality should be sufficient to protect public health and welfare with an adequate margin for safety; that is, there should be no adverse health effects on any one person from any air pollutant. Such an arbitrary standard cannot avoid being refined by benefit/cost analyses.

How does one define zero health effects with an adequate margin for safety? First, one must determine just exactly what "zero health effects" means. If someone gets a cold who might not have if the air or water had been cleaner, is that above the threshold of zero health effects? Would any level of environmental quality generate zero health effects? The answer is yes. There is one level of human emissions into the environment that would produce no adverse health effects. That is zero emissions. Zero emissions necessarily implies zero consumption of food, water, and air, and therefore zero human population. This is clearly too big a price to pay. So what price is appropriate? Which health effects do we count and which ones do we ignore? In answering this question, analysts are inevitably making an implicit benefit/cost analysis. Similarly, the adequacy of a margin of safety depends on how costly it is to provide that safety; if it is cheap, a lot can be provided. This too is a benefit/cost analysis. There is just no way to avoid it.

Cost Effectiveness

We have already discussed cost effectiveness analysis briefly, but it is worthwhile to discuss it further here. All cost effectiveness means is that we should find the least costly method of obtaining a desired result. The definition of the desired result is outside the analysis. We could use cost effectiveness analysis to determine the least costly combination of controls of emitting sources to obtain a desired environmental quality. We would, of course, use the equal marginal cost of control rule presented in Chapter 4.

The standard for the desired level of environmental quality is the result of political and policy decisions. Suppose an analyst were told to determine the most cost-effective way of meeting a particular environmental quality standard. In doing the analysis, she determines that the cost is $1 million per person. That little bit of information would undoubtedly find its way into the political arena and result in a change in the environmental quality standards. Again, we have a benefit/cost trade-off. We do not seem to be able to avoid it. Cost effectiveness is, in fact, a scaled-down version of benefit/cost analysis. Might it not be better simply to adopt the more explicit form?

Policy Trade-Off Analysis

One problem with benefit/cost analysis is that it is expensive to attempt to quantify all benefits and costs. Moreover, when such a quantification has been completed it is subject to criticism because of differences of opinion about how such items as the value of a human life should be treated. These factors compound the uncertainty we have already discussed. Consequently, we cannot expect a definitive answer about the desired level of environmental quality from benefit/cost analysis. What benefit/cost analysis can do — and does — is eliminate policy options that are clearly outside a range like the one shown in Figure 5.3.

To solve or reduce the problems associated with placing monetary values on benefits and costs, and to present decision-makers with a better sense of what the issues and uncertainties are, I would suggest a modification of benefit/cost analysis which I call policy trade-off analysis. A policy trade-off analysis takes a close look at several options with the goal of quantifying as much information as possible in monetary terms. Items that cannot be measured in dollars can be viewed in other quantitative terms, or in qualitative terms if that is all that can be done. The object is to present decision-makers with as much information as possible in a relatively simple form. In fact, it is typical in such federal agencies as EPA for decision memoranda presented to the agency head to be limited to one or two typed pages. This leaves little room for elaboration.

An example of the results of a policy trade-off analysis is presented in Table 5.1, which presents alternatives for controlling emissions and reducing photochemical oxidant (smog) air pollution in Los Angeles. The study was completed in 1974 and presents three levels of control to be reached by 1977. The minimal plan represents a substantial increase in control above the levels aimed at by the state of California. The intermediate and stringent plans are successively more ambitious. The cost estimates were derived from linear programming analysis, with some judgmental adjustments. Ninety dollars per family per year represents the *MCC* of moving from the air quality generated by the California plan to 0.28 ppm oxidants. The *MCC* of moving from 0.28 to 0.19 ppm would be $410 per family per year ($500 − $90).

The minimal plan generates some unquantified costs for reduction in ease of travel. This is the result of a shift of some trips from automobile to bus. People prefer to drive their cars rather than take a bus, so there is some loss to society from reducing or eliminating the private car alternative. Debate on how to value such a loss has continued among transportation planners over the past thirty or more years. Consequently, no dollar estimate of these losses was made. This leaves it up to the decision-maker to evaluate these losses relative to the potential gains. The gains of completing the minimal plan appear to be substantial. Most serious short-term health effects would be virtually eliminated if a peak oxidant of 0.28 ppm were reached. Visibility would be substantially improved and plant damage would be reduced. Some adverse health affects, visibility reductions, and plant damage remain, however.

The intermediate plan would generate even more improvements in health, visibility, and plant condition, but at a substantial increase in costs. To the *MCC* of $410 per family per year we add a greater reduction in mobility and an increase in another pollutant, platinum oxides, which come from catalytic converters on automobiles and which are thought to have adverse health effects. The stringent plan further reduces health damages, but at a very high cost. The average cost per family is $1,250 per year, which was over 20 percent of average family income in 1974. The *MCC* of $750 per family per year, along with further loss of mobility and increased platinum oxide problems, might be too much to pay for the relatively minor gains in health, visibility, and plant condition. Note, however, that the stringent plan does not even come close to meet-

TABLE 5.1 Rough Benefit/Cost Comparison for Alternative Plans

Plan	Peak Oxidant (ppm)	Annual Cost (dollars per family)	Health and Aesthetic Benefits
Minimal	0.28 (0.15–0.40)[a]	90.00 Some reduction in ease of movement, but no trips forgone.	Virtual elimination of lung constriction and throat irritation. Elimination of decreased pulmonary function effects. Reduced possible radiomimetic effects. Substantial increase in number of clear days and virtual elimination of days with very poor visibility. Substantial reduction in visible damage to pine trees, ornamental plants, etc.
Intermediate	0.19 (0.10–0.30)[a]	500.00 Greater reduction in mobility and a relatively minor number of trips forgone. Possible increases in platinum oxide particles, which are a health hazard.	Substantially reduce (if not eliminate) increased aging of red blood cells, structural damage to heart muscles, increased chromosomal abnormalities, decreased visual activity, asthmatic attacks, coughing, chest discomfort. Further reduce chances of radiomimetic effects. Even greater increases in visibility. Even greater improvement in conditions of plants.

TABLE 5.1 Rough Benefit/Cost Comparison for Alternative Plans *(Cont.)*

Plan	Peak Oxidant (ppm)	Annual Cost (dollars per family)	Health and Aesthetic Benefits
Stringent	0.15 (0.08–0.25)[a]	1,250.00 Substantial reduction in mobility and at least a 20% reduction in number of trips taken. Even greater levels of platinum oxide particles.	Substantially reduce but not eliminate susceptibility to infections, eye irritations, neonatal mortality. Further reduce chances of radiomimetic effects. Still greater improvements in visibility, but some unclear days remain. Still greater improvements in the condition of plants, but some visible damage and crop loss will remain.

Source: Adapted from Paul B. Downing, "Controlling Oxidants in Los Angeles," *Environmental Affairs* 4 (Fall 1975): 733–734.

[a] This represents the author's highly judgmental assessment of the possible range of outcomes of each plan. For comparison, note that 0.27 ppm is the first alert stage for oxidant in Riverside County. At readings above this level, schoolchildren cannot go outside to play at recess or participate in physical education classes.

ing the federal oxidant standard of 0.08 ppm, set in 1971 as required by the Clean Air Act of 1970. Nor would the current oxidant standard of 0.12 ppm be met unless the more optimistic ETF estimate is correct.

My purpose here is not to decide what level of control should have been adopted in Los Angeles in 1977, but to demonstrate some of the issues a policy trade-off analysis might raise. The results reported in Table 5.1 suggest that there was substantial uncertainty about the air quality improvements generated by each plan — and note that the range in each plan overlaps the best estimate of the next plan. So uncertainties exist even in this method. But one advantage of policy trade-off analysis is that it makes these uncertainties explicit.

SUMMARY

Benefit/cost analysis has a simple logic: If the benefits do not exceed the costs, the project should not be undertaken. But this simple logic can run into difficulties when applied to the real world. Costs can be estimated in various ways, all of which will contain uncertainty. Likewise, there are numerous techniques for estimating benefits, each of which has its strengths and weaknesses. The result is substantial uncertainty in outcomes.

Alternatives to benefit/cost analysis have been suggested. Arbitrary standards and measures of cost effectiveness cannot avoid benefit/cost considerations. Given uncertain information and difficulty in quantifying benefits and costs, a variant called policy trade-off analysis can be used. This technique has the advantage of making uncertainties and value judgments explicit while retaining the central logic of benefit/cost analysis.

One last point should be stressed. In spite of the practical difficulties encountered in implementing benefit/cost analysis, the weighing of benefits and costs cannot be avoided. Nor do such alternative techniques as cost effectiveness avoid the practical problems of measurement and quantification. It seems preferable to recognize these unavoidable issues explicitly and find appropriate ways to work with them. Unfortunately, the general tendency in public policy has been to ignore these problems rather than to deal with them forthrightly.

STUDY QUESTIONS

1. The appropriate interest rate to employ in calculating present values is the social rate of time preference, that is, the willingness of all society to give up current consumption for greater future consumption. In an unregulated economy such time preference would be measured by the market rate of interest; however, we have active regulation of banks and the credit market. How might such regulation affect the choice of interest rate used in analyzing control policy and the choice of control projects?
2. What evidence exists that suggests that the MCC function is shaped as pictured in this chapter?
3. The values society places on loss of life differ substantially, depending on the circumstances. The loss of life by an auto race driver is considered less serious than that of a spectator. The difference seems to relate to whether the individuals voluntarily placed themselves at risk or were placed at risk through the action of others. What is the appropriate perspective for valuing life in pollution situations? How will this perspective affect efficient control choices as compared to the alternative perspective?
4. What are the advantages and disadvantages of using property value differences vs. epidemiological studies as a measure of the benefits of pollution control?
5. Uncertainty in the range of benefit and cost estimate can be reduced by additional expenditure of resources on research. Develop a rule for the efficient expenditure of such research funds.

SUGGESTED READINGS

1. E. M. Gramlich, *Benefit/Cost Analysis of Government Programs* (Englewood Cliffs, N.J.: Prentice-Hall, 1981) presents a discussion of the practical problems encountered in the application of benefit/cost analysis.
2. L. Needelman, "Valuing Other People's Lives," *The Manchester School of Economics and Social Studies* 44 (December 1976): 330 discusses the difficult problems of valuing human life.
3. L. B. Lave and E. P. Seskin, *Air Pollution and Human Health* (Baltimore: Johns Hopkins University Press, 1977) presents the

results of numerous epidemiological studies of the benefits of air pollution control.
4. A. M. Freeman III, *The Benefits of Environmental Improvement* (Baltimore: Johns Hopkins University Press, 1979) summarizes and critiques current theory and practice in benefit estimation.

6

Government Action to Control Pollution

In Chapter 3 we looked at the reasons the private market does not control pollution efficiently. These reasons justify some form of government action to achieve control. In Chapter 4 and Chapter 5 we saw how the efficient level of pollution control might be determined. In this chapter we will combine elements of political science and economics to see how government actually accomplishes pollution control. The term we use for this kind of study is political economy. We will find that there are several economic reasons why government will not necessarily be led to seek the efficient environmental quality.

GOVERNMENT ACTION

We have seen that the private market will not allocate resources toward pollution control efficiently, primarily because there are externalities involved in the cost of pollution and pollution control is by nature a public good. The private market, in the absence of government intervention, allows emitters to reduce their *out-of-pocket costs* by releasing wastes that damage the environment and harm people. When they do not have to pay for these damages, firms will emit an excessive amount. Because environmental quality is a public good, people who are damaged tend to avoid efforts to control emissions. They realize that such individual efforts also benefit others who do not share in the negotiation costs. In the absence of private efforts, society turns to government to solve the problem.

The Balancing of Interests and Power

There are two basic models of the way government functions. One, called *elitism*, argues that public policy decisions are made not by society through a system of election and representation, but rather by a few leaders, the elite. This model holds that all societies have two classes, the few who govern and the masses who are governed. This phenomenon is not a product only of capitalism and the free market; socialism has its ruling elite as well. The elite are the members of the upper class, who have more resources, power, wealth, education, prestige, information, knowledge of political process, and ability. The prime characteristic of the elite is their consensus about the fundamental norms of society and their vested interest in the continuation of the system. Members of the lower class can move up, but by doing so they become part of the elite, sharing their values and goals. For the elite to continue in power, the masses must be uninterested or inactive in public policy. "Elitism," say political scientists T. R. Dye and L. H. Zeigler, "implies that public policy does not reflect the demands of 'the people' so much as it reflects the interests and values of elite."[1] The elite determine who is elected to office and who is appointed to powerful policy-making positions, and thus what policy will be chosen. They either ignore public opinion or mold it through the news media, which they also control.

The second basic model of public decision-making is called *pluralism*. Pluralists do not argue that each individual actually participates directly in public policy, but rather that public policy is the result of a complex interactive bargaining process that attempts to achieve compromises among competing groups of concerned citizens. Individuals can influence public policy through their choice of political representatives. Their primary influence, however, is through participation in special interest groups. An individual can gain access to decision-making by spending personal resources — time and money. Any individual's power depends on his or her level of interest in the issue, and thus on the amount of resources the individual is willing to expend, as well as on his or her skills in leadership, information about issues, knowledge of the political process, and skill in public relations and organization. Because of differences in the degree of interest individuals have in various issues, those who exercise power in one public policy area will not necessarily exercise

---

[1] T. R. Dye and L. H. Zeigler, *The Irony of Democracy*, 6th ed. (Scituate, Mass.: Duxbury Press, 1984), p. 5. This book provides an excellent discussion of both models of political decision-making.

power in another. The result of this complex interaction is not majority rule but an equilibrium that balances the interests of various groups. These groups represent the important demands of society, so the public policy that results from this balancing is a reasonable approximation of society's preferences — or so the pluralist argument goes.

In this book I will generally adopt the pluralist view of government, although some elements of the elitist interpretation will be employed where they seem valid. Figure 6.1 presents the balancing of public policy interests in pollution control as a ride on a seesaw. The horizontal board represents the stringency, or lack of it, in pollution control policy. One group, the emitters, have an interest in less stringent pollution control laws because this lowers their costs and thereby increases their profits. The recipients, those who feel the negative effects of pollution, prefer a stringent control policy because it reduces their damages. The balance that is struck between these competing interests, represented by the fulcrum, depends on the relative strengths of the groups. Power, represented by the size of each box, is shown to be greater for the anticontrol interests than for the procontrol groups. Because pollution control policy is biased toward the more powerful group, less stringent controls would be adopted if the situation were as it is in our example. Changes in the political power of one or both groups would change the balance.

Utility Maximization in Government

The basic behavioral assumption of economics is that individuals seek to maximize their utility. We can apply this reasoning to each individual's behavior with respect to public policy. Recipients may find that they can maximize their utility by acting politically to influence pollution policy. This increases the size (and thus the power) of the procontrol group, and shifts policy. Emitters also have an incentive to act politically to reduce control, in order to increase their firms' profits and their individual utility.

Individuals in government also act to maximize their utility. Politicians seeking to be re-elected or to be elected to higher office will seek to establish public policies that increase their vote-getting ability. The position individual politicians take on pollution policy will depend on the relative power of procontrol and anticontrol groups in their districts (or expected districts, if they are seeking higher office). We can expect, and in fact can observe, that proen-

FIGURE 6.1 Balancing Interests in Pollution Control Policy

The balancing of political interests in environmental policy can be envisioned as a seesaw, with the strength of competing groups represented by the size of the boxes on each end of the board. For the policy to balance the relative weight of the groups, the fulcrum represented by the triangle must be closer to the group with the larger influence (the one with the large box).

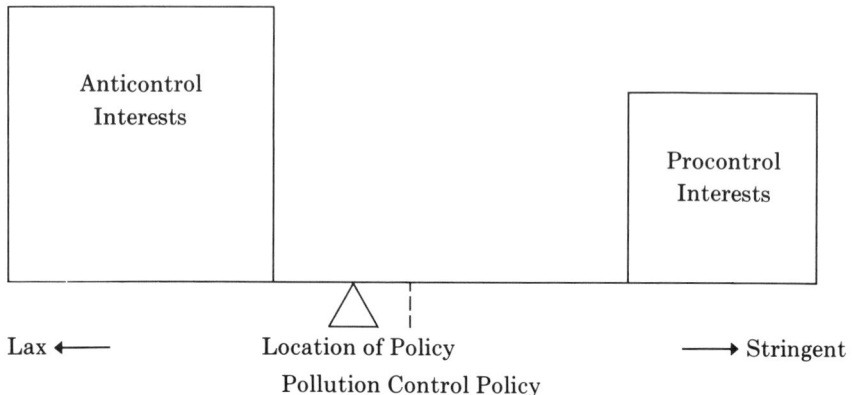

Source: Adapted from T.R. Dye, *Understanding Public Policy* (Englewood Cliffs, N.J.: Prentice-Hall, 1981), Figure 2-2.

vironmental politicians come from such states as Oregon and Wisconsin, which have strong procontrol groups, while anticontrol politicians come from such states as Michigan and Ohio, which have strong industry influences.

Bureaucrats also act to maximize their own utility. An individual bureaucrat might be totally indifferent to the policy output of his agency. Maximizing utility for such an individual might simply mean attempting to increase income, wealth, and power. Advocates of *bureaucracy theory* argue that bureaucrats obtain more income, wealth, and power through the expansion of the size and scope of their agencies, which is achieved by maximizing the agency budget.[2] This expansion would tend to increase the stringency of

[2] See, for example, W. A. Niskanen, Jr., *Bureaucracy and Representative Government* (Aldine, 1971).

pollution control policy, because more control implies a need for more employees and a higher budget.

A second possibility is that bureaucrats are very interested in the policy output of the agencies. (After all, what drew them to that line of work?) Increasing or enhancing that policy output necessitates an increase in the size and budget of the agency. This again leads to budget maximization and more stringent control. Under either behavioral assumption, the bureaucrat will enlist the help of the procontrol groups and politicians, and will have to overcome the resistance of the anticontrol interests.

In either case, bureaucrats will have a general bias toward more stringent controls. This is combined politically with the strength of the procontrol groups. The weighting of these two procontrol groups against the anticontrol groups determines the stringency of pollution control policy.

POLITICAL PRESSURES IN POLLUTION CONTROL

The balancing of interest group pressures can generate a policy that does not necessarily lead to efficiency in pollution control. In this section I explain the incentives that motivate each interest group.

The Emitters' Lobby

The goal of a firm's owner is to make as much profit as possible. One of the ways a firm can maximize its profits is to produce its output at the lowest possible cost to itself. It is costly to control emissions of wastes into the environment, and the firm can avoid costs by not controlling emissions. Thus self-imposed emission controls are not consistent with the firm's goal of cost minimization. As we saw in Chapter 3, this leads to too much pollution and too much production of the goods whose production processes generate pollution. We shall call these firms *emitters*.

Before government took action to control emissions, firms made production decisions on the assumption that release of unwanted wastes into the environment was costless to them. Under these circumstances, market forces generated an equilibrium in which firms were operating at the low point on an average cost (AC) function that did not include the environmental costs imposed on others. Such an equilibrium, where AC and MC do not include environmental costs, is depicted in Figure 6.2. The firm is just covering all its

FIGURE 6.2 One Firm's Reaction to Pollution Control

When government initiates efforts to control emissions the firm's marginal cost of producing its final good will increase to MC', and its average cost to AC'. The firm will adjust to this increase in costs by producing a smaller output (q'_x). Under these circumstances it loses money equal to area P_xABC. It will not stay in business unless market prices adjust.

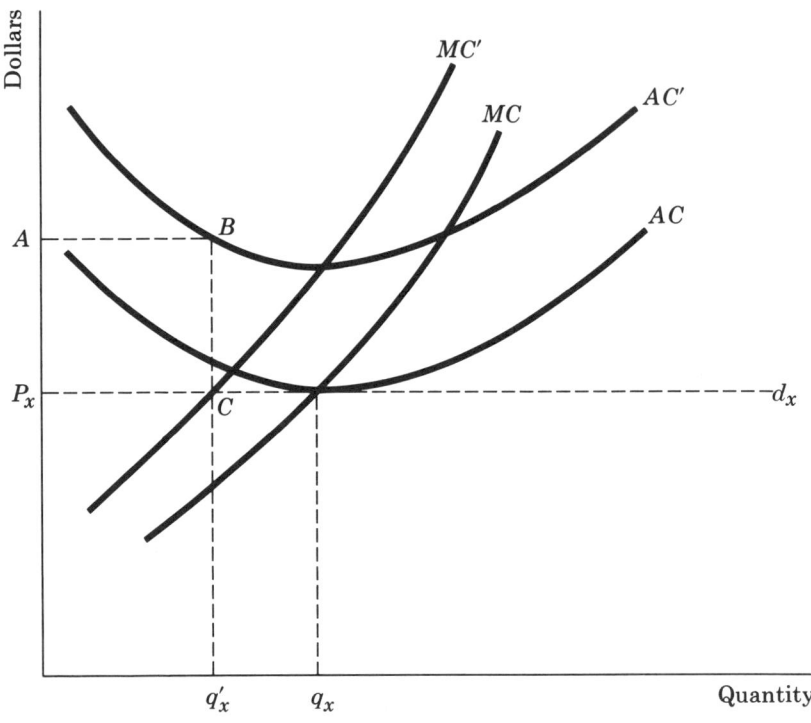

costs at a price P_X and profit-maximizing output q_X. The market for X is in equilibrium.

If a pollution control law were passed, the firm would incur additional costs to control waste emissions. This increase would shift the cost curves to AC' and MC'. The firm's initial reaction would be to reduce output of X to q'_X. This is the new profit-maximizing output for the firm in the short run. Profit, however, is negative. The firm will lose the amount represented graphically in area $P_X ABC$. What happens in the long run depends on the universality of the pollution control law. If this firm were the only one affected by the law, its increase in costs and reduction in supply would have little influence on the market. Price would remain at P_X and eventually the controlled firm would go out of business, at least at the controlled location.

If the pollution law were universal, so all firms producing X had similar increases in their costs, the result would be somewhat different. The reductions in supply from each firm would result in a noticeable reduction in supply in the market. This shift of market supply to the left would cause an increase in price. The shift would take place slowly and would not be sufficient to offset the increase in costs fully. Consequently, some firms would stop producing X. Those who stopped producing and those who remained in the market for X would lose profits during the adjustment period.

After adjusting to this pollution law, firms would still be in a tentative position. Passage of more stringent laws would again reduce their profit. Similarly, any move that would reduce the stringency of existing pollution control laws would generate an increase in profit, at least for a while. These transitional gains and losses cause firm owners to seek ways to influence political action on pollution control laws.[3]

Such individual political action undertaken to influence pollution legislation and control agency activity is a public good. If firm A is successful in reducing the stringency of pollution laws, other firms share in the savings of control costs without having shared in the lobbying costs. This being the case, individual action faces the problem of free riders and the result is an undersupply of effort to change pollution control policy — an undersupply relative to the amount the firms would expend to maximize profits if there were no free rider problem. In an effort to control the free rider problem, firms have organized into trade associations. The benefits of membership in a trade association are many and varied. The association may be able to exclude nonmembers from some highly beneficial activities, such as flows of information. Furthermore, the association may be able to impose economic sanctions against nonmembers. In these ways it may be able to reduce, if not eliminate, the free rider problem, and to encourage firms to join in its efforts. These circumstances produce a relatively strong group of lobbyists seeking reduc-

---

[3] G. Tullock, "The Transitional Gains Trap," *Bell Journal of Economics* 6 (Autumn 1975): 671–678.

tions in pollution control laws. Some of the better-known trade associations include the National Association of Manufacturers, the Business Roundtable, and the American Automobile Manufacturers Association.

It is natural to blame others for a problem, so politicians and individual citizens blame firms for pollution. What they neglect is the fact that every individual faces the same incentives the firm faces and behaves in the same way. Given a limited budget, an individual will seek to maximize his or her own satisfaction. To do this the individual will ignore the costs imposed on others in society. We all pollute the environment because we ourselves do not bear all the costs of pollution. The private costs of waste disposal do not reflect its social costs; so, equating our private marginal costs with our marginal benefit, we choose to release an inefficiently high volume of waste into the environment. Littering is just one example of the individual as polluter; there are many more that we need not list. It is sufficient to note that individuals are part of the problem as well as part of the solution.

The net effect of the economic incentives faced by polluters is resistance to imposed controls. This provides the incentive to act politically to reduce control. This political action may be undertaken by individuals or individual firms, but firms will often find it advantageous to join together to lobby against imposed pollution controls. Throughout this book I will lump all this effort into one category — the emitters' lobby.

Before we proceed, it is important to note that the emitters' lobby need not be anticontrol. It is a matter of incentives. If the costs of control are imposed on polluters, as under current laws, the emitters' lobby will resist control. If, instead, the costs of control were paid by others, emitters would have no incentive to resist. In fact, firm owners and managers, being individuals who are adversely affected by pollution, would favor more controls.

We shall adopt the assumption that pollution control laws impose costs on emitters, which is consistent with the existing situation. Consequently, the emitters' lobby resists pollution control laws. Keep in mind, however, that other incentives could change the emitters' lobby's attitude.

The Recipients' Lobby

Citizens are adversely affected by pollution. As individuals, their health and welfare are endangered; as productive economic agents, their productivity is reduced. I will call *recipients* all people who are damaged either directly (as are the elderly and those in poor health) or indirectly (as are firm owners) by pollution.

Recipients will seek to reduce damages in various ways. One method is to act politically to encourage government action requiring firms to control emissions. Individuals will assess the benefits and costs and extend their political action to the point where their private marginal benefit equals their marginal cost. As we saw in Chapter 3, however, pollution control and government action to generate control have the characteristics of a public good. Any political action taken by one recipient that successfully improves environmental quality also makes other recipients better off. Each recipient has an incentive to act as a free rider. The result, as with any public good, is a less than efficient level of political action favoring emission controls.

Recipients, particularly those who are not firm owners, might well feel that political activity is not worthwhile even if free riding were not a problem. An individual might argue that he or she is only one of many voters, and that his or her influence is likely to be very small. Thus the potential benefits of control are reduced by negative expectations of the outcome of political action. In other words, folks tend not to do what they think can't be done.

Recipients, like emitters, have an alternative to individual action: They can join together to influence policy. Many organizations, including the Sierra Club, the Natural Resources Defense Council, and the Friends of the Earth, have been formed to take joint action. These groups are generally made up of individual citizens who are interested in the same issue, and are called *citizen interest groups* (CIGs). Since these CIGs produce public goods, the incentive to act as a free rider remains. The increased potential effect on policy that such joint effort provides is, however, sufficient incentive for some individuals, who might otherwise be free riders, to become active members of one or more proenvironmental CIGs.

CIGs lobby to provide political support for the goals of their members. Still, the nature of their output as a public good and the lack of a coercive mechanism for attracting members will cause these groups to be relatively underfunded. The recipients' lobby can be expected to be less fully financed than the emitters' lobby. This does not necessarily imply, however, that it will be less effective. Political effectiveness depends on money *and* votes. The recipients' lobby may have less money, but it does appear to have more votes.

The incentive to act as a free rider is present in both the emitters' group and the recipients' group, yet we depicted the emitters' group as more powerful in Figure 6.1. You might well wonder why.

The incentive to join a lobbying group depends on the cost of joining and the benefits of doing so. In comparison to the number of recipients, the number of potential members of the emitters' lobby is relatively small, and the potential benefit to each is relatively large. This gives emitters a greater incentive to join the lobbying effort. In addition, the lobbying association provides a number of other benefits of membership, such as information and lobbying on other issues. This provides additional incentive to ignore the free rider incentive and join the group. The recipient faces a greater incentive to act as a free rider. The number of potential members of the recipients' lobby is large (the entire population, at the limit). Furthermore, the benefit of a policy change to any one recipient is usually quite small. It is expensive to join the lobby. Because the potential benefit is small, relatively few recipients will join. Realizing this, CIGs have attempted to overcome the free rider problem by offering other benefits to members, such as newsletters, magazines, books, and nature trips. While these incentives undoubtedly bring in more members, they do not appear to be highly successful. Consequently, the recipients' lobby tends to be underfunded and less powerful than the emitters' lobby. This can lead to the imbalance in control policy depicted in Figure 6.1.

It is important to note, however, that this imbalance can change with the situation. An oil spill can lead a recipient to perceive a very high benefit. This can overcome the free rider problem and lead to the formation of a powerful recipients' group concerned with the issue of oil spills. After the issue is settled, the incentive to join the group is dissipated and the group loses strength. Local environmental issues appear to provide a better basis for the formation of a strong recipients' lobby, because benefits are more immediate. At the same time, emitters are not as capable of forming a group because there is less commonality of interest outside the environmental issue. There is no local equivalent of the American Automobile Manufacturers Association. There are, however, local business groups that serve as informal lobbies for the diverse firms in their areas.

What this suggests is that the relative strengths of the two groups will differ from case to case and from location to location.

Political Pressures and Pollution Policy

Public policy on pollution control is the result of a complex set of interactions among the emitters' lobby, the recipients' lobby, and the government.[4] The emitters' lobby and the recipients' lobby can affect government policy through direct negotiation and political pressure on the control agency and its budget. They can also affect control agency policy through court actions. Figure 6.3 illustrates some of the possible interactions, flows of information, and reactions of each group.

Let us explore a few examples of efforts to influence government policy. If the recipients' lobby wanted to improve environmental quality, it could do this in several ways. It could put political pressure on the control agency to increase the stringency of its regulations. It could attempt to increase the agency's budget so as to provide more resources for effective implementation and enforcement of existing regulations. Or it could go to court to force the agency to issue more stringent regulations or to force a source to control its emissions further. The recipients' lobby will select the set of actions that maximizes its goals, given its current budget. It will compare the marginal productivity of each action that affects policy (productivity being improved environmental quality in this example) with the cost of that action. Like the firm discussed in Chapter 3, the recipients' lobby will achieve maximization at the point where the marginal productivity per dollar for all actions that affect policy is equal and where it has expended its entire budget.

The emitters' lobby does much the same thing. It applies political pressure on the agency to adopt less stringent regulations. It attempts to reduce the agency's budget in order to render its control efforts less effective. It goes to court to attempt to avoid agency requirements. And, like the recipients' lobby, it allocates resources among these activities so as to maximize its goals.

The results of these complex interactions will depend on the relative strengths of the two lobbies. The emitters' lobby appears to have an advantage in money. This would tend to reduce pollution control. The recipients' lobby appears to have an advantage in votes. The bureaucracy also favors increased pollution control, both because it prefers an improved environment and because it increases agency budgets. The balance achieved by these procontrol and an-

---

[4] This section summarizes the findings of a number of studies conducted by political scientists, lawyers, and economists. A good summary of this research can be found in A. Marcus, "Environmental Protection Agency," in J. Q. Wilson, ed., *The Politics of Regulation* (New York: Basic Books, 1980). Other books that provide useful insights into this political process include J. Krier and E. Ursin, *Pollution and Policy* (Berkeley: University of California Press, 1977); J. Quarles, *Cleaning Up America* (Boston: Houghton Mifflin, 1976); and W. Rosenbaum, *The Politics of Environmental Concern* (New York: Praeger, 1973).

FIGURE 6.3 Interactions of Principal Actors in Pollution Control Implementation

Environmental policy is formed as a result of a complex set of interactions among affected parties. A simple representation of these interactions is shown in this figure. An arrow represents the direction of influence. A word that labels a line of influence represents the mechanism for influence. A box represents the thing that is influenced or that does the influencing. Thus, for example, an emitters' lobby influences the control agency budget by using political pressure.

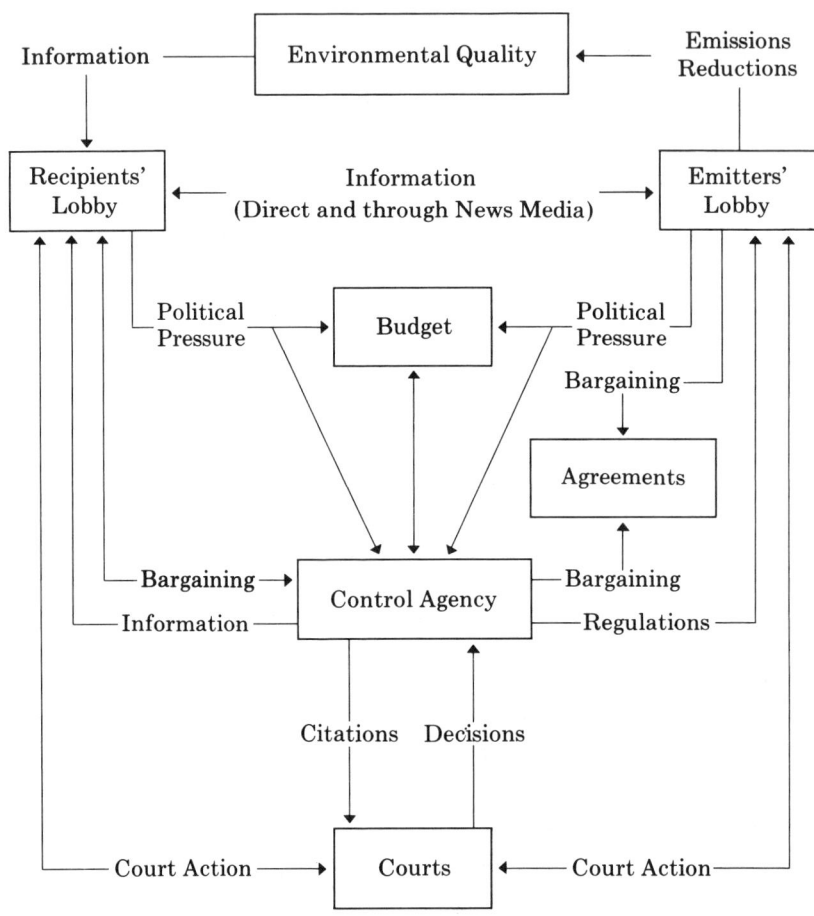

ticontrol political pressures may yield more or less control than is efficient.

Note that each group, in pursuing its self-interest, maximizes its own utility, not society's. Thus the recipients' lobby will seek additional control because recipients benefit from an improved environment. It will prefer methods of achieving this control that place the costs of control on emitters. In this way, recipients get the benefits without bearing the costs. Because they do not bear the costs, it is in their self-interest to lobby for an excessive (inefficient) level of environmental quality. They will push additional control to the point where the marginal benefit of additional control *to them* equals their marginal cost of obtaining that control. But theirs are not the only benefits, and under our current regulatory control system, theirs are not the only costs. They neglect the pollution control costs of the emitters entirely.

The emitters' lobby faces the opposite incentive. They do not get much benefit from control, but the regulatory approach allocates much of the cost of control to them. Consequently, they will allocate funds to lobbying against control to the point where the marginal benefit of control *to them* equals their marginal cost of control. This would occur at a low level of control.

The government is faced with the difficult task of mediating between these strongly divergent interests. At the same time, individuals in the government act in their own self-interest. They may be more or less sympathetic to the environmental issue. They may find action on this issue a method of building power or a constituency. In other words, like any other policy issue, pollution control is subject to political maneuvering. The end result of the balancing of the desires of these three interest groups will vary from case to case because the costs and benefits to each differ from case to case. But none of these groups' actions represents the true benefits and costs to the public. Power politics and special interests make it unlikely that the complex bargaining of these self-interested groups and the individuals in them will lead to efficient public policy.

Ways to Change Control Efforts After Passage of a Law

The political process has resulted in the passage of very stringent federal air and water pollution control laws. This suggests that the recipients' lobby had more political power at the time of the passage of these laws. But we observed in Chapter 1 that actual policy has not achieved the goals set in the law. This suggests that the balance is struck differently in applying these laws than it was in their passage. Power at one point in the political process does not necessarily imply power at another point. In this section we will explore some of the sources of change in policy.

Organizational inadequacies. Environmental quality transcends the individual environmental media of air, water, and land. Control of air pollution can lead sources to release wastes into the water or onto the land. Consequently, control efforts must be coordinated to take effects on other media into consideration. Within a single medium, environmental quality depends on emissions from all sources. Independent control of different types of sources can lead to inefficient control. Coordination is the key to successful, efficient control.

In fact, however, a coordinated effort at pollution control has not been developed. While EPA appears to have general jurisdiction and could perform this coordinating function, it does not do so. Its organization, dictated by the federal laws, splits responsibility between air and water pollution groups. States also split jurisdiction. California even goes one step further. There the responsibility for air pollution control is divided among jurisdictions, stationary sources being controlled by local air pollution control districts while mobile sources are controlled by the state. Splits in political jurisdiction also occur. One of the main reasons for the lack of success of the Delaware River Basin Commission's water pollution control efforts is the jurisdictional conflicts of its members, who represent various states and cities along the river.[5]

Splits in jurisdiction, type of source, and medium tend to reduce coordination. Instead of seeking the least costly solutions, each jurisdiction attempts to act as a free rider. Those responsible for controlling one type of source blame those responsible for another type when pollution remains. Officials who regulate one medium will attempt to solve their pollution problems regardless of the effects on other media, or will blame the actions of agencies that are attempting to control another pollutant for their lack of success.

The result of these organizational inadequacies is a great deal of political bickering instead of efforts to improve the environment. Lack of coordination also wastes resources, because control of emissions into one medium may increase the costs of control for another

---

[5] B. A. Ackerman et al., *The Uncertain Search for Environmental Quality* (New York: The Free Press, 1974).

medium. In fact, it can be technically impossible to meet all the pollution control requirements of air and water agencies simultaneously. Compliance with one set of regulations may preclude compliance with those designed to control emissions into another medium.

Funding inadequacies. Another way a pollution control law can be weakened is by inadequate funding of the agencies responsible for implementing and enforcing its requirements. When pollution control laws are passed, they include authorization to spend money for implementation; the money is not available, however, until a budget appropriation is made. This means that those favoring a pollution control law must fight two political battles: in Congress and in the executive branch. They must get the law passed *and* funded. The second battle may be more difficult, because many other interests are also seeking scarce federal budget dollars. Competition is keen. The emitters' lobby can take advantage of this circumstance to reduce funding. In fact, agencies habitually complain about a lack of funds. While there are other possible reasons for them to fall back on this complaint, the lack of funds may indeed be real.

Time inadequacies. An agency needs time as well as money to implement pollution laws effectively. When it does not have enough time it makes decisions with poor information, and those decisions are likely to be wrong or inefficient. Even if correct, they may be difficult to support in a systematic or scientifically acceptable way. This faulty decision-making subjects agencies to challenges on its policies. These challenges can come from the emitters' lobby, the recipients' lobby, or both. It is not uncommon for EPA to be sued simultaneously by procontrol groups seeking to strengthen a regulation and anticontrol groups seeking to weaken it. The end result is no action at all, which eliminates the effectiveness of the regulation until the court case is settled.

The Clean Air Act of 1970 required a sequence of actions following a very rigid schedule. It can be argued that lack of adequate time caused EPA to make inappropriate choices. It chose a photochemical oxidant (ozone) standard of 0.08 ppm in part because it did not have time to review available data on health effects carefully. Errors in the interpretation of health effects studies led to overly stringent hazard levels, which were much lower than the data actually indicated to be necessary. This drastic error led to drastic measures. EPA even went so far as to require many cities to adopt traffic controls in order to reduce automotive pollution. If the data on health effects had been interpreted correctly, some of those cities would not have had to control emissions at all, or certainly not with so severe a measure as traffic controls. The cities refused to comply with EPA's requirements. Fighting this massive refusal cost EPA and other agencies a lot of money. After a number of years, EPA reviewed the available data on health effects and reduced the stringency of the standard, increasing the acceptable level to 0.12 ppm. In the meantime, however, resources had been wasted, and control had not moved forward as rapidly as it might have had the error not been made.

Enforcement difficulties. The enforcement of regulations issued to implement pollution control laws is provided for in those laws. In all cases, federal legislation is to be enforced through common civil and criminal procedures. The enforcement process must follow several steps. First, violations must be detected. In the case of excess emissions, this is not necessarily an easy task. It is often technologically difficult to measure a source's emissions, and especially difficult to measure emissions without the source's knowledge. Knowing that they are being monitored, sources can temporarily alter their behavior. Second, once a violation has been detected, a case must be brought against the source. The pollution control agency usually does not have the power to bring legal action. Instead, it must request that the attorney general bring the case, which he or she may not wish to do because of certain political and resource constraints. Third, if and when the case has been filed, the source is entitled to all the procedural protections of the legal system. These include the rules of evidence, trial by jury, and the right to appeal. The source can cause delays of perhaps several years while it continues to pollute. The result of this enforcement procedure is a reduction in the effectiveness of the law.

A further cause of enforcement difficulties arises from the incentives faced by control agency personnel. The control agency depends on the legislature and the executive branches for its funding; hence it is very sensitive to political pressures. These pressures can be direct, but they are more often indirect. Inquiries from a member of Congress about enforcement actions against a source in his or her district convey a message to the agency. The agency will find it useful to be certain that the case is important enough and the facts strong enough to risk offending the representative. Such subtle pressures as these can substantially weaken the effectiveness of a pollution control law. On the other hand, informal supervision by members of CIGs can generate political pressure to enforce effectively. While CIGs have concentrated on the issuance of regulations in the past, they are beginning to become active in enforcement.

Individual self-interest may cause agency personnel to go slowly in taking enforcement actions against sources. Typically, enforcement personnel are young engineers who are in their first jobs. Their expectation is to stay in the job a short time while learning pollution control engineering. Having acquired this knowledge, they then expect to move to industry at a higher salary. This outlook makes enforcement personnel reluctant to pursue cases against firms that are potential employers, or firms that potential employers might contact. The general result is additional pressure to go slowly in enforcement.

DOES THE SYSTEM OVERSUPPLY OR UNDERSUPPLY POLLUTION CONTROL?

The argument we have presented suggests that an agency would want to expand its budget. But the marginal value of an additional dollar of budget will decline as more budget dollars are available. Either the value to the bureaucrat of improvements in environmental quality declines, or the increases in budget provide smaller increases in income and power. The agency bureaucracy therefore has a demand curve for budget that slopes downward to the right. The agency demand curve is shown as D_A in Figure 6.4.

The agency will be supported by the recipients' lobby in its efforts to get budget funds. The marginal value for the recipients' lobby of an increase in an agency's budget will decline as a higher budget is provided. The higher budget allows the agency to be more effective, but the marginal value of an improved environment to the recipients declines as the agency moves to the higher control levels the budget allows. Thus the demand of the recipients' lobby (D_R), which is this lobby's willingness to pay for political action that increases the agency's budget and provides benefits for the recipients, also slopes downward. The total demand (D_T) for budget is the vertical sum of D_A and D_R, because the agency budget is a public good.

To obtain funds, the agency and the recipients' lobby must overcome resistance from the emitters' lobby and from other fund-seeking groups, which want to see less spent on pollution control and more spent on their own interests. The emitters' lobby is ad-

FIGURE 6.4 Demand and Supply of Control Agency Budget

The demand for agency budget (D_T) is made up of the vertical sum of the demands of the agency (D_A) and of the recipients' lobby (D_R). The marginal cost of supplying additional budget (MC_T) is the vertical sum of the marginal cost of overcoming emitter resistance (MC_E) and of overcoming the resistance of groups that wish to spend limited government funds for other purposes (MC_O). The compromise budget is B^*.

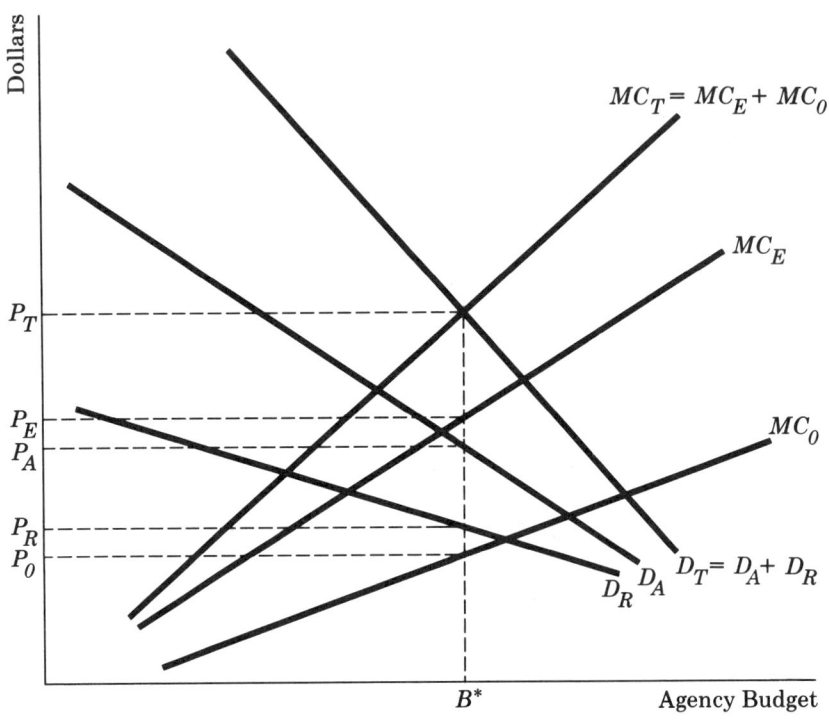

versely affected by a higher budget because an increase in the effectiveness of the control agency means an increase in the cost of control for emitters. The emitters' lobby will spend resources to fight budget increases. The higher the budget, the more expensive the controls are and the more it is worth for emitters to fight. To overcome this resistance, the agency and the recipients' lobby must spend their resources on political action. The greater the budget, the more resistance there will be to each additional dollar of budget; thus the marginal cost of overcoming the resistance of the emitters' lobby (MC_E) slopes upward.

The second group that resists increases in agency budgets is made up of all the other interest groups seeking government expenditures on their projects. Thus the recipients' lobby and the agency must overcome resistance from the agricultural lobby, the housing lobby, the consumers' lobby, and every other lobby. The cost of doing so increases as the agency budget increases. MC_O represents this cost. The total marginal cost of overcoming both sources of resistance is MC_T which equals the vertical sum of MC_E and MC_O. (Fighting budget increases is also a public good.)

The equilibrium budget is B^*, where the sum of the marginal benefits of increases in the budget to the agency and to the recipients' lobby just equals the marginal costs to them of affecting budget allocations through the political process. Note that the efficient sharing of these lobbying costs occurs when the agency pays P_A and the recipients' lobby pays P_R. (These amounts represent the different groups Lindahl taxes, which we discussed in Chapter 3, on page 57.) There is no explicit bargaining between the two groups, so both could attempt to act as free riders, thus reducing the actual budget below B^*. Note also that the efficient combination of expenditures would be P_O to counteract other demands for funds and P_E to counteract the emitters' lobby.

There is no reason to believe that B^*, or the ultimate budget decided upon if free riding reduces the budget, is in fact the budget that would lead to a public policy that maximized the net benefit of pollution control. The bureaucracy argument would suggest that the budget would be excessive. The nature of the budget as a public good, and the consequent free rider problem, leads to an inconclusive prediction. Since both the emitters' lobby and the recipients' lobby are subject to the free rider problem, both MC_E and D_R in Figure 6.4 will be lower than the underlying costs and benefits of budget increases. It is then a matter of who is more likely to be affected by free rider problems. Earlier we argued that the emitters' lobby has more mechanisms to enforce joining and contributions. If this is true, MC_E would be less understated than D_R, and the agency budget would be lowered.

With bureaucratic biases favoring increases in budget and net biases in political pressure favoring decreases, it is impossible to tell whether the agency budget is excessive or insufficient. Another element that might help resolve the debate should be added to the discussion. *Bureaucracy theory* suggests that the agency will seek an excessive budget *and* that it will spend part of its budget pursuing goals other than its assigned duties. That is, it will spend money inefficiently. This suggests that whatever budget is decided upon will not produce as much environmental quality as it could.

Figure 6.4 is a more formal way of presenting the political balance first illustrated in Figure 6.1. The balance depends on the power and the demands of each group. If the anticontrol lobby obtains more power, the positions of D_R, D_A, MC_E, and MC_O in Figure 6.4 would be located more upward and to the left. Other things being equal, this would lead to a lower agency budget. Greater power for the recipients would shift D_R upward to the right, yielding a higher agency budget. This reflects both the willingness to pay for political actions and the effectiveness of those actions. Effectiveness depends on political power.

STUDY QUESTIONS

1. In Figure 6.1, I characterized pollution control policy as a balance among competing groups. How might each of these groups alter the balance? If one group attempts to alter the balance in their favor, what is the other group likely to do?
2. Political action to control pollution is a public good with a consequent free rider problem. How might pro-control and anti-control lobbies overcome the free rider problem? Is there any reason to believe that one lobby will be better than another at overcoming the free rider problem? Hint: Do you as a recipient of reduced environmental quality belong to a pro-control lobby, such as the Sierra Club?
3. All the political interplay discussed in this chapter does not necessarily lead to efficient policy decisions. How could the system be adjusted to cause the political incentives of both groups to move toward the efficient solution?

SUGGESTED READINGS

1. T. R. Dye and L. H. Zeigler, *The Irony of Democracy*, 6th ed. (Scituate, Mass.: Duxbury Press, 1984) provides an excellent discussion of the politics of public decision-making as political scientists see it.

2. J. Buchanan and G. Tullock, *The Calculus of Consent* (Ann Arbor: University of Michigan Press, 1962) is one of the classic works by economists on the interaction between politics and economics.
3. E. Green, "Obstacles to Taming Corporate Polluters: Water Pollution Politics in Gary, Indiana," *Environmental Affairs* 3 (1974): 199–221, provides a case study of the difficulties faced in controlling pollution.
4. E. Haefle, ed., *The Governance of Common Property Resources* (Baltimore: Johns Hopkins University Press, 1974) while more focused on natural resource issues presents the basic problems of governmental control encountered in pollution control policy.
5. D.C. Mueller, *Public Choice* (New York: Cambridge University Press, 1979) contains a summary of current thinking among economists on the interrelationship between economics, politics, and public policy.

7

Some Recent Policy Issues

In previous chapters I argued that environmental quality improvements are a public good and that the private market will not produce the efficient level of environmental quality. Reliance on government to control pollution, however, has also been fraught with difficulties. Power politics and the self-interest of individuals lead to inefficient government solutions. In this chapter we will discover some of the substance of the economic and political difficulties of formulating and implementing environmental policy by reviewing three important policy issues: the control of hazardous and toxic wastes, benefit/cost analysis as it is currently practiced, and the issue of acid rain.

HAZARDOUS WASTES

One of the most serious pollution problems facing our industrial world is the production and disposal of hazardous wastes. Nuclear wastes, for instance, not only cause severe health problems, they also cannot be neutralized by treatment, and they do not naturally degrade for generations. But nuclear wastes are not the only by-products of our industrial age to pose serious problems. The cancer-causing qualities of asbestos are made even more alarming because of the many sources of exposure. Oil spills kill fish and wildlife and spoil miles of shoreline. Eagles are threatened with extinction by the effects of DDT on their egg production. Humans are made ill and animals are killed by the powerful carcinogen dioxin.

Nearly every week sees newly discovered waste dumps added to EPA's list, which numbered 435 sites early in 1983. Leaching of wastes through the soil and into surface and underground water supplies is increasing exposure to these highly toxic chemicals. The problem appears to be of huge proportions, and may be the most serious pollution problem faced in the United States in the last quarter of this century. The Comprehensive Environmental Response, Compensation, and Liability Act of 1980 requires that new disposals of hazardous wastes be accomplished under strict supervision and that past dumps be cleaned up if their wastes create a health hazard. The passage of this law was stimulated by the problem at Love Canal in Niagara Falls, New York. An area that had been used as a disposal site for hazardous wastes was subsequently converted into a housing development. When wastes started leaking out of the ground, the area was abandoned and numerous homeowners lost their investments.[1] The federal law was designed to correct such situations. The implementation of this law, however, has been beset by controversy, which has led to the firing or resignation of many top EPA officials, including Administrator Anne (Gorsuch) Burford.

In this section we will explore the use of benefit/cost analysis in decisions to dispose of hazardous wastes. We will discuss the theoretical issues involved, including whether it is appropriate to prohibit production and release of hazardous wastes, and the difference between new releases and previously released wastes.

THE APPROPRIATENESS OF BENEFIT/COST ANALYSIS

While it may not appear at first that benefit/cost analysis is applicable to issues of hazardous waste, I show in this section that efficiency is an issue in the control of hazardous waste and that benefit/cost analysis can be quite useful in formulating public policy in this area.

Damages Are Not Infinite (Usually)

It is common to think that death will be the result when people, plants, and animals are exposed to hazardous wastes. We quickly leap to the conclusion that damages are infinite and should be

---

[1] For an excellent discussion, see "Love Canal: The Truth Seeps Out," *Reason* (February 1981).

stopped at all costs. But this is incorrect in all but a few cases, because, as we have seen, life is not valued infinitely. Furthermore, low concentrations of toxic wastes may do little or no damage, and may in fact be a necessary component of our diet in some cases.

Current medical opinion suggests that the physical damage function for a hazardous or toxic waste has three segments. At very low concentrations the damages are negligible. As the concentration increases, adverse effects begin to appear. Their point of first appearance is called the *threshold of damages*. After this threshold is reached, damages increase rapidly until they cause death. After this point, damages do not increase.

A representation of this damage function appears in Figure 7.1, panel A. At exposures below the threshold (T), no damage occurs. As

FIGURE 7.1 Toxic Waste Control

Panel A shows a marginal damage (*MD*) function for exposure to toxic wastes. At exposures below some threshold (T), additional exposure does not generate additional damage. As exposures increase beyond T, marginal damages increase, eventually causing death (D). Panel B represents the translation of the *MD* function into a *MBC* function and the determination of an efficient level (E) of exposure to hazardous wastes.

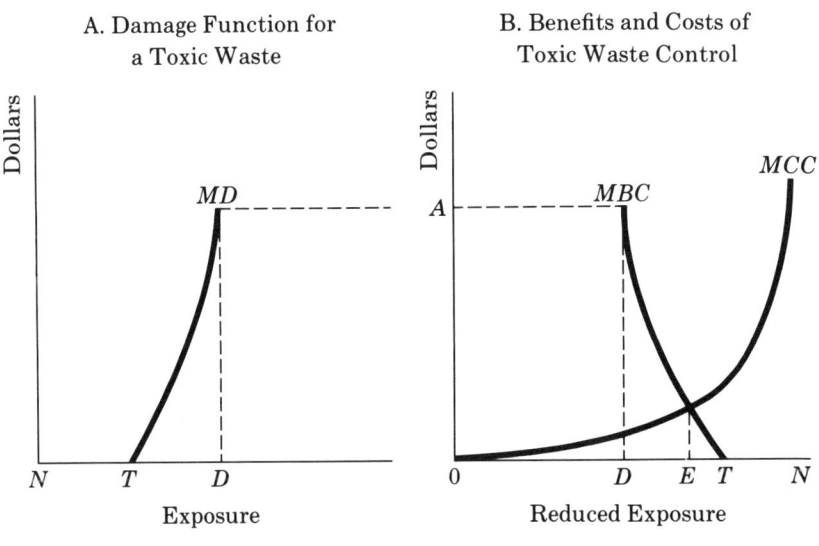

exposure increases, total damages and marginal damages (MD) increase rapidly until death (D). At still higher exposures to a toxic substance, an increase in exposure does not cause an increase in damages. Total damage does not increase, so the marginal damage of additional exposures beyond D is zero. This is indicated by a flat broken line extending the marginal damage function.

This damage function can be thought of in two ways. One is the traditional way we have talked about in previous chapters. Low levels of exposure cause some sickness, such as loss of energy and reduced mental agility. Higher exposures increase this damage until, at some point, it is sufficient to cause death. This traditional damage function does not reflect the situation in toxic waste exposure fully. Individuals do not universally become ill at some level of exposure and die at some other. The reaction depends on several factors, including the individual's exposure to other pollutants and resistance to the toxic substance. Not all people who smoke a pack of cigarettes a day get lung cancer, and not all people who get the disease die from it. Thus a second way of thinking of the damage function is according to probabilities. Suppose one person in every 10,000 exposed to a specified level of a carcinogen contracted cancer and died. Then the probability of any individual contracting cancer at this exposure is one in ten thousand (0.0001). The damage from the disease includes the cost of care and the value of the life lost. Assume that this damage equals $80,000 per person afflicted. For a population of 1 million exposed to this level of the toxic waste, the total number of people who can be expected to contract cancer and die is 100. Of course it may be greater or less than this in any specific instance, but assume that studies show that this is the expected average. Total damage for the population at this exposure would be $8,000,000. Now suppose that an increase in exposure to this toxic material increased the probability of getting cancer to two in 10,000 (0.0002). We could then expect that on average 200 people in a population of 1 million would contract cancer and die. The total damage would increase to $16,000,000 and the marginal damage of the increase in exposure would be $8,000,000. The marginal damage function reflects the probability of a certain percentage of a population getting the disease, not the actuality. This marginal damage function is the one employed in policy analysis for hazardous waste control.

Translating the marginal damage function into a marginal benefit of control (MBC) function is a straightforward process. In Figure 7.1, panel B, the exposure resulting from no control of toxic waste releases (0) causes death to the entire population. As control increases there is no reduction in deaths until D, which is the control level that generates the exposure D in panel A. For additional control, the MBC is zero until D and then jumps to A. As additional control is achieved, damages and MBC decline until they reach the threshold level (T). Beyond this point the MBC is again zero.

Costs of Controlling Toxic Waste Release

There are three ways to reduce the release of toxic and hazardous wastes into the environment: Reduce their production through reduction in final output and through changes in production processes; treat them to reduce their damaging effects; or collect them and dispose of them.

The costs of these control options have the same general characteristics as those for controlling other wastes. Costs increase at an increasing rate once controls have been established, so the MCC function has its typical shape. Such a function is depicted in panel B. The efficient course of action would be to reduce emissions so that exposure is at E. At this level in Figure 7.1, some exposure remains. This does not necessarily mean that people are dying from the toxic pollution; it only means that the probability of someone dying has not been reduced to zero. In the example shown, it is efficient to take the risk that some people in society will die rather than to incur additional control costs.

Prohibition May Be Efficient

While some release of toxic wastes may be efficient under the circumstances depicted in Figure 7.1, in some situations a complete prohibition of release is efficient. There are two ways to do this: the prohibition of all releases into a particular environmental medium on the one hand, and the prohibition of production of the toxic material on the other. Prohibition of release into the air or water can be efficient if the total benefit from eliminating this form of release is greater than the total cost of an alternative method of disposal. Nuclear wastes provide an example. Damages from nuclear wastes can be controlled by packaging the wastes in leak-proof containers and storing them where they will not be released into environmental media and exposed to people, plants, and animals. This method of control, if properly carried out, would reduce exposures to below T and conceivably to none at all (N). The total cost of special disposal in salt mines is presumed by public policy-makers to be lower than the total benefits of avoiding exposure to the general population.

In a previous chapter I pointed out that an efficient policy must pass two criteria: It must equate *MBC* to *MCC, and* total net benefit must be positive. Let us now add another criterion: Total net benefit must be higher than for any other option. The efficient goal of society is to maximize the excess of benefits over costs, or total net benefit. A control level like E in Figure 7.1, panel B, equates *MBC* to *MCC* and has a positive net benefit, but it may not be the efficient level of control if the total net benefit of controlling to E is lower than the total net benefit of the no-release option (N). Prohibition would be efficient in this case.

Efficient prohibition usually takes the form of a decision not to release into a particular environmental medium or media and disposal in some controlled way, such as the salt mine solution for nuclear wastes. There are, however, circumstances where prohibition of production might be justified. If control of releases into the environment were not possible, the net benefit of zero production and the consequent absence of releases could be greater than the net benefit of production and release. This implies that society values the products, the production of which generates the toxic waste, less than it values the freedom from damage.

POLICY APPLICATIONS

Having explored the appropriateness of benefit/cost analysis in formulating control policy for hazardous waste, we now discuss the application of this analytic technique to some specific policy.

The Control of New Releases

We have identified three possible policies for the control of hazardous and toxic wastes. Sources could control to the point where *MBC* equals *MCC* and release some of the remaining wastes into environmental media. Sources could be prohibited from releasing any of the toxic waste into the environment, instead containing them to eliminate environmental exposure. Finally, it could be efficient to prohibit the production of toxic wastes. While these policy alternatives seem straightforward, their application can at times be very complicated.

The biggest problem with a policy for controlling toxic wastes is that there is great uncertainty about the effects of various materials. Damages are often subtle and may not become known for years after the initial production. The pesticide DDT was in wide use for many years before its adverse effects were understood. How should policy-makers treat chemicals whose future effects are unknown? A first step would be to require the testing of these chemicals before their release. This is the technique employed in therapeutic drug regulation. The damaging side effects of some drugs, however, were not discovered despite extensive testing. Only mass exposures demonstrated the adverse consequences. Testing can provide evidence of adverse effects, but it is not foolproof.

Recognizing the element of uncertainty, some analysts argue that new chemicals should not be released into the environment when the risk of damage is unknown. In other words, we should presume the worst unless we have evidence to suggest that a new compound is harmless. This argument suffers from two defects. First, the prohibition of new waste compounds can eliminate the positive benefits of the products that generate them. Suppose a new product has the potential of saving thousands of lives each year but its production generates a new form of waste that may cause damage to the environment. The value of the high probability of immediate benefit could exceed the cost of the low probability of future damage. Presuming the worst and prohibiting all new compounds with any potential to cause environmental damage is just too costly in reducing current benefits, so some future damage must be risked. Second, even if tests indicate that there will be no damage from the compound, errors are made, as drug testing has shown. Again, there is no way of allowing change without risking some future damage.

Realizing that risk is inevitable, what policy might we adopt to reduce the resultant damage? Clearly, continual monitoring of the environment to find early warnings of unexpected effects is one method of controlling damages. A second method is cleaning up the wastes that have been released once the damage has been discovered. There are several problems with this solution, the primary one being that *damages may not be reversible*; that is, a cleanup may do no good. An extinct species cannot be reproduced or replaced; no amount of cleanup will revive it. In some cases, cleanup measures can cause even further damage: The kepone at the bottom of the Chesapeake Bay would be spread over an even larger area if an attempt were made to remove it by dredging. Cleanup makes sense where the benefits of cleaning up exceed the costs. If the compound is widespread, not easily contacted by people, plants, or animals, and in low concentrations in the environment, the cost of removing it may be greater than the benefit of eliminating its damages.

Cleanup has one other problem: It requires the dedication of resources (that is, it costs money). Where do these resources come from? One logical source would be the individual or company that released the waste. But suppose the cost of cleanup is so large as to exceed the company's ability to pay, or suppose the firm no longer exists. Beneficiaries of the cleanup may logically argue that the pollution is not their fault and that they should not have to pay. Current policy employs a combination of resources from companies that release the waste and funds that come from the public through the government.

Current Policy

The Comprehensive Environmental Response, Compensation, and Liability Act of 1980 places the financial liability for the cleanup of toxic waste disposal sites on the firm or individual who released the wastes. If the responsible party cannot be identified, however, or does not have the means to finance the cleanup, a special cleanup fund called the *Superfund* may be tapped.[2] Liability has been defined narrowly as strict liability, meaning that the producer of a toxic waste is liable for damages if it released the waste, but not if someone else released it. Thus, if source A hired another firm (B) to dispose of the waste, and the method of disposal caused widespread damage, B (not A) would be liable for cleanup costs. The Superfund is financed in part by taxes on oil, specified chemical compounds, and certain heavy metals. Costs that can be charged to the fund or the polluter include government's cost of pollution removal, other necessary costs of responding to pollution incidents, and damages to the natural environment. Thus both the cost of cleanup *and* the residual damages to the environment are collectible.

The problem the Superfund is intended to solve has potentially staggering proportions. EPA has identified (as of the beginning of 1983) 435 sites where hazardous wastes have been released and cleanup is required. In all, EPA has listed over 7,000 potentially hazardous waste disposal sites.[3] Current EPA regulations require

---

[2] J. Trauberman, "Superfund: A Legal Update," *Environment* 23 (March 1981): 25.
[3] For a complete listing of these sites, see S. Epstein, L. Brown, and C. Pope, *Hazardous Waste in America* (San Francisco: Sierra Club Books, 1982), Appendix X.

that new hazardous waste disposal sites be lined to prevent the leaching of wastes into ground and surface waters. But these regulations, issued after a long delay in 1982 under the Resource Conservation and Recovery Act of 1976, and subject to substantial political compromise, do not require that existing sites install liners. David Lennett, staff attorney for the Environmental Defense Fund (an environmental lobby), argues that more than 2,000 existing sites should put in liners unless the installation of liners is not feasible or would increase health or environmental hazards. EPA says that it does not have the resources or personnel to deal with these existing sites case by case.[4]

As staggering as these statistics are, they do not cover the whole story. There may be thousands of additional sites where hazardous and toxic wastes have been released. A recent case in Missouri provides an example. Late in 1971 Judy Platt had her horse arena sprayed with oil to control dust. The oil caused her to become ill and caused several of her horses to die. It was determined the oil contained dioxin, one of the most toxic chemicals known.[5] Furthermore, oil containing dioxin was spread over parking lots, roads, and other areas throughout the state. At least fourteen sites have been confirmed and more than 100 are suspected. The company that spread the waste oil contends that it did nothing illegal, and that this waste disposal method was common practice. At the time they may not have been aware that the oil contained dioxin or that it was as dangerous as it turned out to be. Recent congressional revelations suggest that organized crime is profiting from the illegal disposal of hazardous wastes, so the Missouri case may be an example of a widespread and continuing problem.[6]

The Superfund legislation may move toward the correction of past hazardous waste disposal problems, even though current levels of funding may be reduced. But does it solve the problem of current releases? The law places liability for any releases of toxic materials on the source. This liability and payment for cleanup does not come into force, however, until the hazard has been uncovered. For it to be uncovered, substantial damage must have occurred. The source can gamble that its releases will not cause harm. This allows them to

---

[4] M. Sun, "EPA Issues Hazardous Waste Rules," *Science* 217 (July 30, 1982): 430–443.
[5] M. Sun, "Missouri's Costly Dioxin Lesson," *Science* 219 (January 28, 1983): 367–369.
[6] "Mob's Role in Toxic-Waste Dumping Called 'Terrifying,' " *Tallahassee* (Fla.) *Democrat*, March 15, 1983.

make a substantial profit at the time of production. At the same time, they are accumulating a substantial potential liability without paying for it. It is possible that a firm could deliberately avoid effective disposal and the associated costs in order to make current profits, realizing that at some future date the liability will be assessed. If the source is a corporation, however, liability is limited to the value of corporate assets. Personal liability would be possible if the individuals involved were shown to have been deliberately negligent. The ability to avoid liability and payment at the time of release will stimulate more than the efficient amount of release of toxic wastes.

Requiring a payment equal to that liability at the time of the production and release of a hazardous waste could solve this problem. The firm would then compare the value (profit) it gets from producing and disposing of the hazardous waste to the cost of disposal and the cost of the liability. If the liability accurately reflects the social cost of the potential damage, the source will be stimulated to make an efficient decision. Total and marginal social costs would be included in the cost of the liability. The liability payment could be handled in one of two ways: The source could be required to place significant money in a special fund to cover future liabilities, or it could be required to take out special liability insurance. The advantage of the insurance alternative would be the ability of several sources to pool their risks. Not every hazardous waste release will cause damage or necessitate an expensive cleanup operation, so an insurance pool would need only enough resources to cover the occasional loss rather than fully covering all potential losses.

The current practice of charging a tax on imported oil and on various chemicals and heavy metals to fund the Superfund serves much the same insurance purpose. All potential sources of wastes pay into the fund, and cleanup costs are paid out of the fund if liability cannot be assigned to the source of the hazardous wastes. But the Superfund does not work quite like insurance. The Superfund tax is paid by all sources, regardless of their operation. It does not stimulate care, and thus is likely to generate more hazardous waste problems than a well-run, risk-related insurance system. A source's insurance premium would depend on the insurance company's assessment of the risk. This risk would depend on the care taken by the source to avoid spills and to properly dispose of hazardous wastes from its operations. Better operations would mean lower insurance premiums so a firm would have an incentive to be more careful.

The political problems generated by this issue — especially by previously released toxic substances — are great. The proenvironmental lobby wants to gain control of toxic wastes at the expense of those who initially disposed of them or of the general public. This leads them to seek greater levels of control than are economically efficient. At the same time, firms who have disposed of toxic wastes in the past in what was then a legal manner argue that they are being treated unfairly. They feel that they should not have to pay for cleanup, but that it should be paid for by those who benefit or by the general public. What both sides are saying is that their self-interest is best served by having someone else pay. Government, facing these interests, seeks to have someone else pay through a general tax on imported hazardous materials and through general fund revenues. In the first case it is singling out a sector of the economy with little political power. In the second, it is spreading the financial burden over millions of taxpayers in a way that does not make them aware of the costs of this policy. The result of this financing scheme is to lower political resistance to the cleanup of hazardous wastes. The end result is more cleanups than would be the case if either the recipients or the emitters paid for the operation. This ability to pass at least part of the cost on to others creates an externality of sorts, which — like other externalities — can lead to inefficiency, in this case excessive cleanup of past disposals of hazardous wastes.

EXECUTIVE ORDER 12291

As one of his first acts as president, Ronald Reagan signed Executive Order (EO) 12291, which requires that all major regulatory acts of the federal government be subjected to benefit/cost analysis before they are adopted, that this analysis demonstrate that "the potential benefits to society outweigh the potential costs to society," and that these regulations seek to maximize total net benefit.[7] In other words, all major regulations have to pass the efficiency tests we have described. This would appear to be a major victory for economic efficiency and a significant improvement in the actual operation of our regulatory apparatus. Like so many other regulatory reforms, however, it has several difficulties when it is applied to environmental policy-making, thus giving the impression that its actual effect is likely to be substantially less than its promise.

[7] Federal Register, February 17, 1981, pp. 13193–13194.

One of the major problems with this approach is that an analysis of a federal environmental regulation that is applicable to emitters across the nation is inappropriate and can lead to inefficient policy. EPA issues emission standards for particular industrial processes. These standards apply universally. All new steel mills must meet the same standards, regardless of their specific local circumstances. They do not take into consideration differences in the relationships between emissions and environmental quality or differences in the benefits of reducing emissions by the regulated amount, both of which are site-specific and vary from location to location. In addition, the efficient set of emission standards for any given basin depends on the location and the *MERC* functions of every emitter in the basin, regardless of the industry to which this emitter belongs. A universal standard can produce a positive net benefit in one location and a negative net benefit in another. The procedure required by EO 12291 would average these benefits. If the result is a positive net benefit *on average*, the regulation would be accepted; yet for some locations it would be inefficient. In fact, the emission standard could be adjusted to make it lower than appropriate in the areas that receive positive net benefits in order to reduce the loss in the areas that receive negative net benefits. Consequently, it could be "efficient" on average but inefficient in every specific case. This is not a clear improvement over decision-making before the order.

The problem, you might argue, is that EPA is producing a single national standard as required by the applicable pollution laws, rather than the individual case-by-case standards that our analysis suggests would be efficient. True — and this points up one of the reasons why reform of environmental policy is sought. But a national benefit/cost analysis puts the cloak of efficiency on an inherently inefficient procedure. It makes reform all the more difficult to achieve. Nor is this the only problem with this policy.

A second major problem with EO 12291 is that it provides agencies with an incentive to exaggerate benefits and hide costs in order to make the net benefit of a regulation appear positive.[8] This systematic bias has long been recognized and is not new to this policy, but the potential for fudging the benefit/cost data in this case is particularly large. As we have seen, benefit estimates are fraught

---

[8] For some discussion of this, see J. Semmens, "Concealed Costs/Bloated Benefits," *Reason* 12 (March 1981): 29–32, and J. Sonstellie and P. Portney, "Truth or Consequences: Cost Revelation and Regulation," *Journal of Policy Analysis and Management* 2 (Winter 1983): 280–295.

with technical difficulties. Application of estimating techniques across basins tends to add to these difficulties, increasing uncertainty. With greater uncertainty comes the chance to justify the systematic but hidden biases in assumptions that lead to high estimates of benefits and low estimates of costs. It is more difficult to show that the estimates are clearly wrong when they are aggregated over all basins in the country. Furthermore, those adversely affected by this fudging are geographically dispersed, which makes political and legal resistance to inefficient regulations and fudged data much more difficult to organize.

On a related point, an analysis of Inflation Impact Statements prepared by EPA and the Occupational Safety and Health Administration (OSHA) under a 1974 executive order shows that these statements systematically ignored some costs that regulations imposed on government agencies and the regulated activities.[9] These costs included the public and private resources employed in the political debate over these regulations, in implementing the regulations, and in enforcing them. These ignored costs have been estimated to be from 22 percent to 29 percent of the direct costs of complying with proposed pollution control regulations. This systematic neglect of costs can cause agencies to show a positive net benefit for a regulation when their inclusion would demonstrate a negative net benefit.

A third problem that leads one to suggest that EO 12291 will not lead to efficient regulations is that it must be enforced. This job has been given to the Office of Management and Budget (OMB).[10] Effective enforcement of this benefit/cost requirement, however, demands a significant commitment of resources and personnel. The approximately ninety staff members assigned to the enforcement effort in OMB are just not adequate to review the regulatory actions of EPA, let alone the regulatory actions of all federal agencies. "Even if all ninety worked round the clock reviewing preliminary and final RIAs [Regulatory Impact Analyses] and performing the other functions EO 12291 entrusts in them," two political scientists reported, "it is hard to see how they could be a match for the federal regula-

---

[9] P. Downing, "Policy Consequences of Indirect Regulatory Costs," *Public Policy* 29 (Fall 1981): 507–526.

[10] The question of the legality of OMB oversight was first raised during the Nixon administration; see J. Quarles, *Cleaning Up America* (Boston: Houghton Mifflin, 1976), Chapter 7. It was recently settled in favor of OMB; see M. Sohn and R. Litan, "Regulatory Oversight Wins in Court," *Regulation* 5 (July/August 1981): 17–24.

tory establishment."[11] The resulting lack of careful oversight allows EPA additional latitude in fudging its data.

ACID RAIN

Acid rain is the result of chemical reactions in the atmosphere that turn sulfur and nitrogen oxides into acids. The common standard for measuring acidity is pH. Pure rain has a pH of 5.6, but the acid rains that have been falling in the northeastern United States and Canada have pH readings of as much as 4.6 — four times as acid as pure rain. Acid rain is falling in every state and province in eastern North America. The problem is also widespread in Europe.[12] In Scandinavia and northern Britain, acid rain collects in surface reservoirs and underground aquifers, killing fish, corroding water mains, and coloring the water. In Sweden, 4,000 lakes are effectively dead because of acidification. Norway has essentially lost its salmon and brown trout fishery. Trees are dying in the forests of East and West Germany, Czechoslovakia, and Poland.

According to many sources, the cause of increased acidity in the rain is the emission of sulfur oxides from electric utility power plants (primarily those burning coal), from other industries, and from automobiles. The sulfur is contained in the fuel these plants burn. A recent report of the National Academy of Sciences recommends a reduction of SO_2 emissions by 50 percent. They predict that this reduction will bring about a reduction in acid rain of 40 percent to 45 percent, but they acknowledge that there is substantial uncertainty in their estimate of the effect of control on actual acid rain and that the result might be a reduction in acid rain of only 10 percent to 15 percent.[13] The cost of achieving this level of control of sulfur has been estimated by various sources at between $3.5 billion and $4.5 billion a year. Compare this staggering cost to estimates of acid rain damage at $3 billion to $4 billion a year.[14]

Reacting to this problem, the United States Senate has been

---

[11] P. Harrison, Jr., and P. Portney, "Regulatory Reform in the Large and Small," in L. Grayner and F. Thompson, eds., *Reforming Social Regulation* (New York: Sage Publications, 1982), p. 221.

[12] F. Pearce, "The Acid Rain Threat," *World Press Review* 29 (October 1982): 26–28.

[13] E. Marshall, "Air Pollution Clouds U.S.–Canadian Relations," *Science* 217 (September 17, 1982): 1118–1119.

[14] "U.S. Damage: $3 Billion a Year," *U.S. News and World Report,* November 29, 1982, p. 44.

debating a bill that would require reductions of 10 million tons per year in sulfur emissions. There is considerable difference of opinion over whether such a massive control effort would produce the desired result. A recent report by the Office of Technology Assessment, for example, states that preliminary data suggest that wet sulfuric rain is not closely correlated with emissions of sulfur. As Professor Mohen of the Atmospheric Sciences Research Center at the State University of New York at Albany noted in 1982: "What limited research has been done to date indicates that the reduction in sulfur dioxide emissions called for by the pending legislation would most likely *not* result in an equivalent reduction in acid deposition in the sensitive areas and might result in no measurable decrease in acid rain in those areas."[15]

This problem has several elements of particular interest. Two methods have been used to reduce sulfur exposures in various air basins. One is to reduce the sulfur content of fuels burned. This emphasis on low-sulfur fuels, particularly low-sulfur oil and coal burned in electric power plants, can reduce local exposure, and the practice is widespread. The second method that has been commonly used to reduce exposure is the construction of tall smokestacks, some more than 300 feet tall. Emissions released into the atmosphere at these heights do not fall on the land immediately downwind of the source. Instead they are dispersed more widely, finally falling in harmlessly low concentrations on relatively unpopulated land — or so it was thought. Now it appears that these high-altitude emissions may be a cause, or even the principal cause, of the increased acidity of rain. Thus the tall smokestack policy has increased local environmental quality at the cost of reducing quality elsewhere. Clearly, the choice of control techniques should be influenced by the effects of emissions on other areas, not just the area of responsibility of the local agency. Existing laws do not control for these cross-boundary effects adequately. The sources and local agencies were not aware of the acid rain problem, however, when this control measure was adopted. This raises the same problem we have discussed in the hazardous waste case. Should sources be required to pay for effects they and the agency had no idea they were causing before the controls were instituted? Who should pay for dismantling the tall stacks, and for the alternative controls? Given that these effects are felt across states and often across countries, it will be very difficult to reach an agreement. Scandinavian

---

[15] I. Peterson, "Acid Rain: Talking Up a Storm," *Science News* 121 (June 5, 1982): 373.

countries blame Great Britain, but Britain's Central Electricity Generating Board claims that high stacks are not causing the problem and that the Scandinavian lakes were dying at the start of the century, long before the high stacks policy was instituted. Canada claims that its acid rain problem is caused by pollution from the United States. Clearly, the United States is going to be more reluctant to expend its resources to reduce a problem in Canada than it would be if these emissions were causing equivalent damage in the United States. On the other hand, Canada is reluctant to pay U.S. firms for control. The problem of deciding who must pay for control is obviously the central issue. There will be no easily available political solution.

SUMMARY

Three specific pollution issues point out various problems in the practical application of benefit/cost analysis. In the case of hazardous wastes, we have found that the simple maxim of equating MB and MC is inadequate. It is necessary to analyze whether the no-emission solution is more efficient. This also raises an equity problem, which arises in the acid rain issue and in other pollution issues as well. Given that a source was acting in what was at the time a legal manner, and that it did not fully understand the implications of its emissions, should it be held liable for the damages created? The answer that has been adopted seems to take a middle ground, where the source is liable under some circumstances but not under others.

The second point raised in this chapter is that analysis of benefits and costs at the national level, and especially rule-by-rule analysis, is inappropriate and does not provide useful criteria for decision-making. Rule-by-rule benefit/cost analysis does not consider the effects of emissions on environmental quality at different locations. Nor does it consider the possible cost reductions from having all sources control at equal marginal cost. Thus current requirements for benefit/cost analysis are not likely to lead to any substantial increase in efficiency.

The third point that has been raised in this chapter is that benefit/cost analysis confined to one basin or environmental medium is likely to neglect benefits (and costs) in other basins and other media. This can cause policy-makers to adopt inefficient policies that neglect these items. At the same time, national analyses are too broad. Basinwide analysis for each medium is needed, but it must consider external costs and benefits where appropriate.

STUDY QUESTIONS

1. Given substantial uncertainty about the long-term environmental effects of new chemical wastes, how should an efficient policy for control of their release be devised?
2. It has been several years since the adoption of Executive Order 12291 requiring that all major regulatory acts of the federal government be subject to benefit/cost analysis. What effect has this order had on environmental regulation?
3. Suppose a substance was discovered that inhibited the cancer-causing effects of air pollutants. How would such a substance affect estimates of the benefits of pollution control?

SUGGESTED READINGS

1. R. Carson, *Silent Spring* (Boston: Houghton Mifflin, 1962) was the book that brought concern for the long-term environmental effects of toxic materials to the popular consciousness.
2. "Love Canal: The Truth Seeps Out," *Reason* (February 1981) provides an excellent discussion of one toxic waste case and the government mismanagement that caused it to become a national issue.
3. S. Epstein, L. Brown, and C. Pope, *Hazardous Wastes in America* (San Francisco: Sierra Club Books, 1982) covers all the issues in this area.
4. J. Sonstellie and P. Portney, "Truth or Consequences: Cost Revelation and Regulation," *Journal of Policy Analysis and Management* 2 (Winter 1983): 280–295 discusses the problems of Executive Order 12291.

8

The Regulatory Approach to Controlling Pollution

Now that we have examined the essence of the political economy of pollution control, and some of its toughest problems, we will complete this discussion by exploring the operation of the approach we currently employ to control pollution. This approach is based on a system of regulation.

THE REGULATORY APPROACH

Regulation is the basic approach to pollution control adopted by governments in the United States and in most other countries. The government defines a desired goal, formulates specific rules or regulations that mandate the action needed to meet that goal and develops an enforcement program to ensure compliance. The logic of this system is quite simple and straightforward; but the implementation of this regulatory approach is not so simple.

Environmental Quality Standards

An environmental quality standard states the minimum level of environmental quality that the air or water must meet. It is usually stated in specific technical terms that include both the time and the location of application. An example is the national air quality standard for photochemical oxidants. This standard requires that the air in any air basin in the United States shall not exceed an hourly average of 0.12 ppm for more than one hour a year. Methods of measurement and acceptable monitoring equipment to be used to perform the measurement are stipulated in the standard. An area is in violation of this standard if any monitor or combination of monitors produces two readings, each averaged over an hour, that exceed 0.12 ppm.

Environmental quality standards are applied to specific geographic sites that are representative of an integrated environmental system, called a basin. A water basin is composed of the land area drained by a given river system. The water basin for the Mississippi River includes most of the land in the Midwest. This is much too large an area to be dealt with effectively, so the Mississippi River basin is divided into several major and minor water basins. The goal is a geographic area small enough to be manageable but large enough to include most of the important effects of pollution. An air basin is composed of a land area within which the air circulates and major pollutant effects are felt. By its nature, an air basin is less well defined than a water basin. There tends to be greater spillover to other basins, and the spillover is more unpredictable because of the variability of the weather.

As scientists have studied the problems of air and water pollution, they have learned that much more pollution crosses these boundaries than was previously thought. Acid rain is a prime example of emissions from one area affecting environmental quality in another, quite distant area. Studies indicate that the increased acidity of rainwater in the Scandinavian countries comes from sulfur dioxide (SO_2) emissions from tall smokestacks in England. This illustrates one way a pollution control policy designed to reduce environmental damage in one basin could produce undesirable effects in another.

Environmental quality standards can be set according to various criteria, which can be classified into three types:

1. Effects on use.
2. Technological feasibility.
3. Economic efficiency.

For water quality, effects on use are defined in several ways. One criterion is that the water be swimmable and fishable. This means that it is safe for swimming and is of such a quality that native game fish will thrive. This simple criterion requires a complex technical definition. In order to be swimmable, the water must be relatively free of such health-damaging materials as viruses and chemicals. Aesthetic standards like color, taste, and smell also come into play. The requirements for being fishable may introduce additional technical criteria.

One use criterion for air quality is the effect on health. The Clean Air Act requires that the air be so clean that it causes no adverse health effects to any individual. Again, this seemingly simple use criterion requires many technical decisions. Adverse health effects must be defined and related to specific exposures of specific pollutants. The relationship between exposures and health effects is particularly difficult to document.

Once use-related measures of environmental quality are determined, policy-makers are often faced with the problem that these desired levels may not be technically — or politically — feasible. The realization of these constraints may cause policy-makers to rely on an alternative criterion: technological feasibility. A technology-based approach would set environmental quality standards according to what is technically possible. This requires an assessment of sources of emissions and of control techniques — by no means a simple task. If a technical process were available that reduced emissions from every source to zero, a standard based on technological feasibility would require that the environment be completely unpolluted. In fact, such a system does exist — all industrial plants could simply be shut down. But that is not feasible, you say. True enough, it is not economically or politically feasible — but technologically it is quite possible. The obvious conclusion, then, is that the determination of technological feasibility must be tempered by economic and political considerations.

If policy-makers are forced to employ economic criteria in setting environmental quality standards, why not do so directly? We saw in Chapter 2 that benefit/cost analysis can be used to determine the efficient level of environmenal quality for an area. The process of comparing benefits and costs automatically requires that effects on use and technological feasibility be considered. It is, therefore, the more complete alternative in that it includes both the use criterion and the technological criterion, and also explicitly provides a mechanism for assessing the value of the standards to society. An economically efficient environmental quality standard would be one determined by the intersection of the *MBC* and *MCC* curves. The implementation of such a standard does not avoid such technical problems as determining methods of measurement, timing, and location. It does, however, place them in a context where the opportunity costs are more obvious. Although environmental quality standards based on economic efficiency are not typically used in practice, their potential should not be ignored.

Environmental quality standards recognize environmental quality as a goal. In our fishing example in Chapter 4, the efficient level of dissolved oxygen at location B was 9.6 ppm. Suppose an environmental quality standard were set at this level. It would have the express advantage of stating the expected output of control policy. The fisherman would know what quality to expect, and thus how much to invest in fishing. But by itself the environmental quality standard is inadequate, because it does not tell the plant at location A how much to control its emissions. Another layer of regulations must be added to state specifically which plants must control and how much. There is no connection between the environmental quality standard and the means of achieving it without this additional regulatory step. This lack of connection between environmental quality standards and specific controls has left policymakers free to ignore real costs and constraints when setting environmental quality standards. They are able to promise a clean environment by setting a strict environmental quality standard because the real cost of this standard is not obvious until the control of specific sources is prescribed. These two steps are usually separated in time and often completed by different agencies. The result has been standards that tend to be excessively stringent. These stringent standards leave a large number of areas in violation a great deal of the time. The consequence of this excessive stringency and repeated violation is that the regulations are transformed from legally binding standards that must be met to goals that will be sought if the costs are not too high. If environmental quality standards are not legally binding and do not state who must control how much, another layer of regulation must be added. The regulatory form typically used is effluent standards. The combination of environmental quality standards and effluent standards is designed to cause sources to control emissions to appropriate levels. This combination comprises the typical regulatory system for pollution control.

Effluent Standards

Effluent standards state that an individual source must take a required action to control its emissions. There are two types: prescriptive regulations and emission standards.

A *prescriptive regulation* states that an emitting source must take a specific technical control action. This action may be the installation of a particular control device, or the use of a particular input. The regulation does not require that this action generate an emission reduction. It presumes that the required action will produce the desired level of control. One of the most common prescriptive regulations is the requirement to burn low-sulfur fuels.

Prescriptive regulations have the important advantage of being relatively easy to enforce. A source's compliance with a prescriptive regulation can be verified merely by determining whether the required input is being used or the required device has been installed and is operative. Prescriptive regulations do have some disadvantages, though. One stems from the fact that control technology is continually changing. When a more effective or less expensive device becomes available, it would be desirable to require its use. New devices, however, must be approved by the regulating agency — a time-consuming and uncertain process that makes prescriptive regulations less flexible than emission standards.

A second problem with prescriptive regulations is that the installation and operation of a control device does not necessarily guarantee that emissions will be reduced to the desired level. Because prescriptive regulations carry no requirements (or monitoring procedures) for a specific level of control, agencies can only presume that the device is effective. This may not be a serious problem in simple cases, but in more complex industrial applications prescriptive regulations are found to be inadequate.

Emission standards require that emissions of a pollutant be controlled to a specified level. In other words, an emission standard states that a source cannot emit more than the specified amount over a certain period. The form of the specification varies. In the 1960s it was common to specify emission standards as concentrations, such as parts per million. The trouble with this form is that a source could meet the standard by simply diluting the effluent rather than actually reducing emissions. This would lead to little or no improvement in environmental quality. The dilution phenomenon stimulated a move to standards based on mass. A typical mass standard is the one for new automobiles, which states that a 1982 car can emit no more than 0.05 grams of hydrocarbons per mile. Such a standard is some improvement, but it still does not determine total emissions from the source. If the car is driven more miles, emissions increase and air quality declines. Another alternative — one that is common in water pollution — is to state emission standards in terms of total mass emissions per hour, per day, or per year.

Emission standards have some significant advantages over prescriptive regulations. They are more flexible in dealing with control technology, because the standard does not specify the form of technology to be used, only the desired level of effectiveness. This allows a source to search for the least expensive combination of changes in inputs, changes in process, and end-of-process controls to meet the standard. It also allows the source to search for technological innovations and adopt them immediately.

Emission standards have some disadvantages as well. They are more difficult to enforce because they require the measurement of actual emissions, often a technically difficult and expensive task. They also tend to be inefficient in their application, because across-the-board standards typically result in some sources paying much less at the margin for control than do others. A third disadvantage is that innovations that reduce the cost of control do not necessarily induce the source to increase control efforts. This leads to less than efficient levels of control and reduces the incentive to innovate.

All these words starting with E may be confusing. To help keep them straight, remember that to get Environmental Quality you must control Emissions. Effluents and emissions are synonymous.

EFFICIENT REGULATION/INEFFICIENT PRACTICE

It is possible to design an efficient regulatory structure for the control of pollution; however, the political pressures of interest groups and the realities of imperfect information cause even the most efficiently designed regulatory system to be inefficient in practice.

Efficient Environmental Quality Standards

It is at least conceptually possible to design a regulation-based control program that will generate the efficient level of environmental quality. The elements are really quite simple, as you can see in Figure 8.1. Panel C, patterned after panel D in Figure 4.4, depicts a benefit/cost analysis for an air or water basin. Based on this analysis, the efficient level of environmental quality is at the intersection of the MBC and MCC curves, or Q. An environmental quality standard could be set at this level.

FIGURE 8.1 Efficient and Inefficient Standards for Environmental Quality

Efficiency in regulation requires that both sources control at equal marginal cost and that their combined marginal costs (*MCC*) equal the *MBC*. The efficient emission standards for these sources are S_1 and S_2.

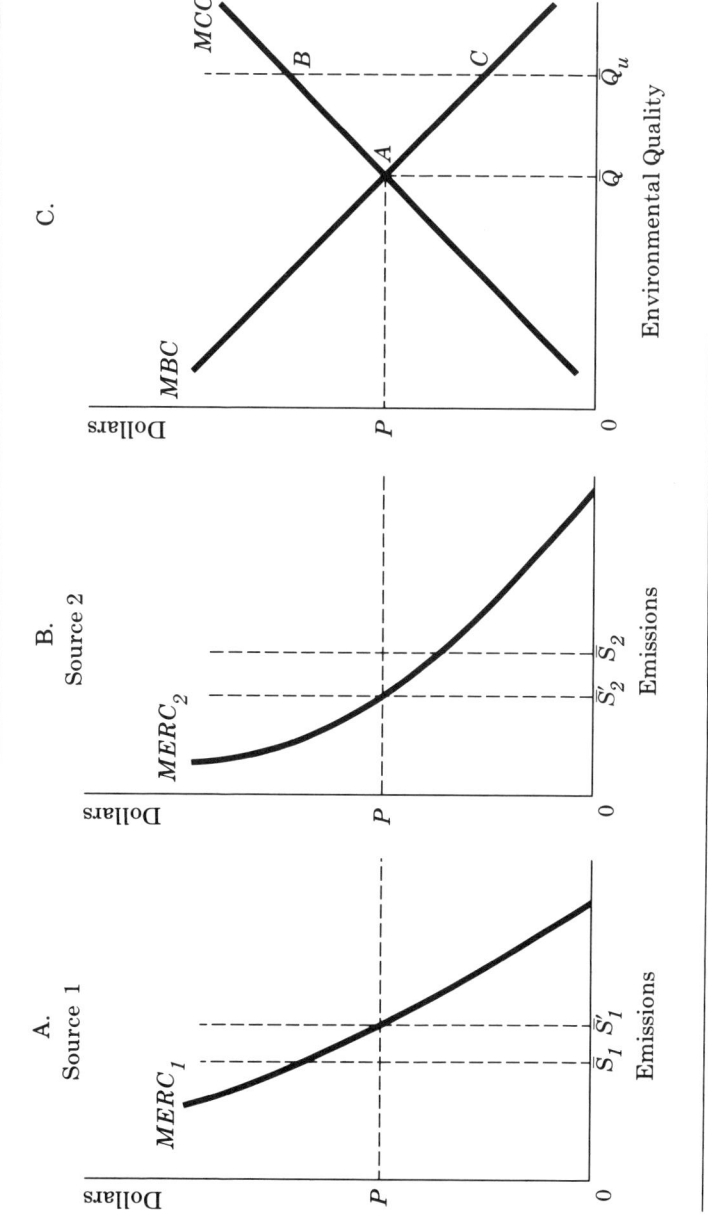

While in theory this regulatory approach could produce the efficient pollution control policy, in practice it does not do so. It has been estimated, for example, that it is much more expensive to meet the national photochemical oxidant standard than the benefits would seem to justify.[1] Such a use-based standard is depicted in panel A as $\overline{Q}_u$.[2] With this standard, MBC is below MCC. This means that the opportunity cost to society of achieving this standard far exceeds the value society places on the achievement of this level of control. Society wastes the resources represented by the triangular area ABC, because the total cost of increasing environmental quality to ($\overline{Q}_u$ is the area $AB\overline{Q}_uQ$ but the total benefit of the increase is only $AC\overline{Q}_u\overline{Q}$. Thus there is a negative net benefit equal to the difference between these two areas, or ABC.

Efficient Emission Standards

Because it is possible to set environmental quality standards at the efficient level, it is also possible to set corresponding efficient emission standards. This can be done by tracing back through the environmental transformation function to the individual marginal emission reduction cost ($MERC$) functions, as we did in Figure 4.4. Suppose there are two sources, 1 and 2, at the same location. Efficiency requires that these sources control at equal marginal costs (see Figure 4.6). For emission standards to be efficient, they would have to be set at efficient levels of control. Panels A and B of Figure 8.1 represent the $MERC$ functions for sources 1 and 2. Note that $MERC_1$ is steeper than $MERC_2$. Efficiency requires that the emission standard for source 1, which is $\overline{S}_1$, be less stringent than the one for source 2, which is $\overline{S}_2$. At these different emission standards, the two sources are controlling at equal marginal cost and the efficient environmental quality Q is achieved. This combination of environmental and emission standards represents an efficient regulatory system.

To demonstrate the efficiency of requiring each source to control at equal marginal cost, let us analyze Figure 8.2. The two adjacent sources, 1 and 2, each emit 100 pounds of BOD per day if uncontrolled, but source 2 has lower control costs. Persuaded by equity arguments that say that equals should be treated equally, the control agency sets emission standards of fifty pounds per day from each

---

[1] See P. B. Downing, "Controlling Oxidants in Los Angeles," *Environmental Affairs* 4 (Fall 1975): 707–743, and L. White, *Reforming Regulation* (Englewood Cliffs, N.J.: Prentice-Hall, 1981), Chapter 4.

FIGURE 8.2 Efficient vs. Inefficient Emission Standards

Inefficient standards (such as a reduction to 50 pounds at each source here) cause sources at the same location to control at different *MERC*s. Costs can be saved by having source 1 reduce emissions to 60 pounds and source 2 reduce emissions to 40 pounds. At this point, $MERC_1 = MERC_2$.

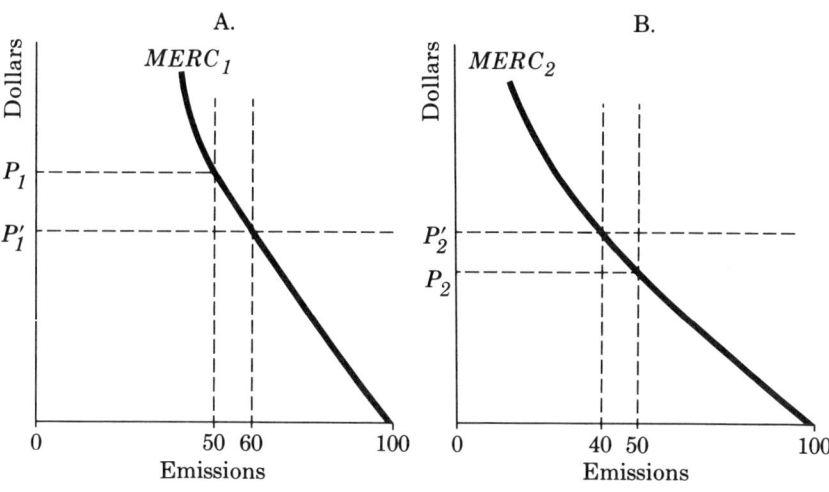

source. At these standards, source 1 is paying P_1 for the last pound of control and source 2 is paying only P_2. Obviously, reducing controls at source 1 by one pound and increasing controls at source 2 by the same amount will save $P_1 - P_2$. It is socially efficient to substitute control of source 2 for control of source 1 until their marginal costs are equal. This happens where marginal cost $P'_1 = P'_2$. At this point source 1 is controlling forty pounds (emitting sixty pounds) and source 2 is controlling sixty pounds (emitting forty pounds). Total emissions are the same as for the previous controls, but society (in this simple case represented by source 1) has saved resources. Compare the area under $MERC_2$ between fifty and forty pounds of emissions with the area under $MERC_1$ between fifty and sixty pounds of emissions. Obviously, the costs saved by source 1 are greater than the increase in costs for source 2. Some resources are saved. The efficient emission standard would be forty pounds of control (sixty pounds of emissions) for source 1 and sixty pounds of control (forty pounds of emissions) for source 2. Of course, source 2 will resist efficient standards because this division of control is more costly.

One study of the process of setting emission standards suggests that it involves a great deal of give and take.[2] In the process of setting "best practicable technology" effluent guidelines for water pollution control, EPA employed a decision-making technique that included detailed technical and economic analyses. Standards were proposed based on these analyses, and a comment period was allowed before final standards were promulgated. The study showed that standards tended to be reduced (made less stringent) when there was adverse comment from firms who would be affected by them. They also had a tendency to move toward a lowest common denominator. That is, sources with low control costs would not be required to control more than sources with high costs. There was no evidence to suggest that EPA was attempting to produce efficient emission standards. Indeed, the final standards suggested that sources would be controlling at vastly different marginal costs.

These inefficient emission standards are depicted in Figure 8.1 as $\bar{S}'_1$ and $\bar{S}'_2$. At these standards, source 1 is controlling at an inefficiently low level while source 2 is controlling too much. Even so, it is possible to obtain the desired level of control of all emissions in the basin so that Q is achieved. But this is accomplished through a waste of resources, as was demonstrated in Figure 8.2. More often, however, not only are the individual emission standards inefficient, but they do not achieve the efficient level of environmental quality, or even the inefficient use-based standard.

Enforcing Emission Standards

Once the efficient emission standards are determined, it is necessary to ensure that each source complies with these standards. Emission control is expensive and reduces profits, so firms will avoid it unless there is a sufficient penalty for doing so. If the penalty for noncompliance is not at least as high as the *MERC*, the source will find it advantageous to control less. The penalty payment would be lower than the savings in control costs, and profit would be increased. The source will find it advantageous to control to the point where the penalty per unit of excess emissions equals *MERC*. In addition, the source will not control at all unless the total penalty for not controlling is greater than the total cost of controlling.

---

[2] A. Krupnick, W. Magat, and W. Harrington, "Understanding Regulatory Decision-Making: An Economic Approach," *Policy Studies Journal* 11 (September 1982): 44–55.

Interrelationships Among Standards

So far we have assumed that each source is emitting only one pollutant and releasing it into only one environmental medium. This is a simplification of the true situation; a typical source emits several pollutants into the air, others into the water, and still others onto the land. In order to ensure that efficiency is achieved, it is necessary to control releases into all media simultaneously. Suppose a control agency regulated water pollution but not air pollution. Sources could change production processes to pollute the air instead of the water. That is just what the pulp and paper manufacturing plants in Wisconsin did in the 1950s. The implementation of tough water pollution laws caused the paper plants to seek inexpensive control efforts. They discovered that a relatively simple process change would dramatically reduce the generation of water pollutants. Unfortunately, it released the wastes into the air. Air quality was not regulated, so these releases were not controlled. The plants adopted the new production technique, releasing sulfur by-products into the air. These sulfur by-products produced a smell like rotten eggs and killed trees for many miles around each plant. The state finally reacted by adopting air pollution laws.

Obviously, a comprehensive approach to environmental regulation is needed. This comprehensive approach must have several components. Regulations must cover all possible emitters — not an easy task. They must also cover all possible pollutants. And they must recognize all possible interactions among emissions. (Two chemicals that are harmless by themselves can interact in the environment to produce a harmful pollutant.) In addition, consistency must be required. It must be possible to meet all emission standards and all environmental quality standards simultaneously. This avoids the possibility of neglecting effects on one environmental medium when controlling pollution in another.

Inefficient Practice

We have seen that efficiency in pollution control requires that sources control at equal marginal costs. The current regulatory system, as implemented, does not require this. Instead, standards are set on the basis of assessments of available technology, and these assessments are subject to political pressures. In one study of the setting of water emission standards, it was shown that the political and economic power of those being regulated reduced the stringency of controls.[3] These adjustments led to substantial differences in *MERC* among sources. Furthermore, these regulations totally ignored the relationship between emissions and environmental quality. In a study designed to determine the cost differences between proposed State Implementation Plan (SIP) strategies for air pollution control in St. Louis and efficient solutions that considered differences in location and the emission transformation function, S. Atkinson and D. Lewis show that the SIP guidelines were six to ten times as costly as the least-cost strategy.[4] A large gain in efficiency appears to be available if we move toward efficient regulations.

IMPLEMENTATION STRUCTURE

Efficient regulation and comprehensive environmental planning are not the norm. EPA represents all media in a single agency, but it does not function comprehensively. Nor is coordination accomplished at the state or local level. Regulation of emissions in one medium is accomplished without much regard for the implications for other media. The tendency is to have separate agencies for control of pollution in each medium. In some cases, in fact, one agency is responsible for air pollutants from such mobile sources as automobiles, and another for such stationary sources as oil refineries. With such separation of jurisdictions, coordination is very difficult if not impossible. In some cases, different jurisdictions set conflicting environmental quality standards for the same pollutant in the same area. Agencies also tend simply to blame one another for pollution problems rather than working jointly toward a solution.[5]

Who Sets Standards?

In the United States, environmental quality standards are set by Congress, by national pollution control agencies, by state agencies, and occasionally by local agencies. The formal bases of environmental standards have been either effects on use or technological feasibility — never economic efficiency. Standards are usually set

[3] Krupnick, Magat, and Harrington.
[4] Krupnick, Magat, and Harrington.
[5] S. Atkinson and D. Lewis, "A Cost-Effectiveness Analysis of Alternative Air Quality Control Strategies," *Journal of Environmental Economics and Management* 1 (November 1974): 249.

by legislative action — a visible test of politicians' commitment to a clean environment.

Emission standards have been set both legislatively and administratively. Congress has set automotive emission standards since 1970. Water and air emission standards based on technological feasibility have been set by EPA and by state agencies. In some cases, such as best practicable technology standards for water, there is no requirement or attempt to set emission standards consistent with environmental quality standards.

Standards set by Congress may contain more political than technical influence. Congress tends to be more proenvironment than a national control agency, and a national control agency tends to be more proenvironment than state and local agencies. Thus there is a political advantage for proenvironment interests in having Congress set standards. There are also some difficulties in this approach. Members of Congress are not technical experts. They have a great deal of technical expertise available to them through EPA, the Congressional Research Service, and private sources, but they have neither the time nor the inclination to inform themselves fully. Consequently, political considerations become paramount. This can lead Congress to set standards that are not technically feasible.

EPA, on the other hand, has a great deal of technical expertise. It is possible for the agency to make an evenhanded technical assessment of control options. They can take into consideration how decisions for one area will affect the environmental quality in other areas. Because of its national constituency, EPA is more likely than state or local agencies to consider both benefits and costs. On the other hand, EPA officials in Washington are somewhat distant from the technical details of individual air and water basins and individual emission sources. Although it is true that regional EPA officials are more aware of local conditions they too tend to lack an understanding of the details of technical differences among sources. They also tend to be unaware of the political forces impinging on state and local areas. These factors make EPA decisions unsatisfactory to state and local agencies and legislative bodies.

State and local agencies excel in knowledge of the specifics of each local area. This allows them to tailor standards to the local situation, thus giving them greater potential for setting efficient standards in the absence of effects on other areas. On the other hand, the costs of control are felt more immediately in the local area. These costs generate political activity by local emitters, who seek relief in order to avoid costs. Local sources tend to concentrate their efforts at the state and local level, where they tend to be more successful at influencing control decisions.

No single institutional choice will set environmental quality standards and emission standards efficiently or objectively. Congress and EPA tend to stress the benefits, which causes them to err toward excessively stringent standards. State and local agencies see the costs and err in the opposite direction. Determining who sets the standards is an important decision; it determines the level and efficiency of control. This is an issue we will return to later.

National versus Regional Standards

Let us first consider the proper geographic level for the setting of environmental quality standards. We saw in Chapter 4 that the costs of controlling emissions depend on the $MERC$ and the ETF. We also saw that the benefits of control are location-specific, and that efficient environmental quality standards will differ from location to location. This is in direct opposition to the presumption of the federal Clean Air Act of 1970, which required the setting of one national standard for each air pollutant. An argument could be made for national environmental quality standards: emissions from one area affect the environmental quality in other areas. These externalities require some national action, but they do not necessarily imply that a single national standard would be efficient. Rather, they suggest that an additional benefit curve should be added to the analysis for any single area: the benefits felt in other regions as a result of control in this region. Still, the result would be different efficient environmental qualities in various air and water basins. With one national standard, environmental quality would be too high in some cases and too low in others. Thus the national photochemical oxidant standard of 0.12 ppm may be too stringent for Los Angeles but too lenient for Albuquerque. Attempting to clean up excessively in some areas and not cleaning up enough in other areas wastes resources in the same way that equal control of sources with different costs wastes resources. Efficiency requires regional variations in environmental quality standards.

A similar situation is faced for the setting of emission standards. Because the location of each source relative to the individuals affected by its emissions differs in every case, efficiency would appear to require emission standards to be set separately for every source. But there are two contrary arguments. One is that standardization of control technology tends to reduce costs. The fixed costs of research and development can be spread over more sources if they all employ the same technology. This lowers the *MERC* for all sources, generating higher efficient levels of control in all areas. The other argument for more standardization of emission standards involves the decision-making costs of setting standards case by case. Decision cost savings could potentially offset the efficiency losses generated by more general emission standards. The choice between individual and general standards is an empirical one; that is, it requires specific study of the benefits and costs of general standards as opposed to individual standards. The results are likely to differ from issue to issue. No general national recommendation can be suggested.

Agency Responsibility

The division of agency responsibility for the various steps involved in implementing a regulatory approach to environmental quality control is complex.[6] Some responsibilities are granted to EPA, some to state control agencies, and some to local agencies. Often two or more agencies can take primary responsibility for a particular element of the implementation process. Take environmental quality standards for air as an example. The primary responsibility rests with EPA, but states do set individual standards for some or all areas of the state. If these standards are more stringent than the national standards, they take precedence; if they are less stringent, the national standards are in force.

The situation varies from case to case, as can be seen from the summary presented in Table 8.1. This table is presented only to provide a general indication of the variations in responsibility found in the environmental quality program in the United States. The situation for enforcement is particularly interesting. Primary responsibility for both air and water pollution control is delegated to the states by the federal legislation. EPA is to supervise the enforcement process, however. If a state is not enforcing to EPA's satisfaction, EPA may become active in any particular case. Sometimes the agency is invited to join the case by the state agency; sometimes it becomes involved even without the state's invitation. In most cases, however, the state is left alone to enforce standards.

---

[6] For a discussion of optimal control agency jurisdictions, see R. Zerbe, "Optimal Environmental Jurisdictions," *Ecology Law Quarterly* 4 (1974).

TABLE 8.1 Division of Responsibility for Environmental Quality among Agencies in the United States

	Federal	State	Local
Air Quality			
Environmental quality standards	Primary	Possible takeover	None
Emission standards			
New	Primary	Possible takeover	None
Existing	Advisory	Primary	Primary or advisory
Monitoring	Advisory	Primary	Primary or advisory
Enforcement	Supervisory and possible takeover	Primary	Primary or advisory
Water Quality			
Environmental quality standards	Advisory	Primary	None
Emission standards	Primary	Advisory	None
Monitoring	Advisory	Primary	None
Enforcement	Supervisory and possible takeover	Primary	None

Some of the entries in Table 8.1 may be a little misleading. States do not, for example, have any responsibility for setting national emission standards in water, but state laws require them to set emission standards. They usually adopt standards that they claim are consistent with the national standards set by EPA. Sometimes EPA does not agree. In such cases, federal law requires that EPA standards take precedence but that the states have primary enforcement responsibility. They would quite naturally have a tendency to enforce their own standards. EPA has the technical authority to take over enforcement, but it lacks the economic resources and political mandate required.

SUMMARY

We employ a regulatory approach to pollution control in the United States, but we do not even attempt to develop the efficient regulatory scheme outlined at the beginning of this chapter. Instead we have a fragmented system, with widespread and sometimes conflicting authority. The end result is a set of inconsistent, uncoordinated, and inefficient standards, and a less than ideal implementation structure. What alternatives would be more efficient? We will turn our attention to some alternatives in the next chapter.

STUDY QUESTIONS

1. What functions does an environmental quality standard perform? What are the effects of emission standards? How can these be combined to produce an effective environmental control program? Can such a program be efficient?
2. There are several methods of increasing the effective control of emissions by a source. Emission standards can be made more stringent. Penalties for noncompliance can be raised. Inspections can be more frequent. Discuss the administrative costs of these options to the control agency and the decision rule for determining the efficient combination of actions.
3. Given your understanding of the interaction between economics and politics, discuss why environmental regulations are inefficient in practice.

SUGGESTED READINGS

1. L. White, *Reforming Regulation* (Englewood Cliffs, N.J.: Prentice-Hall, 1981) has an especially interesting insider's story about the changing of the photochemical oxidant standard.
2. P. B. Downing, "Controlling Oxidants in Los Angeles," *Environmental Affairs* 4 (Fall 1975): 707–743, presents the story of the setting of the initial photochemical oxidant standard. You might note the similarities in these stories and wonder why people did not learn from the earlier experience.
3. A. Krupnick, W. Magat, and W. Harrington, "Understanding Regulatory Decision-Making," *Policy Studies Journal* 11 (September 1982: 44–55, summarizes a study of the emission standard setting process for sources of water pollution.
4. P. B. Downing and J. N. Kimball, "Enforcing Pollution Control Laws in the U.S.," *Policy Studies Journal* 11 (September 1982): 55–64, reviews the practical issues in enforcement while P. B. Downing and W. D. Watson, Jr., "The Economics of Enforcing Air Pollution Controls," *Journal of Environmental Economics and Management* 1 (November 1974) presents a theoretical analysis of enforcement incentives.
5. P. B. Downing, "Policy Consequences of Indirect Regulatory Costs," *Public Policy* 29 (Fall 1981): 507–526 calculates the administrative costs of environmental regulation and finds them quite large.

9

An Economic Incentive System for Pollution Control

The regulatory approach to pollution control as it is implemented in the United States leads to an inefficient effort to control emissions. This system wastes resources that could be used in other ways to generate higher levels of environmental quality or to provide other goods and services. An alternate system can reduce the inefficiencies inherent in a regulatory approach. This system fits under the general heading of "economic incentives," and is usually seen in a particular form called an effluent fee. In this chapter we will first discuss the effluent fee in some detail and then turn our attention to other economic incentive systems.

EFFLUENT FEES

Pollution is an externality for which the emitting source does not pay. The private market, responding to this lack of costs, releases excessive emissions. Producers do not, however, waste resources for which they have to pay. Costs cause them to weigh their use of resources carefully. It follows that one solution to the pollution problem is to make the emission of pollutants costly to the source. In other words, there should be a charge for emissions into the environment. Such a charge is referred to as an *effluent fee*. In this way the private market is stimulated to economize on waste release, just as it is stimulated to economize on other costly resources.

Effect of Effluent Fees on Control Efforts

The operation of the effluent fee or charge can be understood with the help of Figure 9.1. This diagram presents a marginal emission reduction cost ($MERC$) function conceptually identical to the one introduced in Figure 4.1. Suppose this source was charged an effluent fee of E for every unit of emissions it released into the environment. Facing such a charge, the source would find it advantageous to control emissions to D. The logic of this can be seen from examining B, the no-control point. At this point the cost of controlling one more unit of pollution is very low (near zero), but if the source does not control it will have to pay a charge of E. E is greater than $MERC$ at this point; so the source saves money by controlling. This is true for

FIGURE 9.1 Efficient Control Under an Effluent Fee

Under an effluent fee of E a source will find it efficient to emit D. At this point it will pay area $0EAD$ in effluent fees and incur area ABD in control costs. If it decided to continue to emit without control (B) it would pay $0ECB$ in effluent fees. Since area ABD is less than area $ACBD$ the source will save money by controlling.

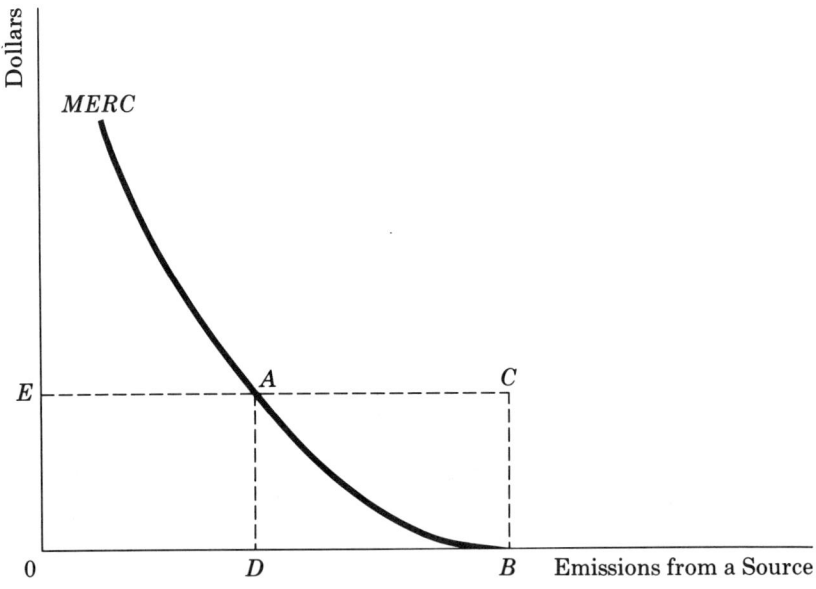

every unit of control to the right of D. To the left of D, the opposite is true. Additional control beyond D does not pay, because the $MERC$ is greater than E. A cost-minimizing source will control to D.

The total payments for pollution control for this source consist of the total emission reduction costs ($TERC$) and the total effluent fee payment. $TERC$ is equal to the roughly triangular area ABD. The total effluent fee payment would equal $0EAD$. The source would control DB emissions and emit $0D$. If the source did not control, it would pay $0ECB$ to the government. $0EAB$ is less than $0ECB$, so it obviously pays to control emissions. Contrary to what some environmentalists say, an effluent fee is not a license to pollute, and the source will not just pay the fee and continue polluting; to do so would be to throw away money (area ABC).

The source will react to variations in the level of the fee by equating the new fee to $MERC$. Thus if the fee were set higher than E, the source would control more than DB. If the fee were lower than E, the source would control less. It is obvious, then, that the control agency can regulate the amount of emissions from any source by varying the level of the effluent fee.

Effect on Firm Output

The control of emissions has the secondary effect of changing the efficient output of final goods of the firm and of the industry in which it operates. The payment of the area $0EAB$ increases the firm's costs to include marginal environmental costs (see Figure 3.6). This increase in costs shifts AC and MC upward to AC' and MC' in Figure 9.2. The initial reaction of the firm is to adjust its final goods output downward and produce at a loss. As a result of the reduction in supply from this and other firms who are now paying effluent charges, the market supply will decrease (to S' in Figure 9.1). This will tend to drive up prices. As prices rise, firms will increase production until they reach a marginal cost equal to the new price. The rise in prices reduces or eliminates the losses generated by the transition to the effluent fee system, depending on the extent of the cost increase generated by the fee and control effort. Sources with more emissions or a higher $MERC$ would incur greater increases in costs. Greater environmental damages would also require higher effluent fees. The end result will be a general reduction in the output of the polluting good, from (Q to Q') which will be brought about by a reduction in the output of some producers and the complete withdrawal of others from the market. Producers with the greatest cost

FIGURE 9.2 Firm and Market Adjustments to an Effluent Charge

When a firm pays an effluent fee, its costs of production increase, rising to MC' and AC'. If all firms in an industry have to pay similar effluent fees, the total industry supply function will shift to S', which now reflects the marginal private costs plus the environmental damages of emissions from plants in the industry. As a result of these changes, some emitters that are in particularly sensitive environments will leave the industry. This will continue until the price rises to P'. At this point all remaining firms will be covering all costs, including the cost of environmental damages from their emissions and the costs of controlling emissions.

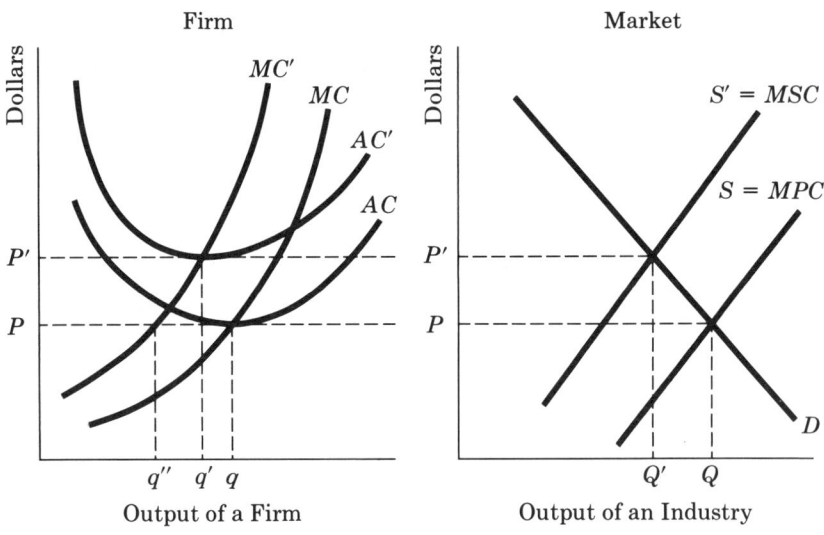

increase will be the ones that stop production. This is, in fact, the efficient choice. The effluent charge reflects the value to society of the environmental resources the firm employs. If the firm cannot continue to produce its final output and cover all costs, including the environmental costs, it should cease production. This releases resources to produce some other, more highly valued good. The effluent fee system automatically removes the least efficient and most environmentally damaging sources from the market.

An effluent fee system can generate the incentive to control emissions. It can also be an incentive for each source to analyze the desirability of continuing to produce the final good and the pollution. Private decision-making will automatically cause relatively "dirty" sources to reduce output or drop out, while relatively "clean" sources will remain to produce in ways that lower environmental damages. An efficient effluent fee system will generate efficient market adjustments.

EFFICIENT EFFLUENT FEES

As with regulation, it is conceptually possible to design a set of efficient effluent fees. In a simple hypothetical example this is quite easy, but in a real world example with many sources and many emissions, efficient effluent charge systems are quite difficult to design.

The Simple Case

In the case of only one emitter at one location, the setting of an efficient effluent fee is a simple matter. Referring again to Figure 4.4, we saw in panel D that the efficient level of environmental quality is produced at a marginal cost of $3,000 per year for the last ppm reduction of dissolved oxygen. This point, at which *MBC equals MCC*, is the efficient effluent fee. The fee must be translated, however, from a charge per unit of environmental quality to a charge per unit of emissions. This is accomplished by working backward through the *ETF* (panel B) to the *MERC* (panel A). If the plant is in operation every day of the year, the appropriate effluent fee would be $3,000/365 pounds/year, or $8.22/pound/day. Note that while policy is expressed in terms of environmental quality, effluent charges are expressed in terms of the pollutant released by the firm, since the firm does not know what effect its emissions have on environmental quality. At this charge, the source would find it efficient to emit sixty pounds per day, and the efficient environmental quality will be produced.

Note that the effluent fee reflects the value of the environment to those adversely affected by pollution. This value is included in *MBC*. Thus the source, in adjusting efficiently to a properly set effluent fee, automatically equates *MBC* with *MCC*. This guarantees that the efficient emission level is achieved. The market for final goods will be brought into efficiency and reflect the full social costs of production. Through the operation of the market mechanism, an efficient effluent charge generates efficient emission decisions, efficient output decisions, and efficient decisions on industrial structure.

Many Sources, Many Emissions

The simple case is just that. The real world is much more complex. Instead of just one source at one location, there are many sources and many locations. Efficiency requires that appropriate fees be set for each individual source. In most cases the efficient effluent fee will be different for each source, reflecting differences in environmental damages. Further, each source will emit several pollutants and will therefore face several different effluent fees. The source must determine the best possible method for minimizing the sum of fees and control costs. This is a rather complex problem, but it does not differ in principle from the simple case discussed above.

Choice of an Efficient Location

The damages done by emissions vary with the location of the emitting source. To determine the efficient location for a source, it is necessary to consider the cost of operation — including the effluent fee — at each alternative location, and to choose the location with the lowest cost. The effluent fee reflects the benefits of control (or the damages of emissions) at each location, and causes the source to consider the environmental implications of its choice of location. Consequently, it lowers the relative costs of the location that is less damaging to the environment. The source will choose the location that minimizes the sum of effluent fees, control costs, and production costs. The efficient effluent fee adjusts costs and induces the choice of an efficient location.

Efficient Timing

The damages done by emissions depend not only on the amount and location of release, but also on the timing of that release. A pound of BOD released into a stream during the spring rains would have less adverse effect on water quality than would that same release late in summer, when flow is down and temperature is up. The release of carbon monoxide from automobiles would cause much less damage at 2:00 A.M. than at 9:00 A.M., when many more people are exposed to it. This suggests that effluent fees should vary with time. A high charge during periods of high potential damage will stimulate more control at those critical times. This control can be obtained in several ways. The source can delay release by collecting and holding its wastes. It can increase the effectiveness of its control technology. Or it can change its production schedule to avoid periods with high effluent costs. The end result would be efficient timing of emissions.

Note, however, that efficiency does not necessarily require continually varying effluent fees. The damages of release are virtually the same at many times. It is costly to administer a complex and frequently changing effluent fee system, so this is useful only if the gain in net benefit is greater than the additional administrative cost.

Dynamic Efficiency

The world is constantly changing. People move into and out of an area; producers do the same. People change their consumption patterns, and consequently their sensitivity to environmental quality. Producers change employment and output. Each change shifts the *MCC* curve, the *MBC* curve, or both. An efficient system for the control of pollution requires that effluent fees adjust to these changes. All things being equal, a new plant moving into an area shifts *MCC* upward to the left. This dictates a higher effluent fee. Population growth shifts *MBC* upward to the right; again, a higher fee is required. As with variations in emissions from one source over time, these dynamic changes need not be reacted to if their effect is small. Only when changes generate inefficiencies greater than the cost of changing the fee is it worthwhile to do so.

REVENUE IMPLICATIONS

The effluent fee system has another desirable attribute: It generates revenue (equal to area 0*EAD* in Figure 9.2) that can be used for various efficiency- or equity-enhancing purposes.

Any system of active government control of pollution requires the expensive process of implementation. A careful benefit/cost analysis must be conducted before the fees are set, and we have seen that this is a difficult and expensive task. Substantial valuable analytical talent is required. Data must be collected and analyzed. Differences of opinion on scientific matters must be settled. Once a fee is determined, the reactions of individual sources must be monitored. In particular, it is necessary to determine the actual emissions of each source in order to levy and collect the fee. There will be other administrative details as well, all of which cost money. The revenue from the effluent fee can be used to offset these administrative costs.

The effluent fee provides a potential source of funds for other efforts as well. One such effort involves the technological enhancement of the capacity of an environmental medium to absorb pollutants. In order to reduce damages from water pollution during periods of low flow and high temperature, for example, flow could be augmented. A dam could be constructed to store the spring runoff for release during critical periods of damage from pollutants. It would pay to adopt such a method in situations where the cost of doing so would be less than the total of pollution damages and control costs saved.

There is a third use for the revenues from effluent fees. At the efficient level of environmental quality, individuals are still suffering damages in the form of adverse health effects, reduced productivity, and diminished aesthetics. Effluent fee revenues can be used to pay for special home air-filtration systems or, in the more serious cases, to subsidize a move to a less polluted area. Funds from the effluent fee could also be used to compensate for such residual damages as soiling or the loss of a view.

The Japanese employ an interesting system of compensation for such damages from pollution. An individual who believes he or she has been damaged by pollution may appeal to a compensation board composed of local physicians, scientists, and engineers. After an investigation, the board determines whether the individual has indeed been damaged by pollution. If the decision is affirmative, the board attempts to determine the source of the pollution, determines just compensation, and assesses the source that amount. In cases where blame cannot be assigned, the board may still award compensation from funds provided by a government agency. Recent experience with this law is limited, but one steel firm has already paid out over $6 million in compensation. There is no evidence on the extent to which emission controls have been stimulated by this compensation program.[1]

---

[1] F. Anderson et al., *Environmental Improvement through Economic Incentives* (Baltimore: Johns Hopkins University Press, 1977), pp. 49–51.

SUBSIDIES

Effluent fees have many desirable characteristics, but they are not the only possible economic incentive system. Let us look at another: *subsidies.*

Under a subsidy system, each source is paid for each unit of pollution it does *not* release. The effects of this payment on the control decision of the source can be seen by referring to Figure 9.1. Suppose a subsidy of E per unit were granted to the source. The source would then find profit maximized by controlling at D. The same reasoning applies here as in the case of effluent fees. To the right of D the subsidy is greater than $MERC$, so profit can be increased by controlling more. To the left of D the subsidy is below $MERC$, so profit would be reduced if the source controlled more than D. At D, the firm incurs total emission reduction costs of ABD. It receives a total subsidy of $ACBD$. Thus there is a net gain to the firm of ACB as a result of the subsidy.

A subsidy will have an effect on a firm's output decisions that is somewhat different from what an effluent fee has. Rather than increasing production costs as does an effluent fee, the subsidy reduces production costs. The initial impact is to generate a profit. The existence of a profit induces other firms to enter the industry. The new entrants increase supply, causing prices for final goods to decline.

A subsidy can make profitable operations that otherwise would not be. The entry of submarginal firms into the market in order to receive the subsidy is inefficient. Another source of inefficiency is generated by a subsidy system. Because the subsidy is paid for every unit of waste not released, it is necessary to determine how much pollution would have been produced without the subsidy and its accompanying control. A source could adopt a more polluting technology in order to gain a greater subsidy even though this dirty technology increased production or pollution control costs. The net effect would be increased profit for the firm if it adopts the dirty technology and is subsidized to control its emissions.

EFFLUENT FEES, SUBSIDIES, AND REGULATIONS COMPARED

Let us compare the results of the three systems we have discussed. This comparison considers the efficient level of control for each system. We are explicitly abstracting from the practical problems each

Emission Level

The efficient emission level for a source can be achieved through any of the three systems. If all the information needed to produce a complete benefit/cost analysis is known, the desired emission level will be the same for all three systems. An effluent standard could be set at D in Figure 9.2. An effluent fee of E would also generate emissions of $0D$, as would a subsidy of E. While there would be no difference in levels of emissions from individual sources in a non-reactive world, the efficient level of control for a basin and the appropriate level of the effluent standard, fee, or subsidy might be different when adjustments in output of final goods and location of plants are considered.

Costs of Control and Residual Payments

While the same emission level can be generated by any of the three approaches, the effects on wealth are very different. The regulatory approach with an effluent standard set at D causes the source to incur pollution control costs of ABD, represented by area 1 in Figure 9.3. An equivalent effluent charge of E would generate this same pollution control expenditure plus an effluent fee payment of $0EAD$ (area 2). Thus an effluent fee generates more out-of-pocket expense for the source than does an equivalent regulation. A subsidy of E causes the source to incur the same pollution control costs, but the source receives a subsidy of $ACBD$ (areas 1 and 3 combined). There is a net gain for the subsidized source of ABC (area 3).

Output of Final Goods and Profit

In comparing the three systems to the circumstances before control, we see that costs to emitters are increased by regulation and even more by effluent fees, but are reduced by subsidies. The comparative effects on the source's output of final goods can be seen in Figure 9.4. The curves labeled AC_B and MC_B represent the cost curves faced by a firm before any effort to control emissions. When a regulatory system is adopted, costs of final goods increase as in curves AC_R and MC_R. The firm's initial reaction will be to reduce its output of final goods from Q_B to Q_R. If an effluent fee system were employed,

FIGURE 9.3 Who Pays under Alternative Pollution Control Systems

Under regulation, a source pays control costs equal to area 1. Under effluent fees a source pays both area 1 and area 2. Under a subsidy system a source pays area 1 for control but receives area 1 and area 3 in subsidy, for a net gain of area 3.

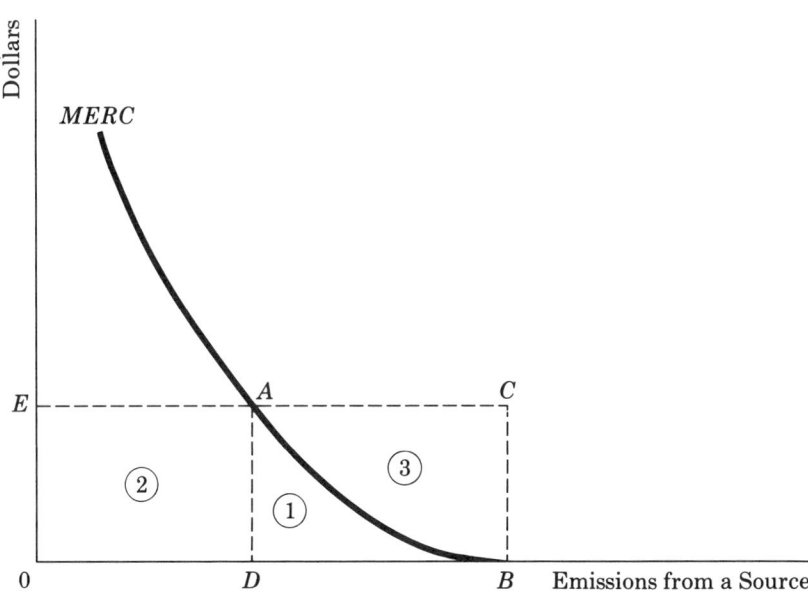

costs would increase even more. The firm would react by reducing final goods output to Q_F, which is even lower than Q_R. In both the regulatory approach and the effluent fee system, the firm will incur at least short-run losses, but the losses will be greater if the effluent fee system is adopted. In the case of a subsidy, the cost curves are actually reduced to AC_S and MC_S. The source will react by increasing production over the precontrol level (from Q_B to Q_S) and will make a profit in the short run.[2]

---

[2] Note that this is only one possible set of shifts in cost functions. For other possibilities, such consistent shifting would not be found and the conclusions would become more uncertain.

FIGURE 9.4 Effect of Alternative Pollution Control Systems on Final Goods Output of a Source

The wealth effects depicted in Figure 9.2 cause the firm's cost curves to shift. Under certain circumstances they will shift as depicted here. A subscript of $_B$ stands for before government action, $_R$ for regulation, $_F$ for effluent fee, and $_S$ for subsidy. Note that a subsidy will actually stimulate a source to increase its output of final goods.

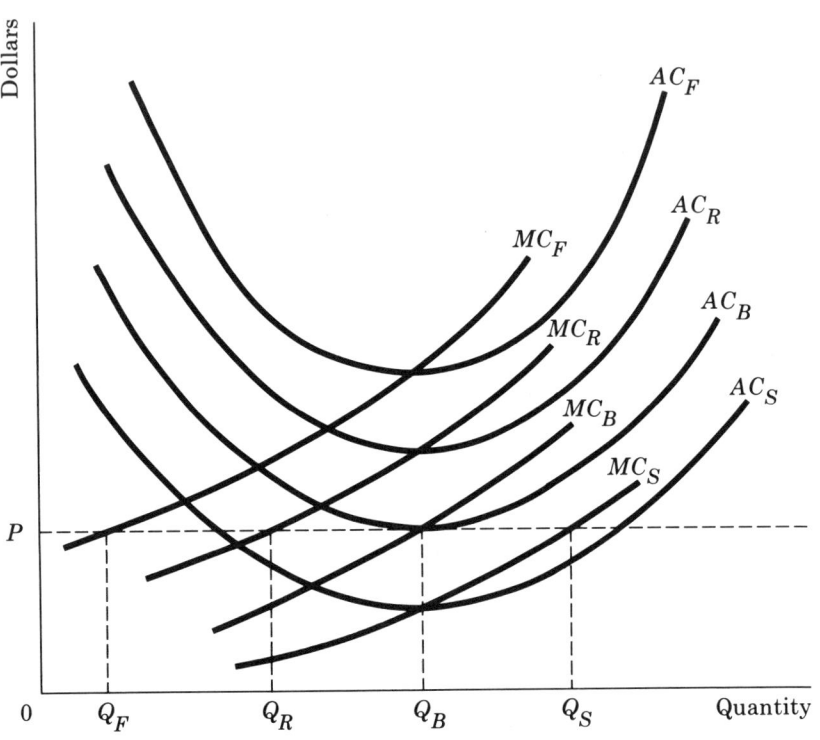

The Market for Final Goods

The short-run adjustments of each source cannot be sustained. There are two extreme possibilities. One is that a source in question is the only one in its industry to be affected by the adoption of a pollution control effort. In this case a regulated firm or a firm facing an effluent fee would continue to suffer losses and eventually go out of business. Given our assumption that no single source has a significant share of the market, this would have virtually no effect on the price or output in the market for final goods. A firm that received a subsidy would continue to produce and earn a profit.

A different circumstance arises when all or a significant number of the firms operating in a market are affected by the pollution control effort. The market supply curve would then shift, generating changes in price and in quantity produced. The market supply curve is the sum of the individual firms' MC curves, so it would be shifted in the same ways as the MC curve by each of the pollution control alternatives. These shifts and their effect on the market quantity and price are presented in Figure 9.5. The quantity adjustments for the market follow the same pattern as for the individual source. The effect on the market price follows as well. A subsidy will lower price, a regulation will increase it, and an effluent fee will increase it still more.

These changes in price will affect the number of firms remaining in the industry. Under regulation, firms with the highest pollution control costs will drop out of the industry. Some firms that would be marginal under regulation would drop out if an effluent fee system were adopted instead. A subsidy would attract firms to the industry because of the profit it made available. The number of firms would be greatest under a subsidy, lowest under a fee, and low — but not quite so low — under regulation.

Shifting of Effluent Fees

These shifts in costs and prices determine who bears the ultimate burden of effluent fees. Let us compare a fee system to regulation, under the assumption that the fee changes the firms' marginal cost of producing the market good. If this is the case, then S_F in Figure 9.6 is above and to the left of S_R, and as we have seen, the market price of the good is increased to P_F. The full cost increase resulting from the fee is $P_B P_F AC$. The price increase from P_R to P_F, however, is less than this amount. After all market adjustments, consumers of the good will pay some of the cost imposed by the fee (area $P_R P_F AD$), and some of the cost will be borne by the owners of the firm (area $P_B P_R DC$). When a firm is able to move some of the burden of the fee

FIGURE 9.5 Market Adjustments Under Alternative Pollution Control Systems

The different pollution control systems have different effects on market price and quantity. An effluent fee system will produce a higher market price (P_F) and lower market output (Q_F) than other controls, while a subsidy actually reduces the market price (P_S) and increases the market output (Q_S).

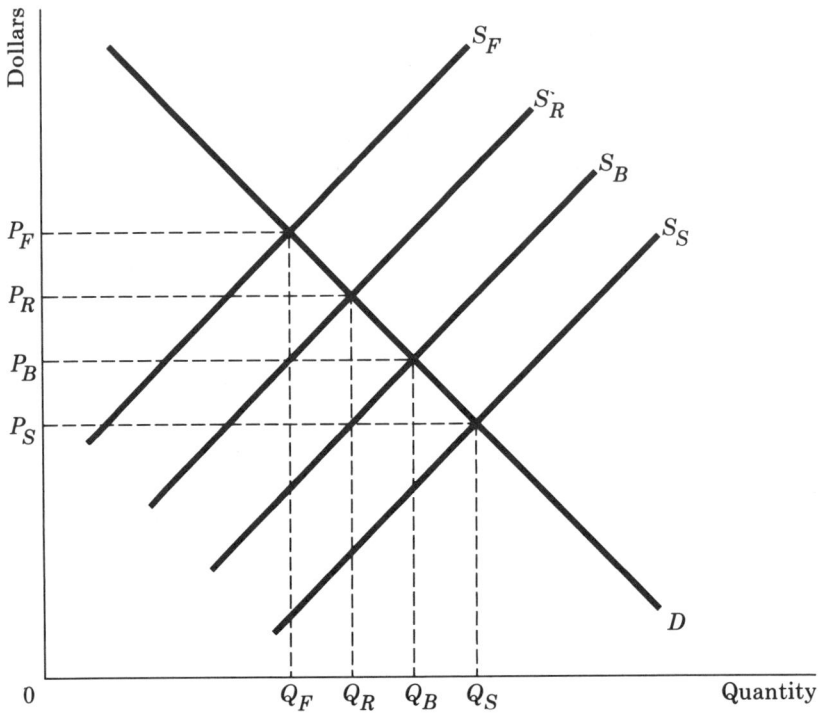

to consumers of the products it produces, it is said to shift the effluent fee. If the effluent fee does not cause a shift in the MC of production for firms in the industry, there is no possibility to shift the fee to consumers.[3]

---

[3] For a complete discussion of shifting and the incidence of taxes see R. Musgrave and P. Musgrave, *Public Finance in Theory and Practice* (New York: McGraw-Hill, 1980), Chapter 12, or any other good public finance text.

FIGURE 9.6 Shifting of an Effluent Fee

A firm that is required to control emissions incurs additional costs. Some of these costs can be passed on to consumers of its products. In this figure, the market reaction to a shift from regulation to effluent fees causes a reduction in output and an increase in price. Part of the additional cost is paid by consumers ($P_R P_F AD$) and part is borne by the firm ($P_B P_R DC$).

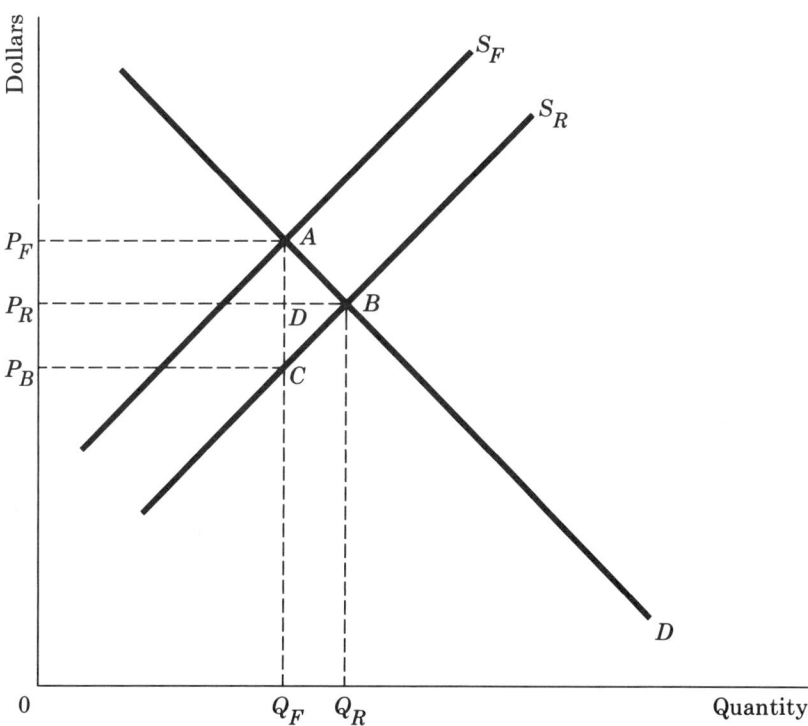

Environmental Quality

Our comparison is based on the assumption that the source will control emissions by the same amount under each system of control. Thus the initial effect on environmental quality would be the same in all three cases. The shifting of costs and its market effects alter this conclusion, however. The MCC curve is derived from the sum of the *MERC*s for each source, translated through the appropriate *ETF*. If a firm drops out of production, *MCC* will shift downward to the right. Thus the number of firms remaining in production will differ under different control systems.[4] Output effects also cause *MERC* to shift — lower output shifting *MERC* to the left. This means that *MCC* will be different under each system, and the appropriate level of environmental quality will change as well.

The efficient level of environmental quality as calculated before the change in the number of firms is taken into consideration is presented as EQ_p in Figure 9.7 (the subscript p representing the planning period). If changes in the number of firms in the area[5] are neglected during planning, EQ_p will be the chosen level of environmental quality. The appropriate effluent fee or subsidy for this level would be E_p.[6] After firms have adjusted to each system, the efficient level of environmental quality will differ. The loss of some emitters under regulation will shift MCC_p to MCC_R and increase EQ_p to EQ_R. Because more firms can be expected to cease production under a system of effluent fees, *MCC* will shift further to the right (to MCC_F) and the efficient level of environmental quality will increase to EQ_F. The efficient effluent fee would be reduced from E_p to E_F. A subsidy system, on the other hand, would attract industry to the area. This would shift *MCC* to the left (to MCC_S). The resultant efficient level of environmental quality would be reduced to EQ_S. The efficient subsidy would be increased to E_S.

The lower effluent fee or the higher subsidy resulting from the adjustment in the number of firms in the area will have an effect on the emission decision. The lower effluent fee will generate a somewhat higher level of emissions than the source adopted initially. The higher subsidy will generate more control. It is efficient to make effluent standards less stringent as sources facing pollution regulations adjust. The downward adjustment in the standard will be smaller, however, than the adjustment caused by an effluent fee, because fewer firms will cease production under regulation.

The effects of all these adjustments are summarized in Table 9.1. Note that if the control agency had perfect information about the costs and market effects of its actions, it could anticipate the

---

[4] The efficient output for each source will also differ as a result of market price effects. This can shift *MERC*. We will ignore these effects, however, because they complicate the analysis unduly.

[5] And their output — see note 4, above.

[6] Remember that this fee or subsidy must be translated through the appropriate *ETF* to determine the appropriate level for each source.

FIGURE 9.7 Environmental Quality Effects Under Alternative Pollution Control Systems

Fewer firms drop out of production under a subsidy system, so the MCC_S, which is a translation of the sum of $MERC$ functions of all emitters, is higher than for other control systems. An effluent fee causes more firms to cease production. As a result, the efficient EQ is higher for an effluent fee than for a subsidy, after all adjustments have been made. Regulation has an intermediate efficient level.

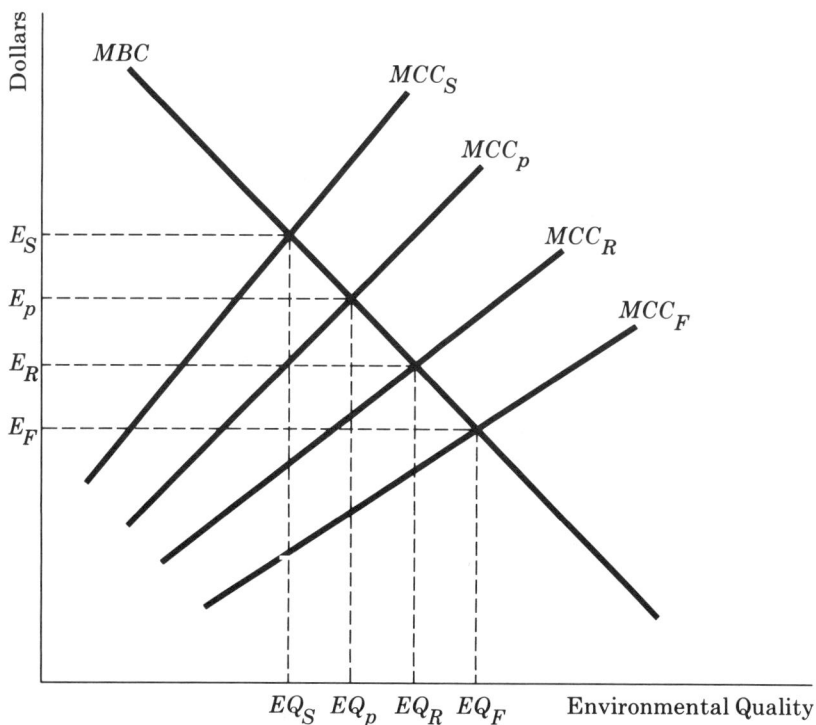

appropriate effluent standard, fee, or subsidy. But as we saw in Chapter 3, this is well beyond the capacity of any agency working in the real world. We will turn to this issue in the next chapter.

Effects on Innovation

We should explore one other effect of these systems. A source will not necessarily retain the control system it initially adopts if it can

TABLE 9.1 Summary of Effects of Alternative Pollution Control Systems

Effect	Type of Pollution Control System		
	Regulation	Effluent Fee	Subsidy
Emission level[a]			
Initial	Lower than before control	Same as regulation	Same as regulation
After all adjustments	Lower than before control	Lower than before control *and* higher than for regulation	Lower than before control *and* lower than for regulation
Control Costs	Loss of area 1 (Fig. 9.2)	Loss of areas 1 and 2 (Fig. 9.2)	Gain of area 3 (Fig. 9.2)
Final goods output	Lower than before control	Lower than before control *and* lower than for regulation	Higher than before control
Profit	Short-run loss	Short-run loss greater than for regulation	Short-run profit
Final goods price	Higher than before control	Higher than before control *and* higher than for regulation	Lower than before control
Number of firms	Fewer than before control	Fewer than before control *and* fewer than for regulation	More than before control
Environmental quality	Higher than originally planned	Higher than originally planned *and* higher than for regulation	Lower than originally planned

[a] For an individual source. The sum of all emissions may be lower for the effluent fee alternative and higher for a subsidy system as compared to regulation. See the entries for "Environmental Quality."

innovate and reduce its costs. A source will find it desirable to adopt a new, innovative pollution control technique if the savings in pollution control costs are greater than the costs of discovering and implementing the innovation. The question is how each of the control systems will stimulate emitters to seek such innovations.

An innovation can take any of several forms. We will view an innovation as any change that reduces the *MERC* for the source. Such a reduction is presented as *MERC'* in Figure 9.8. For initial simplicity, let us assume that this one source is so small that the change in emissions generated by the innovation does not affect environmental quality in an appreciable way.

Let us first see how the regulatory system reacts to this innovation. An effluent standard is initially set at *D*. Should an innovation be available, the source would save pollution control costs equal to the area *ABF* in Figure 9.8, and would retain the same level of emissions (*0D*). If the cost of innovating were less than *ABF*, it would pay for the firm to search for and adopt the innovation. Thus it pays to innovate under regulation in cases where there is no increase in the applicable effluent standard.

Under an effluent fee system, a source using the same innovation will react by increasing its level of control to *G*, the efficient point given an effluent fee of *E*. The source will expend *BGH* in pollution control costs (an increase of *DGHF*), but it will save *DGHA* in effluent fees (a net saving of *AFH*) and *ABF* in its cost of meeting the initial standard, for a total saving of *ABH*. Thus the savings from a given innovation are greater under an effluent fee than under regulation — and emissions are reduced still further. Obviously, innovations costing slightly more than *ABF* will be adopted under the effluent fee because they offer larger savings.

The lower innovation rate under regulation will also be inefficient. Recall that *E* represents the value to society of additional emission reductions from this source. Thus at *D* the new *MERC'* curve is below *E*. It costs less to control after innovation than the value society places on that control, so more control should be forthcoming.

Suppose the control agency, realizing this difference, increases the required level of control to *G*. This reaction is called *ratcheting*. Under this ratcheting, the source saves *ABF* but its costs of control increase by *DGHF*. The net effect can actually be a loss if area *DGHF* is larger than *ABF*. Even if it is smaller, the risk of a loss will reduce the stimulus to innovate and innovation will be inefficiently low.

FIGURE 9.8 Rewards to Pollution Control Innovation

Under regulation at emission level D, a source that innovates ($MERC'$ represents the lower cost resulting from innovation) saves area ABF and continues to control at D. Under an effluent fee, the source would control at G and save ABH. Thus there can be a greater stimulus to innovate under effluent fees than under regulation.

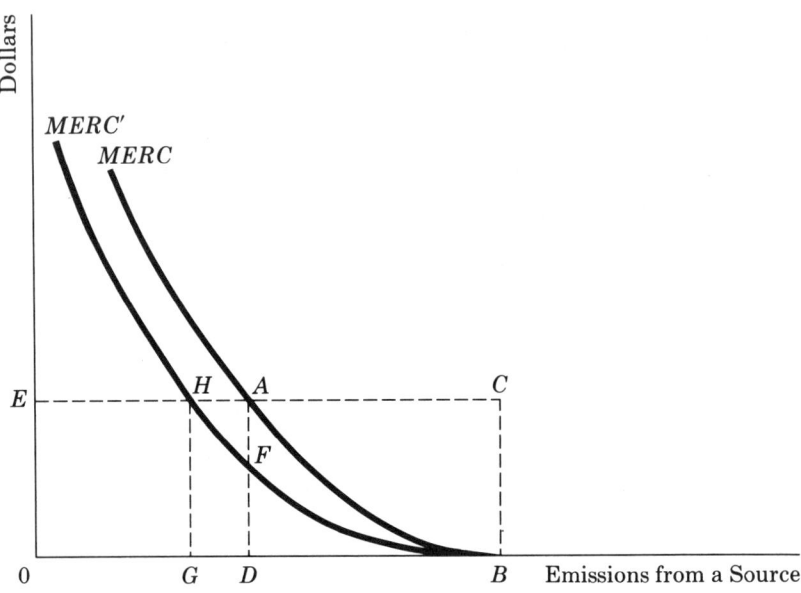

Under a subsidy system, innovation will be stimulated to the same degree as under the effluent fee. The source will save ABH, which is the net of control cost savings of ABF plus additional subsidies of $DGHA$, less additional control costs of $DGHF$. The innovation level and the emission level will be efficient.

If the source has a nonmarginal effect on emissions and environmental quality, conclusions about the efficiency of each system in stimulating innovation must be altered. If all appropriate changes are made in the effluent fee, effluent standard, or subsidy, emission levels will be efficient in all cases, except that regulation will understimulate innovation as discussed above. If adjustments are not made appropriately, however, the effluent fee system can stimulate excessive innovation. This can be seen by envisioning the appropriate adjustment to a substantial reduction in *MCC*. The appropriate reaction would be to reduce E (the effluent fee) somewhat. This would reduce the control cost savings available from innovation, thus reducing the incentive to the efficient level; but at the same time the source would save effluent charges on intramarginal emissions. Consequently, the total savings to the firm would be greater than the social gain, and the source would be stimulated to adopt inefficient innovations.[7]

PROPERTY RIGHTS IMPLICATIONS

When someone owns a piece of real estate, a car, or some other form of property, certain rights and obligations are attached to that ownership. The property can be used for any purpose the owner wishes, consistent with social rules. The right to use property and the constraints that society imposes on its use are lumped together under the general term *property rights*.

The property rights of the owner of an automobile, in the absence of pollution control requirements, might include the right to release unwanted wastes into the environment. Likewise, the owner of real property might have the right to emit wastes into the air or water running through that property in the absence of controls. This would suggest that owners of these types of property have a right to pollute the environment. On the other hand, it might be argued that the owner of property downwind or downstream has the right to clean, unpolluted air and water. Are property rights to the environment vested in the emitter or, alternately, vested in the recipient?[8] The judgment society makes as to who owns the environment has serious implications. It determines who has the responsibility for paying for pollution control.[9]

---

[7] For further discussion, see P. B. Downing and L. J. White, "Innovation in Pollution Control," in preparation.

[8] You or I might believe that property rights should be held by one or another of these groups. That is our personal value judgment. It is no more important than the opinion that orange is a better color than blue. You and I can differ on either of these issues, and nobody can prove that one position is correct.

[9] R. H. Coase has shown that under certain conditions the ownership of property rights will have no influence on the generation of an efficient level of an externality. See R. H. Coase, "The Problem of Social Costs," *Journal of Law and Economics* (October 1960).

Each of the pollution control systems we have discussed rests on certain assumptions about the ownership of property rights to the environment. The effluent fee system implies that property rights are owned by recipients, while the subsidy system implies that property rights are owned by the emitter. The regulatory system is an intermediate system, according to which property rights are shared. The degree of sharing varies from case to case, however, depending on the stringency of regulations.

The effluent fee system requires that the source control its emissions to reduce the environmental damages felt by recipients. It does not, however, require that those damages be reduced to zero. Instead, a payment must be made to cover the value of the environmental damages imposed on others. This is equivalent to saying that the recipients own the right to a clean environment. The emitter must clean up to the efficient level *and* pay recipients for residual damages.

The subsidy system allows the emitter to release as much pollution as it wishes. To induce the emitter to control, a subsidy is paid. We have not been specific about who pays the subsidy, but assume that it is paid by recipients. Recipients then pay for control *and* suffer the residual damages, while sources emit at will and must be paid to reduce emissions. This implies that emitters have all the rights to the environment.

The regulatory system offers an intermediate allocation of property rights. The emitter is required to control and to pay for that control. The emitter does not, however, have to pay for the residual damages suffered by the recipient. The emitter has the right to emit some and the recipient has the right to a somewhat clean environment.

SUMMARY

Where a control agency has perfect information about the costs and benefits of control, it is possible to develop an efficient control system under any one of three alternatives: effluent fees, subsidies, or the regulatory approach.

The effluent fee system leads to efficient outcomes and implies that recipients have the right to a perfectly clean environment. The damages that remain when emissions are controlled efficiently are compensated for by the payment of the fee. The revenue from this fee can be used to help clean up the environment, to administer the program, and to compensate those who are damaged by the remaining emissions. An efficient effluent fee will provide the incentives necessary to induce efficient choices of location, timing, and mix of pollutants, but only if the fee is adjusted appropriately. Thus far we have not discussed the practicality of such a system. Clearly this is a serious issue; we will turn to it in the next chapter.

Subsidies have many of the same desirable characteristics as effluent fees, and can also be made efficient. Subsidies imply that the rights to the environment are owned by emitters — including you and me as owners or users of automobiles. The difference between paying fees for residual damages and being paid subsidies to control emissions leads to quite different reactions by firms. Each firm will control at the efficient level for the given system. Firms will be stimulated to enter the subsidized industry and induced to leave the industry that is required to pay a fee. This results in more firms and more pollution under the subsidy system. Efficiency will still be achieved, given the implicit value judgment about who owns the rights to the environment.

The regulatory approach now employed in the United States can also be efficient. This approach implies that property rights are shared by emitters and recipients. The regulatory approach is used nearly worldwide, so it would seem that this shared responsibility is a universal judgment, or at least the politically necessary compromise between emitters and recipients. There is, however, another possible interpretation of this fact. It may be that the practical difficulties of implementing the regulatory system are less than those of the other systems. This issue will be addressed in the next chapter.

STUDY QUESTIONS

1. Effluent charges are stated in terms of the pollutants emitted rather than the environmental quality intended. Trace the process of determining the appropriate effluent charges for two sources located at different points upstream from a city adversely affected by water pollution. The efficient charges for the two sources differ. What economic effects result from the differences? Are these effects desirable?
2. Innovation causes firms to have lower pollution control costs and lower output costs. Under an effluent charge system what would you expect to happen over time to the output of polluting firms,

their industry, and the environments in which the plants are located? How will this result compare to that of regulation?
3. Since it is possible to design an efficient control system under regulation or effluent charges, is there any reason to prefer one over the other? Be careful to separate value judgments from positive analysis.

SUGGESTED READINGS

1. R. H. Coase, "The Problem of Social Costs," *Journal of Law and Economics* (October 1960): 1–44 offers the perspective that the allocation of property rights to one party or the other will not affect the efficient outcome when it is costless for the two parties to interact and reach an agreement. In most pollution control issues, however, decision-making is costly so the allocation of property rights to the environment does make a difference.
2. Allen Kneese discusses effluent charges in several books including A. Kneese and B. Bower, *Managing Water Quality: Economics, Technology, Institutions* (Baltimore: Johns Hopkins University Press, 1968) and A. Kneese and C. Schultz, *Pollution, Prices, and Public Policy* (Washington, D.C.: The Brookings Institution, 1975).
3. W. J. Baumol and W. E. Oates, *The Theory of Environmental Policy* (Englewood Cliffs, N.J.: Prentice-Hall, 1975) presents a detailed theoretical discussion of effluent charges.
4. J. Buchanan and G. Tullock, "Polluter's Profits and Political Response," *American Economic Review* (1975) argues that the incentives generated by the extra payment required of firms as an effluent fee will cause these firms to favor the regulatory form of control.

10
Practical Problems in Pollution Control

In comparing the operation of regulatory and economic-incentive approaches to pollution control, we have assumed that the control agency in charge has complete and correct information on all aspects of the problem, that its institutional structure allows it to react appropriately, and that it has the incentive to maximize the net benefit of pollution control. Our earlier discussion of the current regulatory approach suggests that these assumptions are not likely to be true in any practical application. In this chapter we will begin to explore such practical issues as the implications of the lack of good information on benefits and costs; the incentives produced by a control system; and the political conflicts such a system can lead to.

IMPERFECT INFORMATION

One of the more serious practical problems in designing any system to control pollution is that there is inevitable uncertainty in the information used to generate policy decisions. In this section I explore the policy problems generated by an uncertain and continually changing world.

Uncertainty in Information

I have argued that environmental quality standards and effluent standards or effluent fees should be based on a careful analysis of the benefits and costs of pollution control. Yet as we saw in Chapter

5, estimating the value of these benefits and costs is a difficult and expensive undertaking. The benefits of pollution control are subject to a great deal of uncertainty, for various technical reasons and because the nature of environmental control as a public good causes people to hide their true preferences. Policy analysts will generate the best estimate of benefits (MBC_B) they can produce given the budget and time constraints they face. Good analysis further requires an attempt to generate a range of uncertainty for this estimate. In other words, the analyst will place a confidence range around this best estimate. This confidence range reflects the degree of uncertainty in the estimate. The analyst expects MBC to be at MBC_B — the best estimate — but it could be as low as the low estimate (MBC_L) or as high as the high estimate (MBC_H). The more uncertainty the analyst finds when making the estimate, the wider will be this range between high and low values.

More time and effort can reduce the uncertainty, but such investments must be weighed against the value of increased accuracy. Errors are costly because they generate inefficiencies in the system, but avoiding them is costly as well. Thus it would be efficient to reduce the uncertainty in the benefit and cost estimates only to the point where the marginal gain in accuracy times the value of increased accuracy equals the marginal cost of the effort to increase accuracy. There will inevitably be a range to the estimates, even after the efficient amount of investigation has taken place. Such a range is presented in Figure 10.1.

There is also uncertainty in the cost estimates for environmental quality. Emission transformation functions (ETFs) are difficult to determine. Marginal emission reduction costs ($MERC$s) require a complicated analysis and still contain substantial uncertainty. Consequently, a policy analyst will produce a best estimate and a range for MCC as well. The difficulties involved in estimating benefits and costs suggests that there will be greater uncertainty in estimating benefits. This will change from issue to issue, however. In cases where control technology is fairly standard and ETFs are relatively well understood, the range of MCC will be relatively small; but for new technology and difficult ETFs, the range could be greater than the benefit range.

The fact that there is a range of uncertainty in both benefits and costs leaves the analyst and the policy-maker in a dilemma. The best estimate of the efficient level of environmental quality is Q_B, where MBC_B and MCC_B intersect. This implies a best estimate for an effluent fee of P_B. The lowest expected efficient level of environ-

FIGURE 10.1 Uncertainty in Estimating Benefits and Costs

Uncertainty in estimating benefit and cost functions can produce a wide range of estimates of the efficient environmental quality and appropriate price. Environmental quality Q_B would be the best estimate of the efficient environmental quality, but uncertainty in estimates of benefits and costs imply that the efficient environmental quality could range between Q_H and Q_L. Likewise, the best estimate of the efficient price is P_B with a range from P_H to P_L.

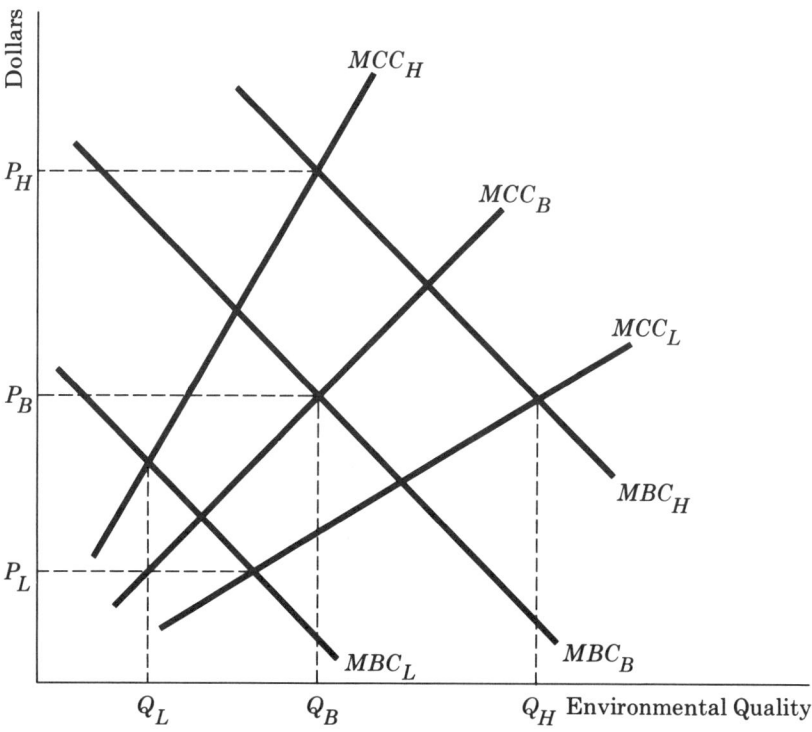

mental quality given this uncertainty is Q_L, the intersection of MCC_H and MBC_L. The highest possible efficient level of environmental quality, the intersection of MCC_L and MBC_H, is Q_H. There is obviously a very substantial range between low and high estimates. This can give policy-makers a great deal of difficulty. The range within which the efficient effluent fee might lie is also quite large, and can generate serious policy problems.

The problems generated by errors and uncertainties, and their implications for the choice between control systems that regulate price (like effluent fees) and systems that regulate quantity (like current regulations) were discussed by M. Weitzman.[1] In his discussion he points out that if errors in the *MBC* function are more costly than errors in the *MCC* function, then it is better to control quantity than to control price. The cost of errors depends on the shape of the functions. A rapidly rising benefit function implies that errors can be very costly. Furthermore, for a given *MCC* function, a more rapidly rising *MBC* function with the same degree of uncertainty as a less rapidly rising function will generate more uncertainty in price and less in quantity. This is demonstrated in Figure 10.2. There we see one set of *MC* curves with high, low, and best estimates, as in Figure 10.1. But there are two different sets of benefit functions. One set is not as steep as the other. The range between the high and low quantity estimates is much higher when the *MBC* function is relatively flat, as in panel A, than is the range of prices. If the benefit function is steeper, as in panel B, the range of uncertainty is greater in price and lower in quantity than for the flatter function. Panel B is the kind of situation that would warrant control of quantity rather than price. Weitzman's assessment is that panel B is more like the true situation for pollution control. If this is the case, an argument can be made for the superiority of quantity-based control systems over price-based systems. This is an important finding, and we must keep it in mind when selecting institutional alternatives. It does not, however, preclude economics-based controls. It only suggests that they should be based on quantity control rather than on price control.

Errors and Adjustments

Two possible sources of error can generate problems for policymakers. One is that the pollution control system finally implemented might not produce the environmental quality aimed at. In other words, something other than Q_B might result when pollution policy is implemented. This can be caused by errors in estimating *MCC* or errors in implementation. Whatever the source, the difference between actual environmental quality and Q_B will be the subject of further policy-making decisions. The other problem is that

---

[1] M. Weitzman, "Prices vs. Quantities," *Review of Economic Studies* 41 (October 1974): 477–491.

FIGURE 10.2 The Effect of the Slope of *MBC* on Uncertainty in Price and Quantity

For any given slope and range of uncertainty in estimates of the *MCC* function, a benefit function with the same degree of uncertainty but with greater elasticity (less slope) will produce a wider range of uncertainty in environmental quality (and a lower range of uncertainty in price) than a less elastic (steeper) benefit estimate.

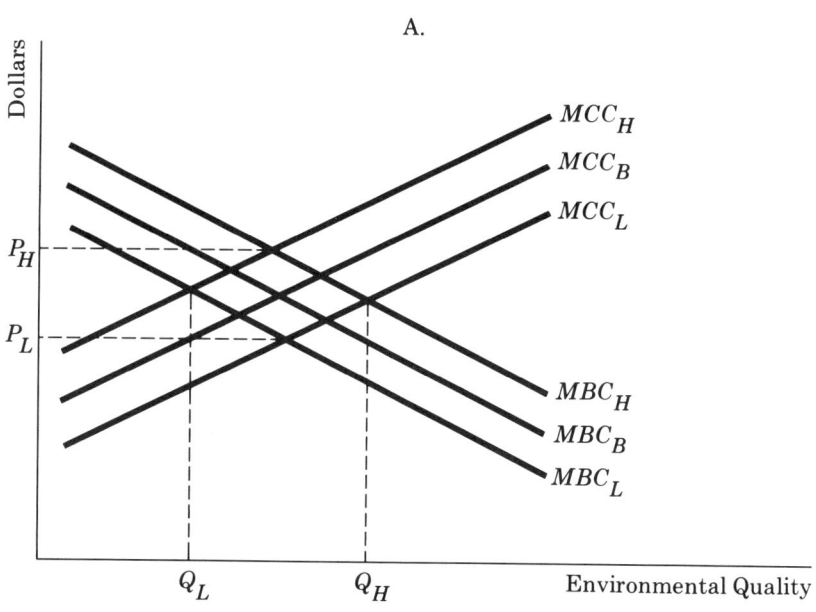

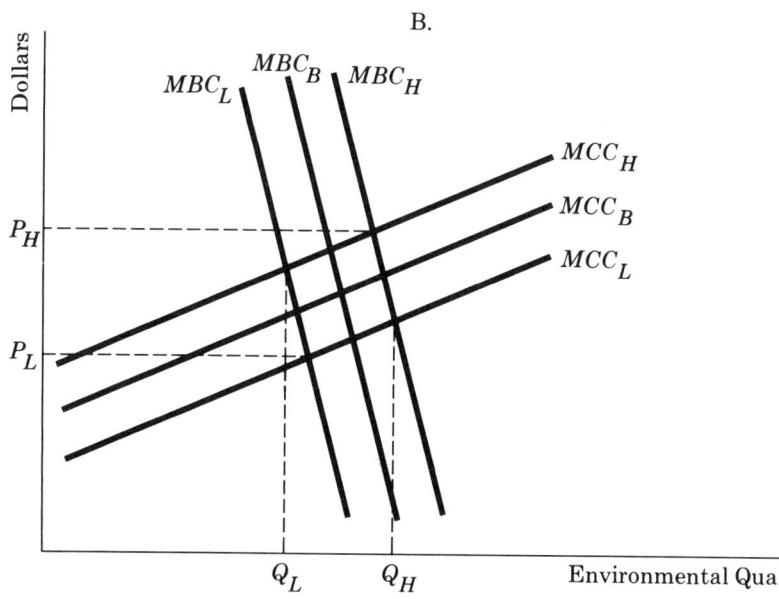

the system as implemented might indeed generate Q_B, but additional information gained during the implementation process might suggest that Q_B is in fact inefficient. This could occur if the true costs or benefits were found to be different from MCC_B or MBC_B.

The simple policy reaction in either event is to adjust something — most likely the environmental quality standard — to make policy right, but there are problems with adjusting policy after it has been implemented. Emitters and recipients make certain adjustments based on environmental policy decisions. An emitter might install a piece of equipment of particular dimensions and capabilities in response to a certain policy. A change in that policy — whether it requires more or less control — would mean changes and costs for the firm. Recipients are also affected by policy changes. An individual might move to an area primarily because of its high environmental quality. If that quality is the result of estimation and policy errors, subsequent correction of the error could create substantial burdens for the individual — in the form of either pollution damage or moving expenses.

Readjustment of policy as a result of discovered errors is costly in another way. The policy causes individuals to form expectations about environmental quality and the costs of control. When these expectations are not realized, the real costs we have already discussed are imposed. In addition, psychological costs are imposed. I feel much worse about a situation if my expectations were high and the realization is low than if my expectations were more in line with the actual result. Once people have adjusted to the realized environmental quality, there will be a psychological cost to changing the situation, which will be translated into political resistance to any change in policy.

Just as surely as there are costs associated with changing a policy, there are also costs if it is not changed. If the environmental quality standard Q_B is discovered to be too high, sources will be paying more for control than recipients benefit (actual MBC will be below MCC). This is a waste of resources. A comparison of estimated gains in efficiency and estimated costs of changing will determine whether a policy change is advisable. Note that this policy analysis itself will involve estimates and the problem of errors.

Flexibility to Change

Individuals and firms move into and out of an area, change locations within an area, and adjust demand for environmental quality because of changes in such underlying factors as income. These changes shift *MBC* and *MCC*, thus altering the efficient level of environmental quality. We have stated in the previous chapters that an efficient system should adjust to these changes. Practical considerations suggest, however, that policy should not be changed unless there is a positive net gain from doing so. This probably will not be the case for small changes, because the short-run adjustment costs are higher than the long-run savings. But as those small

FIGURE 10.3 Adjustments over Time

When growth occurs in an area, it is appropriate to adjust that area's environmental quality standard, individual emission standards, or effluent fees. Economic growth increases potential emissions and shifts *MCC* up to *MCC'*. Growth in population causes *MBC* to shift up to *MBC'*. Only if they both shift by the same amount is it appropriate *not* to adjust environmental quality standards. But even under these circumstances, emission standards or effluent fees would have to be adjusted.

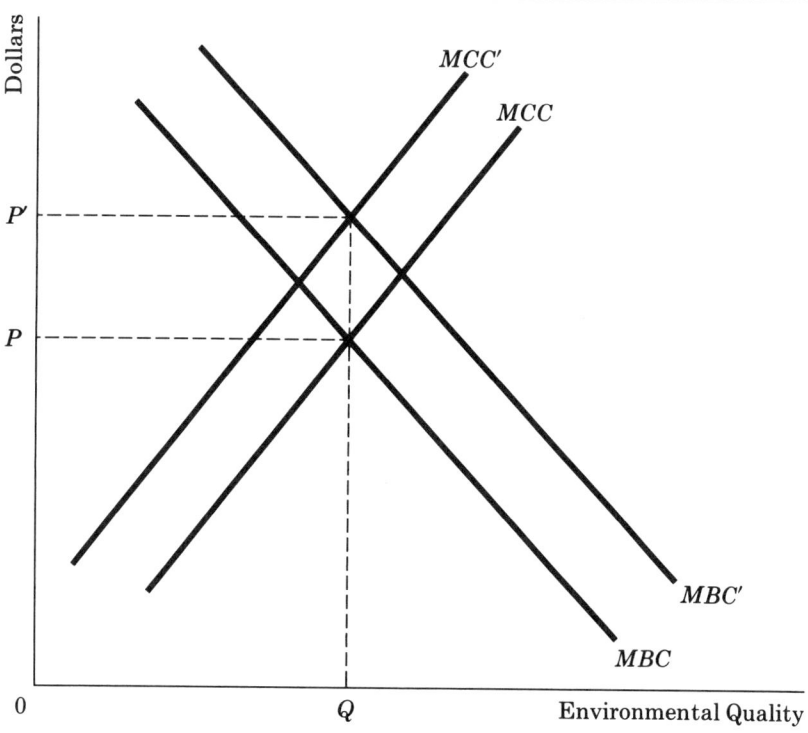

changes begin to add up, there will come a time when it is efficient to change the environmental quality standard and the effluent standards or fees.

It is conceptually possible to anticipate all future changes and to adjust standards and fees so as to produce efficient emission and location choices.[2] But the practicality of such a proposition is seriously in doubt. It would require that an analyst make an accurate prediction of all movements into and out of an area, and of changes in production and consumption that will take place. Such accuracy is not attainable. Probably nothing more than a very general trend can be predicted. Nevertheless, it may be worth the effort.

Suppose that the analyst predicts with some accuracy that the activity and number of emitters will be increasing over time. This shifts *MCC* upward to *MCC'* in Figure 10.3. Suppose that she also predicts an increase in population, which means an increase in the number of recipients. This shifts *MBC* upward to *MBC'*. If the shift in these two curves is about the same, it is unambiguously appropriate to adjust individual effluent standards or fees upward in anticipation. What could be done is to announce that at some year or years in the future the standards or fees will be increased to approximately *P'*. This information allows emitters and recipients to adjust their investments in light of these future changes. A larger change in *MBC* or *MCC* would suggest both an increase in the individual effluent standard or fee and a change in the environmental quality standard. There is more or less the same advantage to announcing expected future changes in environmental quality standards as there is to announcing future effluent fees or standards. Recipients are able to adjust behavior in anticipation of the change. This can save resources.

SOME PRACTICAL ALTERNATIVES

Economists have observed the workings of the existing regulatory approach and have concluded that it functions very inefficiently. In particular, they find that the information problems we have discussed cause decision-makers to resort to inefficient rules of thumb. One that has been commonly cited is the tendency to set equal effluent standards for all sources regardless of differences in *MERC*.

---

[2] This has been shown in W. Baumol and W. Oates, *The Theory of Environmental Policy* (Englewood Cliffs, N.J.: Prentice-Hall, 1975) p. 43 *n.* 17.

Numerous studies have shown that these across-the-board standards are much more expensive than the efficient combination of controls would be. One typical study of water pollution control concludes that across-the-board standards are at least twice as expensive as efficient control.[3] Because charging all sources the same effluent fee would automatically cause each source to control at the same $MERC$, it would reduce the inefficiencies of the across-the-board effluent standard. For this and other reasons, economists have argued that the regulatory approach should be replaced with an effluent fee system.[4] After analyzing the practical problems of implementing a full system of effluent fees and attempting to set fees that would generate the efficient level of environmental quality, several economists have suggested practical systems based on effluent fees but requiring less information than the full "ideal" system. The argument each of these economists makes is that the proposed system is better than the existing regulatory approach. We will now turn to one of the frequently advocated practical alternatives.

Transferable Permits

The transferable permit idea has been advocated by many economists and policy-makers, but it is most commonly associated with Professor J. H. Dales.[5] The system he proposes works in the following way: First, the pollution control agency determines a desired level of environmental quality and sets a standard at that level. The standard could be determined by benefit/cost analysis, as we have suggested, and would cover a basin or perhaps even a larger area. Next, the agency determines the number of units of a given pollutant that can be allowed in order to achieve that environmental quality standard. This requires the same knowledge of the ETF that is required to produce the benefit/cost analysis. Once the allowed total of emissions has been determined, permits to emit the pollut-

---

[3] H. Herzog, Jr., *The Economics of Regional Water Quality Management: A Case Study of River Quality in the Chesapeake Bay Region* (Ph.D. diss., University of Maryland, 1974).

[4] This position was eloquently expounded by Allen Kneese in *The Economics of Regional Water Quality Management* (Baltimore: Johns Hopkins University Press, 1960), where he also introduced the effluent charge system in the Ruhr River area of West Germany. Many others have followed his lead.

[5] J. H. Dales, *Pollution, Property, and Prices* (Toronto: University of Toronto Press, 1968).

ant are auctioned in an open market. After the initial sale, permits can be traded in the same way stocks are traded on Wall Street. When a buyer and a seller agree on a price, the permit is transferred and the new owner of the permit can increase emissions while the previous owner reduces emissions.

The price for permits in this market reflects the total supply of permits and the *MERC* for each potential source, and therefore the *MCC*. Each source will purchase the number of permits needed to equate the permit price (P) with its *MERC*. In panel A of Figure 10.4 this amount is $0D$. The reason for this level of purchase is that at any fewer than $0D$ permits the cost of controlling the emission is greater than the cost of purchasing the permit. The source would lose money if it did not purchase $0D$ permits. The market for permits is determined by the behavior of all firms. The $MERC_T$ (total MERC for the area) curve in panel B represents the willingness of all firms

FIGURE 10.4 The Market for Transferable Permits

Suppose there were S transferable permits available in an area. Individual emitters would bid up the price of permits until it equals the price at which the $MERC_T$ function intersects the permit supply quantity. At this point, total demand for permits would equal supply. Individual sources would have purchased permits up to point D, where the price (P) equals the individual MERC.

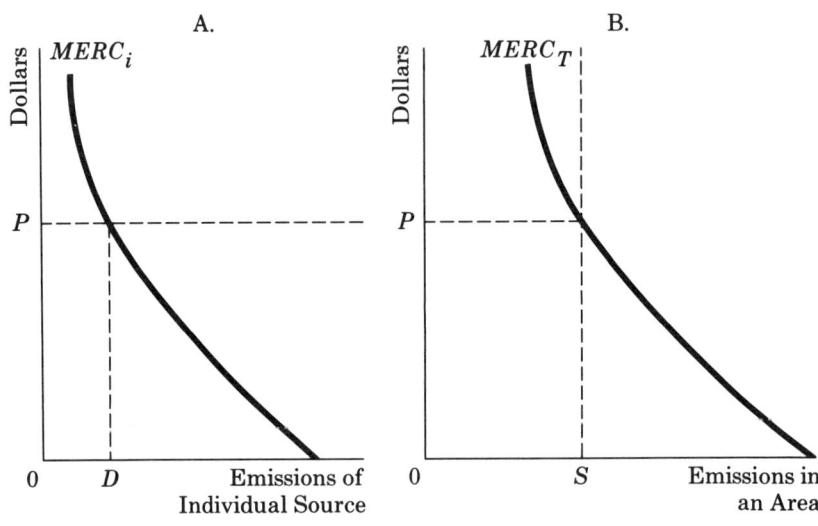

to purchase permits. It is the horizontal sum of all the individual *MERC* curves. The vertical line at S represents the number of permits sold in the area, and is derived from the *ETF* and the environmental quality standard. P represents the market clearing price for permits. At this price, all permits are sold and each individual emitter has exactly the number of permits desired.

There are several advantages to the transferable permit system. The most important is that it causes sources to reveal their true *MERC* function, or at least one point on it. In the system Dales proposes, the total number of permits is determined by estimates of *MERC* rather than actual values. The market clearing price for permits provides direct information on the intersection between the actual $MERC_T$ and the quantity $0S$. What is more, this information is voluntarily produced by the source before any permits are issued. This allows policy-makers to adjust the number of permits before any permits are sold if large errors are discovered.

The second advantage of the transferable permit is that it provides efficient incentives to control and to innovate, in the same way that an effluent fee does. Sources will equate their individual *MERC* with P and therefore with the control cost functions of other sources. This guarantees that all sources are producing the efficient level of environmental quality at the lowest cost. This can result in a great savings when compared to an across-the-board effluent standard. When a source innovates it will reduce its emissions and sell permits. This allows other sources to increase emissions, saving resources in the process. All of this results from the workings of the market. It is not necessary for the control agency to become involved as they do in a regulatory system. The sale of permits, like the payment of effluent fees, would provide the agency with revenue to be used for environmental enhancement, administrative costs, and compensation for residual damages.

A third advantage is that the permits can be purchased by anyone. This allows proenvironmentalists to express their preferences for an improved environment directly by purchasing permits and retiring them. This would reduce total emissions and improve environmental quality. Individuals could do this themselves or through a citizen interest group. There would be a free rider problem, which might lead to the underrevealing of preferences for an improved environment, but some corrections of potential errors in estimating *MBC* might be made. If the analyst significantly underestimated *MBC*, the environmental quality standard would be inefficiently lax. By purchasing permits, recipients could partially correct this error and in the process provide better information on the location of *MBC*. Actually, considering the free rider problem, the information provided by recipient purchases provides the lower limit of the true *MBC* function.

Fourth, the transferable permit system does not require the setting and implementation of individual effluent standards, thus reducing at least some of the administrative burden and expense of a regulatory program. The information given out by emitters and recipients during the initial bidding for permits can also be used to generate more accurate estimates of the efficient level of environmental quality with less analytical effort. Consequently, we can expect that the transferable permit system would be less expensive to administer than a similar regulatory system.

Finally, if Weitzman's argument is correct, the transferable permit system takes advantage of the desire to regulate quantity while retaining the efficiency of an economic incentive system.

Along with these advantages of the transferable permit system, there are some problems that should be considered as well. The primary difficulty with the system arises from two interacting effects. We have shown that the effects of emissions vary with location and timing. This suggests that a permit must be specifically designed for each individual source. Suppose source A, which is upstream, purchases a permit from downstream source Z. The damage from a pound of BOD emissions at A will not be equivalent to the damages from a pound at Z. If a number of permits were sold by a low-damage emitter to a high-damage emitter, environmental quality would deteriorate, even with the same number of permits in circulation. Obviously, this is not how the system is intended to work.

Designating small permit-exchange areas is one way to maintain marginal damages from various emitters at approximately equal levels. But this might mean that there would be too few sources to allow the permit market to function efficiently. A larger market is needed, one that at least partially allows for locational differences in the effects of emissions. Suppose that factory A is in a low-damage area and factory Z is in an area that suffers twice as much damage per pound of emissions. The control agency would generate a rule that a permit for one pound of emissions at A can be used for only half a pound of emissions at Z. This ratio system would increase the size of the market and its efficiency. The agency could establish several such subareas and the trade ratios between them. In each subarea, sources (and recipients) would purchase permits based on their costs and benefits and the amount they would be allowed to emit (or prevent from being emitted) per permit. There would be one price for a permit anywhere in the area, but the amount of emissions that price would buy would vary.

This system has the added advantage of providing existing and potential emitters with better information about location alternatives. A new source could purchase 100 permits in the market for a given area and choose among locations within that area depending on the volume of emissions allowed by these permits in each subarea. Comparing permit costs and allowed emission levels in different locations with other location variables, the source can make an efficient choice for itself. At the same time, it will internalize the environmental damages its choices impose on others because it will pay for the permits whose price reflects *MBC*.

A second problem with the transferable permit system stems from the fact that it begins with the sale of a fixed number of permits. For various reasons, the agency might learn that this number is inappropriate. It could determine that its estimates of *MBC* or *MERC* were in error, or that it misestimated the *ETF*. Or, as time went on, the *MBC* and *MCC* curves could shift because of the movement of emitters in and out of the area. Any of these reasons could cause the agency to want to adjust the number of permits in circulation. The agency could accomplish this adjustment by purchasing or selling permits in the market. Alternatively, the agency could limit the life of permits so some would come up for renewal periodically, at which time the agency could make decisions about the efficient supply. This would allow for fine-tuning over time. The periodic renewal approach has its drawbacks, however. For one, it runs into the adjustment cost problem discussed earlier. And it lays the agency open to all sorts of political maneuvering by procontrol and anticontrol groups. The end result could well be a drift away from efficient environmental quality rather than a movement toward it. The same problem arises in the current regulatory system, where environmental quality standards become inappropriate as conditions change.

Finally, the transferable permit system allocates resources the same way an effluent fee does, in that it requires sources to pay a lump sum which reflects the residual damages of their emissions. This implies that property rights are held by recipients. If this is not the correct interpretation of society's value judgments, there will be political difficulties in obtaining the adoption of such a system. The fact that we now employ a regulatory approach, which implies that property rights are shared, suggests that a transferable permit system would have tough political sledding.[6] A different system could overcome this problem, however. Suppose that instead of being auctioned, permits were allocated to existing emitters in proportion to their current emissions. Then there would not be the significant transfer of wealth found in the Dales system. This could make transferable permits more politically acceptable.

Practical Effluent Fees

While the effluent fee works well in theory, there are some practical problems with implementing it in a world where information is imperfect and incomplete.[7] The same sort of practical problems that led Dales to suggest transferable permits have led others to suggest one or another form of a system of practical effluent fees. While the proposals differ in detail,[8] they generally take the following form: 1) The control agency determines an environmental quality standard in some way. (Some authors even suggest that there may not be much economic input in this determination.) However the standard is determined, 2) the agency then sets an effluent fee based on this standard. It is commonly the case that those who suggest practical fees ignore locational variations, so the fee would be the same for all sources in a basin. 3) This fee system is then applied to each source. If after a reasonable period of time the fee does not generate the desired level of environmental quality, authors suggest that it be adjusted until the standard is met.

One advantage of this system is that it tends to generate lower control costs for achieving any given level of environmental quality than does the regulatory system. In the presence of differences in

---

[6] For further discussion of marketable permits, see Roger Noll, "Implementing Marketable Emission Permits," *American Economic Review* 71 (May 1982): 120–124. A most interesting paper comparing alternative designs of transferable permits is Scott Atkinson and T. H. Tietenberg, "The Empirical Properties of Two Classes of Designs for Transferable Discharge Permit Markets," *Journal of Environmental Economics and Management* 9 (June 1982): 101–121.

[7] For a further discussion of the practical difficulties, see Susan Rose-Ackerman, "Effluent Charges: A Critique," *Canadian Journal of Economics* 6 (November 1973).

[8] See, for example, A. Kneese and B. Bower, *Managing Water Quality: Economics, Technology, Institutions* (Baltimore: Johns Hopkins University Press, 1968); W. Baumol and W. Oates, "The Use of Standards and Prices for Protection of the Environment," *Swedish Journal of Economics* 73 (March 1971); W. Baumol, "On Taxation and the Control of Externalities," *American Economic Review* (1972); and A. Kneese and C. Schultz, *Pollution, Prices, and Public Policy* (Washington, D.C.: The Brookings Institution, 1975).

effects on the environment among sources, however, some inefficiency remains. All sources should be controlling at equal marginal costs per unit of impact on the environmental quality. Because this system ignores locational differences, it would not do this. Instead all sources control at equal *MERC*. This can lead to waste in the same way incorrect standards do (as we saw in Chapter 8). As in the cases of regulatory standards and transferable permits, it is expensive to gather and process the data needed to set fees at appropriate levels for sources whose emissions create different potential damages. This expense tends to offset somewhat the efficiency gains from specific fees. A compromise will save resources. Practicality may require that differences in fees be set for broad areas of a basin. There is no reason to believe that the efficient compromise will always be an identical fee for all sources. This issue cannot be settled by some general prescription. Instead, a detailed analysis of each case will be required.

Another advantage of the practical effluent fee system is that it allows the agency to adjust incentives to meet the environmental quality standard with relative ease. All that need be done is to change the general level of the fee. This leads to the same sort of adjustment costs discussed for the transferable permit system. Periodic adjustment of the fee causes higher costs for emitters. To reduce these adjustment costs, E. Mills and L. White suggest that the initial fee be set for each of the coming five years.[9] At the end of each year the agency would announce the fee for the fifth year hence. In 1985 the agency would set the fee for 1989; in 1986, for 1990 and so on. This preannouncement of fees allows sources to adjust over time to changes in fees and can lead to savings in control costs. This gain in efficiency comes at the cost of flexibility. The agency will be unable to adjust the fee as quickly as it might like when new information becomes available. An efficient compromise between adjustment costs and flexibility might suggest that some period other than five years would be desirable.

The Sulfur Tax

One practical effluent fee gained presidential and some congressional support: the tax on sulfur proposed by the Nixon administra-

---

[9] E. Mills and L. White, "Government Policies toward Automotive Emissions Control," in A. Friedlaender, ed., *Approaches to Controlling Air Pollution* (Cambridge, Mass.: MIT Press, 1978).

tion in 1971 and 1972. The plan called for every source of sulfur emissions in the country to pay a tax (fee) of ten cents per pound for emissions. The level of the fee was based on a general benefit/cost analysis for the country that eschewed issues of local variation. The argument was that the tax would provide more effective incentives for control and innovation than the current regulatory system provided. At the same time, it would save substantial administrative expense because (it was argued) it was far simpler to implement than the regulatory approach.

The tax was not adopted for various reasons. Proenvironmentalists opposed it because it did not guarantee a clean environment. They argued that sources would merely pay the tax and continue polluting — showing their lack of understanding of the economics of fees. They also argued that even if sources did control as predicted there was no guarantee that air would reach the environmental quality standards set by EPA. This certainly was true, since the proposal did not explicitly relate the tax to air quality. It was not adjustable. Any errors would be set in perpetuity or would require a new law. Sources and industry representatives argued against the tax because it created an "unfair financial burden" and would cause industries with high levels of emission to suffer disproportionately. In other words, it might work. In the face of political resistance from both sides, the tax was shelved. It is interesting to speculate about the effect on present levels of air quality, and especially of acid rain, if this simple proposal had been adopted in 1972. I doubt that we would be in worse shape than we are now.

Economic Incentives in the Clean Air Act of 1977

The sulfur tax failed, but some new plans have appeared that employ economic incentives. Two that are gaining prominence are the *bubble concept* and *emission offsets*.

Previously, separate emission standards were set for each process in a plant. This resulted in highly variable standards that did not equate *MERC* for each source within a plant. The bubble concept would allow a regulatory agency to treat all the emissions as if they were one source, thus allowing the source to choose the level at which it would control each process. With this freedom, the source could equate *MERC* among processes, reducing its costs of control while generating the same overall emissions.

The bubble concept could be extended to all the sources in a basin. This has not been possible, primarily because all sources are not owned by the same firm, but an alternative that has some of the desirable characteristics of a transferable permit has been adopted in heavily polluted air basins. For a new source to locate in a basin that exceeds the national primary air quality standards, it must control at least to the applicable emission standards for new sources and obtain a reduction of emissions from an existing source equal to (or greater than) the increase in emissions resulting from its operations (an *emission offset*). To obtain this reduction, the new firm must generally pay an existing firm to reduce its emissions. The payment must cover at least the additional control costs of the existing source or it will not agree to the additional control. The new source will seek existing sources with low *MERC*s. If the *MCC* for higher levels of control than the emission standard for new sources is lower than the payment it would have to make to an existing firm, it would pay to control more and purchase less control from existing sources. This system does not guarantee that all sources will be controlling at equal *MERC*, but it does move toward the efficient solution.[10]

POLITICAL IMPLICATIONS OF ECONOMIC INCENTIVE SYSTEMS

Like a regulatory system, an economic incentive system will lead people to act politically to affect decisions. Sources will attempt to reduce the cost of the system to them, and environmentalists will attempt to make the system as stringent as possible. Two issues are central to these political maneuverings: Who pays, and who receives the revenue.

Who Pays?

Both practical effluent fees and transferable permits answer the question of who owns the rights to the environment by vesting the rights in recipients and requiring emitters to pay for residual damages. The transferable permit does this by requiring sources to bid for permits. This requirement generates resistance from emitters, who feel that the existing regulatory system at least gives them some rights to emit. The adoption of an economic incentive system

[10] For more discussion, see R. Liroff, *Air Pollution Offsets* (New York: The Conservation Foundation, 1980).

like the one we have presented would take these rights from emitters. To solve this problem, both systems could be adjusted.

One method of overcoming emitter resistance to transferable permits is to allocate the permits initially at no cost. Subsequently, permits could be traded and the system would work as described. There is the inevitable problem of deciding who receives the initial permits. To recognize the implicit rights that the existing regulatory system has given to sources, permits could be allocated in proportion to the existing emission standards for each source. If the existing standards were sufficient to meet the environmental quality standard, the proportion would be one to one. If the existing emission standards were too lenient, a lower factor would be used. Such a method of initial allocation would blunt the major political resistance to adopting transferable permits, but it would not solve all the political problems. Some sources would inevitably claim that the existing standards were unfair, and some environmentalists would argue that sources were allowed to emit too much. A politically viable compromise probably could be worked out, however.

A practical effluent fee system is a little more messy, but it does offer a potential solution to the allocation of property rights.[11] This alternative combines fees and subsidies. Suppose that three sources with different costs previously faced an emission standard of $\bar{S}$ (in Figure 10.5). All three would control at the same level, but at different $MERC$s. Their $MERC$s are designated as low (L), medium (M), and high (H). Now suppose we adopted a system where a source would be charged a fee of P if it emitted more than $\bar{S}$. The firm with high costs would find it advantageous to control to E and pay a fee of $BCE\bar{S}$. This firm saves in two ways. It lowers costs by reducing controls and it pays a fee that is lower than its control cost savings. It also gains explicit property rights to emit $\bar{S}$, thus avoiding the transfer of wealth usually associated with an effluent fee. Suppose, in addition, that a source is given a subsidy if it controls more than $\bar{S}$. The source with low costs would find it advantageous to control at D and receive a subsidy of $AB\bar{S}D$, which would be greater than its additional costs of control. This source receives property rights to $\bar{S}$ and is compensated for controlling more. The middle source controls at $\bar{S}$ and neither pays a fee nor receives a subsidy. Those who pay the fee provide the revenue for subsidies paid to low emitters.

In this system, property rights are shared in the same way they

---

[11] This solution was suggested by G. Mumy, "Long-Run Efficiency and Property Rights Sharing for Pollution Control," *Public Choice* (35): 59–74.

FIGURE 10.5 Shared Property Rights Under an Economic Incentive System

An economic incentive system can be devised that shares property rights, as current regulations do. In such a system, a source that has a medium level of *MERC* (*M*) will control at *S*. A source with a low *MERC* (*L*) will control at *D* and receive a subsidy, and a source with a high *MERC* (*H*) will control at *E* and pay an effluent fee. The proceeds from the fees can be used to help offset the expense of the subsidies.

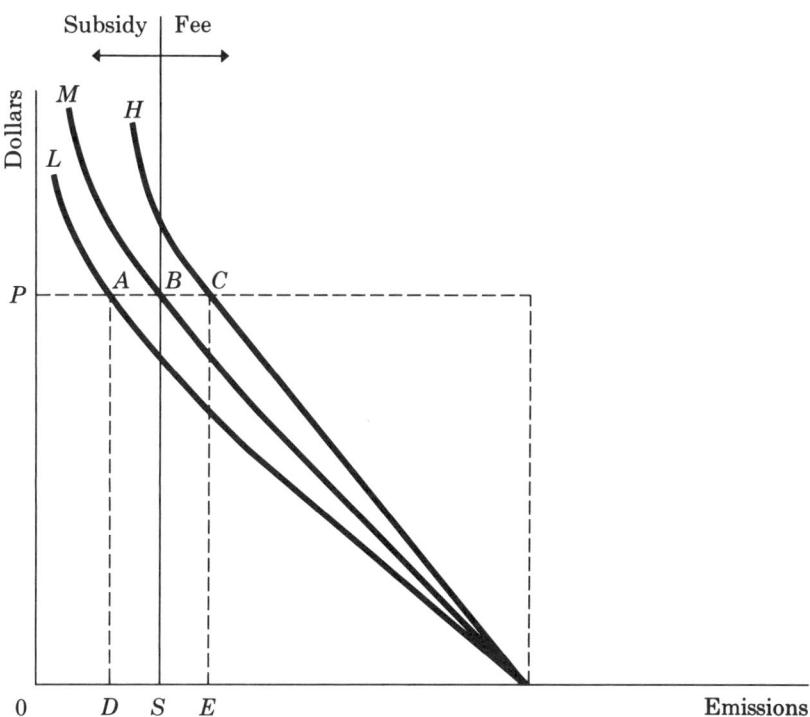

are under regulation. There is no net flow of funds to or from recipients. But this fee/subsidy system has the advantages of achieving efficient levels of control for all sources and of stimulating innovation in the same way an effluent fee does. Because of the shared property rights, this system could also be a politically viable alternative to the current regulatory system.

Who Receives the Revenue?

The revenue from a transferable permit or an effluent fee could be used to pay administrative costs, control environmental quality, and compensate individuals for residual damages. In theory this is desirable if the recipients own the rights to the environment. But there is a practical difficulty to this generation of revenue. The potential for receiving revenue alters the incentives of the control agency managers. Bureaucracy theory argues that these managers will seek to maximize their budget.[12] When given the power to raise their own revenue, they might set the effluent fee or the number of transferable permits at the level that maximizes their revenue rather than at the efficient level.[13] The revenue-maximizing level for an effluent fee would be the point at which the MERC has elasticity of one — that is, where it is at a 45 degree angle. Moving to the unit elastic fee would generate a reduction in the fee and in the level of control at the same time that it would generate an increase in revenue from fees.

Such a situation is depicted in Figure 10.6. The efficient fee is E. At that fee, the source pays 0EAB to the agency. The revenue-maximizing fee is R, at which the source pays 0RCD. Moving from E to R saves total payments of REAF but increases payments by BECD. Because the second area is larger than the first, revenue to the agency is increased.

There are several possible solutions. One would be to require that the agency set the fee efficiently. The substantial uncertainty faced in estimating the efficient level for any one source, however, makes such a requirement difficult to enforce. The agency can argue that its interpretation of the data requires the fee it has selected. It is then a matter of interpretation, and agencies have traditionally been able to sustain their decisions in cases of administrative discretion. It is interesting to ask who has the incentive to monitor the fee-setting process in this case. Recipients will receive less environmental quality, but they will receive some of the proceeds of the fee. On net they will be worse off, because the result is inefficient and because the agency cannot compensate them for all damages — the revenues will not be sufficient. But the payments would reduce the

---

[12] W. Niskanen, *Bureaucracy and Representative Government* (Chicago: Aldine-Atherton, 1971).

[13] C. Goetz, "Political Equilibrium vs. Economic Efficiency in Effluent Pricing," in J. R. Conner and E. Loehman, eds., *Economics and Decision Making for Environmental Quality* (Gainsville: University of Florida Press, 1974).

FIGURE 10.6 Revenue-Maximizing Fees and Efficient Fees Compared

Suppose the efficient effluent fee is E. If the control agency is allowed to keep the proceeds from the fee, it will have an incentive to set the fee on the basis of its revenue potential rather than at its efficient level. The revenue-maximizing effluent fee is at some point like R.

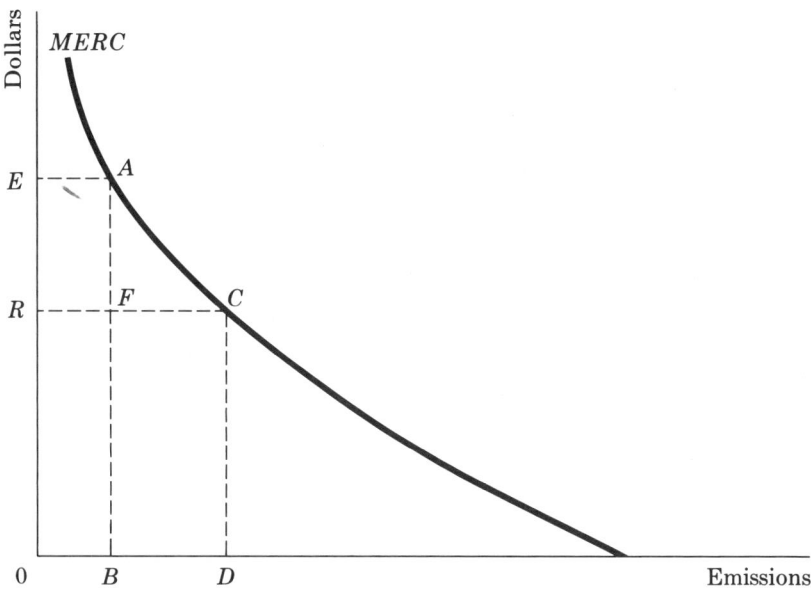

incentive damaged parties feel to pursue the issue. A clever bureaucrat would use a portion of fee revenue to compensate those who would be most likely to cause trouble — that is, the most vocal proenvironmentalists.

It might appear that the emitter would seek to change the fee, because it is paying more to the agency; but this would not be the case. The reduction in fee saves the emitter both fee area $REAF$ and control cost area $BACD$. Because $BACD$ is larger than $BFCD$ by area FAC, the emitter saves from a lowering of the fee. Thus the agency, pursuing its own goals, would be relatively immune from political pressure to seek the efficient solution.

An alternative solution would be to place the revenue in the general fund, thus removing the agency's revenue-maximizing incentive. There would still be indirect pressures on the agency to maximize revenue. Other agencies could use the funds generated by the fee. This would make it easier for politicians to increase the budgets of all agencies, including the control agency. In fact, the control agency's argument for more funds might include the claim that it needs more resources to collect the fee effectively. Thus revenue maximization is blunted, but not eliminated. There is yet another problem with this solution: Without the fee revenue, the agency might not be able to control environmental damage through projects. This would reduce the efficiency of the solution. As with so many other issues, there is no simple solution. Detailed comparisons would have to be made before an alternative was chosen.

PRACTICAL SOLUTIONS WITH PRACTICAL PROBLEMS

Implementing any effort to control emissions presents serious informational problems. Uncertainties in benefits and costs lead to a wide range of possible outcomes. Practical systems, whether based on regulation or on economic incentives, cannot avoid these problems. Rather, it is a matter of searching for an alternative that will minimize them. Of primary concern in the search for a practical system are the errors that might result from its operation, and the cost of adjusting to these errors. As conditions change in a basin, however, it is efficient to make adjustments. Thus reduction of initial errors, costs of adjustment, and flexibility when faced with changes in circumstances are important criteria for judging a pollution control system. Many economists have argued that the current regulatory system does not perform these tasks effectively and that a practical economic incentive system would work better.

One such system is the transferable permit. A primary advantage of this system is that it causes sources to reveal their *MERC* functions voluntarily. This reduces uncertainty on the cost side, but does not eliminate it because the *ETF* is not well understood in many cases. This system reacts like a theoretical effluent fee in its inducement to innovate — providing more incentive than does a regulatory system. It allows proenvironmental groups to express demand, and it avoids individual standards, thus moving toward greater economic efficiency. But because of uncertainty in the *ETF*, errors and inefficiencies are still possible. A practical system would have to be designed to reduce these problems. The number of permits sold could be adjusted over time to take into consideration changing conditions and errors in setting the initial environmental quality standard. A political problem with the transferable permit is that it allocates property rights in the environment to recipients. It may be difficult to get any system adopted that takes property rights away from a group that now has them. Solving the problem of who pays is potentially easy. All that is needed is to give the permits to emitters initially. This also solves the problem of bureaucrats setting fees or permit costs so as to maximize their agencies' revenue.

The marketable permit appears to be a desirable alternative to the current regulatory system. But before we decide to pressure Congress to adopt it, many more practical and political issues must be addressed. One way we can learn about how such a system might work is to investigate how the existing system works. In the past several chapters we have done this in general terms. Various researchers have learned, however, that the process of implementing a pollution control system alters its operation. A system simply does not work the way it was intended or thought to work when the law was passed. In West Germany, this slippage has been termed the implementation deficit. It is an inevitable part of the policy process, and one that should not be ignored. In an effort to understand the implementation process we will explore the implementation of the Clean Air Act of 1970 in the next three chapters. Armed with that information, we can then turn to designing a system that is politically feasible and that will work well when adopted.

UNCERTAINTY AND INFORMATION UNDER POLICY ALTERNATIVES

Before we proceed, let us look more carefully at the incentives faced by the two principal groups affected by government control efforts: recipients and emitters. Suppose an agency were to announce that it was going to use a regulatory approach whereby it would determine an environmental quality standard on the basis of benefit/cost analysis and then set emission standards for individual sources to meet this standard. One of the primary sources of information is, unavoidably, the emitter. Knowing that the agency will set environmental quality standards and effluent standards on the basis of the information provided, the emitter will seek to interpret cost data in a way favorable to its own interests. Its control costs can be reduced by presenting biased data that overestimate the *MCC*. This overestimation would lead the agency to set a less stringent environmental quality standard. In addition, the source will argue that its emissions do not really affect environmental quality that much. To the extent that the emitter's data influence the agency's setting of standards, this bias will reduce the effective effluent standard for the source and save it money.

The mechanism for this can be seen in Figure 10.7. Suppose the firm was successful in convincing the agency that its emissions were less damaging to the environment and more costly to control. In making its benefit/cost analysis, the agency would then employ cost curve $MERC_R$ and transformation function ETF_R. This would cause the agency to derive an *MCC* curve that would be incorrectly high (MCC_R). The agency would set a less stringent environmental quality standard (EQ_R) and a less stringent emission standard (E_R). This lower emission standard would save the firm ABE_RE^* in pollution control costs — the area under the real *MERC* function between the efficient standard (E^*) and the inefficient one (E_R). So long as the cost of influencing the agency by providing misinformation is less than this savings, it pays for the firm to misinform the agency.

Now suppose instead that the agency was going to set an environmental quality standard based on benefit/cost analysis and employ an effluent charge to meet this standard. The incentive for the firm to produce cost information would be substantially changed. In our discussions of practical effluent fees I suggested that the agency might want to set the fees for some period of time and revise them after new information on the *MERC* and *ETF* was gathered. Whatever the timing of the new analysis, there will be a delay in revision of fees. Thus any errors resulting from the initial setting of fees will persist over some time. Realizing this, the firm will find it advantageous to provide misinformation suggesting that the *MERC* function is lower than it actually is — just the opposite of the incentive under regulation. A low *MERC* will generate an estimated *MCC* function to the right of the true function. This would lead the agency initially to set an excessively clean environmental quality standard but an excessively low effluent fee.

The net result of this error for the firm's payments can be seen in Figure 10.8. The true control cost function is *MERC*, but the firm presents its costs as $MERC_F$. The agency sets a lower fee (F_F) instead of the efficient fee (F^*), expecting $\hat{E}$ emissions. Given fee F_F, the source controls at E_F. It pays BME_F in control costs and $0F_FBE_F$ in effluent fees. At the efficient fee the source would pay AME^* in

FIGURE 10.7 Firm Incentives to Provide Inaccurate Information Under Regulation

An emitter has some control over the information it provides to the regulatory agency, and it can use this control to reduce the costs imposed on it. It can argue that it has a higher cost ($MERC_R$) than its true cost of control ($MERC$) and that its emissions have a lower effect on the environment (ETF_R) than the true effect (ETF). This incorrect information will cause the agency to believe that the correct environmental cost function is MCC_R rather than MCC. The agency then sets a lower environmental quality standard (E_R) than is efficient. Under this lower standard the firm saves E^*ABE_R, a large part of the area under its true cost function.

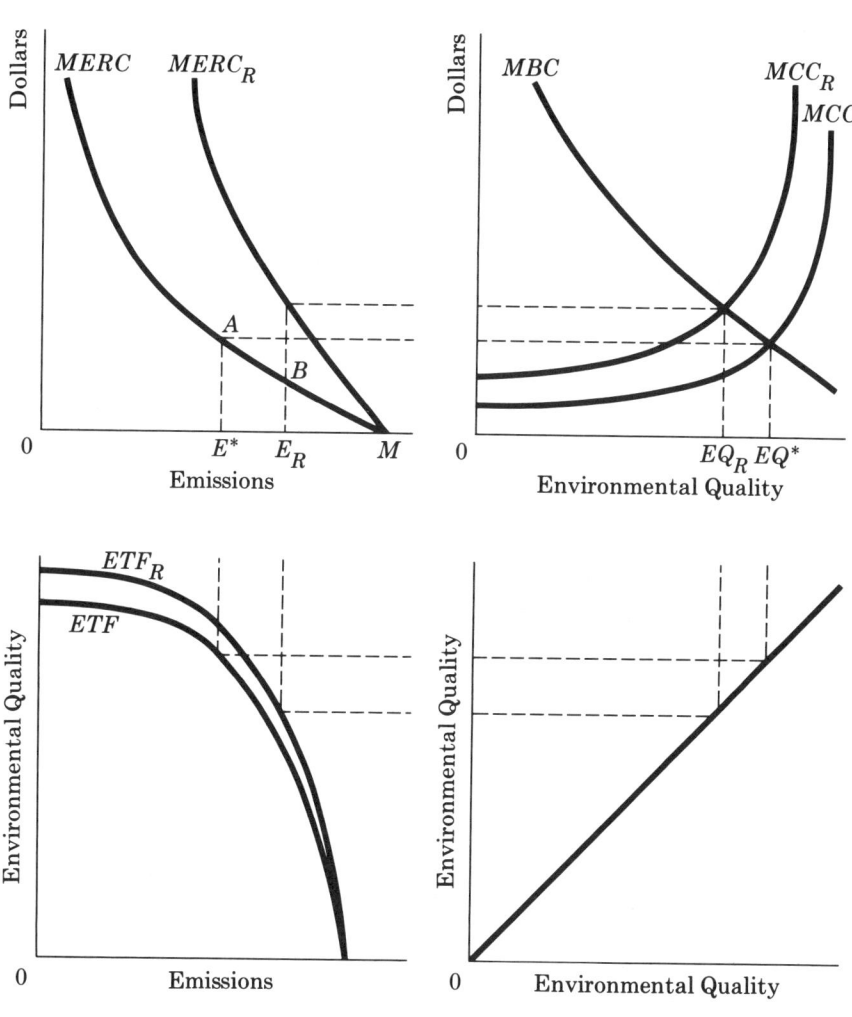

FIGURE 10.8 Firm Incentives to Provide Inaccurate Information Under Effluent Fees

Under a system of effluent charges, the emitter's incentive is to argue that control costs are lower than they actually are ($MERC_F$ is lower than true cost $MERC$). This causes the agency to set a lower effluent fee (F_F). Under the lower fee the source will control at E_F and save area F^*ABF_F.

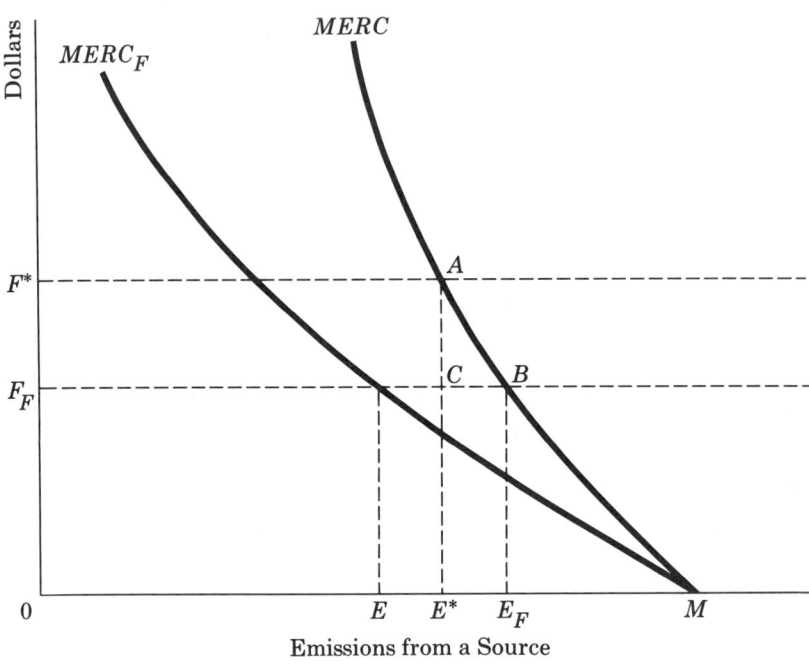

control costs and $0F^*AE^*$ in effluent fees. Thus the firm saves F^*ABF_F by providing the misinformation. After some period of time the misinformation will be perceived and the effluent fee corrected, but the firm will have enjoyed this saving in the meantime.

Clearly, the type of control system employed will have an effect on the flow of information from firms. But emitting firms are not the only ones with an incentive to provide misinformation. Recipients will find it advantageous to provide biased information on the adverse effects of pollution. Whether regulation or effluent fees are employed, it will be advantageous to overstate pollution damages.

This would cause the agency to set an inefficiently stringent environmental quality standard. The higher standard would increase the total benefit to the recipients.

The combination of these two misinformation incentives is of interest. Under the regulatory approach the firm-produced bias would lead to an inefficiently lax environmental quality standard while the recipient's bias would lead to an inefficiently stringent environmental standard. These effects are contradictory, so the resulting policy might not differ greatly from the efficient standard. A similar result would be found for the effluent fee alternative. The environmental quality standard would tend toward the correct level, and the effluent fee would also tend to move toward the efficient level. The end result will depend on the degree to which the agency believes one group or the other, and there is no way to assess this analytically. It will depend on the skill of the leaders of these respective groups, the skill of the agency personnel, and the political power of each.

SUMMARY: THERE IS NO PERFECT SYSTEM

There are some practical problems with alternatives to the existing regulatory system. Imperfect information makes the specification of a single price or quantity subject to substantial error. The likely errors and the shapes of the *MBC* and *MCC* functions suggest that it would be efficient to regulate quantity rather than price. The other problems encountered by practical economic incentive systems can be overcome by careful design. The problem of political resistance to fees or transferable permits as a result of the implicit redistribution of wealth the systems imply can be overcome by combining a fee system with a subsidy system or by simple transfer of permits to sources. In either case, the primary advantages of an economic incentive system can be maintained.

It should now be obvious that there is no perfect system. Indeed, there is no obvious choice among systems. Furthermore, the details of design will have different implications for the desirability of each alternative. The working of a transferable permit system will depend on how widely the permits can be traded, the emission value of a permit at different locations, and the adjustment to new information that is generated by permit prices and observed environmental quality. To select an alternative, we must first specify all the various details of design for each alternative and analyze their implications. One eye must be kept on efficiency, the second on practicality, and the third on political acceptability. But we only have two eyes. Obviously, there are trade-offs to be made, and any system will be a compromise.

STUDY QUESTIONS

1. Given M. Weitzman's arguments, is there a reason to prefer effluent fees over regulation?
2. Various authors have suggested that errors in the setting of environmental quality standards or effluent fees can be easily adjusted as they are identified. How will a policy of adjusting for errors affect the information emitters provide, and how will recipients provide the control agency with information with which it makes decisions about appropriate adjustments?
3. Transferable permits have some advantages over both practical regulation and practical effluent fees. What are they? Why haven't we adopted such a system?
4. Given your understanding of the advantages of alternative systems, which system would you prefer and why?

SUGGESTED READINGS

1. S. Rose-Ackerman, "Effluent Charges: A Critique," *Canadian Journal of Economics* 6 (November 1973) was one of the first to argue that there were some serious problems with effluent charges.
2. J. H. Dales, *Pollution, Property, and Prices* (Toronto: University of Toronto Press, 1968) presents a careful argument for the transferable permit concept.
3. R. Noll, "Implementing Marketable Emission Permits," *American Economic Review* 71 (May 1982): 120–124 reports on a study of the practicability of transferable permits if applied in Los Angeles.
4. M. Weitzman, "Prices vs. Quantities," *Review of Economic Studies* 41 (October 1974): 477–491 presents a detailed discussion of the effects of uncertainty on the choice of control instruments.

5. E. Mills and L. White, "Government Policies toward Control of Automotive Emission Control," in A. Friedlaender, ed., *Approaches to Controlling Air Pollution* (Cambridge, Mass.: MIT Press, 1978) offers a practical system for employing effluent charges to control automotive emissions. I proposed a similar system to Administrator Ruckelshaus in 1973 without success.

11

Pollution Control Policy in Practice

The federal pollution control program is not working as well as it might. Goals set early in the 1970s have yet to be met. I have offered two possible explanations for this failure, particularly emphasizing the lack of economic efficiency inherent in current pollution control laws. These regulation-based laws do not require a balancing of benefits and costs, provide trade-offs among controls in various environmental media, or induce efficient levels of control and innovation. The result is inefficiency in all aspects of the pollution control effort. The second explanation, closely related to the first, is that politicians, bureaucrats, emitters' lobbies, and recipients' lobbies act in their own self-interest and do not necessarily pursue the most efficient level of control for society as a whole. The control agency bureaucrat is willing to trade off improvements in environmental quality for a higher discretionary budget. The citizen interest group is willing to give up some improvements in environmental quality for political power and prestige. Others modify social goals accordingly, both at the time of passage of control laws and during their implementation.

In the last two chapters we have explored the advantages and limits of economic approaches to pollution control. At this point you undoubtedly have an alternative in mind that would improve governmental efforts to control pollution — I certainly do. But before we can proceed to design a detailed plan that is an improvement over the existing situation and is politically practical, we need a more detailed understanding of the political process of passage and implementation of pollution laws. To ensure that the system embodied in your new pollution law is the system you envisioned, you must anticipate the goals and incentives of significant parties to the legislative process. To ensure that the law will work as you anticipate, you must take into consideration, while designing your law, the process of implementation and the incentives individuals will feel to act in their own self-interest while implementing that law. In the next three chapters we will study the passage and implementation of existing pollution control laws in an effort to learn more about these design considerations.

PASSAGE OF A POLLUTION CONTROL LAW

In this section we will discuss the passage of federal pollution control laws, with special emphasis on the Clean Air Act of 1970. Passage of this Act marked the beginning of a new era of major federal involvement in environmental issues. It also marked the beginning of a new era of social regulation on several fronts, including occupational safety and health. We will focus on pollution legislation, but the lessons are applicable to other social regulation as well.

Perceived Benefits and Shifting Costs

When considering a proposal, a legislator goes through a personal benefit/cost analysis. Benefits and costs can come in many forms, but they generally focus on the reactions of the politician's constituents. A politician who wants to be re-elected or elected to a higher office will consider how the proposed legislation will affect various groups of constituents. Winning the support of groups requires that the politician gain passage of legislation that benefits his constituency. The politician will, at the same time, seek to avoid imposing costs on large groups of constituents. Organized efforts to unseat a politician because of costs imposed by legislation can seriously threaten a re-election campaign. It pays a politician to maximize the benefits, or at least the perceived benefits, of public programs to one group (the recipients) and to minimize the perceived costs to the other group (the emitters). It is not possible to do both simultaneously, but the politician will seek the combination that maximizes his or her self-interest. Voters react according to their perceptions, not necessarily according to reality. An accomplished politician can take advantage of this fact.

The goal of maximizing perceived benefits and minimizing perceived costs to constituents can be achieved in several ways. One is to design legislation so that benefits appear large and immediate while costs appear small and remote. Another is to have others pay the costs. A third way is to leave the determination of who pays the costs up to someone else, usually the agency in charge of implementing the new law. A fourth way is to cause the benefits to be concentrated on a specific group while spreading the costs over a large portion of the population, as is often the case with special interest legislation. All these techniques were used in designing the Clean Air Act of 1970.

Legislators are not the only ones who propose new laws. Government agencies and the office of the president are active on Capitol Hill. It is not uncommon for an agency to write a proposed legislative package that it will administer if it is passed. Various interest groups also become involved in writing legislation. In all these cases, the proposed legislation is introduced by a legislator who is convinced that the legislation will benefit his political future. No matter the origin, the legislation will be designed to maximize the perception that there are large benefits to be gained from its passage, while fostering the perception that costs are small and paid by someone else.

This does not imply that politicians or others involved in the passage of pollution control laws are money-hungry or seek to impose costs on others to their own advantage. It is perfectly consistent for an individual politician to be sincerely interested in furthering social well-being as he perceives it and to use the misperceptions of others to obtain that altruistic goal. I am not suggesting that politically active individuals acting in their own self-interest are any different from you or me. They may very well have lofty motives. Whether their motives are lofty or base, the incentives presented by the current political structure induce the same type of behavior.

Distribution of Costs and Benefits in the Passage of the Clean Air Act of 1970

The groundwork for the 1970 Act was laid in the passage and implementation of the Clean Air Act of 1967, which was in reality a set of amendments to the original Clean Air Act of 1955, although the 1955 Act had been amended and expanded numerous times before 1970. The 1970 Amendments, then, reflect both the new ideas and concerns of Congress and the administration and the old successes and failures of previous legislative efforts.

The unchanged purpose of the Clean Air Act is to "protect the health and welfare" of the public. The original 1955 Act and all the succeeding sets of amendments emphasize as a basic principle the central role of the states in establishing an air quality control program. Initially, the federal role was seen as gathering and disseminating information. As the external effects of state policies on other states became more obvious, the federal role was expanded to one of coordination of control efforts, and finally to federal preemption. Congress demonstrated increasing impatience with the states for failing to take faster, more aggressive action. The states were criticized for not establishing control regions, emission standards, and air quality standards in a timely fashion. These perceived inadequacies were used to justify a progressive federalization of the control process. In the 1967 Act the law could still be described as "cooperative federalism," but the federal government had assumed the power to define the role of the states and some authority to force the states to fulfill it.

The 1970 Amendments followed the basic format of the previous legislation, but modified its content in two significant areas. First, the 1970 Act strengthened and clarified the 1967 provisions on air quality control regions, air quality standards, and state-formulated implementation plans. Air quality control regions and air quality standards were now to be set at the federal level. The states were required to produce plans, called State Implementation Plans (SIPs), to meet these national air quality standards for each control region by 1975, or 1977 at the latest. The failure of a state to produce an acceptable SIP would be met with a federal takeover of the responsibility. The intent was to force the states to take action to control pollution, and to do so by the specified date. The 1970 Act also provided for citizen enforcement, so EPA could not avoid the takeover requirement. This mechanism for forcing action provides the appearance of immediate and unavoidable benefits; but as we will see later, appearances can be deceiving.

The second significant departure from the 1967 Act was the provision that EPA set emission standards for all new stationary sources. Previously, states set these standards. The result was vastly different control requirements among states. The argument for national emission standards presented during the debate on the 1970 Act was that industry could use the different standards to blackmail states into lowering control requirements by threatening to move to another state. But this seems implausible. It is difficult to imagine that a firm would close down a plant worth billions of dollars to save a few million in pollution control expenditures. In reality, this provision served an important political function reducing the growth potential of the South and West in order to protect the Northeast and Midwest.

These two major provisions of the 1970 Act, the date certain provisions with mechanisms for forcing action and the performance standards for new sources, effectively allowed costs to be shifted from the federal politicians to the states and EPA while retaining the appearance that Congress had provided the benefit.[1] In proposing SIPs, state officials and politicians would incur substantial political costs from having to tell powerful industries that they would have to control at substantial cost. Virtually no cost would be imposed on national politicians, though. Members of Congress could always claim that the state was imposing those costs and hint that there were other alternatives. The costs of stringent controls in Los Angeles became obvious when a proposed SIP called for gas consumption to be reduced by 90 percent. California's Democratic Senator John Tunney suggested (somewhat inaccurately) that these high costs could be avoided if the automobile manufacturers would clean up new cars.

The air pollution issue provided a convenient vehicle for building a procontrol constituency, and Democratic Senator Edmund Muskie of Maine made use of this opportunity. By "guaranteeing," through the action-forcing mechanism, that the nation would have clean air by 1977, Senator Muskie was able to confer large perceived benefits on all citizens, especially organized proenvironmental citizen groups. Citizen interest groups (CIGs) and federal bureaucrats, as well as federal politicians, would certainly favor the shifting of the political costs of proposing controls to the state level.[2]

The action-forcing mechanism gave CIGs a cost-effective means of applying pressure to the state agencies. If the state did not act, EPA would take over. If EPA did not take over as required, the CIGs could (and did) sue EPA for failure to perform a nondiscretionary

---

[1] This discussion draws on P. B. Downing and G. L. Brady, "Constrained Self-Interest and the Formation of Public Policy," *Public Choice* 34 (1975): 15–28.

[2] A citizen interest group is a voluntary membership organization of private citizens seeking a common goal, in this case pollution control. They presumably represent the public interest, but we shall see in Chapter 12 that this is not the case. They are biased toward improved environmental quality.

duty. This was accomplished through a new provision of the Act, Section 304, which permits any citizen to sue EPA to force it to fulfill its nondiscretionary duties. In this way the CIGs obtained a tougher antipollution law than had been possible through political efforts at the state level. In exchange, federal politicians obtained the support of proenvironmental CIGs.

Another argument for the political advantage of including a federal preemption provision might also be advanced. It is possible that state agency personnel might favor the federal legislation, although they could not reveal this publicly. A state agency bureaucrat might favor stringent control of emissions, for example, but feel constrained by state politics. Reasons for this support might include the state bureaucrat's desire to obtain a larger budget or more power to control emissions. For these reasons, the state bureaucrat might favor a federal law imposing a countervailing threat of federal preemption of state activities. In the end, a compromise solution might emerge in which the state bureaucrat obtained a higher level of control than would have been the case in the absence of the federal role. Dealing with the federal preemptive threat might also lead to "defensive" action by legislators to increase the budget and staff of the state agency. In addition, a provision in the federal law provided federal money for state implementation efforts, thus increasing the state bureaucrats' support of the federal law.

Bureaucrats at the federal level also stood to be net gainers from the new law. The 1970 Act represented a major shift in emphasis from its antecedents. It was no longer necessary for the federal regulators to wait for the states to produce air quality standards and then come up with suitable control strategies to meet the standards. A state's failure to act expeditiously placed EPA in the position of having to preempt the state's control activities. A shift of intergovernmental rights gave the federal agency many tasks that had previously been vested in the states, among them the important task of setting air quality standards. These additional responsibilities permitted an expansion of budget and employment levels, and an increase of power for the federal bureaucracy.

John Middleton, in his role as head of the National Air Pollution Control Agency (NAPCA, a precursor agency to EPA), lobbied actively for an increased federal role. He endorsed the action-forcing provisions in the 1970 Amendments. But when Democratic Senator Thomas Eagleton of Missouri advocated requiring the states to meet air quality standards by 1975, Middleton mounted strong opposition to this date certain approach. Adoption of the date certain provisions would mean that, should the states falter, Middleton would be left to bear the costs of trying to achieve the air quality goals NAPCA had set under the 1967 Act. These goals required very stringent control of stationary and mobile sources of pollutants and a reduction in automobile driving of at least 75 percent in most major urban areas. It is reasonable to assume that Middleton knew it would not be possible to clean up the air to this extent by 1975, and that he would bear substantial political costs for the failure. He did, however, stand to achieve substantial net gains through the concomitant expansion of his budget and power, and the day of reckoning was more than five years away.

Even before debate on the 1970 Amendments was initiated, Middleton appeared to be attempting to build a constituency supporting stringent air quality standards in the development of SIPs and, ultimately, the federalization of the control effort. NAPCA made grants to various national organizations to conduct air quality workshops in major cities during 1969 and 1970. The program had three announced goals. First, it was to increase political pressure on the states to submit adequate air quality standards under the 1967 Act. Second, it was seen as a means of increasing citizen support for NAPCA's goal of air pollution control sufficient to protect public health. Finally, it was to promote more extensive and informed citizen participation in pollution control policy. Given these general objectives, the program sought first to stimulate public participation at the air quality hearings (required in the 1967 Act) and then to encourage the formation of local coalitions capable of monitoring the long and complex process of implementing the standards. In short, rather than seeking scattered support from the general public, NAPCA attempted to mobilize support from specific segments of the population. Nor was this effort exclusive to NAPCA. Members of Senator Muskie's staff were reported to have participated in some of the workshops.

The net effect of the NAPCA program is not clear, but its true intent comes through in testimony by Frank Partee, technical director of the Kentucky Air Pollution Control Commission, at the 1972 Oversight Hearing. He testified as follows:

> As the time for public hearings (required in the 1967 Act) approached, this NAPCA involvement with citizen groups which earlier had been so constructive, took on another color. Representatives were sent by NAPCA, out of its Washington offices. These representatives often appeared without knowledge of State officials and even without knowledge of NAPCA's own regional offices.

They carried a strange message. They said, *"Don't trust your State agency. It won't act in your best interest."* People were coached on how to present testimony, and opinion was prejudiced against State proposals even before they were publicly released.³

NAPCA even took its argument to Congress. Middleton had some of the NAPCA-funded CIGs send telegrams to Senator Muskie during the hearings before the passage of the 1970 Act. The telegrams complained of CIGs having been excluded from state hearings on the setting of air quality standards.

Regional Development and Passage of the 1970 Act

The narrow distribution and immediate impact of benefits and the widespread and distant nature of costs provide opportunities for political entrepreneurs to develop special interest legislation like the Clean Air Act of 1970. A coalition of people with similar interests can design laws that confer benefits on some special interest while imposing costs on some other group. The law must be designed so more legislators benefit than lose. Under majority rule it is possible to pass a law that produces more costs than benefits. Suppose a legislative body consists of ten people and six of them gain a benefit of ten dollars each from a particular law. That law could be adopted even if the remaining four legislators bore a cost of forty dollars each. Such a situation may have taken place in the passage of the Clean Air Act of 1970 and its 1977 Amendments.

The introduction of performance standards for new sources in the 1970 Act substantially increased the cost of new industrial development in the relatively unpolluted and rapidly developing areas of the Sunbelt. These additional costs had the effect of reducing the incentive for industries to relocate from the Northeast and Midwest. At the same time, rapidly developing rural areas would be disadvantaged relative to the old, established urban centers. We could expect political support for this provision to come primarily from the advantaged regions.

There cannot be a direct empirical test for the 1970 Act, because virtually all senators and representatives voted for the bill, reacting to the national sense of the urgency of environmental improvements. The amendments to the law proposed in 1976 and adopted in 1977, however, dealt explicitly with regional develop-

---

³ U.S. Senate, Committee on Public Works, *Oversight Hearings*, 92nd Cong., 2nd sess., February 16, 1972, p. 168.

ment. The issue revolved around the provision of nondegradation in areas already cleaner than the federal law required. If these areas were allowed to deteriorate, the cost of new industrial development would be lower than if deterioration were strictly controlled. In a study of legislative voting on the nondegradation amendments to the Clean Air Act in 1976 and 1977, B. Peter Pashigian shows that the overwhelming support for these issues came from the Northeast and Midwest, while southern and western legislators did not favor them.[4] More than 79 percent of the representatives and 90 percent of the senators from the Northeast favored the proposed nondegradation legislation in 1976 and 1977. Support from the Middle Atlantic and East North Central areas was somewhat lower, but still a majority. Support from the South Atlantic, East South Central, and West South Central was generally less than 30 percent, with a low of 10 percent. This provides strong empirical support for the regional self-interest hypothesis.

In comparing the votes of urban and rural representatives, Pashigian also finds substantial support for the hypothesis. Comparing votes of representatives from areas with high and low densities of development (a proxy for urbanization), he found that fewer than 34 percent of the ones from the areas of lowest population density supported the nondegradation amendments. Even in highly developed states in the Northeast and Midwest, the majority of representatives from the more rural areas did not favor nondegradation provisions overwhelmingly.

As further evidence that the Clean Air Act of 1970 has a substantial negative impact on development in the Sunbelt, Pashigian compares the costs of air pollution abatement per $1,000 of value added in various census regions. He finds that the East South Central, West South Central, Mountain, and Pacific regions bear a higher than average cost burden, but the Northeast and Midwest bear a lower than average burden. Comparing the cost burden to regional voting in Congress is particularly instructive. The New England area bears a cost per $1,000 of value added that is only 39 percent of what the nation as a whole bears. Its senators and representatives, led by Senator Muskie, were virtually unanimous in favoring nondegradation.

[4] B. Peter Pashigian, *The Political Economy of the Clean Air Act: Regional Self-Interest in Environmental Legislation* (St. Louis: Center for the Study of American Business, Washington University, 1982).

It would appear that a political coalition was formed among politicians in developed areas to impose differentially higher pollution control costs on the less developed and rapidly developing areas of the Sunbelt. It would appear that the purpose of this coalition was to reduce competition from these areas and to save jobs and profit for the older, declining industrial areas. Note that as a result the marginal cost of control in relatively dirty areas is lower than in newly developing areas. This is in direct contradiction to what one might expect if the provisions of the Act were based on economic efficiency.

IMPLEMENTING THE CLEAN AIR ACT

Once a law has been passed it is still subject to political maneuvering. The legislature must provide funds to implement the act. An agency (or agencies) must act to put the rules into force and to ensure compliance with their provisions. During this implementation process, the give-and-take of political activity continues. At some points, decisions critical to particular interests are made. It pays for those interests to become active when these critical decisions are being debated. After the decision is made they can spend their scarce resources pursuing other critical decisions rather than following this one to its conclusion. Other groups will find another point or points in the process critical and will be active then. The result is a continual shift in the actors affecting the implementation of a policy. Each group, acting in its own self-interest, will pick those points in the implementation process that tend to maximize its ability to change the outcome in ways it deems favorable. The implementation of the Clean Air Act of 1970 is a case in point.

One of the first events required by the action-forcing mechanism of the 1970 Act was the proposal of federal air quality standards. EPA proposed an oxidant standard of 0.06 ppm, the level suggested by NAPCA before the passage of the Act. This proposed standard met with considerable opposition, particularly from the California Air Resources Board (CARB). CARB argued that there were no demonstrated health effects below 0.10 ppm. The Criteria Document issued by NAPCA, which summarizes and evaluates existing research on the adverse health and welfare effects of pollutants, appeared to be in substantial agreement with the CARB argument.

Why, then, was the 0.06 figure chosen? Our self-interest perspective yields substantial insights into the emergence of this decision. First, recall that before the passage of the 1970 Act, Middleton was apparently attempting to build a constituency for a federal role through NAPCA funding of CIGs. To gain the support of California-based CIGs and to put pressure on CARB to adopt more stringent air quality standards under the 1967 Act, NAPCA had to look tougher than CARB. It makes sense that Middleton advocated a tougher air quality standard than the one already in effect in California in order to accomplish this task.

By previously committing the federal agency to a stringent standard, Middleton made it difficult for EPA to back down without losing the constituency he had built. Furthermore, the 1970 Act created an additional incentive to be tougher than California. If EPA adopted a standard less stringent than California's, EPA's power to affect control policy in California would be significantly reduced. Any SIP submitted by CARB that showed compliance with its own standard would easily demonstrate compliance with the federal standard. EPA would have no choice but to accept it without change. In doing so it would forfeit the power to affect the choice of policy options in California, the state with the most severe oxidant problem and the source of most of the citizen support for the federalization of pollution control activities.

The potential for loss of control in California also explains the consistently pessimistic assessment of technical options by EPA analysts, who repeatedly claimed that technology already in use was not proven.[5] Given the action-forcing mechanism, the more pessimistic the EPA stance on the effectiveness of control efforts, the more control would be required to meet any standard. Hence EPA could obtain the power to dictate the state's control policy. The ability to reject SIPs and the threat of federal preemption represented a significant augmentation of EPA's bargaining power. By defining the problem pessimistically, EPA increased the scope of its bargaining power with a state. The continued contractual and grant support of the CIG participation program throughout the implementation process was a key element of EPA's bargaining strategy. The promotion — by CIGs under contract to EPA — of the Clean Air Act of 1970 as a binding legal constraint increased the political viability of EPA policies at the state level. During implementation EPA compromised with CARB at a point halfway between its proposed stan-

---

[5] See discussion in P. B. Downing, "Controlling Oxidants in Los Angeles," *Environmental Affairs* 4 (Fall 1975): 707–743.

dard (0.06) and CARBs existing standard (0.10) setting a standard of 0.08 ppm oxidants.

The years 1971 and 1972 may be characterized as an attempt by EPA to transform the 1970 Act from a set of stringent requirements with little discretion into a tool for bargaining with the various states to achieve higher levels of control than the states would have been willing to adopt voluntarily. The pessimistic interpretations of technical factors and the stringent air quality standards created and expanded existing areas over which EPA could bargain with the states. To be able to bargain effectively, EPA had to interpret the 1970 Act as allowing for some degree of flexibility, even though Congress appeared to prescribe the limits of permissible bargaining narrowly. This explains the inclusion of economic and technical feasibility in EPA discussions of the development and approval of SIPs, even though the Act was designed by Congress to take an explicit "cost be damned" approach.[6]

Through the passage of the 1970 Act, EPA acquired real power to affect resource allocation. The power to impose costs on politically powerful groups led to efforts to constrain that power. Through Office of Management and Budget (OMB) review of EPA regulations, President Nixon sought to check and limit EPA's use of power. EPA Administrator Ruckelshaus attempted to retain this power, but was ultimately unsuccessful.[7] Senator Muskie and others attempted to gain the same type of control over EPA. They met with some success, primarily because of their power over legislation and funding. It is important to note that Senator Muskie, in addition to his position on the Public Works Committee, was chairman of the Budget Committee and a leading candidate for the Democratic nomination for president in 1972. A third group, the CIGs, were also engaged in attempts to curtail the use of power by EPA and the states and to increase their relative power. In a case brought by the Natural Resources Defense Council (NRDC), the court ruled that

---

[6] The oxidant standard was made less stringent in 1978 after requests for review from the American Petroleum Institute and the city of Houston. It was argued that EPA had misinterpreted studies of health effects and that the 0.08 ppm standard set in 1971 was not justified. This fact was common knowledge within EPA as early as 1973. See Downing, "Controlling Oxidants in Los Angeles," (note 5). The long delay in acting on this information and the resistance to change within EPA even then suggest the strong symbolic function these standards serve. For an insider's discussion of the 1978 revision, see L. White, *Reforming Regulation* (Englewood Cliffs, N.J.: Prentice-Hall, 1981), Chapter 4.

[7] For a discussion of the politics involved, see J. Quarles, *Cleaning Up America* (Boston: Houghton Mifflin, 1976), pp. 79ff.

sources and states cannot agree to individual changes or delays (variances) in emission control after EPA has approved a SIP. In another case, NRDC was successful in reducing its costs by forcing all court reviews of SIPs to be held in the U.S. Court of Appeals for the District of Columbia. This accomplished another goal, in that this court had traditionally been more sympathetic to the environmental cause than had other circuit courts.

EPA's efforts to establish grounds for and constraints on permissible bargaining with the states, and politically motivated attempts to place constraints on EPA, were abruptly halted in their early stages by CIG action in the court case *Riverside* v. *Ruckelshaus*.

Shortly after the passage of the 1970 Act, CARB adopted the attitude that key provisions of the Act were totally unreasonable and that it would not ask the people of California to comply with such a law. CARB submitted a SIP that argued that the air in Los Angeles would never be as clean as the federal air quality standard. EPA had no choice but to reject the SIP. They gave CARB six months, however (until February 15, 1973) to submit a revised SIP.

According to the 1970 Act, disapproval of the initial SIP submitted by California shifted the responsibility for correction of deficiencies to the federal level. In *Riverside*, the court held that EPA had failed to perform a nondiscretionary duty and was required to adhere to the statutory requirement to promulgate a SIP for Los Angeles. The court ruling meant that EPA threats were no longer a viable means of "encouraging" the states to produce more effective plans. The court required EPA to produce an acceptable SIP. It produced a plan that required stringent controls of mobile and stationary sources and reducing gas consumption by more than 80 percent. After EPA proposed the gas rationing plan in 1973, CARB's opposition became politically viable because the costs of EPA policies became clear to the residents of California. The political pressure was removed from CARB and placed instead on EPA. And the shifting of pressure was in large measure the result of previous EPA decisions. In an effort to gain power over CARB decisions, EPA had interpreted scientific studies pessimistically. This decision had the effect of translating the task of controlling oxidants in Los Angeles and other major cities across the country from a difficult but achievable task to a totally unreasonable requirement. Furthermore, the institutional structure of the Act made it a mandate.

It is interesting to note that the group that helped obtain the augmentation of power for EPA eventually caused EPA to have to exercise its power unwillingly. One of several significant provisions,

Section 304, was inserted into the 1970 Act during the final stages of passage. One might argue that it proved to be the most significant section of the Act, because it laid the institutional foundation for the Act's failure. It was the actions of CIGs, acting in their own self-interest, that killed the Act. The action-forcing provisions of the Act provided that opportunity. CIGs sought to increase their property rights to clean air by imposing control costs on a reluctant CARB and Los Angeles County Air Pollution Control District (LACAPCD). The result of the ensuing litigation was the opposite. Those costs were imposed on EPA, which was expected to be their benefactor. Defensively seeking to retrieve its bargaining stance after it promulgated the Los Angeles SIP, EPA argued that the state would have to enforce the SIP. EPA reasoned that requiring the state to enforce the plan would create an incentive to produce a reasonable alternative to the EPA version. This last attempt to shift the decision-making costs to the state failed, however. The plan promulgated by EPA was sufficiently stringent that CARB could obtain political support by openly fighting its imposition. CARB's attempt to shift the burden imposed by EPA came to fruition in *EPA* v. *Brown*.

In *Brown*, the court ruled that CARB need not enforce the SIP, thus placing all the costs back on EPA. Because the costs were politically unbearable, EPA chose to violate the requirements of the Act openly. Finally, the CIGs realized that they were powerless to engage either the state or EPA in further litigation to require implementation and enforcement of the SIP, even though EPA was in violation of the mandate of *Riverside*. The Clean Air Act of 1970 was dead — killed by the self-interest that had shaped it. The decision-making power was returned to the states, where it had been before the passage of the 1970 Act. Attempts to resurrect EPA's power to affect decisions took the form of a new act, the Clean Air Act of 1977.

The new Act did not solve the basic political problem. At the legislative level, the same sorts of actors were involved again who were the principals in the design of the 1970 Act. EPA argued for more discretion and relief from the action-forcing provisions of the law. Firms, now realizing more fully the potential costs of the Act, provided organized resistance. The costs were made more obvious by the SIPs, many of which included gasoline rationing and severe restrictions on private automobile travel in large urban areas. Provisions that imposed large costs on developed urban areas were relaxed or delayed. At the same time the nondegradation provisions, which controlled regional competition for growth and jobs, were strengthened. But the basic structure of the law remained the same. The approach is regulatory, with only passing reference to economic efficiency.

The story does not stop here. The 1977 Act and newly proposed environmental legislation is subject to the same self-interested actions and political maneuvering.[8]

COMPLEX BARGAINING

In this brief discussion of the incentives individuals face when contemplating the passage and implementation of a pollution control law, we have seen a complex interactive process taking place over time and among a continually shifting set of actors. This process might be termed bargaining. I do not mean that all of the involved parties sit down across a table and bargain until an agreement is reached, although this sometimes happens. Rather, the bargaining process is more subtle and indirect. Suppose a federal policy-maker is contemplating a performance standard for new sources. How might he or she develop this standard? The first step would be to collect relevant data on the technology of control, the costs and benefits of control, and the economic effect of the possible regulations on the industry.[9] This information is produced by consulting firms and in-house researchers, both of which depend on the firms being regulated for much of their basic data. This provides the regulated firms with an opportunity to influence the outcome. By strategic release of data they can attempt to influence the agency's decision. It pays for the firms to make control look as expensive and technically difficult as possible. At the same time, it pays for proenvironmental groups to present data that makes the costs look small and the benefits large. Information is not the only indirect bargaining tool. Attempts to influence budget, or at least threats to do so, can alter an agency's behavior. A politically appointed bureaucrat is especially vulnerable to the possibility of removal or reduction of authority. In short, there are many subtle and indirect ways to influence the implementation process. In Chapter 1, I summarized

---

[8] For another recent view of this passage-and-implementation process, see B. Ackerman and G. Hassler, *Clean Coal/Dirty Air* (New Haven, Conn.: Yale University Press, 1981).

[9] This process is analyzed in A. Krupnick, W. Magat, and W. Harrington, "Understanding Regulatory Decision-Making: An Economic Approach," *Policy Studies Journal* 11 (September 1982): 44–54.

some of these as reasons the current system has not performed as well as had been hoped. In Chapter 6, I added more detail in discussing ways to change control efforts after a law is passed. I also showed an example of group activity affecting the demand for and supply of agency budget. We will look at the choices facing one group interested in changing an agency's behavior, the proenvironmental citizen interest group, in the next chapter.

Before leaving the subject of complex bargaining, it is useful to point out that this is not a unique result of the American system of implementing pollution control. In a series of studies of implementation of pollution laws in various countries, every author, whether discussing the situation in one country or in several countries, pointed out the phenomenon of complex bargaining.[10] The institutional details and the primary actors differ from case to case, but the end result is the same. The complex bargaining process inherent in the implementation of pollution laws leads to compromises, which make the final outcome of a policy less control than was originally proposed in the law.

The reason for this universal finding is clear. Federal politicians (or any politicians operating at a national level) have an incentive to promise more control, and therefore more benefits, to procontrol lobbyists than they can possibly deliver. During implementation, costs become more obvious. State and local agencies (or any local governmental actors), reacting to the pressures they feel from the constituents who bear the costs, find it necessary to compromise. This reduces the required level of control for each source. Some sources, being more politically powerful, will have a greater effect on the controlling agency and will receive more lenient standards.

SUMMARY

Political incentives cause federal politicians to select provisions for pollution legislation that promise large benefits and hide costs. Administrators, faced with implementing the resulting laws, attempt to pass the political costs of forcing firms to control on to others, usually state agencies. The state agencies attempt to reduce these costs by compromising with the sources. The result is a lower level of control than was originally promised. At various stages in this proc-

---

[10] See P. Downing and K. Hanf, eds., *International Comparisons in Implementing Environmental Laws* (Boston: Kluwer-Nijhoff, 1983).

ess, different affected groups find it advantageous to become active in the policy-making process. This process of changing policy over time is called complex bargaining.

In previous chapters we have seen that the existing regulatory system, as implemented, is not efficient. Marginal benefits and marginal costs are not equated. Now we know why: Political incentives dictate the estimating of large perceived benefits and hide or ignore costs. Sources are not controlled at efficient levels because the compromise inherent in any political system allows some sources to have a greater ability to affect policy in ways they find favorable. In other words, political compromise makes the divergence from an efficient outcome almost inevitable under the regulatory approach. It remains to be seen whether an alternative approach, based on an economic incentive system, will overcome this difficulty.

STUDY QUESTIONS

1. We have described the self-interest that motivated politicians, bureaucrats, procontrol lobbyists, and anticontrol lobbyists in the passage of previous legislation. If a new pollution control law were being considered today, how would you expect self-interest to affect the political actions of these groups?
2. The benefits and costs of attempting to influence pollution policy differ depending on the type of policy and the location of the policy decision. Discuss which groups are likely to find it advantageous to be heavily involved during passage of a federal law, during the development of federal emission and environmental quality regulations, during state implementation of those regulations, during state or federal enforcement of individual source emission regulations, and during court battles on any of these issues.

SUGGESTED READINGS

1. This chapter summarizes my thinking based on several papers including P. B. Downing, "Controlling Oxidants in Los Angeles," *Environmental Affairs* 4 (Fall 1975): 707–743 and P. B. Downing and G. L. Brady, "Constrained Self-Interest and the Formation of Public Policy," *Public Choice* 34 (1975): 15–28.

2. B. Ackerman and G. Hassler, *Clean Coal/Dirty Air* (New Haven, Conn.: Yale University Press, 1981) reviews the issues surrounding the passage of the 1977 Amendments to the Clean Air Act.
3. R. McKean, "The Unseen Hand in Government," *American Economic Review* 5 (June 1965) develops the self-interest model in government decision-making.
4. B. P. Pashigian, *The Political Economy of the Clean Air Act: Regional Self-Interest in Environmental Legislation*, Publication No. 51 (St. Louis: Center for the Study of American Business, Washington University, 1982) analyzes who voted for air pollution legislation in terms of the geographic interests politicians represent.

12
The Political Economy of Implementation

In previous chapters we have discussed the interactive nature of policy-making. We discussed the balancing of interests and the activity of interest groups in general terms. We discussed the incentives lawmakers have for passing legislation and the complex bargaining that causes policy to be altered during the implementation process, again in general terms. In this chapter we will examine implementation in more detail, first by looking at the decisions of control agencies and then by studying the organization of the pro-control citizens' lobbies.

THE BEHAVIOR OF POLICY-MAKERS

Policy-making can be subjected to the same analysis that we use in analyzing the economic behavior of firms or consumers. In this section the principles of economic analysis are used to explain control agency behavior.

Agency Behavior

Let us first explore the actions available to a control agency. It is useful to distinguish between a federal agency and a state agency. In either case the agency faces costs and constraints and has various policy options, so the general form of a model of their behavior is identical. But state agencies face a different set of opportunities and costs.

Minimizing costs. The control agency has resources available to it with which to affect environmental quality. These resources are depicted graphically in Figure 12.1. They include the laws and legal structure, including precedents (L); the budget, together with constraints on how it can be used (B); and personnel representing a substantial portion of the agency's technical expertise (P). With these resources, the agency will attempt to produce the combination of outputs that will maximize its utility. We will assume for the moment that the agency's sole goal is to maximize its effect on environmental quality.

The agency is not able to improve the environment directly. Only emitters can do so, by controlling emissions. Instead, the agency produces various intermediate outputs which in turn affect the behavior of emitters. The control agency can produce information (I) on the quality of the environment, sources of emissions, the technology of control and its costs, and other relevant issues, and to disseminate this information so as to put pressure on sources to control emissions. Using this information, it can issue regulations (R) specifying emitter behavior. It can negotiate agreements (A) with emitters to move them toward greater or more timely control. It can issue citations (C) and other legal papers to initiate legal action against sources who do not comply readily with its regulations. And it can refer a case to the appropriate legal authority, usually the attorney general, for further legal action (LA) designed to force recalcitrant sources to control.

The agency faces a complex problem of resource allocation. It must decide how to allocate its limited supply of L, B, and P so as to produce the intermediate outputs that will maximize its effect on environmental quality (EQ). The principle is quite simple. The agency would equate the ratio of marginal product of each intermediate output that affects EQ to its respective costs in L, B, and P. This is the same rule firms use to minimize the costs of production. In equating these ratios, the agency would produce the maximum level of EQ for any budget level, with higher budget levels allowing greater levels of control. By varying the budget, the agency could develop a cost function for administering pollution control laws. Such a function, which we shall call the marginal cost of administration (*MCA* in Figure 12.2), represents the lowest possible administrative cost of producing improvements in EQ.

While this process seems simple in theory, it is quite difficult in practice. The agency must control many sources. Each source has its own characteristics and presents its own unique challenge. Some

FIGURE 12.1 Inputs and Policy Outputs of Control Agencies

The goal of the pollution control agency is to produce the final outputs listed on the right. To do this, it has the inputs listed on the left available. It cannot, however, produce its output goals directly. Instead it can produce various intermediate outputs, which stimulate others to behave in ways that will produce its final output goals.

Inputs	Intermediate outputs	Final output goals
Laws (L)	Information (I)	Environmental Quality (EQ) (often measured by emission reductions or equipment installation)
Budget (B)	Regulations (R)	Political Support for Budget (PSB)
Personnel (P)	Agreements with the Emitter (A)	Political Support for New Legislation (PSL)
	Citations (C)	Legal Precedents (LP)
	Discretionary Spending (DS)	Discretionary Activity (DA)

FIGURE 12.2 Cost of Administering Environmental Laws

The marginal costs of administration (*MCA*) for the control agency represent the least expensive combinations of input resources to produce the intermediate outputs that will generate improved environmental quality. As higher level of environmental quality is sought, administrative costs increase because of the greater difficulty in implementing more stringent and complex regulations. If an agency is a discretionary budget maximizer, the cost of administration will appear to be higher than the true cost (MCA_d being the apparent cost and *MCA* the true cost).

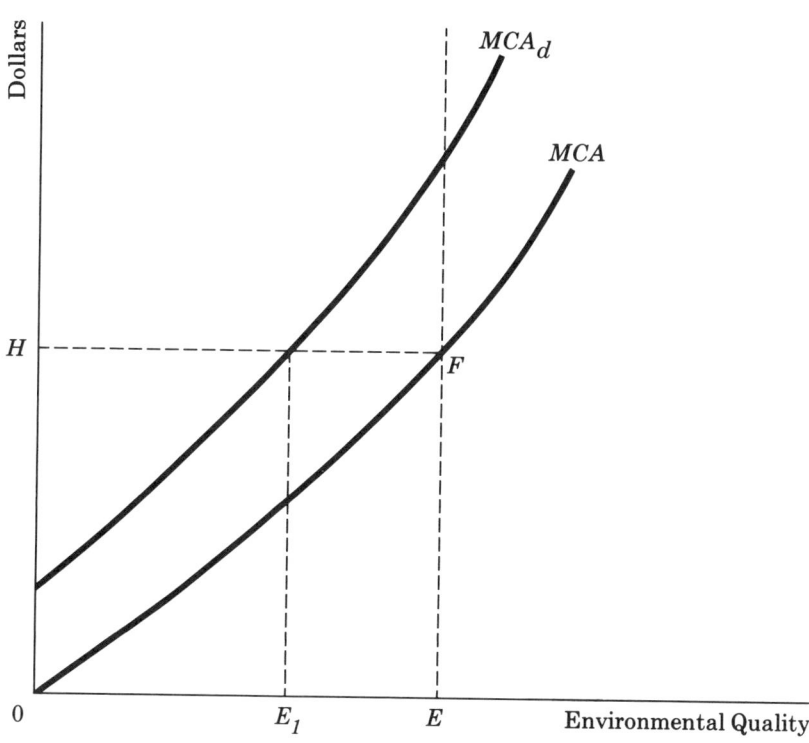

sources comply readily; others prove difficult to deal with. The combination of intermediate outputs that minimizes costs in one case may not in another. This variance requires differentiation of strategies by class of source and perhaps by individual source as well. Second, the productivity of particular intermediate outputs will differ from case to case. Information and regulations may be all that is needed to generate source control in some cases; in others, even the agency spending all its budget on information and regulations would produce no increase in EQ. Third, the cost of producing intermediate outputs varies among sources. This is true for two reasons. The source affects the costs by its reaction to the regulatory effort. A resistant source will cause the agency to have to spend more time and budget resources in order to reach an agreement. At the same time, more detailed study and analysis may be needed to produce effective regulations for this source. In addition, the agency may be constrained politically from employing the most effective methods for obtaining control. Suppose a source was closely connected to the chairman of the legislative committee overseeing the control agency. This political power makes the cost to the agency of certain actions higher. Suppose the source is recalcitrant and the agency contemplates issuing citations and referring the case to the attorney general. Getting the source upset leads to getting the chairman upset, which could lead to less effective laws or a lower budget next year. Political connections affect laws and budget and tend to constrain agency behavior. But the source is not the only interested party with political power. Proenvironmental citizen interest groups (CIGs) attempt to affect the agency's choice of intermediate outputs. The tendency of an agency is to go slow against a politically powerful source, but the CIG will push it to go faster and to require more stringent controls. CIGs affect agency behavior through the courts. As we saw in Chapter 11, in the discussion of the *Riverside* v. *Ruckelshaus* case, a CIG lawsuit can force an agency to take actions it would not otherwise have taken.

All of this leads one to have a great deal of sympathy for the agency bureaucrat, who, armed with a limited budget, faces a large number of diverse sources and all sorts of political and legal constraints. Proenvironmental CIGs are pushing in one direction, sources are pulling in another — and politicians are actively assisting both sides. The balancing act needed to run a control agency successfully is quite incredible.

Discretionary budget. Thus far we have assumed that the goal of the agency bureaucrat is to maximize attainable environmental quality. This may seem logical, but it is contradicted by existing studies of bureaucratic behavior. Bureaucrats are shown in these studies to be primarily interested in personal advancement, individual economic well-being (money), and agency survival — not improved environmental quality. The literature argues that a bureaucrat will seek these objectives through the pursuit of discretionary budget.[1] Discretionary budget is the amount of money expended by the agency in excess of the minimum required to produce the agency's output. We have defined the minimum cost of administering the control program in the above discussion and termed it MCA. If an agency could produce a specific level of EQ according to the MCA function for $1 million but actually spends $1.5 million to produce that level, the additional expense of $500,000 is discretionary budget. This new function is shown as MCA_d in Figure 12.2.

Discretionary budget can be spent in various ways. It can be spent on trips to Hawaii, carpeting, and other personal items generally called the perquisites of office. Or it can be used to generate political support for the agency. This support might be support for budget, support for agency policy, or support for new legislation that increases the power and prestige of the agency, and thus of the bureaucrat.[2] An example of discretionary spending is the grants NAPCA and EPA made to CIGs late in the 1960s and early in the 1970s. This discretionary spending led to more political support for federalization of the pollution control programs in the Act and subsequently to more power and budget for the agency. However these discretionary funds are used, they take resources away from the pursuit of improved environmental quality in the year for which the budget is provided. Bureaucracy theory argues that the bureaucrat will attempt to maximize discretionary budget at the expense of agency output.

One might ask why an agency can operate with a discretionary budget. W. A. Niskanen argues that the bureaucrat has a monopoly over information on the cost function for administering agency programs (MCA).[3] The politicians who oversee the agency have less information, so they are not able to determine if the costs they are presented with (MCA_d) are the least expensive solution to the administrative problem. Consequently politicians assume that MCA_d is the correct cost function, at least according to Niskanen. He also

---

[1] W. A. Niskanen, "Bureaucrats and Politicians," *Journal of Law and Economics* (December 1975).
[2] The bureaucrat can use agency experience as a springboard to a more prestigious or better paying position in government or in the private sector. It is not at all uncommon for the head of a big agency to resign and go to work for a private firm at substantially higher pay.
[3] Niskanen, "Bureaucrats and Politicians."

argues, however, that it is not necessarily in the politician's interest to eliminate the discretionary budget of the agency. Some of the benefit of this discretionary spending can accrue to the politician. Discretionary spending on a CIG in a representative's district, for example, can be used by that representative to gain additional political support. Thus it does not pay for the politician to monitor agency spending too closely. Another reason offered for discretionary expenditure is that most agency heads are not being paid their opportunity cost, the sum they would make in the private economy. It is necessary, therefore, to pay them indirectly through these perquisites of office. Finally, it is not easy to distinguish discretionary spending from efficient spending. It may well be that the availability of a limousine and driver allows the bureaucrat time away from the pressures of office to think about the issues of the day. This may make that bureaucrat more productive, so the net benefit of the expenditure in raising the level of environmental quality is positive.

A counterargument suggests that competition among bureaus will drive discretionary spending to zero.[4] Competition can take the form of takeover bids, where a competitive agency offers to do tasks currently done by another agency at a lower cost than that agency. The reason for the competition is that bureaucrats gain income and power — just the goals Niskanen attributed to bureaucrats — from a larger agency with more responsibility. There can also be takeover bids from outside the bureaucracy. Suppose the agency head pushes discretionary activities too far, so they become obvious. Politicians might seek to replace the bureaucrat with someone who will waste fewer resources (or at least appear to waste fewer) because of the political pressure generated by others who favor more output from the agency or who want to use the funds that will be freed up for other purposes. Proenvironmental CIGs would find it advantageous to resist discretionary spending, because resources currently being wasted could be used to improve environmental quality. For the same reason, anticontrol firms would find it advantageous to encourage wasteful discretionary spending, which reduces pressure on them to control.

While these competition theories are a useful modification of the discretionary budget maximization hypothesis, they do not solve the basic problem. Individuals outside the agency cannot have the qual-

---

[4] A. Breton and R. Wintrobe, *The Logic of Bureaucratic Conduct* (New York: Cambridge University Press, 1982).

ity of information the bureaucrat has. These outsiders are not as capable of determining what are necessary expenditures as is the agency. Thus they are at a competitive disadvantage. This suggests that the bureaucrat will be able to pursue discretionary budget, but will be constrained by outside pressure.

Goal trade-offs. We now have two distinct and contradictory theories of how a bureaucrat will behave: environmental quality maximization and discretionary budget maximization. I believe that bureaucrats in fact compromise between these goals. In other words, they are led by self-interest or by the feedbacks in the system to a trade-off between these goals. To show this, I will develop an alternative model of bureaucratic behavior.

The trade-off central to this model is depicted in Figure 12.3, where the horizontal axis represents the attainable level of environmental quality and the vertical axis represents discretionary activity, or the nonenvironmental activities mentioned above. For any specific total agency budget, the agency could produce some maximum level of environmental quality. We depict this quantity as E. It represents a point on the MCA curve because it is the least expensive combination of inputs needed to produce improvements in environmental quality. (This point is designated as F in Figure 12.2.) As the bureaucrat spends resources on discretionary activity, the amount of such activity increases while the amount of improvement in environmental quality declines, moving along the budget line DE. Note that at some low level of environmental quality (E_0) the budget line becomes horizontal. At this point, low levels of agency performance are likely to lead to dismissal of the bureaucrat. In other words there is a limit to any bureaucrat's ability to produce discretionary activity, and that limit falls at a point where the agency is still producing some improvements in environmental quality.

Now suppose the bureaucrat gains utility from both improvements in environmental quality and discretionary activity, so he or she is willing to trade off between these two goals. This willingness to trade off is represented by an indifference curve (I), which traces a locus of combinations of discretionary activity and improvements in environmental quality that make the bureaucrat equally well off. The point of tangency between I and DE designated as (G) is the combination of discretionary activity and environmental improvements that maximizes the bureaucrat's utility. Note that something less than the maximum level of environmental quality is

FIGURE 12.3 Control Agency Output Choices

The agency head has preferences for environmental quality and for discretionary activity represented by indifference curve I. Her budget constraint is DE, which is a 45° line to the right of E_0, because every dollar spent on environmental quality is a dollar lost to discretionary activity. At a point like E_0, the agency head cannot increase discretionary activity without risking removal from office. The agency head will maximize her own utility by devoting budget resources to produce E_1 and D_1.

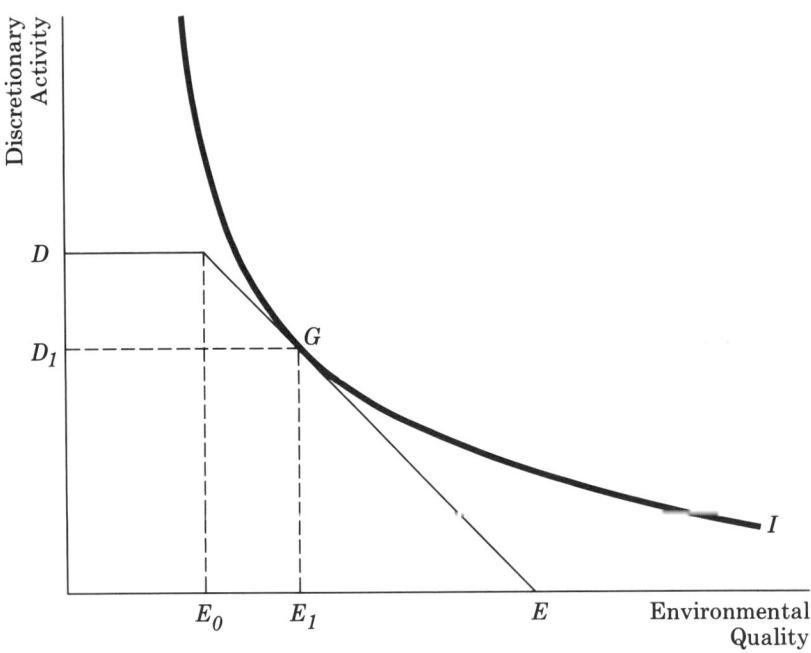

produced. Referring to Figure 12.2, this output represents a point above the minimum marginal cost of administration (*MCA*). Thus at a given cost of $0H$ the agency is producing environmental quality at E_1 instead of E. This makes *MCA* appear higher than it actually is. We could vary the size of the budget and trace out combinations of discretionary activity and environmental improvements that would be produced given the type of trade-off depicted in Figure 12.3. The result would be the new, higher curve in Figure 12.2, which we designate as MCA_d (the subscript indicates the inclusion of discretionary spending). The distance between MCA_d and MCA represents discretionary spending.

We have assumed that the bureaucrat wants (gets utility from) improvements in environmental quality as well as increases in discretionary activity. This is not necessary to obtain the result that the bureaucrat will choose a combination between E_0 and E. Let us look first at a pure discretionary budget maximizer. If the bureaucrat truly obtained no utility from environmental quality, his indifference curves would be horizontal lines. Maximizing utility would lead the discretionary budget maximizer to produce E_0, the minimum level of environmental quality. The bureaucrat's choice may, however, affect the next year's budget. A low level of environmental quality will lead CIGs to mobilize efforts to remove the bureaucrat from office or, failing this, to give the responsibility to another agency. Facing this kind of pressure, politicians will tend to push bureaucrats toward production of more environmental quality. Thus a bureaucrat who wants to maximize discretionary budget but intends to be in the agency next year or intends to use the agency's reputation next year will have a derived demand for environmental quality. In other words, he will behave in the way we have depicted in Figure 12.3.

Now suppose that the bureaucrat is a pure environmental quality maximizer and has no desire for discretionary budget. Her indifference curves would be vertical lines, and the highest utility attainable in this period would be E. But this might not be the most desirable combination if next year's budget is considered. The bureaucrat can allocate some resources this year to producing political support for the agency's budget next year. This means that she is not maximizing environmental quality. Again, the bureaucrat is stimulated by the system to behave as if she has positive preferences for both environmental quality and discretionary activity.

Source Behavior

The problem faced by an emitting source is much like the problem faced by the agency. The firm faces a budget constraint and a set of laws and regulations, and has personnel with which it can produce various intermediate outputs, including emission reductions. These in turn produce the final output of environmental quality. The firm selects among these intermediate outputs on the basis of productivity, costs, and constraints, using the same maximizing rule the agency bureaucrat employs. The goal function of a firm is usually assumed to be to maximize profit. This, we have seen above, is inconsistent with improvements in environmental quality. The broader perspective we are now employing suggests, however, that a firm may be willing to spend some of its resources on items that do not maximize its current profit in order to obtain a higher profit in the future. A profit-maximizing firm might behave as if it had a positive preference for environmental quality in order to preserve profit in the future. The firm would also expend resources in an effort to modify future laws and to reduce the budget of the agency, so as to reduce the effectiveness — and hence the cost to the firm — of agency control requirements.

We introduce this trade-off possibility here for completeness; we will explore firm behavior more completely in the following chapter, in which we discuss the enforcement process.

CIG Formation and Behavior

Every individual who is adversely affected by poor environmental quality has the potential to gain by becoming active in public policy formation. It will be in the interest of the individual to expend resources on political activity to the point where the benefit derived by the individual equals the costs. The costs of being effective in the political debate over environmental policy, however, are high. Because of these high costs, most individuals will not find it desirable to mount an individual effort to influence policy.

As an alternative to independent action, the individual can join a CIG and share the costs. In this way, the nature of political activity as a public good can be partially offset. The policy output of the CIG is available to all people in society, regardless of whether or not they have paid a share of the CIG's costs. When a CIG has a large membership, the costs of political action are reduced and the likelihood of effectiveness is increased, so still more individuals will join. Thus the free rider problem is partially overcome, but not completely solved.

A CIG will attempt to maximize the goals of its members. We can assume that the goal of the members is an improvement in environmental quality. In the same way that the agency and the firms select actions, the CIG will compare the costs and productivity of different options and select the combination of intermediate outputs that maximizes the level of environmental quality. Its efforts can be aimed at affecting a source's emitting behavior directly or indirectly through the control agency and the courts. The intermediate outputs of the CIG include political pressure, court action, bargaining with the agency, and providing information. A CIG bureaucrat may also find it advantageous to give up some environmental quality in this period in order to obtain some political power that can be used later. In other words, CIG behavior is much like agency and source behavior.

Since the goal function of a CIG depends on its membership, we will explore the membership decision in greater detail here.[5] Every citizen has more or less strongly held preferences for improved environmental quality. These preferences are tempered by the actual environmental quality they enjoy and the cost to them of improving that quality. It is possible to think of all individuals in society as being arrayed along a line representing their relative environmental preferences (the strength of their desire for an improved environment). Such an array is represented in Figure 12.4. For convenience we assume that individuals are evenly distributed along this continuum at the level AA. We can designate the actual level of environmental quality as some point on this continuum labeled E. The location we have chosen is to the left of the midpoint of the distribution, so more than half of society would prefer stronger environmental control, while a minority would prefer less control.

Suppose a CIG favoring an improved environment is formed. Who might join such an organization? Clearly anyone who favored less than the current level of quality, such as an individual at L, would not join, because the purpose of the CIG is to move actual quality away from L. Individuals to the right of E are potential candidates, but even they will compare the benefits of joining with the costs of membership. Suppose an individual located at M is considering membership. The benefits he or she receives are a movement to the right of E as a result of CIG activity. The greater the increase in environmental quality and the further away M is from E, the greater this benefit will be. Thus someone at N would get a greater benefit than someone at M, and would be more likely to join the CIG. The benefit also depends on the effectiveness of the CIG, which in turn depends on its size and funding. Thus M is more likely

---

[5] This model of CIG membership is derived from P. B. Downing and G. L. Brady, "The Role of Citizen Interest Groups in Environmental Policy Formation," in M. White, ed., *Nonprofit Firms in a Three-Sector Economy, COUPE Papers on Public Economics,* Vol. 6 (Washington, D.C.: The Urban Institute, 1981).

FIGURE 12.4 Societal and CIG Preferences with Regard to Environmental Quality

Assume that various members of society have various preferences for environmental quality, which range from lower to higher levels of quality and are distributed evenly along the line AA. The median of society's preferences is M. Suppose E is the current level of environmental quality. People with preferences for higher levels will want to move to the right in this range. Some of them will join a proenvironmental organization. Their membership is represented by C, and the median preference of the organization members (N) is to the left of the median for the whole population (M). If they are successful in improving environmental quality (to E'), group membership will decline (to C') and the median preferences of the group will become more extreme (N').

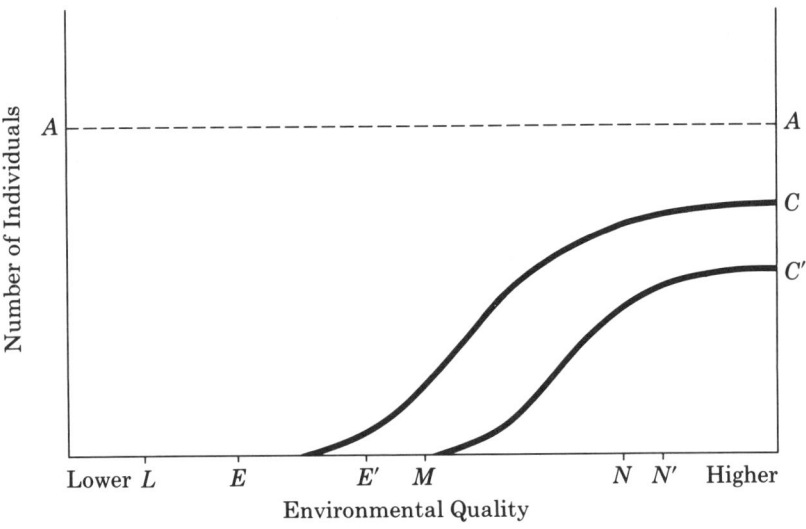

to join a large, well-funded CIG, all other things being equal. The cost of joining the CIG must be compared to this benefit.

If membership costs are lower than expected benefits, the individual at M could gain from joining the group. But that does not mean that he or she will join. Recall that political action to move E is a public good. M will therefore have an incentive to act as a free rider. This incentive will be stronger when net benefits are lower. Consequently, M is more likely to be a free rider than is N.

We can now trace out a distribution of actual members (C). There are no members near E because the cost of membership exceeds the benefit. At some point there is a net gain to joining the CIG, but this net benefit is low, so a large number of potential members act as free riders. As we move to the left, more and more people overcome the free rider tendency and join.

The effect of this economic incentive to join the CIG is that the average member has more extreme preferences for environmental quality than society as a whole. Suppose individual M is exactly in the middle of the social preference for environmental quality. He or she would then represent the position that would be favored over any other if the environmental issue were put to a referendum vote of all of society.[6] A similar vote of the membership of the CIG, however, would produce a preferred environmental quality to the right of M. If group leaders followed the preferences of their membership, they would push for more control than society would prefer. In fact, the leadership of the CIG would probably be even more extreme in their preferences than the membership, because leadership positions take up more time and resources than simple membership and require larger potential benefits to overcome this additional cost.[7] The conclusion we reach from this model of CIG membership is that the members will have greater preferences for improvements than society as a whole, and that the leadership will have still greater preferences. By their very nature, proenvironmental CIGs do not represent the general public.

There is one additional point we should discuss. Suppose the CIG is successful in moving policy and actual environmental quality to the right (E'). This will reduce the potential benefit of membership to all individuals. Some people who were to the right of E find themselves to the left of E' and will not join the CIG. Others, facing lower potential benefits, will have a greater incentive to act as free riders. Thus membership will decline (shown as C' in Figure 12.4) and the median preference of members will move to a more extreme position (N'). This is a phenomenon we observe frequently. CIGs are formed, attract membership, and are successful in moving public policy toward their preferred position. The CIG becomes more extreme in its position, and its membership declines. In some cases the

---

[6] For a discussion of the median voter concept, see R. Wagner, *Public Finance: Revenues and Expenditures in a Democratic Society* (Boston: Little, Brown, 1983), Chapter 4.

[7] M. Olson, *The Logic of Collective Action* (Cambridge, Mass.: Harvard University Press, 1965).

CIG dies from its own success. In other cases it remains active through the formation of counterlobbies.

All this pressure toward improved environmental quality can stimulate anticontrol groups to form an opposing CIG. That is, they form a group of "citizens" to argue that proenvironmental CIGs are not representative of the public and are seeking excessively stringent controls. The further policy is moved toward that preferred by the proenvironmental CIGs, the more incentive there is for anticontrol CIGs to form. Perhaps this is an explanation for the recent rise of corporation-backed political action committees.

INTERACTION AND BARGAINING

Bargaining by its nature implies a give-and-take that reaches an ultimate conclusion. I have characterized this process by using the analogy of balancing a teeter-totter. In this section I develop more fully the process by which such a balance is obtained.

Toward Equilibrium

Each of the three groups discussed above will act politically to affect environmental policy. The principal means of interacting are providing information, either directly or through the news media; political pressure on the agency, directly and through the budget process; direct interaction and bargaining; and court action. These interactions take place over time and were previously illustrated in Figure 6.3.

In the model of group behavior discussed above, we have seen that a group will choose among actions based on costs and productivity. The behavior of other groups can affect these factors. The productivity of a CIG attempting to increase an agency's budget through political pressure depends on both the help it gets from the agency and the resistance it gets from emitters and demanders of other services. The costs of a court case also depend on the expenditures of other groups. The more an opponent spends, the less productive will be a dollar spent by the other side.

This give-and-take was presented as the interaction of the demand for and the supply of control agency budget in Figure 6.4. The total demand for the agency budget (D_T) was shown to be the sum of the demand of the agency (D_A) and the demand of recipients and their lobby (D_R). We now know more about the formation and position of the recipients' lobby (the CIGs) and about their efforts on behalf of the agency budget. They clearly favor a larger agency budget, because even with discretionary spending, increases in budget lead to improvements in environmental quality. The CIG has other opportunities to influence environmental quality. It compares the productivity of support for agency budget per dollar of expenditure with these other opportunities, and equates them at the margin. The demand curve D_R represents the result of this analysis.

The equilibrium budget B^* in Figure 6.4 is the result of the interaction between these demand forces and the groups that resist the budget (emitters and others). To see how a group might react to a change in policy by another group, let us assume that for some reason emitters become more resistant to the agency budget. (This could be because the bureaucrats spent some of their discretionary budget to support a politician unfavorable to business.) This would shift MC_E and MC_T upward. The result would be a lower agency budget. The CIG would react to the change in emitter policy in two ways. A lower budget implies lower environmental quality, so the CIG would find that the potential gain from a budget increase is now greater. At the same time, the greater resistance by emitters would make the productivity per dollar decline. Facing a decline in productivity per dollar, the CIG would find that at the margin it would be advantageous to shift some expenditure away from budget support and to other opportunities, because the marginal productivities of each activity per dollar are no longer equal. The end result of emitter efforts to reduce the agency's budget would be a lower budget, but not so low as might be, because the CIG would increase its efforts (as would the agency) and other CIGs would take action on other fronts, such as in the courts.

It can be seen from this example that the end product of policy formation is the result of a set of very complex reactions. When one group pushes on one aspect of the process, be it budgets or courts, other groups will react on that front and on other fronts as well. The complex bargaining we talked about in Chapter 11 is the result of this reaction to the economics of political action. The interaction of all these forces can lead to a sort of uneasy equilibrium.[8]

Political Benefit/Cost Analysis

Throughout this book we have talked about benefit/cost analysis of environmental quality based on the actual benefits and costs. We

---

[8] P. B. Downing, "A Political Economy Model of Implementing Pollution Laws," *Journal of Environmental Economics and Management* 8 (September 1981): 255–271.

now realize that the political debate is not conducted in these terms. Rather, the meaningful benefits are the benefits to politically active groups, and the relevant costs are those borne by politically powerful emitters.

Let us look first at the demand side. The nature of pollution control as a public good leads individuals to act as free riders, so articulated or effective demand would be systematically below the true demand or MBC. The CIGs partially overcome this free rider problem by providing a relatively inexpensive method of political expression of recipient demand. The politically effective demand of the CIG is based on its membership and budget, but is adversely affected by the free rider problem. The net result is that the recipients' demand is presented in extreme form (D_R in Figure 12.5) as a result of the bias in member preferences, but is underfunded. The agency also favors control and is biased toward more, because increased control implies both more environmental benefits and more discretionary budget. Its estimate of the social demand curve is likely to be biased upward (D_A). The demand function emitters would present (D_E) is biased downward from true demand because less demand means less control and more profit.

The final politically effective demand (D_p) is the weighted average of these demands. It is difficult to know what this average is relative to the true demand. The politically effective demand depends on the relative weights given these different groups in the political process. It is my assessment that at the federal level the political demand is above the true level, while at the state and local level the opposite is often the case.

The politically effective cost function is also potentially different from the true cost function. Recipients will tend to present control costs as low (MC_R) and emitters will tend to present them as high (MC_E) relative to the true MCC. The agency faces an interesting problem. Wishing to increase the level of control and its budget, it will tend to underestimate the true cost of control to emitters. At the same time, its own efforts to obtain discretionary budget increase administrative costs to MCA_d in Figure 12.2. In addition, the inefficient use of regulations causes MCC to be higher than is necessary. The net effect is uncertain, but I feel that at the federal level the net effect is toward overestimating costs (MC_A). The weighted sum of the politically effective cost functions is again indeterminate, but I feel it has been weighted toward overestimation (MC_p). The intersection of the politically effective demand and supply curves could result in an environmental policy more or less stringent than

FIGURE 12.5 Political Benefit/Cost Analysis

Each group involved in policy-making has an incentive to manipulate the environmental benefit/cost analysis in ways that will be more conducive to its preferences. This involves overestimating one factor in the issue and underestimating another. The recipients might, for example, systematically overestimate the benefits of control (D_R instead of D, which is the true benefit) and underestimate the costs of control (MC_R instead of the true cost MCC). They would then argue that the correct policy was E_R rather than the efficient result (E). The emitters, having opposite incentives, underestimate benefits (D_E) and overestimate costs (MC_E), thus concluding that E_E is the preferred policy. The agency has intermediate incentives. The political compromise for costs (MC_p) and benefits (D_p) leads to a policy (E_p) that is not necessarily efficient and which lead to a higher or lower level of environmental quality than is efficient.

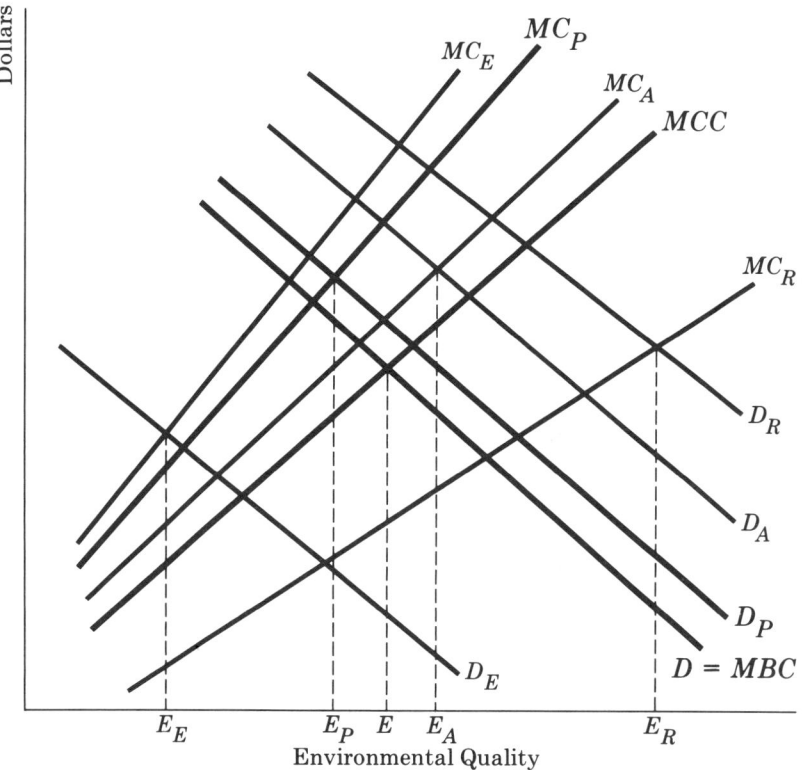

the efficient level. Figure 12.5 represents the politically efficient environmental quality (E_p) at the federal level as lower than the efficient level. I believe this is true in general, but it is not true in all cases. State policy generally leads to control at a lower than efficient level, but even here there are exceptions. Thus while the political rhetoric may be high, the actual level of control is low relative to the efficient level.

There is an interesting feature to political benefit/cost analysis. Each group will seek ways to obtain its own ends. This can be done by carefully designing control requirements to provide benefits to the more politically powerful proenvironmental groups or to reduce the costs of control to powerful emitter groups. Increasing procontrol group benefits shifts D_R and D_p to the right. Reducing costs to some emitters shifts MC_E and MC_p to the right. The end result is that judicious design of policy can move the political equilibrium E_p. The regional and urban support for the Clean Air Act of 1970, which we discussed in the last chapter, is an example of how this political shifting of benefits and costs can affect policy.

An empirical test. A recent study by Bruce Yandle has produced a test of this political economy model of environmental decision-making.[9] As Yandle states, efforts to regulate will be:

1. Less stringent, the greater the number of workers employed in environmentally intensive industries.
2. More stringent, the larger the total income derived from property. (Because land is adversely affected by pollution.)
3. More stringent, the larger the proportion of the manufacturing labor force that is unionized.

Using budget as a proxy for stringency of regulation, he produced a regression showing that factors 1 and 2 are supported by actual experience in pollution control, while factor 3 is not supported by the data. These results confirm the arguments I have made in this chapter. The more powerful polluting industries are and the more they are affected by regulations, the less stringent will be the regulations they face. The more powerful the recipients of pollution are and the more they are adversely affected by pollution, the more stringent regulations will be.

---

[9] B. Yandle, "Economic Agents and the Level of Pollution Control," *Public Choice* 40 (1983): 105–109.

THE ORIGIN AND FUNDING OF CIGs

In the above discussion we examined a model of membership in a CIG, but we did not see how the group was initially formed. It is difficult to start a CIG because the potential benefits to individuals are small and the total benefit, even if large, is widely dispersed over a population. At the same time, the startup costs are high. These two problems can be overcome in one of three ways. A strong central figure, deeply committed to the goals of the CIG, can bear the startup costs. Or a group that wants to produce the political action can finance the startup costs by selling another related product and using the profit. This is called a tie-in sale. Or a group can receive funds from an outside source, such as the government or a private foundation. A study of CIG formation demonstrated that all three of these techniques have been used in the formation of proenvironmental CIGs.[10]

The Friends of the Earth (FOE) is an example of a CIG formed by a powerful and committed individual. FOE was founded in 1969 by David Brower. Brower had left the Sierra Club because of internal policy differences and the loss of the club's tax-exempt status (attributable, it would seem, to his lobbying efforts). Brower had been an important force in developing the Sierra Club's activist stance since he became the Sierra Club's first executive director in 1952. He was also responsible for expanding revenues by developing and marketing Sierra Club products and services. When he left, he took with him at least some of the funding sources he had developed at the Sierra Club.

FOE and the FOE Foundation developed rapidly. It had grown to a membership of 20,000 by 1977, with local branches and state chapters in sixty cities and locations around the country. The FOE Foundation was incorporated separately in 1972 as a tax-exempt and donor-deductible organization to support environmental research. In 1977 FOE had a budget of $670,000, while the FOE Foundation had expenditures of more than $300,000. Members pay dues of twenty dollars per year and receive a biweekly magazine. Members' dues are the primary source of funding for FOE, while the FOE Foundation is supported by both individual contributors and such foundations as the Rockefeller Family Fund.

The Sierra Club was founded in 1892 by John Muir, a renowned

---

[10] Downing and Brady, "The Role of Citizen Interest Groups."

environmentalist and a skilled politician who knew how to marshal public opinion through the press. Throughout its history the Sierra Club has provided a package of recreational benefits in the form of inexpensive retreats, equipment, and meetings on nature preservation. In the 1950s the Sierra Club began to publish books and magazines, which have provided substantial revenues, as has advertising in the club magazine.

In 1976, the Sierra Club had a budget of $6.5 million. Approximately 32 percent of the funding is from the annual membership fee of twenty dollars, which entitles the member to ten issues of the club magazine. The Sierra Club Foundation was incorporated in 1960 and acts as a funding arm for the educational and research activities of the Sierra Club. The Sierra Club Legal Defense Fund (SCLDF) was established in 1970 to pursue policy formation through the courts. In recent years the Ford Foundation made grants of $98,000 (1971), $143,000 (1972), and $192,000 (1974) to SCLDF. The Ford Foundation announced its intention of discontinuing support of public interest law firms in 1974, but it nonetheless provided an additional grant of $85,000 to the Sierra Club Legal Defense Fund in 1976, and continued its funding through at least 1979.

Until the 1960s most of the Sierra Club's 15,000 members were located in California. By 1970 the number of members had grown to 107,000 nationwide, and by 1977 to 180,000. The club is organized into forty-nine chapters and 237 local groups. The Sierra Club spent at least 22 percent of its income in 1978 and 1979 on "studying and influencing public policy" — that is, on lobbying. If "information and education" are included, the total is 56 percent of expenditures. A comparison of expenditures and funding reveals support for the hypothesis that members pay for some lobbying as well as for the private goods they receive. Expenditures on the membership and their share of administrative expenses are far less than members' contributions.[11] Lobbying is supported by membership fees, book revenues, and contributions. Thus the Sierra Club is an example of a CIG funded through tie-in sales. Contributions from the Sierra Club Foundation and the Sierra Club Legal Defense Fund are a major source of its information and lobbying funds. Both of these organizations are constrained from "excess" lobbying. Through contributions

---

[11] Burton Weisbrod, *Public Interest Law* (Berkeley: University of California Press, 1978) reports the results of a survey that indicated that many members joined the Sierra Club to support the environmental preservation effort (the public good) and did not participate in club activities.

to their sister organization, however, they can reduce the effect of this constraint. Both organizations get a large portion of their funds from the Ford Foundation. The implication is that at least some of the Ford money is being used for lobbying, and a substantial portion of the Ford money given to the SCLDF is used for court cases.

The Center for Law in the Public Interest (CLPI) was organized in 1971 using Ford Foundation "seed money." Ford provided about half of the center's $375,000 budget in 1976. In 1976 a direct mail campaign resulted in 3,500 contributions; donations are small, however, compared to foundation support. The center now focuses on other issues, but in the past it played a prominent role in environmental decision-making.

CLPI is one of several prominent national environmental CIGs that received seed money from the Ford Foundation. Others are the Natural Resources Defense Council (NRDC), the Environmental Defense Fund (EDF), and the Center for Law and Social Policy. It is interesting to note that several of the founders of these CIGs, as well as the founders of CLPI, were members of the Yale Law School class of 1969, suggesting that the informational advantage of this association may have facilitated the organization and funding of the CIGs.

The Environmental Defense Fund (EDF) was established in 1967 and achieved early success in having DDT and other insecticides banned. EDF funding of $1.7 million in 1976 came from membership dues and foundations. Approximately 50 percent of its total funding came from the annual dues payments of fifteen dollars from its 45,000 members. The Ford Foundation contributed $300,000 in 1973 and $285,000 in 1976. In 1976, other foundation support came from such sources as the Rockefeller Foundation, the Van Amerigen Foundation, the Bingham Foundation, and the Edna Clark McConnell Foundation.

The National Resources Defense Council (NRDC) was incorporated in 1969 by a group of recent Yale Law School graduates and by several New York lawyers and conservationists. It was started as a nonmembership organization with substantial grants from the Ford Foundation. Now, however, it has a membership of approximately 35,000. For 1978, NRDC had a $2 million budget, of which foundations contributed 75 to 80 percent, with donations and membership dues covering the rest. Seventy-five foundations have contributed approximately $9,000,000 to NRDC over the past ten years. The Ford Foundation, however, has been by far the largest single source of funding. NRDC received $1,075,000 from Ford in its infancy, and another $800,000 in 1974. In 1977 Ford provided $340,000. In 1972,

NRDC received a three-year grant of $450,000 from the Josephine H. McIntosh Foundation for water conservation work. It is interesting to note that for fiscal year 1975, NRDC's litigation budget was $926,204 — out of a total budget of $1,372,012. This suggests that court action was its preferred method of influencing public policy.

The federal government has also become an important source of seed money in the formation of environmental CIGs. The citizen participation program discussed in Chapter 11 was based on the idea that the limited success of past air pollution laws could be attributed to a lack of constituency support for aggressive policies. This lack of constituency support was assumed to be the result of a lack of information and encouragement. To remedy this, EPA and its predecessor organizations provided seed money to encourage national organizations and coalitions to coordinate the activities of their local units, thus building constituency support for EPA policies. The Clean Air Constituency, a Los Angeles based CIG, is one example of a CIG that was specifically set up with such federal money.

The program has developed through three distinct phases. Phase I, conducted under NAPCA from 1968 through 1970, involved grants to a number of prestigious national organizations to hold air quality workshops. NAPCA's objective was to build an adamant antipollution constituency at the local level. Phase II was conducted under the Clean Air Act of 1970, and was a continuation of what came to be known as "the Breather's Lobby." EPA contracted local units of national CIGs or special-purpose CIGs to supply the information necessary for "effective" citizen participation at state implementation plan hearings, workshops, and seminars. A second phase of this program was intended to train local air pollution CIGs to monitor the development and enforcement of state implementation plans by focusing news media attention on polluters and on ineffective state and local control officials. This phase was scrapped in May 1972 in response to opposition from within EPA and from industry. Phase III, the most ambitious part of the program, continued through 1976. CIGs were awarded grants to provide information to local citizens in order to assist in implementing the transportation control strategies promulgated by EPA in thirteen of the most severely polluted cities. These plans were developed by EPA under court orders resulting from the *Riverside* v. *Ruckelshaus* case. During 1974 and 1975 a total of $348,200 was spent on these grants. Some of the transportation control strategies that groups like the Clean Air Constituency were to promote included the following:

1. Gas rationing to cut vehicle miles traveled by some designated amount.
2. Designation of mandatory bus or carpool lanes.
3. Limitations on future construction of off-street parking.
4. Elimination of off-street parking in certain metropolitan areas.
5. Semiannual inspection and maintenance of exhaust systems by specified dates.
6. Altitude modification and tuning specifications for cars in model years 1968 to 1975.

It is important to note that all of these provisions were developed by EPA as replacements for the state implementation plans (SIPs) for these areas, which had been submitted by the states and rejected as inadequate by EPA.

The citizen participation program was terminated by EPA in 1976, but the same sort of activity continued under a different name. In 1978 the National Coalition for Clean Air (NCCA), which has three member organizations — the Sierra Club, Friends of the Earth, and the American Lung Association — received a $200,000 contract from EPA. The contract required NCCA to organize and conduct sixty-five workshops whose purpose was to bring 150 CIGs up to date on the 1977 Amendments to the Clean Air Act and on how they related to local problems.

The formation and operation of CIGs has resulted from strong personalities, tie-in sales, and foundation and government grants. The last sources are somewhat disturbing because of the freedom from membership constraints they allow. In a membership CIG, if the leadership does not pursue policies favored by the membership, the leaders are removed or the membership declines. Through this informal enforcement mechanism at least some relationship is maintained between the CIG's policy and general social preferences. When a CIG is primarily funded by a foundation, it is likely to reflect the preferences of a small set of foundation directors. This is the kind of control of policy that the elitist theory of political activity talks about. Under these circumstances it can hardly be said that a so-called citizen interest group reflects general citizen interest.

Government grants and contracts have much the same effect. Group leaders follow EPA policy (indeed, they are co-opted to do so) because these grants are their major source of funds. In these cases as well it is no longer possible to agree that the CIG represents general citizen preferences. Rather, it represents the interests of the federal bureaucracy in the guise of a "citizen interest group."

SUMMARY

The implementation of pollution control laws can be seen as a complex bargaining process in which each actor seeks to maximize his or her own self-interest but is constrained by the reactions of others. I have argued that each group will have some positive preference for environmental quality and for one other variable. (This has been for the sake of simplicity; there are obviously many elements in the goal function of each individual.) The conclusion that can be reached from this discussion is that each individual will seek to use the system to achieve his or her best interest. This behavior is exactly like what is assumed for the individual consumer maximizing his or her own utility when choosing among consumption choices. I would not argue that one or another group is base, nor would I argue that one or another has superior ethics. In the next chapter we will explore how this model works in the enforcement of pollution laws. Here the focus will be more on firm behavior, which has been neglected, relatively, in this presentation.

STUDY QUESTIONS

1. There are at least two motives for bureaucrats' behavior (narrow self-interest and pure altruism) as well as combinations of these motives. How will the maximizing behavior of bureaucrats be affected by their motives? What effect will this have on pollution control policy?
2. If all these CIGs receive a large proportion of their funding from private foundations, whose interests will they represent? How does this affect the attainment of efficient environmental policy?

SUGGESTED READINGS

1. P. B. Downing, "A Political Economy Model of Implementing Pollution Laws," *Journal of Environmental Economics and Management* 8 (September 1981): 255–271 develops an extended version of the model discussed in this chapter.
2. W. A. Niskanen, Jr., *Bureaucracy and Representative Government* (Chicago: Aldine, 1971) presents the basic model of bureaucracy theory.

3. A. Breton and R. Wintrobe, *The Logic of Bureaucratic Conduct* (Cambridge, England: Cambridge University Press, 1982) offers an alternative model of bureaucratic behavior.
4. P. B. Downing and G. L. Brady, "The Role of Citizen Interest Groups in Environmental Policy Formation" in M. White, ed., *Nonprofit Firms in a Three Sector Economy, COUPE Papers on Public Economics* Vol. 6 (Washington, D.C.: The Urban Institute, 1981) develops a more detailed model of CIG behavior.
5. B. Yandle, "Economic Agents and the Level of Pollution Control," *Public Choice* 40 (1983): 105–109 further develops and tests the self-interest explanation for pollution policy.

13

Enforcing Pollution Control Laws

The complex interactive bargaining that generates pollution control policy continues during the implementation of that policy. The most critical phase of implementation is the enforcement of regulations (or fees) applicable to individual sources. This is the crucial point where emissions are controlled. There is considerable room for further bargaining at this point because of the case-by-case enforcement on highly technical issues and the frequent involvement of confidential "industrial secrets." In this chapter we will explore the process of enforcement in three steps. First we will discuss the economic incentives to control emissions under the enforcement system currently employed in conjunction with the regulatory approach. Then we will discuss this system in practice. Finally, we will use the lessons learned to explore ways a practical economic incentive system might be enforced.

THE ECONOMICS OF ENFORCEMENT

Enforcement is not just a matter of telling polluters that they must control emissions. Economic incentives must be provided before polluters find it efficient to comply. In this section the case of economic incentives to generate compliance is analyzed.

Incentives to Comply

A source facing a regulatory requirement to control emissions will compare the cost of complying with the cost of violating the law and choose the less expensive course of action. There are two kinds of relevant costs. First, the decision to comply or not depends on whether the total cost of noncompliance is higher or lower than the cost of controlling. Second, the decision about what level of emission reductions to maintain depends on the relationship between the marginal cost of controlling emissions and the marginal cost of noncompliance. The key to both the total and the marginal compliance decisions of the source is the effective penalty the source faces.

To understand the effect of penalties on a source's decision to comply with agency regulations, we will again employ the marginal emission reduction cost ($MERC$) function introduced in Chapter 4. Let us suppose that the control agency sets an effluent standard at $\bar{S}$ in Figure 13.1. The firm's efficient level of emissions in the absence of control is B. The total cost of complying with the standard is the area $\bar{S}AB$. To be induced to comply, the source must face a total penalty of at least this amount. Suppose the penalty for noncompliance was P_0 per unit of emissions for all emissions greater than $\bar{S}$. The total cost of noncompliance for the source would be $\bar{S}ACB$, which is greater than the cost of compliance. A rational source would choose to comply because that is the least costly option (assuming the source continues to produce). Now suppose the effective penalty was P_1. The cost of noncompliance would be $SDFB$. But the cost of reducing emissions to J only would be $SDEB$ (a penalty of $SDEJ$ and control costs of EBJ), for a savings of DAE over the cost of full compliance. So a source facing a penalty per unit of P_1 would reduce emissions to J. For a penalty of P_2, it would make sense to reduce emissions only to K. With the fine this low, full compliance would result in extra payments of ALH. Complete noncompliance would result in extra payments of HIB. Controlling until the cost of control per unit equals the penalty per unit results in the lowest possible payment, $SLHB$. For any given fine per unit, it makes sense to control until $MERC$ equals that fine.

There is another possible form of penalty. Suppose that the penalty were lower than P_0 per unit but any level of emissions greater than $\bar{S}$ would make the source liable for a total penalty of the distance $\bar{S}B$ times the per unit penalty, what might be called a flat-fee penalty. It can then be the case that a penalty level can generate either full compliance or zero control. Suppose, for example, that the penalty was P_2 per unit. The total penalty would be $\bar{S}LIB$ for noncompliance while the total cost of compliance would be $\bar{S}AB$. If $\bar{S}AB$ is greater than $\bar{S}LIB$, it will be cheaper for the source to emit at B and pay the penalty. It will not pay to control at some intermediate level since the total penalty $\bar{S}LIB$ will be incurred regardless of

FIGURE 13.1 Economic Incentives to Comply with an Effluent Standard

To provide an effective incentive to comply with an emission standard ($\bar{S}$), an agency must assess a penalty (P_0) for noncompliance. If the penalty is lower than P_0, then a source may find it advantageous to emit more than the standard and pay the penalty. At a penalty of P_1, for example, the source would find it advantageous to control at J and pay a penalty of $SDEJ$. This saves area AED.

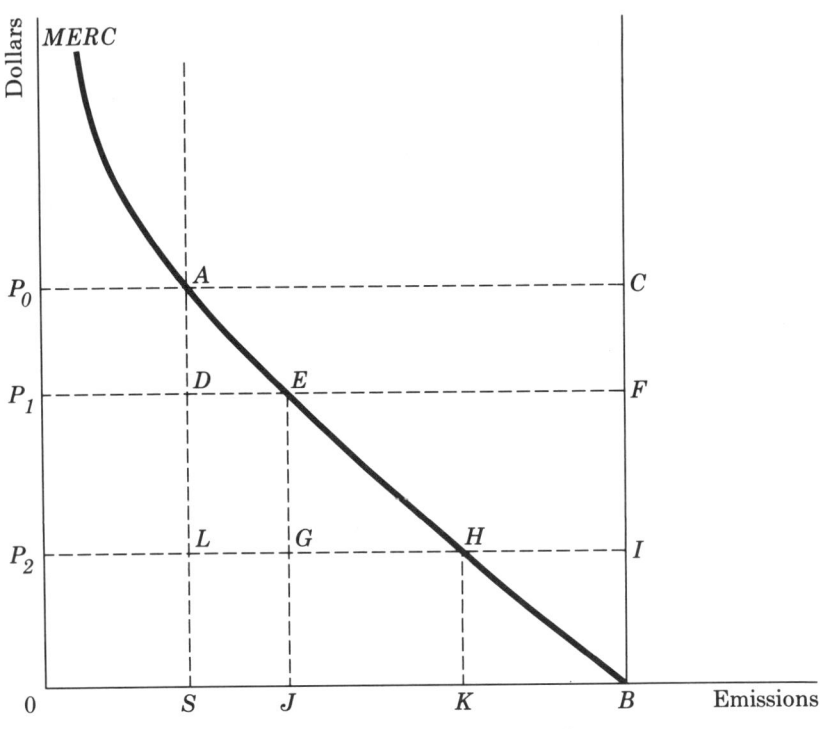

emission level as long as emissions exceed $\bar{S}$. With this form of penalty it will be cheaper to emit and pay the fine and not control if LAH (the surplus of control costs over fine) is greater than HIB (the surplus of fine over control costs). In Figure 13.1, it would appear that a penalty of $\bar{S}LIB$ would not produce emission control while a penalty of $\bar{S}DEB$ would generate control at $\bar{S}$.

Effective Penalty

We have assumed that the source wishes to minimize its pollution control costs so as to maximize its profit. It will do so by equating its marginal penalty for noncompliance with its *MERC* and determining the relationship between total penalties for noncompliance and the total cost of compliance at the efficient level. When the penalty is zero, it does not pay to comply. High penalties tend to generate more compliance, so it is obvious that the penalties applied to violators of emission regulations are of great importance in stimulating control.

But announced penalties are not necessarily effective penalties. Anyone who has ever driven more than 55 miles per hour knows that the penalty for speeding is not the penalty announced by law authorities. First, an officer must detect the violation. Next, the case must be prosecuted and won by the state. Finally, a judge or jury must impose the penalty. Consequently, the effective penalty is much less than the announced penalty. Suppose the announced penalty for driving 70 mph in a 55 mph zone is $100 plus three points toward license suspension. If we assume that the expected rate of detection of speeding is once in every 100 trips, the expected penalty is reduced to one dollar for each trip on which one speeds. Now suppose that resisting the charges in the court can be successful. I know you do not speed but — I admit it — I have been known to, on occasion. (Frequently, actually.) Suppose I was detected speeding. If I could convince the arresting officer that I was making an emergency trip or that her detection was in error, she might not proceed, or she might reduce the charge to 65 mph. In either case, my effective penalty would be reduced. Now suppose I contest the charge in court, claiming that radar is highly inaccurate. (It has been known to clock houses at 70 mph and trees at 46 mph.) The judge or jury might reduce my penalty or throw the case out of court. Being detected driving 70 mph does not necessarily mean that I will pay the $100 fine. Thus the effective fine is lower than a dollar per trip. There can be more to the penalty than the fine, however, I might lose my driving privileges, or my insurance premium might increase. The effective penalty takes all these indirect penalties into account as well.

Detecting violations of emission control requirements is much like detecting speeders. An inspector must observe the violation, usually while within or in close proximity to the plant. The probability of a source being detected in violation depends on the frequency of inspections, just as the probability of detecting speeders depends on the number of officers patrolling the road. It also depends on the accuracy of the detection equipment employed. Like radar, pollution detection devices are subject to equipment and operator error. This causes inspectors to allow some leeway between measured violations and citations for violations. If a source is detected being only a little bit over the standard, it might well not be cited for a violation. Of course, violations depend on the level of the standard, as they do on the speed limit. Equally obvious is the fact that the detection of violations depends on the source's actual emissions, as it does on a driver's actual speed.

Once a violation is detected, a source can influence the probability of its being convicted and paying the fine. Informal negotiations with the agency, like negotiations with the traffic officer, can lead to reduction or withdrawal of the charges. Failing in this effort, the source can carry its argument to the courts. The source will find it advantageous to carry on these forms of negotiation to the point where an additional dollar spent on negotiations equals a dollar of savings in penalty.

A hypothetical set of numbers can help us see the effect of these negotiations on the effective penalty. Suppose a source violates its effluent standard half of the time ($V = 0.5$). Given agency efforts, one out of every ten violations is detected. The probability of being detected is one in ten ($D = 0.1$). The probability of conviction, given both source and agency efforts to pursue the case, is also one in ten ($C = 0.1$). Finally, once the emitter is convicted, the probability of it convincing the judge or jury to reduce or eliminate the penalty is one in two ($R = 0.5$). So an announced fine (F) of $1,000 per violation reduces to an effective penalty of $2.50. The arithmetic of this result can be seen in Equation 13.1.

$$EF = F(V)(D)(C)(R) \qquad 13.1$$
$$\$2.50 = \$1,000\ (.5)(.1)(.1)(.5)$$

where

EF = Effective penalty.
F = Announced fine.
D = Probability of detection.
C = Probability of conviction.
R = Probability of a fine reduction.

To summarize, the effective penalty a source faces is much less than the announced legal maximum. Furthermore, the effective penalty can be reduced by source actions. It will pay for the source to employ personnel and legal resources in efforts to reduce the effective penalty up to the point where an additional dollar spent on such negotiations saves just one dollar. These calculations of the efficient level of negotiation depend on the reactions of the control agency — an issue to which we now turn.

Agency Response

There are several ways the control agency can increase the effective penalty and thereby generate greater compliance. An increase in the effluent standard would heighten the frequency of violations and increase the effective penalty. The agency could step up its effort to detect violations by hiring more inspectors, training them better, equipping them with more accurate means of detection, or conducting unannounced inspections. Announced inspections are more frequent than one might expect, and they tend to reduce detected violations (just as CB radio "good buddies" tend to keep one another from being caught speeding). Once violations are detected, the agency can increase the probability of conviction by spending more resources — especially personnel resources — on the preparation and conduct of the court case. Once in court, the agency can argue for the maximum fine. The agency can impose an indirect penalty by creating adverse publicity for violators. The resulting unfavorable image for the source can provide additional political and economic pressure to comply. This indirect penalty can be important in a source's decision-making, as we shall see in the following discussion of actual enforcement practice.

CURRENT PRACTICE IN ENFORCEMENT

The control agency determines the required action and issues the appropriate regulations. Sources subject to the regulations are expected to comply. If the control agency determines that they have not complied they are fined, either by the agency or the court. The fine and the court action cause the firm to comply.

In practice, the typical case goes as follows: First, the control agency and the firm bargain over the level of the effluent standard. Then, after the firm is given time to install the required equipment or make the required process modifications, the agency determines whether the requirements have been met. If not, the agency has two options. One is to renegotiate the timing of the installation or the level of control; the other is to take the firm to court. The second option is employed only in rare cases when a firm has repeatedly refused to meet deadlines. In fact, the typical action is to grant further delays if some evidence of progress is exhibited.

Once the required equipment has been installed, the agency must ensure its proper operation. This requires self-monitoring by the firm and periodic inspections by the agency. When violations are detected, the agency will initiate some remedial action. If the noncompliance continues, the agency will move from informal measures, such as phone calls and visits, to any of several formal remedies. The agency can issue administrative orders that outline prescribed abatement measures, compliance schedules, and other requirements; or it can issue a cease-and-desist order. Consent orders are essentially identical to administrative orders, except that they are easier to enforce in court because the emitter signs the negotiated agreement. In some cases the agency can issue civil administrative penalties or fines, and it also has the authority — though it is rarely used — to revoke or suspend a permit previously issued. One unique form of achieving compliance is to modify the existing permit to make the effluent standard less stringent; thus noncompliance becomes compliance without additional control. The ultimate administrative remedy is referral to the courts, pursued in most cases through the Department of Justice. Courts have various remedies available: injunctions, orders, and civil or criminal fines. In the United States, very few cases get to court; even when they do, fines are rare and generally minimal.

Enforcement agencies seem to adopt some common attitudes toward enforcement. First, they attempt to maintain a cooperative relationship with emitters, sometimes even forgiving past violations if compliance is achieved or in the offing. They weigh technical and economic feasibility in decisions on hard-line enforcement. Finally, they often grant repeated opportunities to comply without assessing penalties for failure.

Setting a Standard

Pollution control laws nominally require that emission standards be set by the control agency, but in fact the standard is subject to negotiation between the agency and the emitting firm. In a study of water pollution enforcement in eight states, the Environmental Law Institute (ELI) concluded that enforcement procedures emphasize "voluntary compliance" (obtaining control without imposing penalties). The first step in the process is bargaining with the firm on the level of control or the date by which the required controls must be installed. The study also concluded that "considerations of technical and economic feasibility continue to play an important role in the choice of appropriate enforcement remedies."[1] The ELI report further implies that this bargaining outcome is subject to political pressures, which reduce the effectiveness of enforcement.

In a review of air pollution enforcement in seven states, the U.S. General Accounting Office also concluded that heavy reliance was placed on voluntary compliance. The study lists long delays in obtaining compliance, citing numerous examples from various states. In many states, there was not even an organized system for identifying potential emitters.[2]

One aspect of the bargaining process in voluntary compliance affects the level of required control. Here the control agency is faced with the argument that the level of control desired is not technically feasible. If the agency does not bargain, the firm can choose to challenge the standard in court. Almost all 1977 federal water pollution emission standards were challenged in court.

Another alternative for the source is to seek a delay in complying with the required standard. Delay can be accomplished through a variance procedure that grants the source permission to emit above the standard temporarily in exchange for a promise to try to meet the standard by installing equipment during the period for which they have been granted the variance. The granting of variances has been very common. One study concludes that the agency's primary response was to grant a variance whenever immediate enforcement appeared to be in the best interest of neither the state nor the polluter seeking the variance.[3] Often variances are granted repeatedly to the same source.[4]

Delay in compliance can be accomplished in a second way. The permit states the date by which control must be achieved. The permit can be modified, however, to delay the date of compliance. The

---

[1] Environmental Law Institute, *Enforcement of Federal and State Water Pollution Controls: A Report to the National Commission on Water Quality* (Washington, D.C.: ELI, 1975), p.6.
[2] U.S. General Accounting Office, *Assessment of Federal and State Enforcement Efforts to Control Air Pollution from Stationary Sources*, Report to the Congress (Washington, D.C.: U.S. Government Printing Office, 1973).
[3] J. G. Laitos, "The Limits of the Law: Functional Failures of the Air Pollution Variance Board," *University of Colorado Law Review* 44 (1973): 513–551.
[4] D. Willick and T. Windle, "Rule Enforcement by the Los Angeles County Air Pollution Control District," *Ecology Law Quarterly* 3 (1973): 507–534.

effect is the same as the variance procedure, but the technical details are different. In this case the source is listed as in compliance with a current emission standard, while in the variance case it is out of compliance with its emission standard but has permission to continue operations. The ELI study shows that such extensions in the date of compliance are very common, often being granted repeatedly to the same source in exchange for a promise to do better. An inspector for the Maryland Bureau of Air Quality and Noise Control suggested, only somewhat facetiously, that each lawyer a firm brought to a conference on permit requirements with bureau personnel was worth an additional year's delay in compliance. Current data on rates of compliance with federal water pollution control permits indicate that the rates are very high, in part because firms that have been granted delays or variances are listed as being in legal compliance even though they are not meeting their standards.

A study conducted by P. B. Downing and J. N. Kimball showed that bargaining in the South Central Region of the Virginia State Water Control Board (SWCB) has taken a similar form.[5] Starting in the 1973, National Pollution Discharge Elimination System (NPDES) permits were issued by the SWCB in response to the Federal Water Pollution Control Act of 1972. These permits set temporary emission standards, to be met at the time the permit was issued or shortly thereafter, and permanent standards to be met by the middle of 1977. Of the companies surveyed, 83 percent stated that they had negotiated their permit limits with the SWCB, and with very few exceptions, the interim limit sought by the firm was the limit granted on the permit. So the firms' applications represented what they were currently discharging, and more than three-fourths of the total number of firms had to make no basic modifications to be in compliance. In other words, more than 75 percent of the surveyed firms were already in compliance with their interim permit limits when those permits were issued.

Detecting Violations

Once a standard has been agreed on the source moves to install the required equipment, and the control agency keeps track of the source's progress. At the due date, the agency will determine by inspection or other communication whether the source has com-

---

[5] P. B. Downing and J. N. Kimball, "Enforcing Pollution Control Laws in the United States," *Policy Studies Journal* 11 (September 1982): 55–64.

plied. In some cases, especially with large sources, some proof of the devices' effectiveness may be required. When devices are tested, the limitations of the test may cause the agency to accept a device as effective even though it does not meet the standards.[6] This is because the control agency may conduct a test that is inadequate to indicate true emissions.

Once a device is installed and certified, the agency must determine that it is operated effectively. This is done in two ways. Most often the control agency inspects each source periodically to determine compliance. Various studies of the frequency of inspection show that it is highly variable among control programs. The most frequent inspection is attributed to the Los Angeles County Air Pollution Control District, which inspects each major source once a month.[7] On the other hand, water treatment inspections in North Carolina are conducted sporadically, and many facilities have not been inspected for years.[8] The reason given for this infrequent inspection is inadequate staffing. In a study of New York City, a staff member of the Air Resources Department was quoted as saying, "There are probably 60,000 violations a day, and we catch only about 600 a month."[9]

In South Central Virginia, inspections were found to be infrequent. According to NPDES regulations, major industries are to be inspected at least twice a year; minor industries, at least once a year. The Downing and Kimball study indicated that in 1976 and 1977 major firms had been inspected, on the average, less than once a year. Two of the twelve firms reported that they had never been inspected by the SWCB. The SWCB staff suggested that they had neither sufficient time nor sufficient personnel to conduct the required inspections. The experience in water pollution control in Virginia is typical of air and water pollution efforts throughout the country. The average frequency of inspections is less than once a year. Inspections are conducted during normal working hours, and are almost always announced. Permission to enter the plant is obtained from the officer of the firm who has dealt with the State Water Control Board previously. Obtaining permission to enter is a

---

[6] W. D. Watson, Jr., and P. B. Downing, "Enforcement of Environmental Standards and the Central Limit Theorem," *Journal of the American Statistical Association* 71 (September 1976): 567–573.

[7] Willick and Windle, "Rule Enforcement by LACAPCD."

[8] T. Schoenbaum, "The Efficiency of Federal and State Control of Water Pollution in Intrastate Streams," *Arizona Law Review* 14 (1972): 1–39.

[9] E. Schachter, *Enforcing Air Pollution Controls* (New York: Praeger, 1974), p. 26.

central part of the voluntary compliance scheme, but it also ensures that each inspection is expected. This procedure effectively announces all inspections and certainly reduces the number of emitters found to be in violation of the law.

The fact that an inspection is conducted does not necessarily mean that all violations will be detected. As long as the control equipment appears to be operating effectively, the inspector is likely to pass it. An inspector may take a sample of the plant's effluent if it seems that the operation is suspect, but bureaucratic rules and budget constraints limit the number of samples inspectors can send to the state laboratory for analysis. Furthermore, the accuracy of the tests (the typical margin of error is at least 25 percent, plus or minus) and the variability of effluent quality over short periods of time make this sampling procedure highly inaccurate. It can only be considered indicative of a potential problem.

The principal method of detecting violations throughout the nation is the firms' self-monitoring reports.[10] Firms are required by their permits to report any violation and to notify the control agency, within five days, of the reason for the violation, the extent of the damage, and the steps taken to correct the problem. Failure to do so constitutes a violation of the permit. Firms are also required to monitor their emissions and submit a monthly report to the agency.

Amazingly, self-monitoring does not produce perfect reported compliance. On average, 90 percent of the 5,977 major air pollution sources were in compliance with state implementation plan requirements in 1980.[11] The range of compliance varied from a high of 97 percent in coal cleaning operations to a low of 13 percent in integrated iron and steel plants. Self-monitoring and certification was used to determine compliance in 57 percent of the complying cases, while inspections were used in 38 percent of the cases and emission tests in only 5 percent. The true level of compliance can only be guessed, but it is certainly lower than the published figures.

The second most frequent source of detection of violations is citizen complaints. By their very nature, citizen complaints will detect only visible or odoriferous pollution, such as smoke and fish kills. Many of the more dangerous pollutants cannot be detected by sensory perception. Consequently, reliance on citizen complaints

---

[10] Council on Environmental Quality, Memorandum to D. Tunderman, Executive Office of the President, 1976, p. 6.
[11] Council on Environmental Quality, *Environmental Quality*, Eleventh Annual Report (Washington, D.C.: U.S. Government Printing Office, 1980), p. 181.

tends to bias enforcement toward solving easily detected violations, drawing attention away from more damaging pollutants.

In summary, we find that the typical agency does not inspect frequently and that what inspections do occur are usually announced. Thus the probability of being found in violation is very small. There are two possible exceptions to this conclusion: third-party reports of violation and source self-reports. Third-party reports constitute the major source of violation detection in air pollution.[12] In cases where violations have been self-reported, no penalty has usually been imposed.

Court Referral and Conviction

Not every detected violation results in court action. Typically, the control agency initiates action through various informal means, such as telephone calls and letters. If these efforts do not generate compliance, more formal actions may be taken. Officials of the emitting firm may be called into the agency's offices for a conference. If this is not successful in generating efforts to comply, a notice of violation may be issued. If there is still no corrective action, court action may be recommended. It is, in fact, very rare that a court case is instituted and even more rare that it is not dropped before the court hands down a decision. It is extremely rare that a source is found guilty and fined.

The administrative process is cumbersome and time-consuming. A study of air compliance in Connecticut provides an example.[13] Of 4,000 premises inspected between 1971 and 1974, 1,469 (37 percent) were found not to be in compliance. After notices of violation were issued, 323 (8 percent of the total number of inspections) did not comply quickly. In these cases, compliance orders were issued. Next, 171 (4 percent of those inspected) failed to meet compliance order deadlines. Twenty-seven of these had delayed for more than fifteen months. Those with long delays were either very large or very small sources. Delays throughout the process were significant. On average, four weeks elapsed between the time of detection and the time when a notice of violation was issued. Almost four months passed from the issuance of a notice of violation to the signing of a compliance order. Seven months passed between the issuance of an

---

[12] See Schachter, *Enforcing Air Pollution Controls*, State of Connecticut, Department of Environmental Protection, *Economic Law Enforcement* (September 1975).
[13] Connecticut, *Economic Law Enforcement*.

order and the scheduled date of compliance. Half of the orders were not completed on time. Delays in compliance averaged over five months. Of the orders that were complied with, 30 percent were met by means other than those proposed in the order. Sources blamed third-party delays for more than 65 percent of all missed compliance schedules. Citizen complaints accounted for 18 percent of the inspections but 46 percent of the detections of a violation. Most of these were for visible emissions — smoke.

Other agencies have had similar experiences. The Minnesota Pollution Control Agency, for example, "disposes of all but a handful of violations informally through the 'twilight zone' process of seeking voluntary compliance and negotiating stipulations."[14] Texas water pollution control agencies try never to use legal sanctions in obtaining compliance.[15] In its study of water pollution enforcement, the Environmental Law Institute concluded in part:

1. Pollution control agencies, particularly at the state level, continue to emphasize informal cooperation — as opposed to issuing warnings, orders, etc. — in their dealings with dischargers.
2. Enforcement is most often a graduated process. Government responses vary with the gravity of the violation and the degree of pressure necessary to bring about compliance.
3. Past violations will usually be forgiven if compliance is in the offing.
4. Considerations of technical and economic feasibility continue to play an important role in the choice of appropriate enforcement remedies.
5. Dischargers will often be given repeated opportunities to comply before serious enforcement action is taken.
6. Negotiation continues to play an important role in enforcement.[16]

Looking again at the Connecticut study, we see that only 22 percent of the sources that were issued notices of violation were also issued compliance orders. The remainder came into compliance "quickly." Of these compliance orders, only 4 percent were referred to the state attorney general. Of these cases, 19 percent were settled out of court, 6 percent were lost by the control agency, 56 percent remained undecided at the end of the study, and 19 percent resulted

---

[14] "Note: The Minnesota Pollution Control Agency — A Study in State Administrative Law," *Minnesota Law Review* 56 (June 1972): 1033.
[15] W. T. Jacks, "Local and Regional Water Pollution Control in Texas," *Texas Law Review* 48 (November 1970): 1287–1383.
[16] ELI, *Enforcement of Federal and State Water Pollution Controls*.

in the court issuing injunctions. No fines or other penalties were levied. Long delays and indecisions in the courts appear elsewhere in the literature. In New York City, by the end of 1970 there were 9,310 cases outstanding out of a total of 12,619 brought to court. Of the 3,309 cases resolved, 325 were dismissed, 282 withdrawn, and 2,702 resulted in convictions.[17]

Fines

I have argued that increasing fines will increase the cost of noncompliance and thus stimulate the firm to comply. Most violators, however, are never fined. Those who are fined pay a very low penalty, given the court's ability and predilection to set a low dollar amount even after a successful prosecution. The ELI report is full of such cases.[18] The average fine in New York City was thirty-five dollars. There are a few exceptions in the literature. In one case in Illinois, a fine of $149,000 levied by the Pollution Control Board was later negotiated down to $50,000.[19]

The case of the Gary Works of the United States Steel Corporation might be considered a highly visible indicator for corporations to judge the economic sanctions imposed by water pollution control agencies.[20] After a conference in March 1965, the state of Indiana gave the Gary Works three years — until December 31, 1968 — to take some significant action toward controlling its water pollution. During this time, the Gary Works did nothing to control its effluent. In mid 1968 the federal government granted U.S. Steel a one-year extension. In January 1969, another conference was held to assess progress. At that time U.S. Steel obtained a second one-year extension — until December 31, 1970. In December 1970, U.S. Steel was demanding a new extension and making no pretense of cooperating with the emission control requirements.

The Department of Justice filed a criminal suit against the Gary Works in February 1970, under the Rivers and Harbors Act of 1899. Initially it appeared that the February 1970 suit was a giant step forward. On June 8, 1972, U.S. Steel was found guilty and fined $5,000. The amount of the fine was much less than the cost of pollu-

[17] Schachter, *Enforcing Air Pollution Controls*, Table A-7.
[18] ELI, *Enforcement of Federal and State Water Pollution Controls*.
[19] D. Currie, "Enforcement under the Illinois Pollution Law," *Northwestern Law Review* 70: 389–485.
[20] E. Greer, "Obstacles to Taming Corporate Polluters: Water Pollution Politics in Gary, Indiana," *Environmental Affairs* 3: 199–221.

tion control equipment to prevent the discharge, and more than four years had elapsed between the alleged offense and conviction. In 1983, EPA and U.S. Steel reached a new agreement whereby the company agreed to pay $250,000 in penalties in exchange for three additional years to comply with federal air pollution standards at seven plants.[21]

The Control Agency's Prosecution Effort

Prosecution effort can be defined as the ability of the control agency to win a successful verdict against a discharger in a court of law. Although very few cases actually go to court, several major obstacles tend to reduce the probability of gaining a successful verdict even in those few. The most important of these obstacles are agency resource constraints, poor coordination between various state agencies, and lack of coordination between state and federal offices.

Resource limitations are probably the largest factor working against successful prosecution. Extensive documentation is required for any judicial action, and the responsibility for gathering the data falls on the regional staff. Usually a control agency has neither the time nor the personnel to gather data on all the dischargers who have violated their permits.

Lack of cooperation between state agencies often frustrates court action. Typically, the control agency cannot pursue the case in court but must convince the attorney general's office to proceed. This office has its own priorities and constraints, and its own political pressure points. The attorney general is either elected or appointed, and thus highly sensitive to political pressures, so a pollution case against a prominent firm could be delayed for political reasons. In addition, the attorney general's office faces budget constraints, which may force it to choose from among a large number of cases. It might well argue that a murder or rape case is more important to pursue. The end result of all these constraints on agency enforcement efforts is the cooperative approach observed throughout the United States and in Europe as well.[22] Cooperation may be the most effective strategy available to obtain control after all, given these constraints.

[21] *USA Today*, Monday, January 3, 1983, p. B-1.
[22] See various chapters in P. B. Downing and K. Hanf, eds., *International Comparisons in Implementing Pollution Control* (Boston: Kluwer-Nijhoff, 1983).

A Source's Decision to Control

At this point you may be wondering, as I do, why sources control at all. The effective penalty is usually very low. Our theory suggests that a cost-minimizing source would choose noncompliance, and some sources do, but the vast majority in fact comply at some level. In this section I will attempt to explain why they do so.

Bargaining. Bargaining between the agency and the source has three effects. First it reduces the standard, either directly or by changing the technical details of the implementation and continued compliance plans. Reducing the defined maximum capacity of the plant, for example, has the effect of reducing the stringency of the standard. Second, bargaining reduces the probability of detecting violations. Self-monitoring agreements are part of the bargain, and they reduce detections. Third, bargaining reduces the agency's efforts to prosecute violations, thus reducing the probability of conviction for violations. In fact, it is so far reduced that only after repeated serious violations can any penalty be expected.

The net result of these three effects of bargaining is that formal penalties cannot be expected for emissions that only exceed the federal standard ($\bar{S}$ in Figure 13.2) by a little. At about point A, formal penalties can be expected to be imposed. There is some reason to believe that direct court-imposed penalties become very large when a source refuses to control at all. So the actual marginal penalty function (P_A) can be expected to rise rapidly at low levels of control. Alternatively, the penalty can be thought of as a fixed-fee penalty taking effect at some level of emissions and having some probability of being applied at emissions of A or greater.

An indirect penalty is also imposed on a firm when a violation is detected. The firm must consult with, negotiate with, and provide documentation to the agency, and expend resources in other ways. This required expenditure is in effect a penalty, though it is not a formal one. This informal penalty will take effect at some point between $\bar{S}$ and A and will increase as the degree and frequency of violations increases. We designate this indirect penalty P_I.

Penalties like these are sufficient to explain why levels of control are lower than required, but what can explain why sources do not pay full penalties? For a full explanation, we must look at several more elements.

FIGURE 13.2 Enforcement in Practice

A source may emit at some level above the standard (say A) because its true out-of-pocket costs ($MERC_{OP}$) are still low and the total penalty for controlling at even lower levels (P_T) would be higher than this cost.

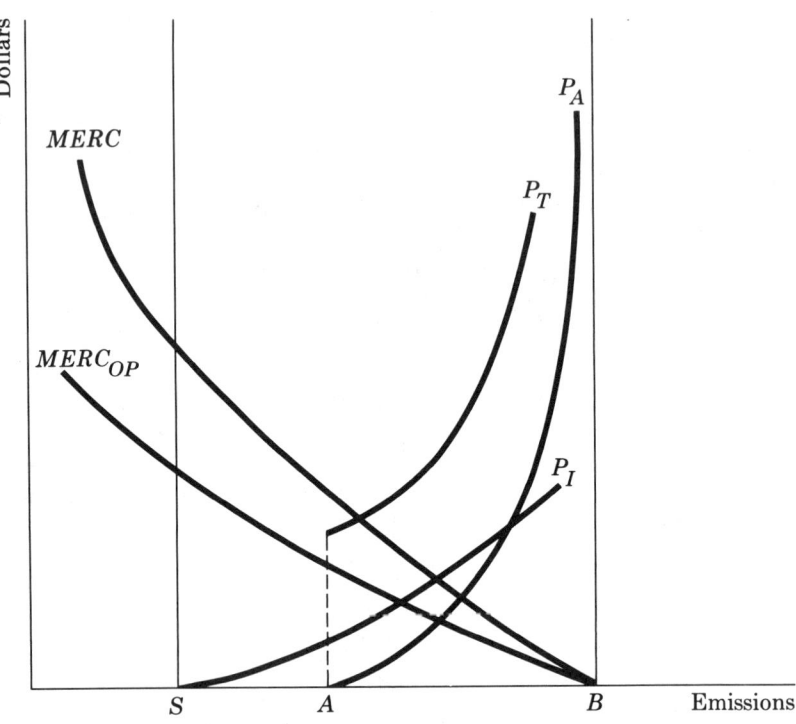

Out-of-pocket expenses. The cost a source considers when comparing control costs to penalties is its out-of-pocket expenses, or the effect of these expenditures on profits. Out-of-pocket expenses are the payments by the firm for the capital, land, and labor it uses to control emissions, less any subsidy the firm might receive for these expenditures. Out-of-pocket expenses represent the net effect on accounting profit (not economic profit) of the firm. Out-of-pocket expenses can be reduced in several ways. These include interest subsidies and tax breaks, which have the effect of reducing out-of-pocket costs by more than 50 percent while not reducing real cost at all. Consequently, the cost of concern to the source ($MERC_{OP}$ in Figure 13.2) are much lower than the real resource costs ($MERC$).

Interest rate subsidies come from a variant of the industrial revenue bond called the Pollution Control Revenue Bond. Bonds are issued through and backed by the municipality in which a plant is located. The plant receives the proceeds and pays back the bondholders at the interest rate negotiated by the municipality. Purchasers of these bonds do not have to pay federal income taxes on earnings from them, so they can be sold at a lower interest rate than the bonds of a corporate borrower. The lower interest rate allows the source to carry pollution control investments at a lower annual cost, just as lower interest rates reduce the monthly payments on a new car. Federal tax regulations require that at least 90 percent of the proceeds of these bonds be used for pollution control. It is very difficult, however, to determine if process changes have been adopted to control pollution or to reduce costs. Thus it is possible for a source to use these bonds to subsidize its regular capital investments. A strong statement by the pollution control agency about the desirable effect of these expenditures on pollution control — which could be generated in the bargaining process — would make the source's case virtually incontestable.

In addition to these bonds, federal and state income tax provisions help reduce the out-of-pocket cost of pollution control equipment. Rapid depreciation and in some cases one-year expensing is allowed for such equipment. This allows the source to reduce its tax payments during the current and next few years. The effect is a substantial reduction in the present value of current and future tax liabilities.

Indirect penalties. Even these reductions in costs are not sufficient to generate compliance at a level where no monetary penalty is generated. To complete the explanation we must add the fact that certain indirect penalties can be imposed on the source. These take at least three forms.

We have suggested (in Chapter 11) that some industries and regions gain from pollution control regulations. Raising the cost of entry for new plants has the effect of reducing competition and keeping prices higher for existing plants. This can cause those existing plants to earn excess profit in the short run. The barrier to entry provided by pollution laws is the requirement that regulations be enforced more stringently against new sources. It would be politically difficult for an existing source to argue for strict control of new sources when it is blatantly not complying. Thus one of the indirect penalties imposed on a source is the loss of potential profit generated by strict enforcement against new sources. In order to encourage such enforcement, the existing source must be listed as in compliance. This can be accomplished at some level of control below $\bar{S}$ but above A.

A second indirect penalty can be the effect on other government agencies of the announcement that a source is not in compliance. Especially in serious cases, other agencies might start to wonder what regulations of theirs the source is ignoring. The result may be increased inspections and expensive preparation of audit records for other agencies, including the tax authorities. The source, not wishing to open a Pandora's box, will control to a level where they are listed as being in compliance, again somewhere between $\bar{S}$ and A.

Finally, firms are concerned about their public image. Managers attempt to be socially responsible, and they rate pollution control second only to equal opportunity as a corporate social priority.[23] The reason for this rating may be the training and political views of corporate managers. They have high incomes and educational levels, and are thus likely to be heavy participants in such environmentally sensitive activities as outdoor sports. In addition, a manager's personal reputation may be tarnished by being associated with a firm that is considered a scofflaw. Corporate executives have a certain amount of discretion — sometimes very great — in deciding on expenditures.

The net effect of all these indirect penalties may be a rather large total penalty, but one that does not start until emissions are near A. Such a total penalty is presented in Figure 13.2 as P_T. A rational source, facing this penalty structure with its reduced control cost function, will choose to control somewhere to the left of A. The source is controlling at less than the standard, but is not cited for violations, or if cited, it does not suffer penalties. The source is listed as being in substantial compliance even though it is out of compliance with the applicable federal standard a large percentage of the time.

[23] Lyman E. Ostlund, "Attitudes of Managers toward Corporate Social Responsibility," *California Management Review* 19 (Summer 1977): 38.

SUMMARY: LESSONS LEARNED

Enforcement of pollution control regulations is based on cooperative negotiation between the source and the agency. The agency is inhibited from being tough on emitters by its political vulnerability and by the high cost of enforcing through the courts. At the same time, procontrol political forces constrain the agency from being too lenient with emitters. Faced with these constraints, the agency finds it advantageous to bargain with the sources. Technical uncertainties provide a reason for such bargaining. Case-by-case decision-making is the result.

The source also finds it advantageous to bargain. By maintaining a "cooperative" attitude, the source is able to obtain delays in compliance, technological concessions, and a virtual guarantee of no penalty for noncompliance. Being listed as in compliance has political and economic benefits for the source as well.

Enforcement is accomplished through a complex bargaining process in a political arena. The political power of the actors affects the results. The outcome is not likely to be a move toward efficiency. Larger, more politically powerful sources are likely to be more effective in the bargaining game even though, in most circumstances, economic efficiency requires that they be controlled more than smaller, less politically powerful firms.

In contemplating the enforcement of transferable discharge permits or practical effluent charges, we must conclude that technical uncertainties will still exist, and will probably become more crucial to the enforcement process. Likewise, we cannot expect the political setting within which the enforcement agency operates to change significantly. This implies that bargaining and case-by-case decision-making will continue. The result will be a move away from the efficient allocations envisioned in economic writings on these alternatives.

The control of environmental externalities generates costs to some and benefits to others. Because government action is required to accomplish control, environmental quality improvement is a political issue. Changing institutional forms will not make it less so. We cannot take the enforcement agency out of a political situation, which requires it to negotiate. We probably cannot establish a system that penalizes emission violations at rates sufficiently high to ensure compliance. If we could, the current regulatory system could be made more effective. The politically and legally active procontrol lobby has not been able to do this under the existing system, and it is not likely to be more than marginally successful if a new institutional form is adopted.

We face a serious political problem in designing a new institutional structure for pollution control. A system that is more effective will impose significant new costs on emitting firms. In the absence of compensation for these costs, the firms will be a very powerful political force to overcome. A compensation requirement would scatter many of the political allies of the procontrol lobby. And the control agency bureaucracy will be reluctant to give up power. In particular, it will attempt to retain case-by-case decision-making.

The problems of designing an alternative system are great indeed. Take the example of spatial differentiation. Greater spatial differentiation increases the potential cost savings of any practical system. At the same time, it increases the amount of information required to implement the system, thus increasing technological uncertainty. Technological uncertainty leaves room for case-by-case decision-making, and thus for bargaining between the source and the agency. The costs of bargaining and the resultant inefficiencies in control reduce or eliminate any cost savings.

In the rest of this book we will turn our attention to the design of a practical and politically feasible system that might work better than the existing regulatory system.

STUDY QUESTIONS

1. How might the effective penalty for violating an emission standard be increased? I am sure you could suggest some very simple steps. Why haven't these steps been taken?
2. Why would firms voluntarily report emission violations on their self-monitoring reports? Would you expect this voluntary admission of excess emissions to continue if the effective marginal penalty were increased to equal *MERC*?
3. How would this enforcement process be altered if an effluent fee system were adopted? A transferable permit system involves other enforcement problems. What are they and how can they be solved?

SUGGESTED READINGS

1. P. B. Downing and J. N. Kimball, "Enforcing Pollution Control Laws in the U.S."; A. A. Ullmann, "The Implementation of Air

Pollution Control in German Industry"; G. Richardson, "The Enforcement of Water Pollution Controls in the United Kingdom"; and G. Brady and B. Bower, "Effectiveness of the U.S. Regulatory Approach to Air Quality Management: Stationary Sources" all in P. B. Downing and K. I. Hanf, ed., *International Comparisons in Implementing Pollution Laws* (Boston: Kluwer-Nijhoff, 1983) present various case studies of the enforcement process that arrive at much the same conclusions.
2. E. Schachter, *Enforcing Air Pollution Controls* (New York: Praeger, 1974) provides a case study of enforcement in New York City.

14

Where Do We Go from Here?

By now you have probably developed a preference for one or another of the pollution control approaches we have discussed. In this chapter I will offer some criteria for judging alternatives to the existing system. Use the issues raised to test your own preference.

Our efforts to determine where to go from here must be grounded in the present. We must work within the confines (or with the advantages) of compromises already struck and agreements already at least tentatively reached on the distribution of rights and responsibilities.

CONSIDERING BASIC ISSUES

In choosing an alternative, we must address certain basic issues. This section presents these basic issues.

The Role of Government

The first decision must be whether government should intervene in the private economy to reallocate resources in order to improve environmental quality. We have seen that an uncontrolled private market that attaches no cost to emitting will overproduce polluting goods and inefficiently degrade the environment. One possible solution to this problem is to determine who owns the environment. Whoever is given the ownership of the environment will have an incentive to use it efficiently.[1] The potential for efficiency was demonstrated by our example of a lake where ownership could be effectively organized and exclusion was possible at a relatively low cost. Unfortunately, however, this simple model does not accommodate most pollution cases. The extent of emissions' effects on a geographic area and on the population involved makes the transaction cost of private negotiations prohibitive. Instead, government is brought in to assist emitters and recipients in resolving conflicts. If it is true that government economizes in the transaction cost of negotiation (and I believe that it does in most, but not all, pollution cases), then there is a role for government in pollution control.

Having decided that there is a role for government, we must decide on the components of that role. One is the provision of information. Information has the characteristics of a public good in that, once it is produced, the marginal cost of providing it to one more person is near zero. While exclusion can be exercised to make information private, I believe that for most pollution issues it would be inefficient to do so. Exclusion causes individuals to refrain from an activity because of the cost involved. In public decisions, uninformed people are less likely to choose the options they would understand to be in their best interest if they knew all the factors. Thus providing information to the public in such areas as environmental quality, the effects of pollution, and the costs of control will lead to a better informed public and more efficient public choices.

Who Owns the Environment?

I have argued that the existing system creates an implicit sharing of ownership between emitters and recipients. Emitters have the right to release unwanted wastes and reduce environmental quality so long as the damage created is not too great. Recipients have the right to a relatively healthful environment but not to a pure one, at least according to current laws. Whatever one might feel about the way things ought to be, that is the way they are at the moment.

The practicality of political interest suggests that ownership rights to the environment cannot be changed drastically except under extraordinary circumstances. The reawakening of interest in the environment in 1970 was just such an extraordinary circumstance. One can view the process of implementation since then as an

[1] R. Coase, "The Problem of Social Costs," *Journal of Law and Economics* 3 (October 1960).

attempt by emitters to regain some of the lost ground and an attempt by environmentalists to maintain their gains. In any case, without another, similar reawakening we cannot expect a substantial shift in public sentiment. Any alternative to the existing system will have to share rights between emitters and recipients more or less the way they are now shared. To insist, as some economists have, that recipients hold the property rights to the environment is to ignore the real world of political conflict resolution. Shared property rights are an essential element if one hopes to reduce political resistance to any change in our pollution control system.

Efficiency and Equity in Pollution Control

Society has two basic goals: to maximize the value of goods and services produced (efficiency), and to treat people in various circumstances fairly (equity). Each individual in our society is willing to give up some control over goods and services in order to provide some equity to others. We see this in our support for public and private charity.

Some consider it equitable that people who have spent money based on the current regulatory structure not be penalized too severely by any change in that structure. Some consider it equitable that those who are most adversely affected by pollution be given a greater say in decisions about its control. Reconciling these two points of view would require that both emitters and recipients make the important social decisions about control. This is politically practical as well.

There is a problem with allowing equity arguments into the pollution issue: What is equitable is a matter of opinion. This inherent fuzziness renders public decision-making vulnerable to manipulation. Individuals can take strongly self-interested positions that would lead to substantial costs to others and argue for them on equity grounds. Political activists will take advantage of this to move policy in directions they prefer. We must be very cautious about agreeing to any equity issue in making public policy choices because of this possible hidden agenda of individual self-interest.

Acting in the Social Interest

How can we get individuals to act in the social interest? We cannot. First of all — lamentable as it is — self-interest is a powerful motivating force, and asking people to act in the social interest when it is against their self-interest is like asking water to flow uphill. The solution is to rearrange the situation so that the individual's self-interest coincides with the social interest.[2] Second, there is no single "best interest" of society; there are only the interests of the individuals who make up society. The problem of aggregating these interests in a consistent way has been the subject of a whole field of economics and political science, called public choice. It cannot be proven that the current political system will produce efficient results, but at the same time, it cannot be shown that any alternative system is preferable.

We must design a system in which the goal of efficient control of pollution is as consistent as possible with the self-interests of the participants. What is needed is a system wherein the self-interest of individuals will cause the emitters to control efficiently, the recipients to seek and enjoy efficient environmental quality, and the agency personnel to be rewarded for helping produce it.

Cost of Errors

Any system will generate errors in determining both the cost of controlling emissions and the desired level of environmental quality. The current system appears to be geared more toward avoiding errors in environmental quality than toward avoiding errors in cost. It would be efficient to design institutions so as to minimize the total costs of both types of error. We have seen that quantity control is generally favored because an emphasis on quantity in pollution control policy will likely reduce the costs of errors in policy. In addition, environmentalists have been very resistant to systems that regulate price and allow environmental quality levels to adjust. Perhaps the reason for this resistance is that they have an implicit understanding of the desirability of control through quantity.

Growth and Change

We live in a dynamic world. Public policy on pollution control should accommodate constantly changing situations. To stimulate efficient relocations, it is necessary to have a source pay all the costs of location in an area. At the same time, any relocation should efficiently affect the level of control by other sources in the area, and

---

[2] R. McKean, "The Unseen Hand in Government," *American Economic Review* 55 (June 1965).

the efficient level of environmental quality. A change in environmental quality can lead to efficient changes in the location decisions and pollution-avoiding behaviors of recipients.

This sort of stimulus should also be generated by recipients' changes in location and demand. When a recipient moves into an area, he or she should elicit the efficient change in the level of environmental quality and the control of emissions by individual sources.

These are complex goals, and difficult ones to achieve, but any system that ignores them completely may be making a substantial error.

A COMPARISON OF OPTIONS

The set of criteria outlined above can be used to select from among proposals for changes in the institutional structure we employ to determine the environmental policy of government. To see how this comparison would work, and to generate some idea of how other systems proposed by economists might fare in comparison with the existing regulatory system, consider the following comparison.

A practical system, such as was proposed by Baumol and Oates as modified by Mills and White (see page 211) will serve as our model for effluent fees. We will call this system the practical effluent fee (PEF). The transferable permit system proposed by Dales (page 205) will serve as our model for that option. We shall call this system the practical transferable permit (PTP).

Both PEF and the PTP fare very poorly on the criteria of not altering property rights drastically. They both require sources to pay a fee or purchase a permit. This significantly increases the cost to emitters, creating the political resistance we discussed earlier. The revenues generated by these payments will be desirable to others, however, and will serve to lessen the net political resistance. But overall, it is likely that such a redistribution of rights will be resisted.

We have discussed possible solutions to this resistance for both alternatives. For the effluent fee we suggested a combined system, where sources are charged if they emit more than the effluent standard and subsidized if they emit less. This system would recognize the existing rights if individual effluent standards were set at or near the standards now in force; not the announced standards, that is, but the actual standards after negotiation between sources and the agency. For the transferable permit system, a solution to this rights problem would be to grant permits to sources in proportion to the effluent standards now in force. This system would also recognize the rights structure now in existence and would not modify it substantially.

Now let us compare these systems on the basis of efficiency. We have discussed three applications of efficiency: the determination of the efficient level of environmental quality; the least costly attainment of any particular level of environmental quality; and the efficient stimulation of innovations. We will look at efficiency in reacting to the changes innovation might produce in a separate discussion of reactions to growth and change.

Both PEF and PTP take the existing environmental quality standard or some other externally chosen standard as given. The originators of both these proposals seem to feel that including a requirement to set environmental quality standards on grounds of efficiency would render their proposals politically unviable. Whether this is true or not, the neglect of this issue casues the proposals to be no more or less efficient in producing environmental quality than the existing system.

On the issue of reaching a given environmental quality standard at the lowest cost, the PEF proposal claims to improve efficiency. There is no explicit recognition in this proposal, however, of the fact that emissions at different locations can cause different damages (or benefits) and it might therefore be efficient to control each at a different $MERC$ or effluent fee. Assuming that the effluent fee would apply universally and that there are differences in damages among sites, the PEF proposal would not cause sources to reach the chosen level of environmental quality at the lowest cost. The PTP proposal states the proposition that the gains in efficiency from explicit recognition of differences in location would not justify the administrative costs of a system that would include them. This may well have been true in the case Dales was discussing when he explored the application of his proposal, but it would depend on the specifics of each situation. In comparing these solutions to the existing system, we must make some assessment of the degree to which the existing effluent standards, negotiated between the sources and the agency, are modified by the environmental damages caused by the emissions. Various studies suggest that one important element in the negotiation process is the effect of emissions on environmental quality.[3] If this is indeed the case, current regulation could prove to be superior to the PEF and PTP proposals.

As we have seen, however, negotiations between the firm and the agency can have the opposite effect. A politically powerful source can have standards reduced, even if this causes substantial environmental damage, while a weak firm that causes less damage per unit of emission might be controlled more stringently. This side of the efficiency argument seems to go in favor of PEF and PTP, because the economic incentives generated by those plans cause sources in like circumstances to control at equal marginal cost. There is no reason to believe, however, that sources will not find it in their interest to negotiate with the agency.[4] Negotiations can take place on several technical issues. The end result might be that individual sources whose emissions cause similar marginal damages will not control at equal marginal cost. Thus it is not possible to say unambiguously whether the PEF or PTP proposals are net improvements of the existing system or not. It is, of course, possible to solve this problem by taking the emission transformation function and the benefits of control explicitly into account in those circumstances where the transaction costs of doing so are not excessive.

On innovation, both PEF and PTP are clearly superior to regulation. Each would stimulate sources to innovate more than does the socially inefficient lower incentive provided by the existing regulatory system. The incentive to innovate under these alternative proposals may not be perfectly efficient, but it appears to be superior to the existing system.

Another element of efficiency is the cost of administering the system. Some systems require more information to operate effectively, so they are more costly to administer. PEF requires more information than the current regulatory system because the entire *MERC* function for each source, as well as the *ETF*, must be estimated before an estimate of the correct fee can be made. All the regulatory system requires is the *ETF* — assuming the agency is not trying to set individual effluent standards so as to minimize cost (and there is plenty of evidence to suggest that it is not). In addition,

---

[3] See, for example, G. Brady and B. Bower, "Effectiveness of the U.S. Regulatory Approach to Air Quality Management: Stationary Sources," and G. Richardson, "Policing Pollution: The Enforcement Process," in *Policy Studies Journal* 11 (September 1982): 66–76, and 153–164, respectively.

[4] P. Downing, "Bargaining in Pollution Control," *Policy Studies Journal* 11 (June 1983): 577–586.

the effluent fee represents an increase in the marginal fine for emitting, so a source will find it advantageous to seek to disguise its true emissions. Voluntary self-monitoring will be less reliable than under the existing system. The result of both of these influences is a higher marginal cost of administration (*MCA*) for PEF than for the existing system. PTP requires somewhat less information than the existing system. The agency need only determine the number of permits that can be issued, which depends on the environmental quality standard that must be met. This requires knowledge of the *ETF*. After permits are issued, trading will take place until prices equalize without further agency action. Enforcement cost may be somewhat higher than for the existing system, but the net *MCA* should be lower.

The authors of these proposals are silent on the incentives they provide agency personnel for acting in the social interest — that is, efficiently. They simply do not consider agency behavior in making their proposals, and they make no provision for ensuring efficient behavior from bureaucrats. We can state some assumptions, however, and draw conclusions from them. In the PEF proposal there is no mention of where the revenue from the charges will be deposited or what they will be used for. I have argued that, whether the funds are kept by the agency or placed in the general fund, there will be pressures on the agency to set fees at a rate that would maximize revenue. Having this source of revenue allows the bureaucrat to seek discretionary budget with less resistance from those with competing demands for government funds. At the same time, the additional revenue allows the agency to spend more on gathering information and on environmental improvement projects. There is little to recommend PEF over the existing regulatory system on this count. The PTP proposal provides the same sort of potential for maximizing revenue and discretionary budget as the PEF, but it has one advantage over the existing system. Proenvironmentalists can express their demand for environmental quality directly by purchasing permits in the open market and retiring them. This increases the probability that bureaucrats will act in the social interest, because it will pay two groups — the firms and the procontrol CIGs — to monitor the permit process. Given this, the PTP proposal should be somewhat superior to either the existing system or PEF in encouraging bureaucratic efficiency.

The next issue is the adjustment of the system to growth in an area and to changes in the demand (*MBC*) for and costs of control. The existing regulatory system does not allow for growth and change to affect the environmental quality standard. In many areas, however, an emission offset policy allows new sources to move in only if they negotiate emission reductions from existing sources equal to or greater than the increase in emissions they will be responsible for. This allows for some movement toward efficiency as growth occurs, in that paying for reductions in emissions from other sources tends to have the same effect as a transferable permit in creating a tendency among sources to equalize their MCC. The PEF proposal would react to growth by increasing the fee so the fixed environmental quality standard would still be met. This would cause all sources to control at the same, now higher, MCC. It is not clear whether this would be an improvement over the current system of regulation with emission offsets. It depends on whether there is a systematic reason in the current system for new sources to locate at sites with low levels of damage and purchase offsets from sources located at sites with high levels of damage. If this is the case there is reason to believe that the regulatory system is superior to PEF, but if not (and I believe it is not) there is little difference between them on this point. The PTP proposal also keeps a fixed level of environmental quality, so if a new source moves in it must purchase permits from existing sources. The price is adjusted automatically. Again, because of the lack of explicit locational variations in price, there is no reason to suppose that there would be a tendency to purchase permits from sources at sites with high damages. Again there is little reason to prefer PTP to the existing system. If the number of recipients grows, however, PTP does provide some mechanism for adjusting environmental quality: the purchase of permits that would result from the combined and increased demand of new and old recipients. This gives PTP a slight edge over the existing system. The problems of growth and change can be solved to some degree in any of these proposals by allowing the environmental quality standard to change over time.

I have argued that it is preferable to regulate quantity rather than price. PEF regulates price, while the existing system and the PTP regulate quantity.

SUMMARY

Many criteria can be used to judge which system is preferable in the real world. We have judged the proposals on the basis of our eight proposed criteria. The results of this judgment are summarized in

TABLE 14.1 The Advantages and Disadvantages of Alternatives to the Existing Regulatory Approach to Pollution Control

Criteria	Practical effluent Fees (PEF)	Practical transferable permits (PTP)
Property rights distribution	−	−
Efficiency in the environmental quality standard	0	0
Least expensive control	0	0
Innovation	+	+
Administrative costs	−	+
Bureaucrats act in social interest	0	+
Growth adjustments	0	+
Cost of errors	−	0

An alternative is given a zero if it is judged to be equivalent to the current regulatory system on the listed criterion; a plus if it is judged better; and a minus if it is judged worse.

Table 14.1. An alternative is given a zero if it is judged to be equivalent to the current regulatory system on the criterion listed, a plus if it is judged superior, and a minus if it is judged inferior.

A simple adding up of the pluses and minuses suggests that there is a strong case for PTP and a relatively weak case for PEF. Furthermore, it is possible to modify PTP to overcome some of its problems. It is possible, for example, to design a PTP system that would set an environmental quality standard based on a benefit/cost analysis and allow it to adjust to growth. In addition, the permits could be allocated initially on the basis of existing implicit property rights. Creating a system whereby permits are traded at ratios that reflect differences in environmental damages at different sites is also possible. If these three modifications were made, the transferable permit system could be superior to the existing system on all grounds.

I have tried to design a system that gives the best results on all these criteria. Such a system would be based on the transferable permit idea. Whether or not it would get all pluses is something for you to decide. It is presented in the Appendix to this chapter. It may not win the Nobel Prize for me, but I believe that it takes some aspects of the real problem of the political economy of pollution control into consideration, which other proposals have not done.

STUDY QUESTIONS

1. As preparation for question 2, analyze the Dales transferable permit and the practical effluent fee systems discussed in Chapters 9 and 10 in terms of the basic issues raised in this chapter. You might also wish to analyze the solution presented in the Appendix to this chapter.
2. Design a set of institutions for pollution control that will work better than the existing system and is politically feasible. Alternatively, explain why the existing system cannot be changed and is, therefore, optimal and efficient.

Appendix to Chapter 14:
A Proposal for a Practical Alternative

THE BASIC SYSTEM

Any system that is to work effectively to control emissions must contain elements of economic incentive and regulation. This proposed system for controlling pollution is based on a transferable permit system, but it has elements of regulation, especially in enforcement. The first section of the proposal will outline its central elements, with subsequent sections providing some detailed discussion and analysis. Please keep in mind that the various elements of the proposal are intended to work together rather than independently. This discussion will pertain to air pollution; the application of the system to water pollution would require some institutional adjustment.[1]

Determining an Environmental Quality Goal

We now have national air quality standards for several pollutants, and it is politically advantageous to maintain these standards. These standards are routinely violated, however: At least 218 counties in thirty-three states were cited by EPA for being in violation of one or more of these standards on December 31, 1982.[2] In the proposed system, interim air quality standards for each federal air quality region would reflect the benefits and costs of air pollution control more accurately. The national standards would remain the long-term goal, but the interim standards would drive the system.

The initial interim standards should be set by local air pollution control agencies. Each agency would be set up as a special district (a separate unit of local government) with the power to tax property (land only). The board of directors would be made up of a number of persons elected area by area (rather than at large), which would provide at least some representation for each area of the control district and provide voters with increased incentive to participate in elections.

The agency staff would be responsible for producing best estimates and ranges of uncertainty for the benefits and costs of each

---

[1] For another view of how pollution control institutions and policy should be changed see Lester Lave and Gilber Omenn, *Clearing the Air: Reforming the Clean Air Act* (Washington, D.C.: The Brookings Institution, 1981).
[2] *The Tallahassee* (Fla.) *Democrat*, February 1, 1983, p. 9A.

standard to be applied in the region. This would include assessments of the technical feasibility of the possible standards, and their compatibility with one another and with other environmental goals. The board of directors would make these estimates public and solicit public comment both in writing and at public hearings. Having completed this process, the board would determine the interim air quality standards to be met over the next five years and the number of emission permits that can be issued to meet this standard.

During the first five years of implementation the agency would gather a great deal of information on the costs of control and the emission transformation function. It should also obtain more information on benefits from studies conducted by the national agency (EPA) and from its own investigations. At the end of the first five-year period the board would determine new interim standards, employing the same procedures. Current holders of permits would be issued new permits in proportion to their current holdings. If the board determines that the number of permits should be reduced by 20 percent, all holders would receive 20 percent fewer new permits. If the number of permits were increased, all would share in the increase equally. Permit holders would not be compensated if they lost permits during this first adjustment, nor would they have to pay if they gained permits, because of the considerable uncertainty in setting the initial interim standards. The experience of the first five years should substantially reduce that uncertainty, so compensation would be paid if a permit holder lost permits in any subsequent five-year adjustments. If new permits were issued at those times, they would be sold on the open market.

The effect of this system would be to share the property rights among emitters and recipients in roughly the same proportion as they are now shared, and to allow future changes only to the extent that one or the other party is willing to pay for the change. After the first five-year adjustment, any increase in the number of permits would be paid for by the emitters who purchase the new permits, and permit holders would suffer some reduction in the price of existing permits. The revenue from the sale of new permits would be passed on to recipients directly or indirectly through reduction of the land value tax. (More on the financing of the agency shortly.)

Transferable Permits

The setting of standards necessarily provides the data for the initial allocation of transferable permits. Estimates of the cost of controlling to the desired level of environmental quality at key locations (MCC) require information on both individual $MERC$ functions and ETF functions. Given a chosen interim standard, it is possible to work backward to obtain the ETF and the number of permits to be allocated to each emitter. There are at least two ways this initial allocation of permits could take place. The simplest and perhaps most politically acceptable alternative would be to give each emitter permits in proportion to its currently allowed emissions, regardless of location or expected effect on air quality at specific recipient locations. Conversion tables would explain the emission value of permits if traded with others. Subsequent to this initial allocation, emitters could trade — and would trade if the price of a permit was different from their $MERC$. Thus actual emissions need not be those initially allocated to the source.

An alternative initial allocation system would be to issue permits based on a source's expected effect on environmental quality, regardless of its current allowed emissions. This method would enable the agency to achieve the desired level of environmental quality with somewhat greater ease. But some sources would receive a number of permits that would exceed their currently allowed emissions, and others would be cut back. This would generate political opposition from emitters who suffer an economic loss because of this allocation. Gains in accuracy may not be worth the loss attributable to this political resistance, so the first method of initial allocation is preferable.

After initial allocation, permits could be traded among emitters at any price they choose, without agency approval. To ensure a large enough market, it will be necessary to develop specific standards for emissions allowed under a one-unit permit at different locations. If the basic unit of an emission permit is one pound per day, a holder might be allowed to emit 1.2 pounds per day at location A and only 0.8 pounds per day at location B. Such a system allows for trading among a larger group of emitters; but it generates a potential problem as well. Emitters in one area might purchase a lot of permits held by firms in other areas. The resultant concentration of emissions might cause violations of interim standards at specific locations. To solve this problem, the agency would have to modify the exchange matrix and the value of a permit in the area of the purchase. This would work as follows: Suppose the total amount of emissions allowed in one area according to the interim standard is 1,000 pounds per day. Initially, 1,000 permits for one pound each would be issued to existing emitters. Let us suppose that one of these emitters, or a new source locating in the area, purchases 100 permits from a source in another area. If these imported permits retained the same allowed emission value, total emissions would be 1,100 pounds per day and the agency would expect the interim environmental quality standard to be violated. To regain the original balance it would be necessary to reduce the allowed amount of emissions for each of the 1,100 permits to 0.909 pounds per day. Thus the total of emissions would remain at 1,000 pounds per day. This reduction in the emission value of permits held by existing emitters would cause them to suffer a loss. The situation for an existing emitter in the area is presented in Figure 14.A. The initial permits at the initial emission value would allow total emissions for this source of E_1. The source would not seek to sell or buy permits because its $MERC$ would equal P_1, the market price of permits. After another source imported permits and the agency reduced the emission value of permits, the first source's current permit holdings would allow total emissions of only E_2. Assuming no other market reactions, the price of permits would rise to P_2 and the source would be in equilibrium again. The source would have incurred additional pollution control costs, however, equal to the area ABE_1E_2. At the same time, the total value of the permits would have changed from P_1BE_10 to P_2AE_20. This might be an increase or a decrease, depending on the elasticity of the $MERC$ function. An inelastic function, which would probably be typical where high levels of control were required, would yield an increase in the value of permits. But adding the additional cost of control to the revaluation of permits would most likely result in a financial loss for the source. To avoid adverse political repercussions on the source and to promote economic efficiency in locational decisions, it would be necessary to charge the permit importer for the real resource costs of the required additional controls for all existing sources (area ABE_1E_2). In this way, the importing source would be faced with all the real resource costs of its movement into the area.

It is interesting to note that emitters in the permit exporting area would gain. Because there would now be fewer permits held in the area, the agency could increase the allowed emissions per permit, thus reducing the real resource costs of emissions for existing sources in the exporting area. This savings would be similar to the area ABE_1E_2 in Figure 14.A, but with the price and emission subscript numbers reversed. For economic efficiency it would be necessary for existing sources in the exporting area to pay the permit purchaser for their cost savings. The net effect on the source trans-

FIGURE 14.A Costs to an Existing Source of Reduction in Permit Emission Values

A reevaluation of permits that previously allowed emissions of E_1 now allows only E_2. With permits at the original market price (P_1), the source will want to continue emitting at E_1. To do so, it will purchase permits in the market. This will increase the price until a new equilibrium is attained with permit prices increased to P_2.

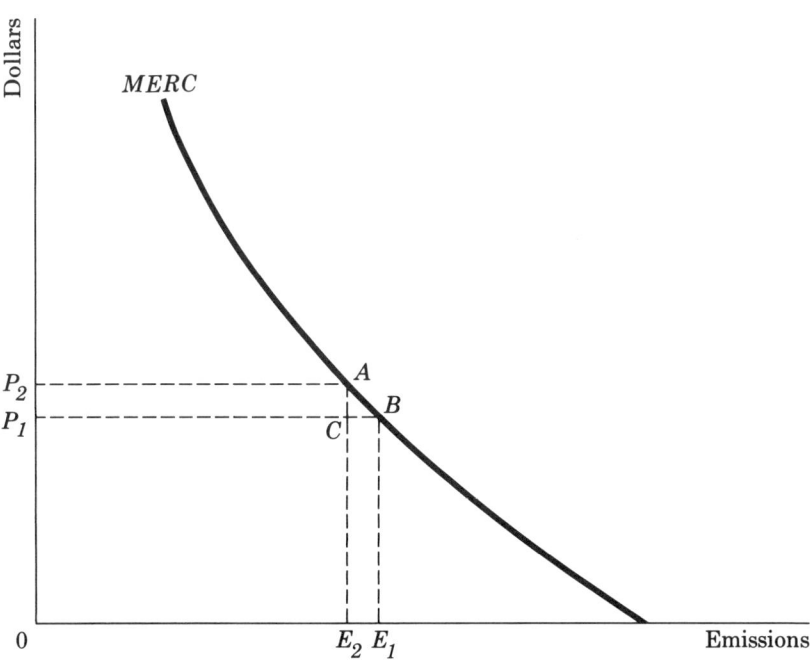

ferring permits would be the cost of the permits plus the cost of compensating the other emitters in the importing area less the compensations from the emitters in the exporting area. At the initial stage it would be possible (perhaps likely) that sources would find such trades advantageous, because the existing regulation-based standards have not been assigned efficiently. Thus the initial allocation of transferable permits, which would be based on the old allowances, would be inefficient. The trading process would move the whole set of emitters toward the efficient solution without major effects on the wealth of the various emitters.

Enforcement

As we have seen, enforcement is not an easy task. First, detection of excess emissions is technically difficult, which means that there will be errors even with a major expenditure of resources on detection. This problem could be solved by assessing the accuracy of the procedures for determining emission and defining a confidence interval around any measure of emissions. This confidence interval could be reduced by more frequent inspections and the use of frequent sampling or continuous self-monitoring. Second, once a violation was detected, the cost of that violation would have to be felt by the emitter. If this cost were not at least as great as the price of a permit, the source might find it advantageous to emit more than its permits allowed without purchasing permits from others. This would result in violations of the interim environmental standards.

To solve these two problems, the agency could adopt an excess emission penalty that reflected both the probability of detecting violations and the opportunity cost of the violation. Suppose a source was allowed to emit 1,000 pounds of a pollutant per day and the total price of its permits was $500 per day. The minimum necessary penalty with perfect detection would be fifty cents per pound per day. If the source were inspected one day per year, the probability of detecting a violation that could occur on any day of the year would be one in 260 (the number of working days for a plant). Thus, the penalty must be fifty cents times 260, or $130 per pound per day, to have the same effect as the permit price. Note that I have assumed that the probability of having to pay the fine is 1 (certainty). The $130 penalty would reflect the opportunity costs or marginal benefits of control, because the interim standard would be set to equate the number of permits in the area their estimated value per unit to the MBC. If the estimates were correct, the price of the permit would equal MBC. If not, the number of permits would have to be adjusted during the five-year revision.

Agency Structure and Financing

Control agencies should serve two functions. They should provide information of various kinds and they should arrange institutions and constraints to stimulate the efficient reallocation of resources toward the goal of improved environmental quality. To accomplish these two tasks, a national agency like EPA would have to oversee state and local (regional) agencies. While both types of agencies would provide some of the inputs necessary for each role, the federal agency's major responsibility would be informational and the state or local agency's primary responsibilities would be regulatory.

Information has the characteristics of a public good since: Once produced, it can be provided to additional individuals at a very low marginal cost. Exclusion could be exercised in this case, but overall efficiency would require free access. EPA's informational roles would not differ substantially from those it now performs, but the importance of this information would be greater. EPA's somewhat reduced regulatory role would allow additional resources to be devoted to the production and distribution of information.

EPA would provide four types of information. They are, in order of importance: a comprehensive and comparable set of current environmental quality data for all areas of the country; data on the health and welfare effects of various levels of environmental quality, presented in such a form that they could be used to estimate *MBC* functions; a systematic and continuing study of the emission transformation functions to be used in estimating *MCC* functions; and research into and dissemination of information on alternative control technologies. The data on current environmental quality should be comparable across communities and over time. We saw in Chapter 1 that such data are not presently available. Furthermore, the data should allow for a direct analysis of the environmental quality.

There is currently an extensive set of monitoring stations across the nation; they are operated by local agencies, however, and their location may be affected by political considerations. With this function under EPA direction, local concerns would be less important in siting choices, and a more accurate reading of true environmental quality would emerge. This would not prevent the local agency from operating its own monitoring network. Monitoring data should be published daily. EPA (or CEQ) should make an annual report that analyzes trends in environmental quality and publishes basic data from the monitoring networks.

One of the most important sets of information needed in benefit/cost analysis would detail the effects of exposures to environmental pollutants on the health and welfare of people, plants, and animals. There exists little private incentive to collect such information now, because there is no organized market. EPA's efforts to date have provided some basic data, but there has been no mandate to develop useful marginal benefit estimates from these data. Instead, the data have been used to determine (justify) current federal quality standards. There has been little effort to place dollar values on damages or to organize the data so marginal calculations can be made. The end product of such information would be a benefit estimation manual, which would detail the marginal effects of exposures together with a methodology for estimating the likely dollar value of damages. This manual could then be used by local agencies to develop the benefit/cost studies required for setting the interim standards.

The relationship between emissions and environmental quality is certainly highly dependent on local circumstances. Certain principles and basic scientific data can, however, be provided most efficiently through a central source like EPA. The state of knowledge about emission transformation functions is relatively poor. The control efforts of various agencies throughout the country would provide new data on which more accurate transformation functions could be built. Thus we could expect greater predictability over time as the EPA developed a greater understanding of the general scientific principles and the local agencies learned how to apply those principles.

Finally, EPA should act as the central clearinghouse for information on control technology. Under the transferable permit system each source would have an incentive to develop new technologies for controlling emissions. The information and experience gained could be useful to other sources seeking new methods of control. Sharing these data through a central clearinghouse would increase their transferability to other firms. As a further incentive to develop new control technologies, inventors would be permitted to patent their inventions and license the rights to use them. The EPA clearinghouse would provide an efficient method of marketing these new technologies. In addition, EPA would conduct its own investigations of the basic science of control. Sources would have neither the resources to conduct such research nor the ability to exclude others from the information generated, so the private supply of such basic research would be inefficiently low. In addition to these informational activities, EPA would be responsible for the control of interregional flows of pollution. This control effort will be discussed later.

The main state and local role would be to generate the incentives for sources to control emissions. The primary agency would be basinwide, with authority over all sources in the basin. This authority would set interim environmental quality standards, issue permits, determine trade-offs among permit values (in units of emissions), and enforce permit restrictions. Obviously, it would be the most important and powerful agency in the pollution control effort.

The basinwide agency would be controlled by a board of directors made up of citizens who represented the various interests in the area. The representation should be geographic within the basin, so upwind and downwind (or upstream and downstream) interests would be represented adequately. The number of elected positions would be based on the population of each municipality. The board of directors would be chaired by a person elected to a four-year term in a general popular election across all areas of the basin. Decisions of the board would be by majority rule, except interim environmental quality standards, which would require a two-thirds majority. This would ensure that all interests were adequately reflected in this most crucial decision. A professional staff headed by a director would report to the board. The director would serve at the pleasure of the board and could be appointed or removed by a two-thirds majority vote. The staff would be responsible for daily operations, including enforcement and monitoring of environmental quality as well as technical analysis of benefits and costs and continuing review of the interim standards and control technology. The basinwide agency would be responsible for controlling all pollution, in the air, in the water, and on the land. This would help produce the coordination of controls for the various environmental media that is currently lacking. The agency would run (or control through lease) all sewage treatment and solid waste disposal facilities.

A state EPA would be formed to oversee the basinwide agencies, provide coordination among them, and provide technical assistance to them. The technical assistance function would be of great importance. The state EPA would assist in assessing transformation functions, benefit and cost functions, and control technology. In an advisory role, it would assist in the running of treatment and disposal facilities, primarily by training personnel and conducting periodic inspections. One of the problems that currently faces local agencies is the lack of technical expertise on their staffs. This would be partly solved by defining a basinwide agency of sufficient size that it could afford to hire competent staff. But when sufficient expertise was not available at this level, the state EPA would provide assistance.

The basinwide agency would be funded by a tax on land value. We have seen that any changes in environmental quality that affect benefits to recipients are capitalized into the value of land. Thus a tax on land to support the control operations of the basinwide agency would amount to a partial recovery of the land wealth generated by the control effort. This financing system would require a separation of real estate values into land and improvements. This would be a logical extension of the effort to estimate benefits. Although conceptually complex, estimation of land value is in fact practical.[3] The land value tax would be paid by both emitters and recipients.

One final aspect of the operation of the basinwide agency must be presented. Board members and professional staff members must be provided with an incentive to control effectively. This could be done by awarding them salary bonuses that depend on how close the actual level of environmental quality comes to the interim standards they set. The bonus would be predetermined and set by law. It would increase the closer actual measured environmental quality came to the interim standard, regardless of whether environmental quality was above or below the standard. This system would provide a direct feedback to those responsible for accomplishing the tasks of the basinwide agency. The bonus would be only a part of each worker's salary; natural variations in weather can affect environmental quality, so success or failure would not be fully under staff control. The presence of a base salary would ensure against a large loss to workers on account of very unusual weather conditions, while the bonus would provide an incentive to do a good job regardless of variations in weather and other conditions.

Interregional Control

A basin cannot confine the adverse effects of its emissions. Some effects are felt by other basins, to which environmental quality reductions are exported. Thus any basin both receives pollution from others (imported pollution) and sends pollution to others (exported pollution). With no contrary mechanism, there would be an incentive to blame current conditions within the basin on imported pollution, and to solve the control problem for the basin by exporting pollution. To change this incentive each basin agency would be charged a pollution export tax, which would reflect the degree to which environmental quality leaving the basin exceeded the national environmental quality standards. This tax would be paid by

---

[3] See Paul B. Downing, "Measuring Urban Land Prices through Regression Analysis of Actual Sales," in *Urban Land Markets* (Washington, D.C.: Urban Land Institute, 1980), pp. 39–54.

the basin exporting the reduced quality and received by the importing basin. In effect, this system would provide each basin with a right to a level of environmental quality at least as high as the national standard. The tax would be based on the estimated damages to the importing basin. The estimates would be made, the tax levied, and proceeds paid by the federal EPA. EPA's role would be necessary because the basins would not necessarily agree on the level of damages. In addition, some of the effects would be widespread and difficult to trace, as exemplified by the acid rain issue.

This system compensates the importing basin for the reduction in the value of its environmental resources and rationalizes the export decisions of the exporting basin. The exporting agency would compare the cost of controlling emissions to the benefits within the basin and the benefits to recipients in other basins. This would lead to greater control than would a neglect of exported pollution's effects. At the same time, the importing basin's agency would be compensated for the additional control that the lower quality made necessary.

AN EXAMPLE OF THE PROPOSAL

An example may provide a more concrete understanding of the workings of the proposed institutional system. Suppose there is an air basin with geographic distributions of emitters and recipients as in Figure 14.B. There is one central city, which contains the majority of the basin's population and a substantial part of its emissions. The basin is divided into five subbasins. For simplicity, let us assume only five stationary emission sources: the central city source (C) and one source for each outlying area (N, E, S, W). Air quality monitors (M-1 through M-10) are strategically placed throughout the basin. Monitors are more heavily concentrated in the central section, where much of the population lives and works, and along the borders of the basin to document imports and exports. The dominant air flow is from west to east.

The first task the basinwide agency must face is setting interim standards. For simplicity, we will assume that only one air pollutant is emitted and that that pollutant does not change physically over time. Pollution concentrations are reduced through dispersion. A typical dispersion cone is shown for emitter S. The concentration of pollution declines linearly with distance. This represents the simplest possible emission transformation function. With this *ETF*,

314   Appendix: A Proposal for a Practical Alternative

FIGURE 14.B Hypothetical Air Basin with Emitters and Recipients

The five emission sources are designated as N,S,E,W,C, and air quality monitors are designated as M–1 through M–10. The effect of any emitter on any monitor follows a dispersion cone. Monitor M–4, for example, is affected only by emissions from W, while monitor M–9 is affected by E,C, and N. (I thought I would give you one complicated diagram before you finished the book.)

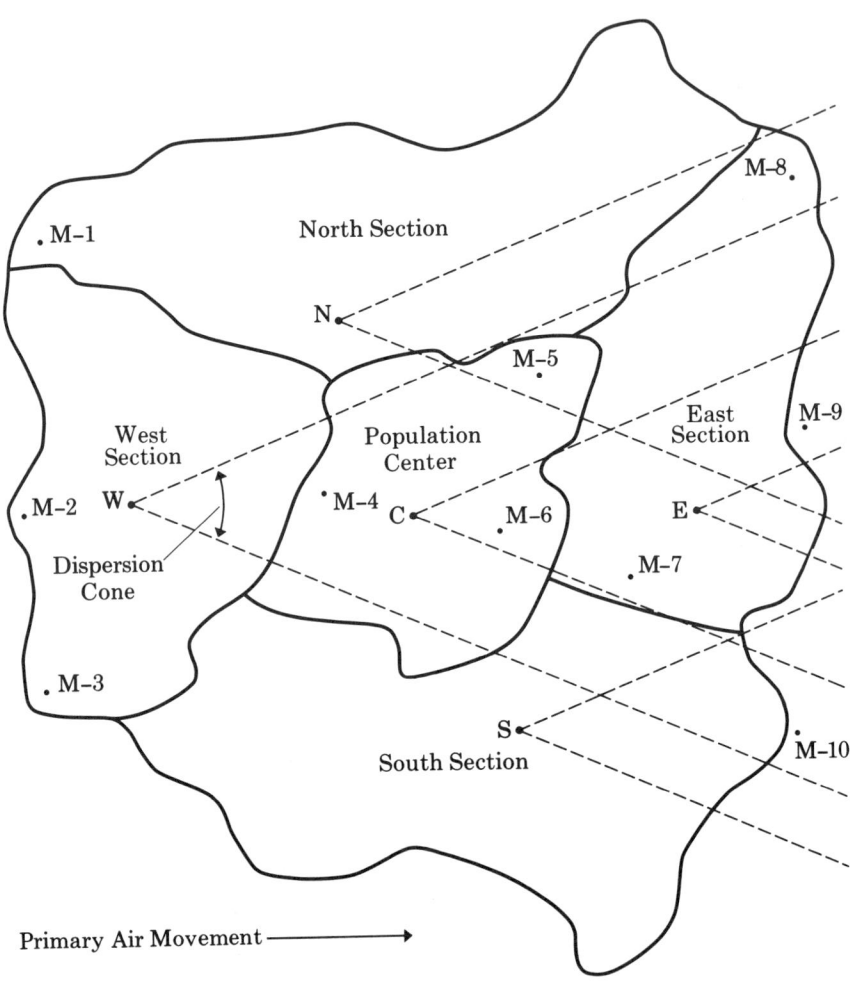

source S affects only a small area of the basin. It does, however, affect the incoming air quality in the next basin by influencing the reading at monitor M-10. The basin agency's task is fairly simple: It must calculate the benefits of control in its own area (the area under the dispersion cone within the basin), add the pollution export tax imposed by EPA (if any), and compare this benefit to the estimated cost of control, setting the interim standard at the intersection of MCC and MBC. The plant is then issued the transferable permits required to meet this interim standard.

The broken lines represent dispersion cones for the other sources. Because of the overlap of these cones, several monitoring sites and a large area of the basin are affected by more than one source's emissions. A listing of monitors and the sources influencing their readings is contained in Table 14.A. Source W affects the largest area of the basin and the most monitoring stations (six). Setting the interim standard for M-4 is just like setting the standard for M-10, because each monitor is only affected by one source. The standard for M-9 is the most complex; it is influenced by all the sources except S. For M-9, source E's emissions are most important per pound because of their close proximity, with C, N, and W being more distant and thus less important. As we saw in Chapter 2, however, the efficient combination of controls depends on the $MERC$ for each source as well as the ETF. Thus, E's efficient level of control may be lower than that of W or C.

TABLE 14.A Emitters Affecting Monitors in Basin

Monitor	Source
M-1	O[a]
M-2	O
M-3	O
M-4	O,W
M-5	O,W,N
M-6	O,W,C
M-7	O,W,C
M-8	O,W,N
M-9	O,W,C,N,E
M-10	O,S

[a] O stands for "other basins."

316   Appendix: A Proposal for a Practical Alternative

Note that source W would hold permits to emit relative to interim standards for monitors M-4 through M-9. Upon receiving its initial allocation of permits it might find that the standards at one particular monitor are binding (place an effective on its total emissions) while permits for other areas allow greater emissions. Source W can improve its situation in such a case by buying permits from others for the restrictive source or by selling extra permits for the ones that are not rigorous. It will continue to buy and sell permits until all standards are equally easy (or difficult) to comply with and the sum of the marginal values (the prices) of the permits just equals the source's *MERC*.

Note also that source W affects a large area and population in the basin. Thus we can expect that the aggregate benefit of controlling W's emissions would be relatively large. The cost of control will be high at this location. These high costs might cause source W to seek a new location. If it moved, source W would have to pay for emission permits at its new location and would receive payments for permits sold. The permits for M-4 are held exclusively by source W. This leads to an interesting problem. Who does W sell them to? If there are no new potential emitters to replace W, it would appear that there is no market. But this answer would provide the wrong incentive, because the population represented by M-4 is not indifferent to the move. The reduced emissions would benefit them. They should be willing to pay W the total benefit of reducing emissions to zero. This can be accomplished by having the basinwide agency purchase the permits at the value of the benefits (or at any lower price it can negotiate) and pay for them out of its land value tax receipts.[4]

This brief example will allow you to think through my proposed system. At this point you probably have said to yourself that the system cannot work because of this or that flaw. Good! I never expected to produce a system that would work perfectly. In fact, I know there is at least one major flaw in my proposal which I have not corrected. Did you find it? My intention was to get you to think the issues through carefully. Perhaps now you are prepared to tackle this problem and design your own system. Good luck! Remember who got you this far, and share your Nobel Prize with your instructor and me.

---

[4] Technically, the basin agency should charge all whose land values increase and subsidize all whose land values decrease but such a system is probably not practical.

CONCLUSION

The system I have proposed is probably not the ideal solution, but there is still hope. *You* can design the ideal solution. You have most of the necessary information about the economics of this design in this book. In addition, you have information on some of the important political and technical aspects of the problem. I would suggest further investigation of these two areas as preparation for your effort. Let me know what you think will work.

Oh, by the way, the fatal flaw. Think about emitter S deciding to sell permits to emitter W. After it sells them, the basinwide agency would readjust the emission value of remaining permits in the area affecting M-10, increasing the value of each permit so total emissions are the same. Thus S, who is the only emitter in the area, gets the same number of pounds of allowed emissions after having sold some permits. This problem becomes trivial when there are a lot of emitters in an area and no one emitter has a large share of all emissions, but there is no guarantee that this will be the case in the real world. This problem can be solved in several ways, some of which I am sure you have already thought of.

Good luck on your Nobel Prize.

Basic Terms

acid rain a decrease in the pH of rainwater, apparently caused by the emission of sulfur oxides into the atmosphere

benefit/cost analysis the systematic comparison of the benefits and costs of undertaking a project to determine the efficient level of activity for that project

bubble concept regulatory concept that allows all sources within a plant to be treated as one source, as if they were in a bubble with only one point of escape

bureaucracy theory the theory that individual bureaucrats, in seeking their own self-interest, will attempt to maximize particular variables, often budget or discretionary budget

citizen interest groups (CIG) a group of individuals who have joined together voluntarily to pool their resources to influence government policy

dose-response function the relationship between exposure to a change in the physical environment and a change in the physical condition of the person, plant, animal, or inanimate object exposed to that change

efficient environmental quality the level of quality of the environment, measured according to some set of physical indicators, that maximizes total net benefit

efficient prohibition the circumstance where any release will generate lower net benefit than no release at all

effluent fee (charge) a charge to each emitter for each unit of a pollutant that it releases

effluent standard the general term used for any rule that attempts to control physical emissions from a source

effluent subsidy a payment to each emitter for each unit of a pollutant that is *not* released

elitism the proposition that public affairs are dictated by a few leaders, the elite, in whose hands are concentrated wealth, power, and access to information

emission offsets the requirement that new sources moving into an area offset the increase in emissions they will generate by negotiating for an equal or greater reduction in emissions from sources already emitting in the area

emission standard (*S*) a rule that states the maximum amount of a pollutant a source is allowed to emit over a specified period of time

emission transformation function (*ETF*) the physical relationship between releases of waste products at one location and time and the level of environmental quality at other locations and times

emitter anyone who releases polluting wastes into the environment

emitters' lobby the informal or formal groups that represent the interests of those who produce pollution in government decision-making

environmental damage the reduction in the value of the environment to society or to an individual as a result of emissions of unwanted by-products

environmental quality standards rules stating that some measure of a physical quality in the environment may not exceed a certain level

exclusion the act of preventing those who do not pay from consuming a good

external cost the cost to third parties who feel the effects of externalities

externality the effect of a resource allocation decision on a party not directly participating in the decisions

free riders individuals with a positive demand for a public good who do not express that demand in order to avoid paying for the supply of the public good

hazardous wastes unwanted by-products that have the potential of causing very serious damages at relatively low concentrations if released into the environment in a way that causes exposure to people, plants, and animals

marginal benefits of control (*MBC*) the reduction in all environmental damages as the next unit of pollution is controlled

marginal costs of control (*MCC*) the increase in total costs of control as environmental quality control is increased by the next small amount.

marginal emission reduction cost (*MERC*) the real resource costs of controlling the production and release of each additional unit of unwanted by-products into an environmental medium or of changing the characteristics of those by-products to an additional small extent to reduce the damages they cause when released

maximizing self-interest the way economists assume each individual behaves to ensure that what he or she believes to be his or her own utility will be as large as possible

nonreversible damages a situation where, after a waste compound is released, it is not possible to return the environment to the state it was in before the release

opportunity cost the amount of access to one good that we must give up in order to acquire a second good

out-of-pocket cost a firm's real resource cost of controlling emissions, less any subsidy or reimbursement of these costs it might receive from others

pluralism the proposition that public policy is the result of a complex interactive bargaining process in which compromise is sought among competing groups of concerned citizens

pollution any change (usually for the worse) in the physical characteristics of the natural environment caused by human activity

prescriptive regulations effluent standards that dictate specified technical control action, such as the installation of a specific control device

present value (*PV*) the value today of some benefit to be received or cost to be incurred at some future date

present value of total net benefit (*PVTNB*) the net value today of all the benefits accruing to a project over its life, less the value today of all the costs of that project over its life

private costs the real resource costs to a firm itself of producing its output; these do not include external costs

private goods goods for which the consumption of a unit by one person precludes the consumption of that same unit by another person

public goods goods for which two or more individuals can consume the same unit at the same time and not reduce its availability to others

recipients all people who are damaged by pollution, directly or indirectly

recipient's lobby the informal or formal groups that represent those damaged by pollution in government decision-making

regulation an approach to the control of pollution that emphasizes the issuance of rules and the enforcement of those rules

scarcity the limited availability of resources and a consequent impossibility of producing everything society desires

social costs the sum of private costs and external costs

Superfund a special fund set up by Congress to pay for cleaning up hazardous wastes that present a serious current or potential threat to human health, when the emitter of those wastes cannot be determined or located, or is unable to bear the cost of such a cleanup

threshold of damages the concentration at which the damages of pollution first start to appear

total benefits of control (*TBC*)   the reduction in all environmental damages as pollution is controlled

total costs of control (*TCC*)   the value to society (opportunity cost) of all resources expended to control pollution

total net benefit (*TNB*)   the difference between total benefits and total costs of control

transferable permits system   a pollution control system according to which a source must hold permits, each of which allows it a specified amount of emissions, and any of which can be bought and sold in an open market

Bibliography

Ackerman, B.A., et al. *The Uncertain Search for Environmental Quality.* New York: The Free Press, 1974.

Ackerman, B., and G. Hassler. *Clean Coal/Dirty Air.* New Haven, Conn.: Yale University Press, 1981.

Anderson, F., et al. *Environmental Improvement through Economic Incentives.* Baltimore: Johns Hopkins University Press, 1977.

Anderson, R.J., and T.D. Crocker. "Air Pollution and Property Values," *Urban Studies* (1971).

Arrow, K. *Social Choice and Individual Values.* New York: Wiley, 1963.

Assessment of Federal and State Enforcement Efforts to Control Air Pollution from Stationary Sources. Report to the Congress. Washington, D.C.: General Accounting Office, 1973.

Atkinson, S., and D. Lewis. "A Cost Effectiveness Analysis of Alternative Air Quality Control Strategies," *Journal of Environmental Economics and Management* 1 (November 1974): 249.

Atkinson, S., and T.H. Tietenberg. "The Empirical Properties of Two Classes of Designs for Transferable Discharge Permit Market," *Journal of Environmental Economics and Management* 9 (June 1982): 101–121.

Bator, F. "The Simple Analytics of Welfare Maximization," *American Economic Review* 47 (March 1957).

Baumol, W.J. "On Taxation and the Control of Externalities," *American Economic Review* 62 (June 1972): 307–319.

Baumol, W.J., and W.E. Oates. *The Theory of Environmental Policy.* Englewood Cliffs, N.J.: Prentice-Hall, 1975.

Baumol, W., and W. Oates. "The Use of Standards and Prices for Protection of the Environment," *Swedish Journal of Economics* 73 (March 1971).

"Behind the Push to Ease Pollution Laws: An Interview with Anne M. Gorsuch, Administrator, EPA," *U.S. News and World Report,* October 19, 1981, p. 48.

Boulding, K. "The Economics of the Coming Spaceship Earth." In H. Jarrett, ed. *Environmental Quality in a Growing Economy.* Baltimore: Johns Hopkins University Press, 1966.

Brady, G., and B. Bower. "Effectiveness of the U.S. Regulatory Approach to Air Quality Management: Stationary Sources," *Policy Studies Journal* 11 (September 1982): 66–76.
Breton, A. *The Economic Theory of Representative Government*. Chicago: Aldine, 1974.
Breton, A., and R. Wintrobe. *The Logic of Bureaucratic Conduct*. New York: Cambridge University Press, 1982.
Brown, G.M. "An Optimum Program for Managing Common Property Resources with Congestion Externalities," *Journal of Political Economy* 82 (1974).
Buchanan, J., and C. Stubblebine. "Externality," *Economica* 29 (1962): 371–384.
Buchanan, J., and G. Tullock. "Polluter's Profits and Political Response," *American Economic Review* (1975).
Buchanan, J., and G. Tullock. *The Calculus of Consent*. Ann Arbor: University of Michigan Press, 1962.
Buchanan, J. "The Institutional Structure of Externality," *Public Choice* 29 (Spring 1973).
Buchanan, J. "An Economic Theory of Clubs," *Economica* (February 1965).
Burrows, P. *The Economic Theory of Pollution Control*. Cambridge, Mass.: MIT Press, 1980.
Calabresi, G. "Transaction Costs, Resource Allocation and Liability Rules," *Journal of Law and Economics* (April 1968).
Calabresi, G., and A. Melamed. "Property Rules, Liability Rules, and Inalienability," *Harvard Law Review* (April 1972).
Carson, R. *Silent Spring*. Boston: Houghton Mifflin, 1962.
Christensen, L.R., D.W. Jorgenson, and L.J. Lau. "Transcendental Logarithmic Production Frontiers," *Review of Economics and Statistics* (1973).
Coase, R.H. "The Problem of Social Cost," *Journal of Law and Economics* 3 (October 1960).
Cooper, B.S., and D.P. Rice. "The Economic Cost of Illness Revisited," *Social Security Bulletin* 39 (1976): 28.
Council on Environmental Quality. *Environmental Quality*, Seventh Annual Report. Washington, D.C.: U.S. Government Printing Office, 1976.
Council on Environmental Quality. *Environmental Quality*, Eleventh Annual Report. Washington, D.C.: U.S. Government Printing Office, 1980.
Crocker, T. "Externalities, Property Rights, and Transaction Costs: An Empirical Study," *Journal of Law and Economics* 14 (October 1971).
Crocker, T., and A. Rogers. *Environmental Economics*. Chicago: Dryden, 1971.
Currie, D. "Enforcement Under the Illinois Pollution Laws," *Northwestern Law Review* 70: 389–485.
Dales, J.H. *Pollution, Property, and Prices*. Toronto: The University of Toronto Press, 1968.
Dewees, D., C. Everson, and W. Sims. *Economic Analysis of Environmental Policies*. Toronto: University of Toronto Press, 1975.

Dorfman, N., and A. Snow. "Who Will Pay for Pollution Control?" *National Tax Journal* 28 (March 1975).
Dorfman, R. "Incidence of the Benefits and Costs of Environmental Programs," *American Economic Review* 67 (February 1977): 333–340.
Dorfman, R. *Prices and Markets*. Englewood Cliffs: Prentice-Hall, 1978.
Dorfman, R., and N. Dorfman, eds. *Economics of the Environmental: Selected Readings*. New York: Norton, 1977.
"Dow Cleans Up Pollution at No Net Cost," *Business Week,* January 1, 1972, pp. 32–34.
Downing, P.B. "Bargaining in Pollution Control," *Policy Studies Journal* 11 (June 1983): 577–586.
Downing, P.B. Controlling Oxidants in Los Angeles," *Environmental Affairs* 4 (Fall 1975): 707–743.
Downing, P.B. "Measuring Urban Land Prices through Regression Analysis of Actual Sales." In *Urban Land Markets*. Washington DC: Urban Land Institute, 1980.
Downing, P.B. "Policy Consequences of Indirect Regulatory Costs," *Public Policy* 29 (Fall 1981): 507–526.
Downing, P.B. "A Political Economy Model of Implementing Pollution Laws," *Journal of Environmental Economics and Management* 8 (September 1981): 255–271.
Downing, P.B., and G.L. Brady. "Constrained Self-Interest and the Formation of Public Policy," *Public Choice* 34 (1975): 15–28.
Downing, P.B., and G.L. Brady. "The Role of Citizen Interest Groups in Environmental Policy Formation." In M. White, ed. *Nonprofit Firms in a Three Sector Economy, COUPE Papers on Public Economics,* Vol. 6. The Urban Institute, 1981.
Downing, P.B., and J.N. Kimball. "Enforcing Pollution Control Laws in the U.S.," *Policy Studies Journal* 11 (September 1982): 55–64.
Downing, P.B., and W.D. Watson, Jr. "The Economics of Enforcing Air Pollution Controls," *Journal of Environmental Economics and Management* 1 (November 1974): 219–236.
Downing, P.B., and K. Hanf, eds. *International Comparisons in Implementing Environmental Laws*. Boston: Kluwer-Nijhoff, 1983.
Downs, A., *Inside Bureaucracy*. Boston: Little, Brown, 1967.
Dye, T.R., and L.H. Zeigler. *The Irony of Democracy*, 4th ed. Scituate, Mass. Duxbury Press, 1978.
Effluent Charges on Air and Water Pollution. Washington, D.C.: Environmental Law Institute, 1973.
Enforcement of Federal and State Water Pollution Controls, A Report to the National Commission on Water Quality. Washington, D.C.: Environmental Law Institute, 1975.
Epstein, S., L. Brown, and C. Pope. *Hazardous Waste in America*. San Francisco: Sierra Club Books, 1982.
Fisher, A., and R. Raucher. "Estimating the Benefits of Improving Environmental Quality: Evidence from the Application of Alternative Models to Specific Waterbodies." Paper presented at the Southern Economics Association Meetings, Atlanta, November 11, 1982.

Freeman, A.M. "Air Pollution and Property Values: A Methodological Comment," *Review of Economics and Statistics* (1971).
Freeman, A.M. *The Benefits of Environmental Improvement: Theory and Practice*. Baltimore: Johns Hopkins University Press, 1979.
Freeman, A.M. "On Estimating Air Pollution Control Benefits from Land Value Studies," *Journal of Environmental Economics and Management* 1 (May 1974).
Furubotn, E., and S. Pejovich. "Property Rights and Economic Theory: A Survey of Recent Literature," *Journal of Economic Literature* 10 (December 1972).
Fuss, M.A. "The Demand for Energy in Canadian Manufacturing: An Example of the Estimation of Production Structures with Many Inputs," *Journal of Econometrics* 5 (January 1977).
Goetz, C.J. "Political Equilibrium vs. Economic Efficiency in Effluent Pricing." In J.R. Conner, and E. Lochman, eds. *Economics and Decision Making for Environmental Quality*. Gainsville: University of Florida Press, 1974.
Gordon, H.S. "The Economic Theory of a Common Property Resource," *Journal of Political Economy* 62 (1954).
Gramlich, E.M. *Benefit/Cost Analysis of Government Programs*. Englewood Cliffs, N.J.: Prentice-Hall, 1981.
Greer, E. "Obstacles to Taming Corporate Polluters: Water Pollution Politics in Gary, Indiana," *Environmental Affairs 3 (1974): 199*–221.
Haefle, E., ed. *The Governance of Common Property Resources*. Baltimore: Johns Hopkins University Press, 1974.
Hardin, G. "The Tragedy of the Commons," *Science* 162 (1968): 1243–1248.
Harrison, D. *Who Pays for Clean Air: The Cost and Benefit Distribution of Federal Automobile Emission Controls*. Cambridge, Mass.: Ballinger, 1975.
Harrison, P., Jr., and P. Portney. "Regulatory Reform in the Large and Small." In L. Grayner and F. Thompson, eds. *Reforming Social Regulation*. New York: Sage Publications, 1982.
Haveman, R.H., and J. Margolis. *Public Expenditure and Policy Analysis*. Boston: Houghton Mifflin, 1983.
Head, J. "Public Goods and Public Policy," *Public Finance* (1962).
Herzog, H., Jr. *The Economics of Regional Water Quality Management: A Case Study of River Quality in the Chesapeake Bay Region*, Ph.D. diss., University of Maryland, 1974.
Hjalte, K., K. Lidgren, and I. Stahl. *Environmental Policy and Welfare Economics*. New York: Cambridge University Press, 1977.
Jacks, W.T. "Local and Regional Water Pollution Control in Texas," *Texas Law Review* 48 (November 1970): 1287–1383.
Kneese, A. *The Economics of Regional Water Quality Management*. Baltimore: Johns Hopkins University Press, 1960.
Kneese, A.V., and B.T. Bower. *Managing Water Quality: Economics, Technology, Institutions*. Baltimore: Johns Hopkins University Press, 1968.

Kneese, A., R. Ayres, and R. d'Arge. *Economics and the Environment: A Materials Balance Approach.* Baltimore: Johns Hopkins University Press, 1970.

Kneese, A.V., and C.L. Schultz. *Pollution, Prices, and Public Policy.* Washington, D.C.: The Brookings Institution, 1975.

Kopp, R., and V.K. Smith. "The Perceived Role of Materials in Neoclassical Models of Production Technology." In V.K. Smith and J. Krutilla, eds. *Explorations in Natural Resources Economics.* Baltimore: Johns Hopkins University Press, 1982.

Krier, J., and E. Ursin. *Pollution and Policy.* Berkeley: University of California Press, 1977.

Krupnick, A.J., and W. Harrington. "Decision Rules Used in the Promulgation of Federal Regulations: The Case of EPA Effluent Discharge Standards." In P.B. Downing and K.I. Hanf, eds. *Implementing Pollution Laws: International Comparisons.* Tallahassee: Florida State University Press, 1981.

Krupnick, A., W. Magat, and W. Harrington. "Understanding Regulatory Decision-Making: An Economic Approach," *Policy Studies Journal* 11 (September 1982): 44–55.

Laitos, J.G. "The Limits of the Law: Functional Failures of the Air Pollution Variance Board," *University of Colorado Law Review* 44 (1973): 513–551.

Lave, L., and E. Seskin. *Air Pollution and Human Health.* Baltimore: Johns Hopkins University Press, 1977.

"Love Canal: The Truth Seeps Out," *Reason* 13 (February 1981).

Marcus, A. "Environmental Protection Agency." In J.Q. Wilson, ed. *The Politics of Regulation.* New York: Basic Books, 1980.

Marshall, E. "Air Pollution Clouds U.S.–Canadian Relations," *Science* 217 (September 17, 1982): 1118–1119.

McKean, R. "The Unseen Hand in Government," *American Economic Review* 55 (June 1965).

Mills, E., ed. *Economic Analysis of Environmental Problems* New York: National Bureau of Economic Research, 1975.

Mills, E., and L. White. "Government Policies toward Automotive Emissions Control." In A. Friedlaender, ed. *Approaches to Controlling Air Pollution.* Cambridge, Mass.: MIT Press, 1978.

Mishan, E. *Cost-Benefit Analysis.* New York: Praeger, various editions.

Mishan, E.J. "The Post War Literature on Externalities: An Interpretive Essay," *Journal of Economic Literature* 9 (March 1971).

"Mob's Role in Toxic-Waste Dumping Called 'Terrifying'," *Tallahassee* (Fla.) *Democrat*, March 15, 1983.

Molotch, H., and R.C. Follett. "Air Pollution as a Problem for Sociological Research." In Paul B. Downing, ed. *Air Pollution and the Social Sciences.* New York: Praeger, 1971.

Montgomery, W.D. "Markets in Licenses and Efficient Pollution Control Programs," *Journal of Economic Theory* 5 (1972).

Mueller, D.C. *Public Choice.* New York: Cambridge University Press, 1979.

Mumy, G. "Long-Run Efficiency and Property Rights Sharing for Pollution Control," *Public Choice* 35 (1980): 59–74.

Musgrave, R., and P. Musgrave. *Public Finance in Theory and Practice.* New York: McGraw-Hill, 1980.

Needelman, L. "Valuing Other People's Lives," *The Manchester School of Economics and Social Studies* 44 (December 1976): 330.

Niskanen, W.A. *Bureaucracy and Representative Government.* Chicago: Aldine, 1971.

Niskanen, W.A. "Bureaucrats and Politicians," *Journal of Law and Economics* (December 1975).

Noll, Roger. "Implementing Marketable Emission Permits," *American Economic Review* 71 (May 1982): 120–124.

Nordhaus, W. "Resources as a Constraint on Growth," *American Economic Review* 64 (1974).

Olson, M. *The Logic of Collective Action.* Cambridge: Harvard University Press, 1971.

Ostlund, L.E. "Attitudes of Managers toward Corporate Social Responsibility," *California Management Review* 19 (Summer 1977): 38.

Pashigian, B.P. *The Political Economy of the Clean Air Act: Regional Self-Interest in Environmental Legislation,* Publication No. 51. St. Louis: Center for the Study of American Business, Washington University, 1982.

Peskin, H.M. "Environmental Policy and the Distribution of Benefits and Costs." In P.R. Portney, ed. *Current Issues in U.S. Environmental Policy.* Baltimore: Johns Hopkins University Press, 1978.

Peskin, H., P. Portney, and A. Kneese, eds. *Environmental Regulation and the U.S. Economy.* Baltimore: Johns Hopkins University Press, 1981.

Peterson, I. "Acid Rain: Talking Up a Storm," *Science News* 121 (June 5, 1982): 373.

Quarles, J. *Cleaning Up America.* Boston: Houghton Mifflin, 1976.

Ridker, R.G., and J.A. Henning. "The Determinants of Residential Property Values with Special Reference to Air Pollution," *Review of Economics and Statistics* 49 (May 1967).

Rose-Ackerman, S. "Effluent Charges: A Critique," *Canadian Journal of Economics* (1973).

Rosenbaum, W. *The Politics of Environmental Concern.* New York: Praeger, 1973.

Russell, C., and W. Vaughan. "The National Recreational Fishing Benefits of Water Pollution Control," *Journal of Environmental Economics and Management* 9 (December 1982): 328–354.

Samuelson, P. "The Pure Theory of Public Expenditure," *Review of Economics and Statistics* 36 (1954): 386–389.

Schachter, E. *Enforcing Air Pollution Controls.* New York: Praeger, 1974.

Schoenbaum, T. "The Efficiency of Federal and State Control of Water Pollution in Intrastate Streams," *Arizona Law Review* 14 (1972): 1–39.

Semmens, J. "Concealed Costs/Bloated Benefits," *Reason* 12 (March 1981): 29–32.

Smith, V.K. *The Economic Consequences of Air Pollution.* Cambridge, Mass.: Ballinger, 1976.

Sohn, M., and R. Litan. "Regulatory Oversight Wins in Court," *Regulation* 5 (July/August 1981): 17–24.

Sonstellie, J., and P. Portney. "Truth or Consequences: Cost Revelation and Regulation," *Journal of Policy Analysis and Management* 2 (Winter 1983): 280–295.

Stern, A., ed. *Air Pollution.* New York: Academic Press, 1968.

E. Stokey, and R. Zeckhauser. *A Primer for Policy Analysis.* New York: W.W. Norton, 1978.

Sun, M. "EPA Issues Hazardous Waste Rules," *Science* 217 (July 30, 1982): 430–443.

Sun, M. "Missouri's Costly Dioxin Lesson," *Science* 219 (January 28, 1983): 367–369.

Teitenberg, T.H. "Derived Decision Rules for Pollution Control in a General Equilibrium Space Economy," *Journal of Environmental Economics and Management* 1 (June 1974): 3–16.

Trauberman, J. "Superfund: A Legal Update," *Environment* 23 (March 1981): 25.

Tullock, G. "The Transitional Gains Trap," *Bell Journal of Economics* 6 (Autumn 1975): 671–678.

"U.S. Damage: $3 Billion a Year," *U.S. News and World Report,* November 29, 1982, p. 44.

U.S. Federal Energy Administration. *National Energy Outlook.* Washington, D.C.: U.S. Government Printing Office, 1976.

U.S. Federal Energy Administration. *Project Independence Report.* Washington, D.C.: U.S. Government Printing Office, 1974.

Waddell, T.E. *The Economic Damages of Air Pollution.* EPA Publication, Socioeconomic Environmental Studies. Washington, D.C.: U.S. Government Printing Office, 1979.

Watson, W.D., Jr., and P.B. Downing. "Enforcement of Environmental Standards and the Central Limit Theory," *Journal of the American Statistical Association* 71 (September 1976): 567–573.

Weisbrod, B. *Public Interest Law.* Berkeley: University of California Press, 1978.

Weitzman, M.L. "Prices vs. Quantities," *Review of Economic Studies* 34 (1974).

White, L. "American Automotive Emissions Control Policy: A Review of Reviews," *Journal of Environmental Economics and Management* 2 (April 1976): 231–246.

White, L. *Reforming Regulation.* Englewood Cliffs, N.J.: Prentice-Hall, 1981.

Willick, D., and T. Windle. "Rule Enforcement by the Los Angeles County Air Pollution Control District," *Ecology Law Quarterly* 3 (1973): 507.

Yandle, B. "Economic Agents and the Level of Pollution Control," *Public Choice* 40 (1983): 105–109.

Zellner, A. "An Efficient Method of Estimating Seemingly Unrelated Regressions and Tests for Aggregation Bias," *Journal of the American Statistical Association* (June 1962).

Zerbe, R. "Optimal Environmental Jurisdictions," *Ecology Law Quarterly* 4 (1974).

INDEX

AC. See Average cost
Acid rain, 18, 151–153, 156
Air pollution. See also Smog
 and property value, 99–102
Air quality, national standards, 3, 155
Albuquerque, 168
American Automobile Manufacturers Association, 124, 126
American Lung Association, 267
Asbestos, 96
Asthma, 29
Atkinson, S., 166
Atmospheric Sciences Research Center, 152
Auto emissions, 91–93
Auto emission standards, 4
Average and marginal cost, 44
Average cost (AC), 121–122, 175–176, 182–183

Bargaining, 240–241, 258–262, 285–286
BAT Standards, 5–6, 107
Behavioral assumptions, 22–23
Beneficiaries of emissions control, 80–82, 84
Benefit/cost analysis, 26–35, 48, 72–85, 86, 109, 149–150, 153–154, 157, 259–262
 alternatives to, 109–114
 appropriateness of, 139–143
 discounting, 86–88
 estimating costs and benefits, 88–104, 106–108
Bingham Foundation, 265
Biochemical oxygen demand (BOD), 67–69, 74, 76, 89–90, 95, 162, 178
BOD. See Biochemical oxygen demand
Boston, 101
BPT Standards, 5–6, 107
"Breather's Lobby," 266
Brower, D., 263
Bubble concept, 7, 212

Bureau of Economic Analysis (BEA), 9, 10
Bureaucracy theory, 120–121, 136, 249–250
 and competition theory, 250, 251
Burford, Anne (Gorsuch), 139
Business Roundtable, 124

California, 130, 264
California Air Resources Board (CARB), 235–236, 238
Carbon monoxides, 3, 13
 standards for, 3
Carcinogens, 138
Carpooling, 267
Catalytic converters, 93
Center for Law and Social Policy, 265
Center for Law in the Public Interest (CLPI), 265
Central Electricity Generating Board (Great Britain), 153
Chesapeake Bay, 144
Chicago, 101
Citizen interest groups (CIGs), 125–126, 133, 230–231, 233, 236–239, 248–250, 253, 299
 formation and behavior, 254–258
 membership, 255–258
 origin and funding of, 263–268
Clean Air Act of 1955, 228–229
Clean Air Act of 1967, 228–229
Clean Air Act of 1970, 2, 9, 92, 109, 114, 131, 157, 168, 219, 227–240, 262, 266–267
 Amendments of 1977, 5, 212, 233, 267
 and auto emission standards, 4
 impracticality of, 4–5
 State Implementation Plan (SIP), 2–4, 166, 229–230, 232, 236–237, 239
 "technology forcing" provisions of, 4
Clean Air Constituency, 266–267
Coal, 94, 95

329

Competition theory, 250, 251
  and bureaucracy theory, 250, 251
Comprehensive Environmental Response, Compensation, and Liability Act of 1980, 2, 8, 139, 145
Congressional Research Service, 167
Connecticut, 281, 282
Constraints, 23
Control agencies, 244–253, 284
  budgeting of, 248–253
  discretionary spending by, 250
  federal vs. state, 244, 284
Cooper, B.S., 99
Cost effectiveness, 109–110
Council on Environmental Quality (CEQ), 9, 11, 13–15, 309
Court action, 127, 281–283
Czechoslovakia, 151

Dales, J.H., 205, 210
DDT, 138, 144, 265
Delaware River Basin Commission, 130
Demand, 29
Detection of emissions violations, 273–274, 278–281
  citizen complaints, 280
  self-monitoring, 280
Dioxin, 138, 146
Discounting, 86–88
Discretionary spending, 250
Distributional equity, 26
Dose-response function, 96–97
Downing, P.B., 278
Dye, T.R., 118

Eagleton, Thomas, 231
East Germany, 151
Economies of scale, 89–90
Edna Clark McConnell Foundation, 265
Efficiency, 23–26, 30–33, 160–166
  vs. equity, 294
Effluent fees, 173–179, 296–300
  compared with subsidies and regulation, 181–185
  and changes in environmental quality, 187–189
  effects on innovation, 189–193
  efficiency of, 177–179
  practical, 210–211
  and property rights, 193–194
  shifting of, 185–187
  sulfur tax, 211–212
  transferable permits and, 209
  use of revenues from, 179–180, 216
Effluent standards, 158–160
Elderly people, 13, 125

Electrostatic precipitators, 94
Elitism, 118
Emission offset, 7, 212–213
Emissions
  auto, 91–93
  benefits of control, 70–72
  control of, in a plant, 62–67
  and environmental quality, 67–70
  from more than one source, 76–80
  sources and locations, 82–83, 178
Emission standards, 159–160, 276–278
Emission transformation function (ETF), 69 fig., 70, 73–75, 80, 84, 93, 114, 168, 177, 188, 198–223, 299, 305, 313–315
Emitters, 121, 253–254
  emitters' lobby, 121–124, 126–129, 133, 226
Enforcement, 132–133, 270–291, 308
  current practice, 275–288
  economics of, 270–272
Environmental Defense Fund, 146, 265
Environmental Law Institute, 276–278, 282
Environmental Protection Agency (EPA), 1–2, 110, 130, 131–132, 139, 145–146, 149, 150, 164, 166–171, 229–231, 235, 236–239, 249, 303–304, 309–312
  political pressure on, 6
Environmental quality (EQ or Q), 31–33, 36, 105–106, 107–108, 188–189, 198–223, 245–253
Environmental quality standards, 155–158
  across-the-board vs. combination of controls, 204–205
  efficiency of, 160–166
  national vs. regional, 168–169
  who sets, 166–171
EPA. See Environmental Protection Agency
EPA v. Brown, 239
Epidemiological studies, 99
EQ. See Environmental quality
Equilibrium, 258–259
  firm, 45, 46
  market, 45, 46
ETF. See Emission transformation function
Exclusion, 56
Executive Order 12291, 148–151
Externalities, 48–53, 148

Factors of production, 42
Feasibility, 91–93

Index   331

Federal Water Pollution Control Act (FWPCA), 2, 5–6, 107, 108
Fines, 283–284
Firm equilibrium, 45, 46
Ford Foundation, 264, 265
Freeman, A.M., III, 101
Free riders, 56–57, 125–126
Friends of the Earth, 125, 263, 267
    FOE foundation, 263
Funding, 131–132

Gary Works, 283
Gasoline rationing, 239, 267
Goal trade-offs, 251–253
Gorsuch. *See* Burford
Great Britain, 151, 153

Hazardous wastes, 8–9, 18, 138–148
Heart disease, 13
Heavy metals, 147
Human life, value of, 96–98
Hydrocarbons (nonmethane), 3, 12, 92, 93
    standards for, 3

Illinois, 283
Indirect penalties, 287–288
Infinite damages, 139
Inflation Impact Statements, 150
Information, imperfect, 197
Interest rates, 88
Interregional control, 312–313
"Invisible hand," 24, 47

Josephine H. McIntosh Foundation, 266

Kansas City (Missouri), 101
Kentucky Air Pollution Commission, 232–233
Kepone, 144
Kimball, J.N., 278

Lave, L.B., 99
Lead, 3
    standards for, 3
Legislation. *See under* Clean Air Act of 1970; Comprehensive Environmental Response, Compensation, and Liability Act of 1980; and Resources Conservation and Recovery Act of 1976
Legislation, inadequacies of, 129–133
Lennett, D., 146
Lewis, D., 166
Lindahl, E., 57
Lindahl taxes, 57

Linear programming, 91–93
Lobbyists, 121–129
    court actions by, 127, 281–283
Local control agencies, 169–171
Los Angeles, 92, 101, 102, 111–114, 168, 266
Los Angeles County Air Pollution Control District (LACAPCD), 239, 279
Love Canal, 8, 139
Lung disease, 13

Marginal benefits, 45, 48, 51, 55, 56, 58–59, 71, 153
Marginal benefits of control, 29–33, 36, 40–41, 72, 74–75, 104–106, 107–108, 141–143, 157, 160–162, 177, 179, 198–223, 299
Marginal cost, 44, 46, 48, 51, 52, 55, 59, 66, 92, 107–108, 121–122, 134–136, 153, 175–176, 182–186, 259–262
Marginal cost of administration (MCA), 245–253, 260, 299
Marginal cost of control, 28–29, 31–33, 36, 65, 73–75, 79, 80, 104–106, 107–108, 111, 142–143, 177, 179, 187, 188–189, 193, 198–223, 260–261, 300, 305, 309, 315
Marginal damages (MD), 141
Marginal emission reduction cost (MERC), 64–67, 73–74, 76–82, 84, 93, 149, 162–164, 166, 168–169, 174–175, 177, 181, 188–193, 198–223, 287, 299, 305–306, 315–316
Marginal externality costs, 50–51
Marginal physical product, 42, 64, 66
Marginal private costs, 50–51
Marginal social cost, 50–51
Marginal utility (MU), 39–40, 71
Market adjustments, 45–48, 176
Market economy, 38–48, 100
Market equilibrium, 45, 46
Materials balance approach, 63
Maximization, 24–25
MB. *See* Marginal benefits
MBC. *See* Marginal benefits of control
MC. *See* Marginal cost
MCA. *See* Marginal cost of administration
MCC. *See* Marginal cost of control
MD. *See* Marginal damages
MEC. *See* Marginal externality costs
MERC. *See* Marginal emission reduction cost
Michigan, 120
Middleton, John 231–233
Minnesota, 282

332 Index

Mississippi River, 156
Missouri, 146
MPC. *See* Marginal private costs
MPP. *See* Marginal physical product
MSC. *See* Marginal social cost
MU. *See* Marginal utility
Muir, John, 263–264
Muskie, Edmund, 230, 233, 234, 237

National Academy of Sciences, 151
National Air Pollution Control Agency (NAPCA), 231–233, 235–236, 249, 266
National Ambient Air Quality Standards, 3
National Association of Manufacturers, 124
National Coalition for Clean Air (NCCA), 267
National Pollution Discharge Elimination System (NPDES), 278–279
Natural Resources Defense Council (NRDC), 125, 237, 265
Net gain from a move (NGM), 83
New York City, 279, 283
  Air Resources Department, 279
NGM. *See* Net gain from a move
Niskanen, W.A., 249–250
Nitrogen dioxide, 3, 13
  standards for, 3
Nitrogen oxides, 11, 92, 93
Nixon, R., 237
North Carolina, 279

Occupational Safety and Health Administration (OSHA), 150
Office of Management and Budget (OMB), 150, 237
Office of Technology Assessment, 152
Ohio, 120
Oil spills, 138
OMB. *See* Office of Management and Budget
Opportunity cost, 21–22, 54, 98
Oregon, 120
Organic wastes, 67
OSHA. *See* Occupational Safety and Health Administration
Out-of-pocket costs, 117, 286–287
Oxygen sag curve, 68 fig.
Ozone (photochemical oxidant), 3, 13, 14, 168
  standards for, 3, 168, 235, 236

Partee, Frank, 232
Particulate matter, 3, 63, 94, 101
  standards for, 3

Pashigian, B. Peter, 234
Penalties, 273–275
Peskin, H.M., 33, 34
Philadelphia, 101
Photochemical oxidant. *See* Ozone
Pittsburgh, 101
Platt, J., 146
Pluralism, 118–119
Poland, 151
Policy trade-off, 110–114
Political pressures, 121–133
Polling and survey techniques, 102
Pollutant mix, 91–93
Pollutants. *See* individual substances
Pollution. *See also* specific types; e.g., Air pollution, Thermal pollution, etc.
  control of, 62–85
  effects of, 29
  positive effects of, 49
Pollution control. *See also* Prevention of pollution
  economic incentives, 173–196
  political implications of, 213–218
  political aspects, 117–137, 213–215
  regulation, 155–172
Pollution control, economics of, 21–37
  benefit/cost analysis, 26–35
  income and, 33–34
Pollution control costs, 9–11
  estimating, 88–95
Pollution control policy, 226–243
  flexibility to change, 202–204
  practical problems, 197–225
  sources of error, 200–202
Practical effluent fee (PEF), 296–300
Practical transferable permit (PTP), 296–300
Prescriptive regulations, 158–159
Present value (PV), 87–88, 97–98
Present value of total net benefit (PVTNB), 88
Prevention of pollution
  benefits of, 29–30, 96–104
  costs of, 27–29, 142
  efficiency in, 30–33
Private goods, 53–54
Profit, 42, 45
  maximizing, 42
Property rights, 193–194
Property value, 99–102
Public goods, 53–59
  environment as, 58–59
  market demand for, 54
  vs. private goods, 53, 54
Pulp and paper manufacturing, 165
PVTNB. *See* Present value of total net benefit

Ratcheting, 191
Reagan, Ronald, 7, 148
Recipients, 124
  recipients' lobby, 124–129, 133, 226
Redistribution of income, 26
Regression analysis, 89
Regulation, 155
Regulatory Impact Analysis, 150
Resource Conservation and Recovery Act of 1976, 2, 8, 146
Resource recovery, 95
Resources, misallocation of, 49–53
Rice, D.P., 99
Rivers and Harbors Act of 1899, 1, 283
Riverside v. Ruckelshaus, 238, 239, 248, 266
Rockefeller Family Fund, 263
Rockefeller Foundation, 265
Ruckelshaus, W., 237, 238
Russell, C., 107

St. Louis, 101, 166
San Mateo County (California), 101
San Onofre nuclear power plant, 49
Scale, economies of, 89–90
Scandinavia, 151, 152–153, 156
Scarcity, 21–22
Self-interest, 18, 22–23, 47
  vs. social interest, 294–295
Seskin, E.P., 99
Sewage, 67
Sewage treatment plants, 89
  regional, 89
Sierra Club, 125, 263–265, 267
  Sierra Club Foundation, 264
  Sierra Club Legal Defense Fund (SCLDF), 264–265
Simulation studies, 94–95
Smith, Adam, 24, 47
Smog, 92, 111–114. *See also* Air pollution
Sources (of emissions), 253–254. *See also* Emitters
South Central Region of the Virginia State Water Control Board, 278–280
State control agencies, 169–171, 284
Subsidies, 181
Sulfate pollution, 101
Sulfur by-products, 165
Sulfur content in fuels, 152
Sulfur oxides, 3, 12, 151, 152
  standards for, 3, 156
Sulfur tax, 211–212
Superfund, 8, 145–148
  compared to insurance, 147
  liability and, 146, 147

Survey techniques, 102–103
Sweden, 151

T. *See* Threshold of damages
TBC. *See* Total benefits of control
TCC. *See* Total cost of control
Technical coefficients, 96–98
TERC. *See* Total emission reduction cost
TGB. *See* Total gain in benefits
Thermal pollution, 49
Threshold of damages (T), 140, 142
Times Beach, Missouri, 9
TLB. *See* Total loss in benefits
Toronto, 101
Total benefits of control, 29–33
Total cost of control, 27, 28, 31–33, 89
Total cost curve, 43
Total emmission reduction cost (TERC), 78, 83, 175
Total gain in benefits (TGB), 83
Total loss in benefits (TLB), 83
Total relocation costs (TRC), 83
Total Suspended Particulates (TSP), 11, 13, 15
Toxic waste. *See also* Hazardous waste
  cleaning up, 144–145, 148
  controlling, 142, 143–145
  liability for, 146, 147
  prohibition, 142–143
Trade associations, 123–124
Transferable permits, 205–210, 218–219, 296–300, 304–308
  and effluent fees, 210–211
  revenues from, 216
TRC. *See* Total relocation costs
Tunney, John, 230

Uncertainty, 104–106, 197–200, 219–223
U.S. Steel, 283
Utility maximization, 119, 129
Utility, personal, 23

Van Amerigen Foundation, 265
Vaughan, W., 107
Virginia, 278–279
  Water Control Board, 278–280

Waddell, T.E., 103
Washington, D.C., 101
Water pollution, 67, 106–108
Water Pollution Control Act of 1972, 2, 5–6, 107, 278
  Amendment of 1977, 7
  proposed further amendments, 7–8

Water quality, 15, 16
Water quality standards, 156–157
Weitzman, M., 200, 208
West Germany, 151, 219

Wisconsin, 120

Yale Law School, 265
Yandle, B., 262

AF